Forensic Anthropology and Medicine

FORENSIC ANTHROPOLOGY AND MEDICINE

Complementary Sciences From Recovery to Cause of Death

Edited by

Aurore Schmitt, PhD

Laboratoire d'Anthropologie des Populations du Passé
Université Bordeaux 1
Talence, France

Eugénia Cunha, PhD

Departamento de Antropologia
Universidade de Coimbra
Coimbra, Portugal

and

João Pinheiro, MD, MSci

Serviço Tanatologia Forense,
Instituto Nacional de Medicina Legal
Coimbra, Portugal

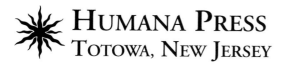

HUMANA PRESS
TOTOWA, NEW JERSEY

Cover design by Patricia F. Cleary

Production Editor: Amy Thau

Cover Illustrations: From left to right: Skull x-ray, by João Pinheiro; Fig. 13, Chapter 14, "Pathology as a Factor of Personal Identity in Forensic Anthropology," by Eugénia Cunha; Fig. 2, Chapter 4, "Biological vs Legal Age of Living Individuals," by Francesco Introna and Carlo P. Campobasso; Fig. 4, Chapter 6, "Understanding the Circumstances of Decomposition When the Body Is Skeletonized," by Henri Duday and Mark Guillon.

For additional copies, pricing for bulk purchases, and/or information about other Humana titles, contact Humana at the above address or at any of the following numbers: Tel: 973-256-1699; Fax: 973-256-8341; E-mail: orders@humanapr.com, or visit our Website at www.humanapress.com

Printed in the United States of America. 10 9 8 7 6 5 4 3 2 1

eISBN: 1-59745-099-5

Library of Congress Cataloging in Publication Data
Forensic anthropology and medicine: complementary sciences from recovery to cause of
  death/ edited by Aurore Schmitt, Eugénia Cunha, and João Pinheiro.
      p. cm.
Includes bibliographical references and index.
ISBN 1-58829-824-8 (alk. paper)
  1. Forensic anthropology. 2. Medical jurisprudence. I. Schmitt, Aurore. II. Cunha,
Eugénia. III. Pinheiro, João.

RA1059.F672 2006
614'.1--dc22
                                                                    2005055082

Preface

Recent political, religious, ethnic, and racial conflicts, as well as mass disasters, have significantly helped to bring to light the almost unknown discipline of forensic anthropology. This science has become particularly useful to forensic pathologists because it aids in solving various puzzles, such as identifying victims and documenting crimes. On topics such as mass disasters and crimes against humanity, teamwork between forensic pathologists and forensic anthropologists has significantly increased over the few last years. This relationship has also improved the study of routine cases in local medicolegal institutes. When human remains are badly decomposed, partially skeletonized, and/or burned, it is particularly useful for the forensic pathologist to be assisted by a forensic anthropologist. It is not a one-way situation: when the forensic anthropologist deals with skeletonized bodies that have some kind of soft tissue, the advice of a forensic pathologist would be welcome.

Forensic anthropology is a subspecialty/field of physical anthropology. Most of the background on skeletal biology was gathered on the basis of skeletal remains from past populations. Physical anthropologists then developed an indisputable "know-how"; nevertheless, one must keep in mind that looking for a missing person or checking an assumed identity is quite a different matter. Pieces of information needed by forensic anthropologists require a higher level of reliability and accuracy than those granted in a general archaeological context. To achieve a positive identification, findings have to match with evidence, particularly when genetic identification is not possible. Forensic anthropology can also be essential in providing details about identification, even if a DNA profile is compiled.

As a consequence, both the potential and limits of forensic anthropology have to be equally taken into account in forensic investigations. However, this perspective is seldom covered in the current forensic literature.

Forensic medicine is a known branch of medicine whose origin is difficult to pinpoint, but is surely at least two or three centuries old. Often considered the "medicine of the dead," it is, however, much more, and today, as in the past, it offers an unquestionable social value to the community, as illustrated in *Forensic*

Anthropology and Medicine: Complementary Sciences From Recovery to Cause of Death. Nevertheless, forensic pathology is undoubtedly the most well-known branch of this specialty, and the one that touches most deeply the aim of *Forensic Anthropology and Medicine: Complementary Sciences From Recovery to Cause of Death*. This is true for many reasons, but it is certainly owing to a recent, successful "marriage" of forensic pathology to forensic anthropology.

There are many textbooks of forensic medicine and pathology, as well as forensic anthropology; however, it is hard to find a reference text that covers all three areas. *Forensic Anthropology and Medicine: Complementary Sciences From Recovery to Cause of Death*, located on the border between forensic anthropology and forensic pathology, aims to fill this gap. It also claims to strengthen the contribution of forensic anthropologists in all the main stages of forensic work, namely recovery, identification, and determination of the cause of death. These goals will be enhanced when fulfilled within multidisciplinary teams. Crossing over these two fields of knowledge will obviously lead to mutual benefits. This enables forensic pathologists to grasp the anthropological background beneath a routine autopsy, and then to increase their knowledge.

Furthermore, we wish *Forensic Anthropology and Medicine: Complementary Sciences From Recovery to Cause of Death* to be a methodological bridge between different countries of Europe and America. We believe that there is an acute need for spreading knowledge of and expertise in its many powerful techniques and methods across continents.

Forensic Anthropology and Medicine: Complementary Sciences From Recovery to Cause of Death is geared particularly toward postgraduate students and researchers in forensic medicine and pathology, forensic anthropology, law sciences, and the police. The topics discussed range from individual recovery and autopsy to specific contexts, such as crimes against humanity and mass disasters.

Part I presents both disciplines—forensic anthropology and forensic medicine focused specially on forensic pathology—starting with a brief historical background leading up to the point where both sciences meet. Chapter 1 also clarifies their goals, quantifies their collaboration, analyzes both professional careers, and discusses the challenges of a common future. The difference between the medicolegal systems and organization of forensic medicine and pathology is debated in Chapter 2, which discusses their pros and cons in order to justify the situation of forensic pathology in many parts of the world.

The presentation of forensic anthropology in Europe (Chapter 3) takes into account the variety of expertises, cases, backgrounds, training, and accreditation in comparison with the United States.

Part II deals with age estimation of living individuals for reasons of imputability, which is one of the growing subfields of forensic anthropology requiring cooperation between forensic physicians and forensic anthropologists. Chapter 4 explores the whole range of techniques and methods available.

The chapters in Part III discuss all the steps of forensic analysis, precisely from recovery to the cause of death. Before starting such an investigation, one must have a comprehensive understanding of the different ways a body can change after death. Among others, a relevant interpretation of the events surrounding a death depends on mastering body decomposition and taphonomic processes. Chapter 5 reviews the states of preservation/decomposition, and through well-illustrated cases, emphasizes both what a forensic pathologist can obtain from a mummified or saponified body, and what a forensic anthropologist can obtain from skeletonized remains.

The recovery scene, where every examination should start, is discussed in Chapter 6, which underlines the importance of an archaeological background, particularly if the remains are dry bones. The presence of forensic anthropologists and/or pathologists should be required in scene examination.

When facing a cadaver that is neither preserved nor completely skeletonized, or is unrecognizable, teamwork (forensic pathologist plus forensic anthropologist) is requested, as are appropriate methodologies to carry out the specific autopsy or examination. Chapter 7 presents a multidisciplinary approach to this issue and the best practices in conducting an investigation, benefiting from the experience the authors gained in different settings.

Chapter 8, which closes Part III, describes in detail the different types of traumatic bone lesions—blunt, sharp, or gunshot wounds—which are discussed as differential diagnoses. The relevance of these injuries to establish the cause of death, and through it, as evidence of crimes against humanity, genocide, and torture, is emphasized.

The main attributes of biological identity are gender, age, stature, and ancestry. Part IV reviews the state of knowledge on assessing these four parameters from skeletal remains. The reliability, accuracy, and limits of the methodologies are covered, and the best approach in legal contexts is recommended. Because the previously mentioned generic factors of identification are, in most instances, not sufficient to achieve identification, the next step is to search for other factors of individualization. Chapter 14 deals with this issue, in particular, with pathological alterations of bones.

Part IV ends with a very useful summary chapter (Chapter 15), which reviews several related points and discusses the advantages and disadvantages of the several methods usually accepted as proof of identification.

Recently, an increasing number of systematic investigations have been launched worldwide following crimes against humanity. The variable preservation of cadavers or body parts requires contributions of both forensic pathologists and forensic anthropologists to provide evidence on the cause and manner of death. This combined effort is also required for expertise on the context of catastrophes, whether natural and/or caused by humans, where identification is the main issue. These crimes against humanity and mass disasters are examined in Part V, which analyzes their different problems. In mass disasters, the cause of death is frequently known, and all efforts are then focused on victims' identification, which is also a key issue for crimes against humanity, where the research of cause of death still remains very important.

Within this context, Chapter 16 presents useful and relevant recommendations for forensic professionals, examining their links with international organizations in the field, such as the United Nations, the Red Cross, or Interpol, whose actualized protocols are displayed.

Although the very beginning of any scientific issue is hard to define, it is undeniable that the South American anthropologists, particularly the Equipo Argentino de Antropologia Forense, are among the world's pioneers in investigating crimes against humanity. Through practical cases, one of this organization's members presents the adequate methodology to investigate these crimes profiting from the group's vast experience on the subject.

Chapter 18 uses a practical case to discuss the organization and procedures that are needed whenever a forensic intervention is necessary in the context of mass disasters.

In all, Part V is a clear example of the real value of a multidisciplinary investigation in these types of cases, showing the pros and cons and reassuming the spirit of *Forensic Anthropology and Medicine: Complementary Sciences From Recovery to Cause of Death*, which is to build a bridge between two complementary sciences—forensic anthropology and forensic medicine—that will grow and develop very closely in the future, whenever humans and humanity have the need.

Aurore Schmitt, PhD
Eugénia Cunha, PhD
João Pinheiro, MD, MSci

Contents

Preface v

Contributors xiii

Part I. Two Sciences, One Objective

CHAPTER *1*

Introduction to Forensic Anthropology 3

Douglas H. Ubelaker

CHAPTER *2*

Introduction to Forensic Medicine and Pathology 13

João Pinheiro

CHAPTER *3*

Forensic Anthropology and Forensic Pathology: *The State of the Art* 39

Eugénia Cunha and Cristina Cattaneo

Part II. Aging Living Young Individuals

CHAPTER *4*

Biological vs Legal Age of Living Individuals 57

Francesco Introna and Carlo P. Campobasso

*Part III. Pathophysiology of Death and Forensic Investigation:
From Recovery to the Cause of Death*

CHAPTER *5*

Decay Process of a Cadaver 85

João Pinheiro

CHAPTER *6*

Understanding the Circumstances of Decomposition When the Body
   Is Skeletonized 117

Henri Duday and Mark Guillon

CHAPTER 7

Forensic Investigation of Corpses in Various States of Decomposition:
  A Multidisciplinary Approach 159
  João Pinheiro and Eugénia Cunha

CHAPTER 8

Identification and Differential Diagnosis of Traumatic Lesions
  of the Skeleton 197
  Conrado Rodríguez-Martín

Part IV. Biological Identity

CHAPTER 9

Methodology and Reliability of Sex Determination From the Skeleton 225
  Jaroslav Bruzek and Pascal Murail

CHAPTER 10

Age Assessment of Child Skeletal Remains in Forensic Contexts 243
  Mary E. Lewis and Ambika Flavel

CHAPTER 11

Determination of Adult Age at Death in the Forensic Context 259
  Eric Baccino and Aurore Schmitt

CHAPTER 12

Is It Possible to Escape Racial Typology in Forensic Identification? 281
  John Albanese and Shelley R. Saunders

CHAPTER 13

Estimation and Evidence in Forensic Anthropology:
  Determining Stature 317
  Lyle W. Konigsberg, Ann H. Ross, and William L. Jungers

CHAPTER 14

Pathology as a Factor of Personal Identity in Forensic Anthropology 333
  Eugénia Cunha

CHAPTER 15

Personal Identification of Cadavers and Human Remains 359
  Cristina Cattaneo, Danilo De Angelis, Davide Porta, and Marco Grandi

Part V. Particular Contexts: Crimes Against Humanity and Mass Disasters

CHAPTER 16

Forensic Investigations Into the Missing: *Recommendations and Operational Best Practices* 383

Morris Tidball-Binz

CHAPTER 17

Crimes Against Humanity 409

Dario M. Olmo

CHAPTER 18

Mass Disasters 431

Cristina Cattaneo, Danilo De Angelis, and Marco Grandi

Index 445

Contributors

JOHN ALBANESE • *Department of Sociology and Anthropology, University of Windsor, Windsor, Ontario, Canada*

ERIC BACCINO • *Médecine Légale, CHU Lapeyronie, Montpellier, France*

JAROSLAV BRUZEK • *UMR 5199, PACEA, Laboratoire d'Anthropologie des Populations du Passé, Université Bordeaux 1, Talence, France*

CARLO P. CAMPOBASSO • *Section of Legal Medicine (DiMIMP), University of Bari, Italy*

CRISTINA CATTANEO • *Laboratorio di Antropologia ed Odontologia Forense (LABANOF), Istituto di Medicina Legale, Università degli Studi, Milan, Italy*

EUGÉNIA CUNHA • *Departamento de Antropologia, Faculdade de Ciéncias e Tecnologia, Instituto Nacional de Medicina Legal, Universidade de Coimbra, Coimbra, Portugal*

DANILO DE ANGELIS • *Laboratorio di Antropologia ed Odontologia Forense (LABANOF), Istituto di Medicina Legale, Università degli Studi, Milan, Italy*

HENRI DUDAY • *UMR 5199, PACEA, Laboratoire d'Anthropologie des Populations du Passé, Université Bordeaux 1, Talence, France*

AMBIKA FLAVEL • *Forensic and Bioarchaeological Science Group, School of Conservation Sciences, Bournemouth University, Bournemouth, United Kingdom*

MARCO GRANDI • *Laboratorio di Antropologia ed Odontologia Forense (LABANOF), Istituto di Medicina Legale, Università degli Studi, Milan, Italy*

MARK GUILLON • *Anthropologie, Institut National de Recherches Archéologiques Préventives, UMR 5199 Laboratoire d'Anthropologie des Populations du Passé, France*

FRANCESCO INTRONA • *Section of Legal Medicine (DiMIMP), University of Bari, Bari, Italy*

WILLIAM L. JUNGERS • *Department of Anatomical Sciences, Health Sciences Center, State University of New York, New York*

LYLE W. KONIGSBERG • *Department of Anthropology, University of Tennessee, Knoxville, TN*

MARY E. LEWIS • *Department of Archaeology, School of Human and Environmental Sciences University of Reading, Reading, United Kingdom*

PASCAL MURAIL • *UMR 5199, PACEA, Laboratoire d'Anthropologie des Populations du Passé, Université Bordeaux 1, Talence, France*

DARIO M. OLMO • *Equipo Argentino de Antropologia Forense, Museo de Antropologia, Córdoba, Argentina*

JOÃO PINHEIRO • *Serviço Tanatologia Forense, Instituto Nacional de Medicina Legal, Coimbra, Portugal*

DAVIDE PORTA • *Laboratorio di Antropologia ed Odontologia Forense (LABANOF), Istituto di Medicina Legale, Università degli Studi, Milano, Italy*

CONRADO RODRÍGUEZ-MARTÍN • *Instituto Canario de Bioantropologia, Organismo Autonomo de Museos y Centros, Santa Cruz de Tenerife, Canarias, Spain*

ANN H. ROSS • *Department of Sociology and Anthropology, North Carolina State University, Raleigh, NC*

SHELLEY R. SAUNDERS • *Department of Anthropology, McMaster University, Hamilton, Ontario, Canada*

AURORE SCHMITT • *UMR 5199, PACEA, Laboratoire d'Anthropologie des Populations du Passé, Université Bordeaux 1, Talence, France*

MORRIS TIDBALL-BINZ • *Forensic Coordination, Assistance Division, International Committee of the Red Cross, Geneva, Switzerland*

DOUGLAS H. UBELAKER • *Department of Anthropology, Smithsonian Institution, NMNH, Washington, DC*

PART I

Two Sciences,
One Objective

Chapter 1

Introduction to Forensic Anthropology

Douglas H. Ubelaker

Summary

The academic roots of modern forensic anthropology can be traced back to contributions of Europeans, beginning in the 18th century. In particular, Jean-Joseph Sue, Matthieu-Joseph-Bonaventure Orfila, Paul Broca, Paul Topinard, Étienne Rollet, Leonce Manouvrier, and Karl Pearson published research on the methodology of stature estimation and related topics.

In North America, Thomas Dwight, Aleš Hrdlička, T. D. Stewart, Wilton Krogman, and Mildred Trotter provided early leadership in forensic anthropology. Key developments were the establishment of the physical anthropology section of the American Academy of Forensic Sciences in 1972 and the American Board of Forensic Anthropology in 1977, as well as many publications focusing specifically on issues of forensic anthropology.

Professional activity in forensic anthropology continues to grow throughout the world. The formation in 2003 of the Forensic Anthropology Society of Europe in association with the International Academy of Legal Medicine demonstrates the strength of such activity, and suggests that through regional research and casework, forensic anthropology will become increasingly sophisticated.

Key Words: Forensic anthropology; physical anthropology; Europe; United States.

From *Forensic Anthropology and Medicine:*
Complementary Sciences From Recovery to Cause of Death
Edited by: A. Schmitt, E. Cunha, and J. Pinheiro © Humana Press Inc., Totowa, NJ

1. INTRODUCTION

Forensic anthropology represents the application of knowledge and techniques of physical anthropology to problems of medicolegal significance. Goals are usually to assist in the identification of human remains and to help determine what happened to the remains, especially with regard to the evidence of foul play. Usually, the material examined consists of largely or completely skeletonized remains, or skeletal evidence that has been removed from fleshed remains. Forensic anthropology brings to a case techniques and experience in the interpretation of skeletal remains as well as a worldwide comparative population perspective. Such a perspective is needed to assess properly the probabilities involved and to avoid errors of interpretation.

2. DEFINITIONS

In 1976, T. D. Stewart (1901–1907) defined forensic anthropology as "that branch of physical anthropology, which, for forensic purposes, deals with the identification of more or less skeletonized remains known to be, or suspected of being, human" *(1)*. This definition reflects the thinking at the time regarding the nature of cases usually examined and the distinction between the comparatively new science of forensic anthropology and the more established science of forensic pathology/forensic medicine.

Snow *(2)* offered a somewhat broader definition of forensic anthropology to include applications to "problems of medical jurisprudence." He agreed with Stewart that skeletal remains constituted the usual object of inquiry; however, on occasion, forensic anthropologists offer opinions on the living, become involved in paternity issues, and otherwise deal with fleshed remains. This broader definition has been reinforced in more recent times, as forensic anthropologists have applied their skills to a variety of problems beyond classic skeletal analysis.

3. HISTORY AND DEVELOPMENT

The history of forensic anthropology is closely linked with that of physical anthropology and related specialties within forensic science. Before the late 18th century and continuing to some extent subsequently, skeletal analysis within a forensic context was mostly an applied area of anatomy. Anatomists and physicians would apply their knowledge of skeletal anatomy and its variation as best they could using general knowledge, the few techniques that existed in textbooks, and their experience.

3.1. European Roots

Seeds of what was to become forensic anthropology were sown in France with the work of Jean-Joseph Sue, an instructor of art anatomy at the Louvre in Paris. In 1755, he published measurements of cadavers ranging in age from fetus to young adult. Although the intention was to provide artists with accurate information on body proportions and how such proportions changed with age, the work launched an important French interest, leading to research on stature calculation (3). Sue's measurements reached a wider audience through publication by Matthieu-Joseph-Bonaventure Orfila in two medicolegal textbooks in the early 19th century (4,5). Orfila supplemented Sue's measurements with his own, and for many years, the two databases comprised the sources used by the medicolegal community to evaluate stature from incomplete remains. As Stewart (6) has noted, some confusion resulted from Sue's use of the old French system of measurement (pied, pouce, ligne, etc.) vs the metric system employed by Orfila, but a nascent science of developing techniques aimed specifically at skeletal analysis was launched.

In 1859, Paul Broca (1824–1880) founded, in Paris, the world's first official organization of physical anthropology, the Société d'Anthropologie de Paris. Broca is perhaps best known for his work in neuroanatomy, and like other founding members of the Société, he was trained in medicine, yet he recognized the need for understanding human variation and putting skeletal interpretation on a more scientific footing. Broca developed new instruments (e.g., the osteometric board, goniometer, and stereograph) for the quantification of skeletal measurements, and initiated training and discussion in comparative skeletal anatomy (7).

Broca's successor, Paul Topinard (1830–1911), included in a new textbook of physical anthropology (8) a section on stature estimation, which strengthened interest in these techniques. This effort was followed by a doctoral thesis in Lyon by Étienne Rollet (9), who compared long-bone lengths with cadaver length in a sample of 50 males and 50 females. These data were then organized into tabular form and published (10) by Leonce Manouvrier (1850–1927) and widely utilized subsequently.

English input into the development of forensic anthropology came in the form of Karl Pearson's regression theory. Like Manouvrier, Pearson (11) utilized Rollet's long-bone/cadaver length data, but presented them in the form of regression equations. Pearson's 1899 monograph, as well as much of the biometrical school that followed, focused on evolutionary issues, but these developments greatly influenced the future development of forensic anthropology. Much of the subsequent effort in Europe in physical anthropology focused on paleoanthropology, growth and development, and studies of archeologically recovered human remains, although anthropologists remained active in modern cases involving issues of paternity *(12)* and other legal problems *(13)*. In an early use of the term "forensic anthropology," Schwidetzky *(12)* described efforts in Germany and Austria to use techniques of physical anthropology to assess the parentage of displaced children and those of disputed paternity. According to Schwidetzky *(12)*, as many as 2500 opinions were presented to the courts by anthropologists each year on these issues. She traces the first such opinion back to Professor Otto Reche in 1926, who was then director of the Anthropological Institute at Vienna. Courts in Austria and Germany subsequently emphasized the importance of anthropological analysis in such cases *(12)*.

3.2. Developments in America

As in Europe, early practitioners of forensic anthropology in the United States represented anatomists and medical specialists who were drawn into casework. A case in point is Jeffries Wyman (1814–1874), the Hersey Professor of Anatomy at Harvard and first curator of the Peabody Museum of American Archaeology and Ethnology in 1866, who studied human remains recovered in a sensational murder investigation at Harvard *(14)*. Dr. George Parkman, a physician and wealthy donor to the university, who also ran a loan business, was murdered by Harvard faculty member John W. Webster, who failed to make loan payments. Apparently, after killing Parkman, Webster removed some body parts and burned them in the furnace of his laboratory. Wyman was called in to identify the burned remains and demonstrate that they were consistent with those parts removed from the body *(14)*.

American research aimed directly at issues of forensic anthropology was initiated by Thomas Dwight (1843–1911), upon whom Stewart *(1)* bestowed the title "Father of American Forensic Anthropology." Like Wyman, Dwight was trained in anatomy and taught at Harvard. In fact, Dwight held the Parkman Professorship of Anatomy at Harvard and taught at the medical school that houses the laboratory where Parkman was killed, which was built on the land Parkman donated. Dwight became the first American anatomist to research issues relative to forensic anthropology. After winning a prize for an essay on the medicolegal identification of the human skeleton in 1878 *(15)*, Dwight published a series of important articles *(16–21)* on issues of estimation of sex, age at death, and stature.

George A. Dorsey (1868–1931) appears to represent the first anthropologically trained professional to become involved in forensic matters. Holding a Harvard doctorate, Dorsey conducted some research on archeologically recovered human remains, and, like Wyman, he participated in at least one high-profile forensic case. Just after joining the faculty at the Field Columbian Museum in Chicago in 1896, Dorsey testified in the trial of a Chicago sausage producer who was accused of murdering his wife and attempting to dispose of the remains by cooking them in a vat at the factory *(22)*. Small fragments were recovered that Dorsey felt were consistent with the missing adult female. His testimony was severely challenged by other experts, and Dorsey did not contribute further to forensic anthropology *(1)*.

3.3. Aleš Hrdlička

Aleš Hrdlička (1869–1943) immigrated to the United States in 1881 from his birthplace in Humpolec, Bohemia. After receiving a medical degree in 1892, Hrdlička gradually shifted his interest from medical subjects to anthropology, and became the first curator of the physical anthropology division at the Smithsonian Institution in Washington, DC, where he worked from 1903 until his death in 1943. While at the Smithsonian, Hrdlička became a major figure in the formation and professionalization of American physical anthropology. He founded the American Association of Physical Anthropology, which met for the first time in 1930, and its journal, the *American Journal of Physical Anthropology*, in 1918. Although Hrdlička was a prodigious researcher, he was generally not well-known for his contributions to forensic anthropology. Largely, Hrdlička's contributions to forensic issues were overshadowed by the magnitude of his work in other areas of anthropology and medicine *(23)*.

In 1896, Hrdlička studied in Paris at Broca's Institute (Ecole d'Anthropologie) and was so impressed that he hoped to found a similar institute in Washington *(24)*. While in Paris, Hrdlička studied with Manouvrier *(6)* and visited the laboratory of Alphonse Bertillon (1853–1914), where anthropometric measurements and observations were utilized for human identification *(23)*.

Hrdlička's court testimony and involvement with forensic issues date back to 1896, when he testified in a jury trial on epilepsy and insanity issues. He offered an opinion on a skeletal forensic case in 1910, while traveling in Argentina. From 1914 to about 1920, Hrdlička was involved in legal issues of ancestry among contemporary American Indians, especially the Chippewa. In 1932, he conducted trauma analysis of a recovered cranium and attempted a skull/photograph comparison to assist identification. In 1936, his expertise came to the attention of his Washington neighbor, the FBI, who subsequently consulted with him on many forensic cases involving skeletal remains. Hrdlička initiated a tradition of consultation between the FBI Headquarters in Washington and the Smithsonian that was maintained after Hrdlička's death by T.

D. Stewart *(25,26)* and J. Lawrence Angel (1915–1986) *[27,28]*), and continues today through the author's consultation.

Hrdlička's research included such forensic-related topics as anatomical evidence (or lack thereof) for insanity and criminal behavior (influenced by the work of the Italian Cesare Lombroso [1835–1909]), anthropometry, and techniques for estimating age, sex, stature, and ancestry. Various revisions of his text *Practical Anthropometry* increasingly included forensic-related material; the 1939 edition acquired a section on "Anthropometry and Medicine" and "Anthropometric Identifications." This edition was published the same year as Wilton Krogman's (1903–1987) *A Guide to the Identification of Human Skeletal Material*, which has been cited as inaugurating a new professional period in the history of American forensic anthropology *(1,14)*. These key 1939 publications presented detailed information on techniques of skeletal analysis and served to inaugurate more general interest in the applications of physical anthropology to forensic issues.

Through Hrdlička's and Krogman's work, and subsequently, that of Stewart *(1)*, research and interest in American forensic anthropology gradually increased. World War II and subsequent military conflicts generated the need to identify recovered human remains; consultations by anthropologists and the formation of identification laboratories followed. These developments documented the recognition of the importance of techniques of forensic anthropology in identification and generated new research. Notable examples of the latter include Trotter's work on improving stature estimation methods *(29)* and McKern and Stewart's classic 1957 monograph on skeletal age changes in young American males who died in the Korean conflict *(30)*.

3.4. Physical Anthropology Section of the American Academy of Forensic Sciences

A key development in the history of forensic anthropology was the 1972 formation of the physical anthropology section of the American Academy of Forensic Sciences (AAFS). Through an effort initiated by Ellis R. Kerley (1924–1998), 14 colleagues agreed to comprise the entry class of the new section of physical anthropology in the world's premier organization of forensic science *(31)*. For the first time, forensic anthropologists could gather to report their research and casework at an annual meeting. The Association's *Journal of Forensic Sciences* became more available to publish research results. Membership in the section grew rapidly and by 2004, reached more than 260 members.

3.5. American Board of Forensic Anthropology

In 1977, the American Board of Forensic Anthropology (ABFA) formed to help develop standards for the recognition of expertise in the field. With an initial membership of only five members, the charge of the ABFA was to regulate the practice of forensic anthropology, promote the acceptance of quality forensic anthropology in the legal system, and accredit individuals qualified as forensic anthropologists *(32)*. By 2004, 68 individuals were certified as diplomates by the ABFA. Certification requires residence in the United States or Canada, a relevant doctorate in anthropology, experience in the field, and successful completion of an examination.

Professional activity with the AAFS and the ABFA has stimulated considerable new research and training. Whereas professional activity intensified in association with the AAFS, it can be argued that the visibility of forensic anthropology was comparatively less in other anthropological associations and journals *(33)*. Public exposure to the field through mass-market volumes and television has greatly stimulated public and student interest, generating increased treatment of the field in university academic departments and medicolegal investigation.

3.6. Back in Europe

Although much of the recent academic growth of forensic anthropology has taken place in North America, European institutions and colleagues shared similar experiences. Growth of the science brought recognition to the worldwide variation in many of the attributes studied and the difficulties inherent in applying research conducted from a sample in one part of the world to forensic cases in another. Regional studies have begun to document aspects of this variation, making forensic anthropology a stronger science *(34)*.

3.7. Forensic Anthropology Society of Europe

In 2003, the Forensic Anthropology Society of Europe (FASE) was formed as a subsection of the International Academy of Legal Medicine. This newly formed organization promises to promote the science in Europe in a manner similar to the ABFA. In 2004, the FASE sponsored its first training seminar in collaboration with the Smithsonian Institution, a follow-up to a series of biannual seminars conducted in previous years by the Smithsonian and institutions in France. The FASE conducted its first scientific meeting in Germany in the fall of 2004.

4. SUMMARY

In its early history, the antecedents of forensic anthropology were components of forensic medicine, practiced by anatomists and physicians. With the birth and growth of physical anthropology/forensic anthropology and the increasing specialization of all fields of forensic science, distinctions have grown. One hundred thirty-eight years have passed since the anatomist Jeffries Wyman was called into court to help identify skeletal remains in Massachusetts. Today, the science of forensic anthropology and other aspects of forensic medicine have created specialists who now collaborate in resolving cases *(35)*, at times working side by side at the autopsy table or in the laboratory.

This book documents the growth, sophistication, and specialization of these fields, but also demonstrates how the distinct expertise and methodology need to be integrated in resolving forensic problems. With such interaction and collaboration, the whole becomes greater than the parts.

REFERENCES

1. Stewart, T. D., Essentials of Forensic Anthropology: Especially as Developed in the United States. Charles C. Thomas Publisher, Springfield, IL, 1979.
2. Snow, C. C. Forensic anthropology. In: Redfield, A., ed., Anthropology Beyond the University, Southern Anthropological Society Proceedings, No. 7. Southern Anthropological Society, Athens, GA, pp. 4–17, 1973.
3. Sue, J.-J. Sur les proportions des squelette de homme, examiné depuis l'âge de plus tendre, jusqu' B celui de vingt cinq, soixante ans, & audel [in French]. Acad. Sci. Paris Mem Mathemat. Phys. Present. Divers Savants 2:572–585, 1755.
4. Orfila, M. J. B. Leáons de Médicine Légale, 2 vols. [In French.] Béchet Jeune, Paris, 1821–1823.
5. Orfila, M. J. B., Lesueur, O. Traité des exhumations juridiques, et considérations sur les changements physiques que les cadavres éprouvent en se pourrissant dans la terre, dans l'eau, dans les fosses d'aisance et dans le fumier, 2 vols. [In French.] Béchet Jeune, Paris, 1831.
6. Stewart, T. D. History of physical anthropology. In: Wallace, A. F. C., ed., Perspectives on Anthropology, 1976. Special publication of the American Anthropology Association, no. 10. American Anthropological Association, Washington, D.C., pp. 70–79, 1977.
7. Spencer, F. Broca, Paul (Pierre) (1824–1880). In: Spencer, F., ed., History of Physical Anthropology, Vol. 1. Garland, New York, NY, pp. 221–222, 1997.
8. Topinard, P. Élements d'anthropologie générale [in French]. Delahaye & Lecrosnier, Paris, 1885.
9. Rollet, É. De la mensuration des os longs des membres dans ses rapports avec l'anthropologie, la clinique et la médicine judiciaire [in French]. Lyon, 1889.

10. Manouvrier, L. La détermination de la taille d'aprés des grands os des membres [in French]. Mem. Soc. Anthropol, Paris, 4 Ser. II:347–402, 1893.
11. Pearson, K. Mathematical contributions to the theory of evolution: on the reconstruction of the stature of prehistoric races. Philos. Trans. R. Soc. 192:169–244, 1899.
12. Schwidetzky, I. Forensic anthropology in Germany. Hum. Biol. 26:1–20, 1954.
13. Rösing, F. W. The forensic relevance of skeletal biology: taxonomy of individuals and kinship reconstruction. In: Bonte, J. W., ed., Advances in Forensic Sciences, Vol. 7: Forensic Ondontology and Anthropology. Köster, Berlin, pp. 1–5, 1995.
14. Stewart, T. D. Forensic anthropology. In: Goldschmidt, W., ed., The Uses of Anthropology, Special Publication of the American Anthropology Association, no. 11. American Anthropological Association, Washington, D.C., pp. 169–183, 1979.
15. Dwight, T. The Identification of the Human Skeleton. A Medico-Legal Study. Boston, 1878.
16. Dwight, T. The sternum as an index of sex and age. J. Anat. Physiol. Lond 15:327–330, 1881.
17. Dwight, T. The sternum as an index of sex, height and age. J. Anat. Physiol. Lond 24:527–535, 1890.
18. Dwight, T. The closure of the cranial sutures as a sign of age. Boston Med. Surg. J. 122:389–392, 1890.
19. Dwight, T. Methods of estimating the height from parts of the skeleton. Med. Rec. 46:293–296, 1894.
20. Dwight, T. The range and significance of variations in the human skeleton. Boston Med. Surg. J. 13:361–389, 1894.
21. Dwight, T. The size of the articular surfaces of the long bones as characteristic of sex: an anthropological study. Am. J. Anat. 4:19–32, 1905.
22. Ubelaker, D. George Amos Dorsey. In: Garraty, J. A., Carnes, M. C., eds., American National Biography, Vol. 6. Oxford University Press, New York, NY, pp. 764–765, 1999.
23. Ubelaker, D. H. Aleš Hrdlička's role in the history of forensic anthropology. J. Forensic Sci. 44:724–730, 1999.
24. Stewart, T. D. Hrdlička's dream of an American institute of physical anthropology. In: Novotný, V. V., ed., Proceedings of the 2nd Anthropological Congress dedicated to Dr. Aleš Hrdlička, held in Prague and Humpolec, 3–7 September 1979. Universitas Carolina Pragensis, Praha, pp. 19–21, 1982.
25. Ubelaker, D. H. The forensic anthropology legacy of T. Dale Stewart (1901–1997). J. Forensic Sci. 45:245–252, 2000.
26. Ubelaker, D. H. T. Dale Stewart's perspective on his career as a forensic anthropologist at the Smithsonian. J. Forensic Sci. 45:269–278, 2000.
27. Ubelaker, D. H. J. Lawrence Angel and the development of forensic anthropology in the United States. In: Buikstra, J. E., ed., A Life in Science: Papers in Honor of J. Lawrence Angel, Scientific Papers 6. Center for American Archeology, Kampsville, IL, pp. 191–200, 1990.
28. Ubelaker, D. H. Angel, J(ohn) Lawrence (1915–1986). In: Spencer, F., ed., History of Physical Anthropology, Vol. 1. Garland Publishing, New York, NY, pp. 76–77, 1997.

29. Trotter, M. Estimation of stature from intact long limb bones. In: Stewart, T. D., ed., Personal Identification in Mass Disasters. National Museum of Natural History, Smithsonian Institution, Washington, D.C., pp. 71–83, 1970.

30. McKern, T. W., Stewart, T. D. Skeletal Age Changes in Young American Males: Analyzed from the Standpoint of Age Identification, Report No. EP-45. Quartermaster Research and Development Center, Environmental Protection Research Division, Natick, MA, 1957.

31. Ubelaker, D. H. Contributions of Ellis R. Kerley to forensic anthropology. J. Forensic Sci. 46:773–776, 2001.

32. Ubelaker, D. H. Skeletons testify: anthropology in forensic science, AAPA luncheon address: April 12, 1996. Yearb. Phys. Anthropol. 39:229–244, 1996.

33. Buikstra, J. E., King, J. L., Nystrom, K. C. Forensic anthropology and bioarchaeology in the American Anthropologist: rare but exquisite gems. Am. Anthropol. 105: 38–52, 2003.

34. Prieto, J. L., Magaña, C., Ubelaker, D. H. Interpretation of postmortem change in cadavers in Spain. J. Forensic Sci. 49:918–923, 2004.

35. Ubelaker, D. H., Smialek, J. E. The interface of forensic anthropology and forensic pathology in trauma interpretation. In: Steadman, D. W., ed., Hard Evidence, Case Studies in Forensic Anthropology. Prentice Hall, Saddle River, NJ, pp. 155–159, 2003.

Chapter 2

Introduction to Forensic Medicine and Pathology

João Pinheiro

Summary

The aim of this chapter is to explain what legal medicine is (from its background to the present), and forensic pathology in particular—what its objectives are, what forensic doctors do, and when, why, how, and for whom. Furthermore, the author aims to identify their main difficulties and expectancies.

Starting from the definition and going through a brief historical contextualization, this chapter reviews the types of autopsies, their objectives and, among them, the distinction between cause, manner, and mechanism of death, with unambiguous examples. The different systems of medicolegal organizations in several countries are also debated, with a more detailed presentation of the one considered most efficient. The state of the art throughout the world is analyzed toward/according to the future that needs to be built, often in conjunction with forensic anthropology, emphasizing the role of a fair legislation, organization, and above all, education and training.

Key Words: Forensic medicine; legal medicine; forensic pathology; autopsies; coroner; medical examination; cause of death; manner of death.

To investigate a medicolegal case without performing an autopsy can be compared to reading a mystery novel with last page torn out.

—Luke Tedeschi, 1980

From *Forensic Anthropology and Medicine:
Complementary Sciences From Recovery to Cause of Death*
Edited by: A. Schmitt, E. Cunha, and J. Pinheiro © Humana Press Inc., Totowa, NJ

1. INTRODUCTION

Forensic medicine today is a large medical field that includes many sub-areas. However, generally, when one speaks or thinks about it, one associates it immediately with death, autopsies, and related problems. Yet, this is only part of legal medicine, as new approaches and subspecialties are realized because of the advances in medical sciences and sociopolitical changes around the world. Forensic anthropology and clinical forensic medicine are perhaps the best examples of these "new sciences."

In a book that aims to build a bridge between two complementary sciences (forensic pathology and forensic anthropology) for anthropologists, medical doctors, and related professions, an introductory section to both sciences seems essential (*see* Chapter 1). What is forensic medicine (from its background to present), and what is forensic pathology in particular? What are its objectives? What do forensic doctors do? When, why, how, and for whom? What are the difficulties, and what is expected for the future? These are all questions that a nonmedical professional might ask and that the author attempts to answer in this chapter.

The origin of forensic medicine remains lost in a distant past, whenever the principles of medical sciences met those of law and justice *(1,2)*. Perhaps it began with the Code of Hammurabi (1792–1750 BCE), which imposed sanctions for errors in medical and surgical practices. The same type of punishment also existed in Persia. Later on, the Visigoths promulgated laws that punished poisoning, infanticide, and homicide.

Described as a medical trunk that serves the administration of justice, forensic medicine has different branches. Forensic pathology is probably the most emblematic one. Known in many Latin countries as tanathology (from the Greek word *thanatos*, meaning "death's god"), definitions of forensic pathology are often so broad that they would fit better into forensic medicine as a whole than in this single branch. For Di Maio *(3)*, it is "a branch of medicine that applies the principles and knowledge of the medical sciences in the field of law." An even larger conception of forensic pathology *(4)* considers it the study of diseases and injuries of the community, because it involves the knowledge of diagnosis and treatment in every medical specialty, but also requires information in many nonmedical areas, such as chemistry, physics, criminalistics and police sciences, motor vehicle and highway conception, politics, sociology, and even the way of life of a society. Closer to its objectives and limits, Williams et al. *(5)* define forensic pathology as a specialized branch of pathology (*pathology* being the study by scientific methods of disease and tissue injury) that relates within a legal framework to the effects of trauma, poisoning, occupational hazards, and natural disease.

Forensic dissections of bodies began in the 13th century at the University of Bologna in Italy by a surgeon and teacher of anatomy, Saliceto *(6)*. Surprisingly, these forensic dissections appeared before the hospital autopsies that started by the end of the 19th century with Rokitansky, Virchow, and the advent of the pathogenesis of diseases and cellular pathology *(6)*. However, some authors *(7)* consider the French surgeon Ambrosio Paré, who in 1575 began a real scientific period in France, the father of legal medicine. This paternity is divided with Zacchia, the Pope's physician, who taught in Italy and wrote in 1601 what can be considered the first medicolegal textbook *(7)*. This was of decisive influence on the development of forensic sciences, as were the European codes of the 16th century *(6)*: the Bamberg Code in 1507 and especially the Caroline Code in 1532, which obliged the courts to call specialized doctors to clarify forensic questions.

Nevertheless, the 19th century was indeed a reference for modern legal medicine, born formally in many countries, almost at the same time: 1855 in Austria *(6)*, 1872 in Hungary *(8)*, 1886 in Brazil *(7)*, 1887 in Great Britain *(9,10)*, and 1889 in Portugal (when legal medicine was first referred to as being legally organized *[11]*). This century was really a golden age for forensic medicine *(1,11)*, which knew a quick but supported growth, especially in France, Italy, and Germany *(11)*. Besides, in German countries, forensic matters were always carefully treated, as can be proved by the early beginning of teaching forensic medicine in some universities in 1720 *(11)*. The posterior development of forensic pathology was processed in accordance with the legal systems and sociopolitical conditions of each country.

At the end of the 19th century, complementary sciences, such as toxicology and histology, were aggregate to forensic pathology, and from that union resulted the constitution of legal medicine institutes similar to the medicolegal units known today, where every type of expertise related to justice may be executed.

Later, in the second half of the 20th century, a new medicolegal problem arose in Europe and wherever roads and cars existed. The traffic accidents and the necessity of civil litigations of the injuries of the victims led to a new medicolegal subspecialty concerning living people: clinical forensic medicine. It started in Belgium and France with Derobert, Roche, Muller, and Rousseau *(12)*. Supported by the Deliberation 75 *(7)* of the Committee of Ministers of the Council of Europe, an "expertise-type" was created *(12,13)* to achieve a global evaluation of consequences resulting from injuries caused by accidents to the body of an individual (as a whole being). This process was crucial for the financial indemnity of the injuries by insurance companies. These ideas, adopted in Portugal by Oliveira Sá, a great enthusiast of this new discipline, were developed and "exported" to Spain through the excellent relationship he had with the forensic physicians in the neighbor country, where a huge development took place; however, it was more as a private medical activity than centralized in medicolegal institutions. The popularity of this new forensic area increased quickly because of the growing number of traffic accidents in the world. Once the Iberian Peninsula was "conquered," the area extended to South and Latin America. The English-speaking countries were the last to develop this new specialty; it has been only within the last several years that the popularity of clinical forensic medicine has exploded in the United States and the United Kingdom.

This specialty has opened the window to economic independence for forensic practitioners (but not for pathologists). Close to victimology, this new area has extended to any act of violence on a living individual: aggressions, sexual assault, age determination, and of course, traffic accidents. Baccino (E. Baccino, personal communication) claims that forensic doctors should be called "violence medicine doctors," as violence, whether lethal or not, is the common ground between those who commit it and those who suffer it. Violence is usually the result of complex interactions between offender and victim, and the evaluation of injuries is similar in living and dead bodies.

Taking these facts into account, some specialists (E. Baccino, personal communication) achieved the incorrect idea, not shared by the authors, that forensic medicine is becoming much more clinical than pathological.

2. AUTOPSIES

2.1. Types of Autopsy: Clinical and Forensic

There are essentially two types of autopsies—the clinical or academic autopsies done at hospitals and the forensic autopsies executed in the medicolegal settings. The aim of the clinical autopsy is to find out, clarify, or confirm diagnoses that remained unknown or are not sufficiently clear during the stay of a patient in a hospital or health institution. The forensic autopsy is performed under the supervision of a legal authority such as a prosecutor, a procurator fiscal, a magistrate, a judge, a coroner, medical examiner, or the police. The forensic or medicolegal autopsy primarily focuses on violent deaths (accidents, suicides, and homicides), although in many situations (35–40% according to the Portuguese experience), it also deals with natural deaths that should be the object of a clinical autopsy. Suspicious and sudden deaths, deaths without medical assistance, and deaths that are litigious or related to surgical or anesthetic procedures, must also to be clarified by a forensic autopsy.

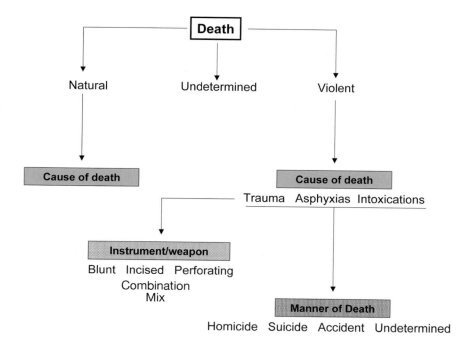

Fig. 1. Categorization of the main objectives of a forensic autopsy.

Usually in the majority of jurisdictions, relatives' permission is not necessary to carry out the autopsy. Eventual obstruction of justice is then avoided. In some regions, the forensic autopsies are divided in two categories *(6)*— criminal deaths (suspicious or because of murder, homicidal suffocation or smothering, infanticide) and noncriminal deaths (suicides, natural deaths, accidents, etc.).

2.2. Objectives of a Forensic Autopsy

The determination of the cause and manner of death has been considered during recent decades the classic objective of a forensic autopsy. Although not new, another goal emerged recently from ethnic conflicts and genocide as important as the first objective: the identification of the victim(s). Thus, cause of death and identification are essentially the two main objectives of a medicolegal autopsy.

When a typical forensic necropsy is performed on an identified corpse, a categorization of goals can be established (Fig. 1). To begin with, it is necessary to diagnose the cause of death and to distinguish it as either a natural or a violent death, which can be achieved often at the same time at the autopsy table, solely based on macroscopy. If the case corresponds to a violent death, three possibilities arise: traumatic injuries, asphyxia, or intoxication. Next, traumatic wounds should be classified according to the instrument/weapon that produced them: blunt, incised and perforating, or a mix. "What was the weapon used?" is precisely one of the first questions the police officers usually ask the pathologist as soon as a crime investigation begins in order to plan the investigation. Incised wounds are produced by sharp instruments, whereas perforating injuries can be the result of different weapons, from pointed, sharp instruments to firearms. One should note that the nomenclature of these wounds is not precise in every country or language, which frequently yields additional difficulties in interpreting an autopsy report.

The final step of a violent death autopsy is the establishment of the manner of death (*see* Fig. 1): homicide, suicide, accident, or undetermined (as explained in Subheading 2.3.). Many cases (intoxications and natural deaths, for example) are not ascertained at the necropsy table and need further investigation, including complementary examinations.

An autopsy also has many other accessory objectives, such as the following:

1. To document (diagnose, describe, and measure) both external and internal injuries.
2. To detect external and internal abnormalities, malformations, and diseases.
3. To attribute the death to a particular event—the nexus of causality, a paramount issue in legal medicine.
4. To determine other causes that might have contributed to death.
5. To collect samples for histological, toxicological, microbiological, or other ancillary analysis.
6. To determine the time of death, when necessary and possible (6).
7. To determine whether a newborn had breathed or not.
8. To keep relevant organs, tissues, or samples as evidence.
9. To provide a full written report of the necropsy findings, giving a serious and competent medicolegal interpretation of the findings.
10. To return the body to the family as well presented as possible.

In certain necropsies, characteristic objectives of a particular type of expertise can be pointed out. When a firearm has been used, it is important to estimate the distance of the shot, the pathway of the bullet, to determine the entry or the exit wound, and the relative position between the aggressor and the victim.

In delayed deaths, it is necessary to establish the causality nexus between an original traumatic event (and correspondent lesions) and the supposed "natural cause" of death ascertained. For example, it is a common mistake that general physicians certify "pulmonary embolism" as a natural cause of death of traffic accident victims who suffered traumatic injuries and died in the hospital with such a complication, obviously linked to the initial traumatic wounds.

2.3. Cause, Manner, and Mechanism of Death

Many people, including some specialists working in the area, have difficulties in distinguishing among cause, manner, and mechanism of death. *Cause of death* means any injury or disease that generates a pathological alteration in the body that leads to the individual's death. Examples are esophageal carcinoma, a myocardial infarction, blunt trauma of the head, or a gunshot wound of the thorax.

The *mechanism of death* signifies the pathological alteration resulting from the cause of death: hemorrhage, infection, fatal arrhythmia. It is possible that a mechanism of death is shared by different causes of death: a hemorrhage may result from blunt trauma, stabbing, or lung carcinoma. The contrary is also true, as the cause of death can give origin to different mechanisms of death: a gunshot wound can produce a hemorrhage, but if the victim had survived, an infectious complication is the mechanism.

The *manner of death* (known in Latin countries as "medicolegal etiology," where it is considered as another objective of the autopsy) means, in violent deaths, the distinction among an accident, suicide, homicide, or an undetermined death. Following the above-mentioned way of thinking, a manner of death can be the result of multiple causes and mechanisms of death. The classic example is the one of a gunshot injury (cause of death), which could be classified as the four manners of death: homicide (someone shot the victim), suicide (the shot was self-inflicted), accident (the shot was self-inflicted unintentionally), and undetermined (there are no witnesses to the events, and the autopsy failed to clarify the manner of death). Mechanism of death could be hypovolemic shock by hemorrhage or, if the person survived, a thromboembolic or infectious complication, such as a bronchopneumonia or peritonitis.

Cause and manner of death determinations often imply laboratory analysis and (always) information about the circumstances of death that can be determined by the police (or other authorities) scene report or by the forensic pathologist, if the pathologist was the one who recovered the body from the site. This is not always simple and easy because the pathologist's statement not infrequently contradicts the scene report or the police story about the case. Moreover, families seldom accept suicide as the cause of death. That is why the pathologist must study each case carefully, must be well informed about

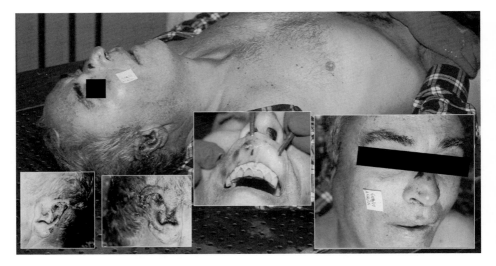

Fig. 2. Homicide without lethal injuries: minor traumatic wounds of the face, inner lips, and tears of the ears caused by the aggressor's bite. Death was attributed to sympathetic-adrenal stimulation on a victim with clinical favorable antecedents such as chronic ischemic disease.

the events surrounding the victim, and document the investigation cautiously to produce the final verdict.

Exceptionally, a natural cause of death can be considered a homicide. The author autopsied a man who was almost caught in his lover's bed by her husband. He ran to the loft of the house and was discovered some minutes later by the husband. After a violent argument, the men fought and suddenly, the lover died. Minor traumatic injuries, not enough to justify the death, were found (Fig. 2). Microscopic sections of the heart revealed a chronic ischemic disease, confirmed by the cardiologist of the victim. Death was attributed to a sympatheticoadrenal stimulation mechanism. This case turned out to be a case study in the courts, but finally, the accused aggressor was dismissed. Other authors have stated similar reports *(3)*, but it is controversial and rare that a homicide is ruled only by psychological stress without any external or internal injuries.

In nonfresh cadavers, i.e., in different states of decomposition (closer to this book's subject), the pathologist and the forensic anthropologist are sometimes not able to ascertain the manner of death, especially in skeletonized bodies. These are the cases that remain undetermined.

Occasionally, a manner of death can be stated without determination of the cause of death. In a documented suicide committed by a nurse who injected herself with an anesthetic product, the toxin was not detected by laboratory analysis. Macroscopy and histology were also nonspecific. However, the circumstances were so evident—the syringe found in the arm, the empty bottle in the wastebasket, and a farewell letter—that a suicide was ruled.

In a case within the context of this book, a young pregnant girl was murdered by her boyfriend, who confessed to the crime. She was buried in soil (*see* Chapters 5 and 7 for more detail on this case) and exhumed 2.5 mo later. The autopsy was conducted by a multidisciplinary team*, but it was impossible to confirm the cause of death because of the decomposition of the body—thoracic organs were skeletonized, and the larynx apparatus and hyoid bone were not found *(14)*. However, the circumstances and all the information collected by the police pointed to a high probability that the death was a homicide.

3. MEDICOLEGAL ORGANIZATIONS

What kinds of deaths are investigated through a medicolegal necropsy? It depends on the country legislation: violent deaths, suspicious deaths or deaths of unknown cause, sudden deaths, deaths without medical assistance, deaths in institutions or in custody, or deaths related to surgical or anesthetic procedures. Apart from the latter and the violent deaths, many of the other deaths fall into the category of natural deaths, which represent the higher volume of work in the majority of medicolegal institutions. Many pathologists complain about it. However, one will be a good forensic pathologist and learn how to recognize a violent death only when one has performed many necropsies of natural deaths.

It is not the purpose of this chapter to make an exhaustive review of the medicolegal systems throughout the world, but to provide examples that illustrate the limits of medicolegal frameworks, pointing out the pros and cons, differences and similarities, realities and expectations.

3.1. United States

Medicolegal systems are different around the world. In the United States, the situation can vary within states from one county to another. However, there are two well-defined main systems, the coroner system and the medical examiner system *(3,4)*.

---

* Team composed of the author, a forensic pathologist, and a forensic anthropologist, E. Cunha.

The coroner system, inspired by the English feudal system *(3)*, is based on the election of someone to the office of coroner. The coroner is in charge of determining the manner of death, with or without physician opinion, in accordance or not with the autopsy report. In the past, it was not necessary to be a physician, but in many areas today, it is required, even if the physician is not a pathologist. The training for coroners varies from none to 1 to 2 wk *(3)*. The variation of the coroner's system is related to the fact that, in the past, the system was introduced in different areas of the British Empire in its pure "English" form, and the rules (and subsequent amendments thereto) of the Coroner's Act (in Great Britain) in recent years have not been adopted in the United States *(10)*.

The medical examiner system introduced in 1877 in Massachusetts *(2,3)* continued to develop until 1918 when, in New York City, the first medical examiner was installed* *(2,3)*. The medical examiner should be a physician experienced in pathology. The concept that can be found in the United States today originates from the New York system, with variations. In the modern systems, the chief medical examiner must be a forensic pathologist.

The medical examiner (in some states) works under the guidelines of the state government agencies or the public health department, either case leading to additional problems because technical and economic independence is essential to perform this work. On the other hand, a nonphysician cannot make medical determinations, no matter what training that person has *(3)*. As a politically elected administrator, the coroner can easily be put under pressure to make a determination, whereas a physician must behave under rigorous ethical rules. Even if the coroner relies on a competent physician, the coroner may be replaced in the next election, for political reasons, by a more convenient person. Whatever the name of the system used—medical examiner, coroner, or medical examiner–coroner— the main issue remains the responsibility and the methods these authorities must assume to assure scientific and professional quality *(4)*.

These systems do not provide a forensic pathologist on every scene examination because the number of forensic pathologists is not sufficient to do so. In the United States, it is attributed to lay investigators employed by the medical examiner's office, who decide whether a death is a medical examiner's case. When a death certificate cannot be obtained, the case is accepted by the office. These professionals then make a report. When the case is not accepted, a physician obligatorily revises the report. If there is a disagreement between the two parts (a rare possibility), the case will then be accepted. The medical examiner decides whether to perform only an external examination, a full autopsy, or other laboratory tests.

---

* It was not until the 1980s that the first "real" medical examiner system, including a central laboratory, was established.

3.2. Northern Europe

The medicolegal external examination system is also used in northern European countries such as Finland and Denmark (15,16). In the latter, the examination is made by a medical officer of health (in the presence or requested by the police), who decides if an autopsy is necessary (16). Presumed cause and manner of death are stated after the external examination, sometimes erroneously (as mentioned under Heading 6).

3.3. Turkey

A similar system is employed in Turkey (17): the prosecutor refers medicolegal deaths to forensic departments, where the medical doctor, after an external examination, may sign the death certificate with the prosecutor, unless a need for an autopsy is decided.

3.4. Great Britain

The development of legal medicine in Great Britain is inseparable from the coroner system (10) that was later adopted in the United States. It began with the election of county coroners in the 12th century and followed through the subsequent centuries, a slow development. The practice of forensic medicine dates from the 17th century, when the first autopsy was recorded, but the first book was published only in the early 19th century. The Coroner's Act of 1887 that regulates the actual British medicolegal system arrived late in comparison with the development of the specialty in Continental Europe (9,10).

The Coroner's Amendment Act of 1926 and other rules and orders updated the original Act. As a result, the coroners now deal with many natural deaths. The coroners are, in some areas, based on university departments, whereas in other regions, Home Office pathologists may be called for cases of homicide and suspicious deaths. Yet, the vast part of the coroners' cases (natural and noncriminal unnatural deaths) are dealt with by consultant pathologists of Britain's National Health Service in general hospitals (10).

3.5. France

In France, the external examination is always requested by the police or a prosecutor. However, a medicolegal autopsy may be ordered only by a prosecutor, who relies on his exclusive decision—French law does not have any provision with which to decide whether to order or deny a forensic necropsy. The general physician who certifies the death generally does not signal a "medicolegal obstacle" on death certificate. The forensic doctor, whose opinion is given later, usually confirms this statement. In this case, there is no autopsy. Therefore, the judicial investigation of a death is directed frequently and easily toward a natural death, a suicide, or an accident, without autopsy *(18)*. That is why, in France, suicides are seldom, unquestionably creating training problems (for example, one cannot perform a good autopsy of strangulation without having been trained by autopsying many suicidal hangings).

The situation is even worse when a fatal accident happens at work—the autopsy is commonly not executed *(18,19)*. Lenoir refers to studies in which when autopsies were performed, in 32% of the cases, the examinations were performed between 3 and 6 mo after death *(19)*, which means they were actually exhumations, extremely limited in terms of diagnostic value when compared with a recent autopsy. Recent autopsies of job accidents or professional diseases were less than 9% *(19)*. Relatives' prejudice in terms of litigation by insurance companies is obvious.

3.6. Spain

In Spain, the *forense* is a kind of medicolegal examiner of a particular area of the country. The *forense* must be able to handle every type of medicolegal expertise from autopsies to psychiatric examinations of prisoners. To obtain the qualifications, medical doctors have to undergo a postgraduate training of 6 mo in all relevant forensic areas: pathology, toxicology, genetics, and law. A positive aspect of this system is good national coverage. On the other hand, *forenses* have excessive power because in practice, they are the ones who decide whether or not an autopsy must be made, and few are performed. Moreover, the minor training in so vast a scientific area is deficient and not appropriate.

3.7. Portugal

Portugal is known to have one of the best medicolegal organizations in Europe (D.N. Viera, personal communication).* As a result, many countries wish to implement and "import" this system. That is the reason why it deserves a detailed presentation and a reference to Duarte Nuno Vieira, the "engineer" of this system, first and actual president of the National Institute of Legal Medicine (NILM).

The NILM, an autonomous administrative branch of the Justice Ministry, is located in the small central town of Coimbra and not in the capital, Lisbon (a good example of political decentralization of institutions). The NILM (Fig. 3) is composed of three main delegations (former independent legal medicine institutes): one in Coimbra and the other two in bigger towns, Lisbon

---

* In 2003, in Bordeaux, the European Economic Community conference of Medico-Legal Institutes acclaimed the Portuguese system as the best in Europe.

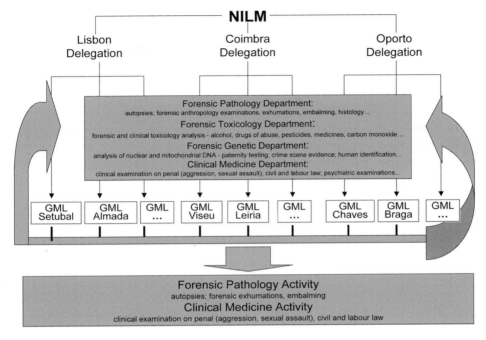

Fig. 3. The Portuguese National Institute of Legal Medicine (NILM). The regional forensic units (Gabinetes Médico-Legais [GML]) perform essential forensic activity, on pathology and clinical medicine areas, and depend technically on the main delegations.

and Oporto. These three delegations are complete "institutes," meaning that almost all types of medicolegal expertise can be executed at each location. Each delegation is divided in departments as follows: forensic pathology (including histopathology), forensic toxicology, forensic genetics, and clinical forensic medicine (which includes the sexual abuse and psychiatry areas). There are also protocols with other institutions, such as the Anthropology Department of the Sciences and Technology Faculty to perform the anthropological examinations,* and hospitals to realize more specific examinations that can be requested during the medicolegal activity. Concerning forensic anthropological examinations, when a forensic pathologist has a nonfresh body as part of routine work, the assistance of forensic anthropologists can be sought (details about the *modus operandi* of this multidisciplinary work are described in Chapter 6). In some cases, when the remains are dry bones, the anthropologist

* The head of the Anthropology Department is E. Cunha.

can do the work. However, if a death certificate is necessary or if the cause of death can be determined, the pathologist is called to participate. This assistance covers nearly the whole country, with few exceptions related to cases dealt with by local practitioners with no communication to the NILM.

In forensic pathology and clinical forensic medicine departments, there are full-time medical doctors who are specialists in forensic medicine after a 5-yr training period, the normal duration of any medical specialty in the country. In the histopathology department, a fully qualified pathologist examines all the microscopic sections from the autopsies performed in the delegation and from the regional forensic units described in the following paragraphs. Biologists, biochemists, pharmacists, and chemists are qualified to work in the laboratories (toxicology and genetics) and they are trained on duty. A psychiatrist, an orthopedist, and a neurologist are part-time specialists who help and give scientific support to the medical examinations, more frequently in clinical forensic medicine departments. X-ray facilities with full-time radiology technicians, essential in all the medical areas, are available at any time; however, the radiologist medical specialist usually works on a part-time basis. The whole institution is managed by an administrative staff that has the inherent logistic facilities to work appropriately.

Regional forensic units called medicolegal offices (Gabinetes Médico-Legais [GML]), created in smaller towns to cover the entire country, aggregate the medicolegal activities of the localities (*see* Fig. 3). They have the minimum requirements to perform all medicolegal functions, such as autopsies, clinical examinations in civil litigation, and sexual or drug abuse, but no laboratories. Samples, when needed, are sent to one of the three main delegations mentioned previously. In these GML, there are medical doctors of other specialties, mostly general practitioners, who obtained (the majority of them) a postgraduate course of 90 h, including the practice of autopsies. It is something, but not sufficient. Thus, this is the challenge the NILM must face in the near future: to improve the quality of training of the "regional" specialists, because now there is a gap between the quality of the medicolegal services in the main delegations (good, at international standards) and the GML.

The main positive aspect of the Portuguese system is the law: all violent deaths or deaths whose cause is unknown are object of a compulsory necropsy.* The decision relies on the prosecutor, who takes into account the police report about the circumstances of death and the hospital information (if the deceased was admitted to a hospital). The prosecutor usually interviews the relatives in order to know the clinical antecedents or other relevant information about the

---

* Law 45/2004, Art. 18. Furthermore, this law provides that autopsies of immediate death after traffic or job accidents must be performed.

case. The prosecutor can always ask the forensic pathologist's opinion to decide whether a necropsy must be done. This system avoids Europe's and the United States' chronic problem: the decline in autopsy numbers. It provides a significant number of postmortem dissections for current times: about 6000 a year for a country with 12 million inhabitants. For 2002, the forensic autopsy incidence was 4.8% of total deaths, whereas in 2003 this figure was 5.1%.

Another service offered by the NILM is the round-the-clock assistance of a forensic doctor in the three main delegations and in many GML, to make scene examinations in case of violent deaths and to examine victims of aggressions (especially those with only minor injuries) or to observe victims of sexual assault, so biological evidence is not lost. This is an important community service, with very good results in terms of helping the criminal investigation that follows the events.

There is a close relationship between the three main delegations and the principal medicine faculties around the country, where the undergraduate teaching of legal medicine is done. Forensic medicine professors are usually jointly appointed by their own faculties and the NILM. The medical and law students of Portuguese universities have to follow a semester or 1 yr of a legal medicine course, and they are obliged to assist with at least two autopsies. This scientific support is also applied to magistrates, prosecutors, and judges, even in their academic training. The NILM and their professionals collaborate with all sorts of forensic training, from criminal police to mortuary technicians. Sometimes, it extends out of the country, as with the postgraduate courses the author with other Portuguese and Danish colleagues taught in Kosovo, under the United Nation auspices, to form Kosovar medical practitioners.

Finally, the medicolegal council composed of university professors of diverse medical specialties and law, representatives of the Portuguese Medical Council, and the directors of the three NILM delegations is a technical scientific consultant body. It assists the courts in medical issues that overcome routine forensic cases and that need deeper and specific studies or discussion, such as medical responsibility. Apart from the permanent members, other specialists may be called to give their opinion in a particular expertise. This council can be requested by the Minister of Justice, the General Prosecutor, the Supreme Council of Justice, and the President of the NILM.

4. QUALITY CONTROL AND FORENSIC PATHOLOGIST QUALIFICATIONS

The requirements about quality control of autopsies are not a recent issue, because in the 19th century, the Austrian decree of 1855 provided very detailed instructions for performing a medicolegal autopsy *(6)*. It occurred in other countries at the same time. In Portugal, a questionnaire and precise instructions were furnished by the famous Decree of February 8, 1900, which lasted until the 1980s, when the law was renovated and a new medicolegal organization implemented, with higher skills and standards.

Modern times necessitated harmonization of procedures, especially inside communities such as the Economic European Community. The United Nations approved in 1991 its model protocol of autopsy (UN Minnesota Protocol) *(20)*, and then, Interpol standardized its Disaster Victim Identification protocol *(21)*. The European Council of Legal Medicine promoted the "Harmonisation of the Performance of the Medicolegal Autopsy," which was approved in 1995 and used as a base to the Recommendation R(99)3 on the "Harmonisation of Medico-Legal Autopsy Rules and Its Explanatory Memorandum," adopted by the Economic European Community Committee of Ministers in 1999 *(6,18)*. In fact, the European countries are obliged to incorporate these rules into their national legislation. However, it is not the case, as far as is known, in the majority of them. It is difficult to harmonize procedures, whereas harmonizing systems and qualifications are not.

The professional qualifications of those who perform medicolegal autopsies vary from place to place and from system to system. Sometimes, as in the United States, it registers regional and intraregional variations. From fully qualified clinical or anatomic pathologists with postgraduate training in forensics (United States, United Kingdom) *(3,4)* and forensic physicians with a full specialty in legal medicine (Portugal), to a minimal half-year training *(forenses* in Spain) or even no formation at all, every stage of qualification is possible.

In the United States, the chief medical examiner is required to be a board-certified forensic pathologist. The chief medical examiner is a physician who has accomplished a series of graduate medical programs and examinations involving the Residence Review Committee, the Accreditation Council for Graduate Medical Education, and the American Board of Pathology *(3)*. A full year of forensic pathology ends this training program.

In the European Union, forensic medicine exists as a medical specialty in 20–25 of its member countries *(22)* with different training programs.

In Yugoslavia *(1)* and Portugal, after the completion of medical studies and 2 yr of general practice, physicians may specialize in forensic medicine for 3 and 5 yr, respectively. A similar medical specialization of 4 yr in forensic medicine can also be followed in the Spanish university hospitals. Only a few candidates make this choice; they need a couple of years to reach the same position as the *forenses,* who trained only half a year postgraduation.

To be a forensic specialist in Hungarian universities, one must take a postgraduate course of 4 yr. A valuable particularity of the Hungarian system is a compulsory short course for each specialist every 5 yr *(8)*, a good example that should be followed in other countries.

In Belgium, legal medicine is a medical specialty recognized by law since 2002, requiring 5 yr of complementary studies *(23)*.

Unfortunately, and apart from these programs and qualifications, there are in too many places people neither sufficiently skilled nor experienced performing important criminal necropsies *(6,18)*. This is not exclusive of poor, undeveloped countries: it happens in Europe and even in the United States. Besides, it is more than an academic question because it determines a deficient administration of justice and creates the possibility for enormous and, sometimes irreparable, justice errors. *A bad opinion is often worse than no opinion at all*, because in the latter case, a magistrate is clearly conscious of the lack of support to his or her decision. With some of the absolutely certain statements of inexperienced pathologists seen, a judge will rely on apparently irrefutable arguments without any kind of scientific justification.

In all, education and training are the decisive battles forensic pathology must win in the near future.

5. THE STATE OF THE ART

The medicolegal systems changed in the last few decades. In the 1980s, law modifications in the United States allowed families to prevent autopsies that do not seem to be homicide, which meant that only autopsies of obvious homicides were authorized.

Every experienced pathologist knows that the problem is never with the cases that appear as homicides, but with those masked as suicides, accidents, or even natural diseases. According to Quatrehomme *(18)*, Brinkmann estimated that for Germany in 1997, 1200 homicides a year were hidden as natural deaths, and that 11,000 of nonnatural deaths were classified as natural ones. The death of an old man found at home 3 wk after he had disappeared, supposedly dead of a natural disease, was attributed after the autopsy to a murder by a blunt trauma of the head *(24)*. It is not always possible to recognize a homicide until an autopsy is performed. There are many examples of this, such as child battering syndrome, suffocations, traffic accidents that were, in fact, cardiac infarcts.

The changes in national legislations brought tremendous consequences everywhere they were applied: United States *(25)*, Finland *(15)*, Denmark *(16)*, and France *(26)*. The number of autopsies has diminished vertiginously in many parts of the world. Diverse arguments have been exposed to justify this dramatic drop, such as the high cost of necropsies *(15,25–27)*, lack of facilities, difficulties in attracting people to the discipline *(15)*, the advent of the modern diagnostic methods *(25,27,28)*, communication problems between pathologists and clinicians—a significant delay to know a necropsy result, the pathologist jargon, and the defensive position, family opposition because of fear of mutilation, religious objections, or economic interest, or other conveniences of morticians *(27)*. Citing these negative approaches that contributed to the removal of the minimum autopsy rate requirement (20%) by the American Joint Commission on Accreditation of Hospitals, Clark *(27)* states that some authors consider hospital autopsies as inefficient, expensive, irrelevant, and unnecessary.

Another non-negligible reason also mentioned by Tedeschi *(25)* is the very little motivation of clinic pathologists to perform postmortem examinations: it is a long task, done while facing bad ergonomic conditions (e.g., standing up, bad odors, an unclean work with a relative risk of contagious disease) and socially not recognized. They prefer the "clean" biopsies of surgical pieces or other more interesting researches. Nevertheless, the question is not only the motivation, but also the inability to answer the question of "Why did he die?", because of the inefficient approach hospital pathologists use to explain the cause and manner of death *(4)*. Taking into account this last development of clinical pathology in the world, it is predictable that, in the near future, clinical pathologists will not be able to perform any type of autopsy.

However, in accordance with many authors *(15,29)*, the authors in this book believe that autopsies (either clinical or forensic) are still necessary to control and correct causes of death and to distinguish the violent deaths under the initial label of natural deaths. It should by no means be substituted by external medical examinations.

In this context, the accuracy of the mortality statistics if autopsies were carried out in well-defined populations must not be forgotten in order to permit the health authorities of each country to adopt adequate measures of preventing and controlling disease, which is, unfortunately, not always the case. This has a perverse result on the society: the mass media bomb the public with official statistics as soon as a particular clinical entity (such as sudden cardiac death) occurs, ignoring that they are not, often, trustable. For example, in a large sequence of 1595 patients, Ambach et al. *(28)* demonstrated that a clinical diagnosis of myocardial infarction based on the modern methods, including typical symptoms, electrocardiographic abnormalities, and enzymology, failed after autopsy in 28% of the cases. Myocardial infarction is overdiagnosed in clinics *(28)*, resulting in mortality statistics 15% higher than the reality. Shockingly, murder by strangulation was found among this series, reinforcing that the *autopsy represents the best opportunity for clinicians to check their diagnostic certainty.* In 1076 consecutive unselected hospital autopsies, Clark *(27)* proved the efficiency and usefulness of the hospital autopsy: 90% of positive determinations for dead on arrival and 9% of significant findings not obtained by other testing methods. He also demonstrated that the fear of some clinicians to be involved in civil litigation because of eventual malpractice is unfounded—a few cases were revealed by the autopsy, and not one was introduced as evidence. On the other hand, families are comforted by the 90% confirmation of clinic information and very satisfied with the 9% of cases clinically unclear that the autopsies ultimately explain. This diminishes many malpractice claims. In terms of real costs, using the College of American Pathologists units, Clark *(27)* arrives at a cost similar to previous authors ($930 per case), concluding that it is not an inexpensive procedure, considering that 200 autopsies (the usual rate for a single pathologist) might prevent 10 malpractices. Hospitals' and physicians' malpractice insurance carriers should consider the autopsy as a valuable investment and should share their costs.

However, pretending to reduce forensic pathology to the restrictive limits of the "little" Europe or North America should be considered a chauvinist position to which the author, by no means, subscribe. In fact, the notorious decline of autopsies in the Old World, probably related to the improvement of the citizenship rights and a general awareness of the human rights by the population, is specific to the so-called developed countries. In Central and South America for instance, autopsy numbers have not declined, and maintain a high level because of the violence those countries face. In São Paolo, Brazil, an average of 40–50 necropsies of all sorts of violent deaths is performed each day in only one of the five local forensic institutes. In Bogotá, Columbia, the institute does not close on weekends because they could not face the accumulation of cadavers on Mondays. In this part of the world, the quality of expertise presents a problem. However, there are good exceptions. The Medicolegal Institute of Bogotá (Colombia) reaches a quality level that many departments of the United States and Europe would like to have. The challenge for the high standard forensic community is to export the know-how to these countries in a global effort to train their human resources. It has already begun in Brazil with Portuguese scientists, and in Argentina[*] and other Latin American countries with Spanish specialists. However, it is limited to

---

[*] Recently, a delegation of the American Academy of Forensic Sciences took charge of a whole Saturday in a National Meeting of Legal Medicine.

the congress or scientific meetings level, which is not enough. This effort needs much more than someone that travels and shows, in different conferences, some pieces of "academic" science. It needs effective cooperation from those who work in the field, perform autopsies everyday, and have the experience and the doubts related therewith. They should cooperate and work there, in short or medium missions with local physicians, helping on a daily basis formation. Unfortunately, this objective is far from being attained. At the same time, it could also be an outstanding opportunity to form professionals of countries like Portugal, where violent deaths are fortunately not frequent: 1 mo spent in a South American institute is equivalent to 4 or 5 yr of local training.

6. THE FUTURE: A CHALLENGE FOR ALL

Quality and training, that is, education, is indeed one of the three major platforms on which forensic pathology needs to build in the future, the other two aims being good legislation and organization. This challenge, on a scientific and quality level, has been emphasized by renowned specialists *(3,4,6,18)*. Truth, work, and experience are crucial to triumph over the well-known bane—reinforced by Saukko and Knight *(6)*—that in many countries, those who teach forensic pathology in universities have not worked on the field for years, sometimes for decades. *It is impossible to be a credible and convincing teacher unless one has continuing practical experience on the subject (6)*. As Arsenio Nunes, a venerable professor of legal medicine in Lisbon in the 1950s said, "Never teach things where you don't dirty your hands everyday."

To build on the other platforms (legislation and organization), it is crucial to prove the usefulness and advantages of legal medicine to communities, governments, and politics, and of course, to opinion makers, such as the mass media.

First, the advantages that result directly from the objectives of a forensic necropsy itself should be pointed out: it is an excellent tool for a better administration of justice, helping police, prosecutors and courts, and serving the community as a whole. Some authors *(29)* cite a 4.5 % margin of error in the manner-of-death determinations in a series of clinical autopsies. However, when referring to medicolegal autopsies, the percentage increases to 23.4% *(16)* when compared with the information given by the medical external examination* and the police. This rate of error has much more serious

---

* In Denmark, an external examination is carried out, and if the police report is in accordance, autopsy can be ruled out.

consequences than clinical errors because it induces legal and insurance implications. Most of the 23.4% of erroneous determinations of death were because of an unknown mode of death. However, if those were excluded, there remained 7.6% of women and 6.9% of men whose autopsies revealed wrong determinations; 6.5% of presumed accidental deaths were natural deaths; 7.5% of natural deaths were accidental; 4% of natural deaths were suicides; and one case was an homicide (*see* Heading 5., in which a similar case of homicide initially labeled as a natural death is discussed). In another series of 600 consecutive cases of forensic necropsies, a 10% margin of error in determining the mode of death and a 29.5% error margin in the cause of death were found *(16)*.

Called "detectives in white coats" *(4)*, forensic pathologists are clearly special practitioners who must be prepared to answer questions in nonmedical fields, such as criminology, criminalistics, engineering, highway design, police science, political science, chemistry, atmospheric physics, electricity, toxicology, and genetics, to list only some. In addition, the forensic pathologist must have a comprehensive awareness of the specificity of the community within which the work is being done in terms of religion, government, society, and politics. No other branch of medicine faces such a stimulating challenge. The contribution of forensic pathology to the community is then relevant, overlapping the direct determination of cause and manner of death — it prevents injury or disease in the whole community *(4)*. In Great Britain, after many incidents of people asphyxiated inside refrigerators, the apparatus was obliged to possess an opening from the inside *(6)*. Rural tractors were mandated to possess a protecting roof to avoid possible traumatic asphyxia by thoracic–abdominal compression when the vehicle overturned on the driver. Immunizations and prophylactic therapies were determined by the findings at autopsies of infectious diseases *(4)*. For individual well-being, forensic pathology contributes to support decisions based on the cause of death, about fortunes, litigations in traffic accidents, or individual rights against police or political power. The forensic pathologist is expected to defend his or her report in court, to discuss reports of colleagues, to know the effects of cardiopulmonary resuscitation or of a particular therapeutic, to study mechanics of motor vehicles, or simply to comfort, as the author does often*, a mother who suddenly and unexpectedly lost her child, victim of sudden infant death syndrome.

A medicolegal autopsy brings still more medical advantages and benefits. The ones presented here are not imaginary, hypothetical, or unrealistic

---

* In a sudden infant death sydnrome research multidisciplinary project conducted after a decade at the Coimbra Delegation of the NILM.

pros of this activity, but true and palpable outcomes of the author's daily medicolegal work on necropsies.

If the department has good practice and is known as a highly skilled center, then it will grant permanent experience for qualified pathologists and provide excellent opportunities for training younger medical doctors. The author's delegation in Coimbra is repeatedly asked to offer stages not only for national physicians, but also to professionals from different countries, such as Brazil, Spain, those in Latin America, Italy, Angola, and Kosovo. The institute is also open to law students, prosecutors, and judges who have the opportunity to assist to autopsies as a part of their academic formation.

Teaching anatomy on the cadaver is also done by the specialists with whom the authors work. Some of them (also professors of anatomy) enhance the basic preparation for a good forensic pathologist. Tedeschi *(25)* suggests that third-party carriers must reimburse the true scientific worth of the autopsy to the medical knowledge.

Concerning investigation, a huge field of opportunities is open, and not only for medicolegal research. There is a wide variety of investigations in different areas that uses the cadavers themselves (like the sudden infant death syndrome project already mentioned or another project in the northern Portugal dealing with sudden cardiac death) or the samples collected, such as the research in pathology, toxicology, pharmaceutics, orthopedics, neurology, tanathochemics. In fact, the author and colleagues collect—strictly following Portuguese law*—samples for scientific purposes (investigation projects, masters or doctoral theses). This "redelineation" of the autopsy has also been pointed out by other authors *(25)* and can be extended to the wide world of the biomechanics of traffic accidents and to physiological, pharmacological, and toxicological research.

It has also been an excellent opportunity for surgeons, who sometimes ask permission to train special surgical techniques on "our" cadavers: samples, such as the petrous portion of temporal bone, are constantly being requested for the practical courses in the middle ear surgery. It is also an opportunity to check the quality of the hospital and the medical care, as many of their necropsies are performed in the authors' facilities.† Some doctors, especially sur-

---

  * Law 12/93 and the decree 274/99 regulates the collection of organs and samples of
    dead donors.
  † Despite the positive aspects of Portuguese law, it presents some limits: it permits
    the family to refuse a clinical autopsy—if stated—until 12 h after the death. As this
    almost always happens, the physicians "transform" a clinical autopsy into a foren-
    sic one, informing the prosecutor it was a death of an unknown cause.

geons and intensivists, usually ask to assist in autopsies of cases they have treated, to clarify clinical doubts. Abundant literature states a margin of error of clinical diagnoses, confirmed by autopsies, ranging from 18 to 50% *(15,26,29)*.

Finally, the Coimbra Delegation of the NILM developed a protocol with the orthopedic department of a national public university hospital to collect bones for transplantation. This process shows how a medicolegal department can serve its community. In addition, other organs, such as kidneys, heart, liver, bone marrow and tissues (corneas, cartilage, skin), can be taken *(25)*. This close relationship among forensic institutions, hospitals, investigation centers, and the community gives a strong feeling of satisfaction to be useful to society, erasing the overlapped and old-fashioned idea that legal medicine is only "the science of the dead."

7. CONCLUSION

Wright and Tate wrote, "Forensic pathology is the last stronghold of the autopsy" *(4)*. Whatever man does, wherever he is living, deaths will continue to occur, often by violence, errors, or mistakes. Forensic pathology is expected to explain these deaths and to propose measures that might have prevented unnecessary deceases. In such a way, forensic pathology might be considered as "community and public safety pathology" *(4)*.

The future will be written with education, legislation, and organization, a magic triangle the author thinks more important than financial support to face the challenge of forensic pathology in the complex and difficult days ahead. The stronger and the more powerful forensic pathology is, the more solid will be the bridge with forensic anthropology, to face the diverse multidisciplinary missions for which they are employed, day after day, in many parts of this ever-changing world.

REFERENCES

1. Kovacevic, S. Forensic medicine in Yugoslavia. J. Forensic Med. Pathol. 10:172–173, 1989.
2. Kaye, S. The rebirth and blooming of forensic medicine. J. Forensic Med. Pathol. 13:299–304, 1992.
3. Di Maio, V. J., Di Maio, D. Forensic Pathology, 2nd Ed. CRC Press, Boca Raton, FL, pp. 1–19, 2001.
4. Wright, R. Forensic pathology: last stronghold of the autopsy. J. Forensic Med. Pathol. 1:57–60, 1980.
5. Williams, D. J., Ansford, A. J., Priday, D. S., Forrest, A. S. Forensic Pathology, Colour Guide. Churchill Livingstone, Edinburgh, pp. 1–7, 1998.

6. Saukko, P., Knight, B. Knight's Forensic Pathology, 3rd Ed. Arnold, London, p p. 1–52; 352–368, 2004.
7. Favero, F. Medicina Legal [in Portuguese], 12th Ed. Belo Horizonte, Villa Rica, pp. 21–32, 1991.
8. Somogyi, E. The history of forensic medicine in Hungary. J. Forensic Med. Pathol. 6:145–147, 1985.
9. Garland, A. N. Forensic medicine in Great Britain. J. Forensic Med. Pathol. 8: 269–272, 1987.
10. Mant, A. K., Forensic medicine in Great Britain: the origins of the British medico-legal system and some historic cases. J. Forensic Med. Pathol. 8:354–361, 1987.
11. Sousa, J. T. Medicina Forense em Portugal, Contributo para o estudo da criminalidade em Coimbra (1899–1917) [in Portuguese]. Mar da Palavra, Coimbra, pp. 25–49, 2003.
12. Sá, F. O. Dano Corporal e Peritagem Médico-Legal. Panorama Português em 1992 [in Portuguese]. Rev. Port. Dano Corp. 1:9–15, 1992.
13. Sá, F. O. Clínica Médico-Legal da Reparação do Dano Corporal em Direito Civil [in Portuguese]. APADAC, Coimbra, pp. 17–25; 70–75, 1992.
14. Pinheiro, J., Cunha, E., Corte Real, F. Adipocere in a Strangulated Young Girl: Lessons about the Decomposition Process. Abstract Book of the Second Mediterranean Academy of Forensic Sciences Congress. Monastir, p. 56, 2005.
15. Virkkunnen, M., Penttila, A., Tenhu, M., et al. Comparative study on the underlying cause and mode of death established prior to and after medico-legal autopsy. Forensic Sci. Int. 5:73–79, 1975.
16. Asnees, S., Paaske, F. The significance of medico-legal autopsy in determining mode and cause of death. Forensic Sci. Int. 14:23–40, 1979.
17. Salaçin, S. An analysis of the medico-legal autopsies performed in Adana, Turkey, in 1983–1988. J. Forensic Med. Pathol. 12:191–193, 1991.
18. Quatrehomme, G., Rougé, G. La Recommandation nº R(99)3 du Comité des Ministres aux États Membres, relative à l'harmonisation des règles en matière d'autopsie médico-légale [in French]. J. Med. Legale Droit Med. 46:249–260, 2003.
19. Lenoir, L. Intérêt et Limites de L'Autopsie des Victimes des Accidents du Travail et des Maladies Professionnelles [in French]. J. Med. Legale Droit Med. 32: 237–241, 1989.
20. UN manual on the effective prevention and investigation of extra-legal, arbitrary and summary executions, 1991. Sales No. E.91.IV.1 (doc.ST/CSDHA/12).
21. Interpol Disaster Victim Identification (DVI) autopsy protocol. Available online at www.INTERPOL.int/Public/Forensic. Last accessed on Feb. 18, 2006.
22. Saukko, P. Accreditation and Quality Assurance in Forensic Medicine. Abstract Book of the Second Mediterranean Academy of Forensic Sciences Congress. Monastir, p. 1, 2005.
23. Beauthier, J. P. Médicine Légale—evolution actuelle et situation en Belgique. Available online [in English] at www.hnbe.com/healthweb/srmlb. Website last accessed May 27, 2005.
24. Pinheiro, J., Cunha, E., Cattaneo, C., Corte Real, F. Forensic Anthropologist and Forensic Pathologist: Why Work Together? Some Illustrative Cases of Homicide.

54th Proceedings of the American Academy of Forensic Sciences, Vol. 11. New Orleans, p. 301, 2005.

25. Tedeschi, L. G. Future of the autopsy: a redelination. J. Forensic Med. Pathol. 1:103–104, 1980.

26. Lancien, G., Devalay-Legueut, M.. Evaluation Actuelle de L'Autopsie Médicale ou Scientifique en Milieu Hospitalier [in French]. J. Med. Legale Droit Med. 28: 169–172, 1985.

27. Clark, M. A. The value of the hospital autopsy: is it worth the cost? J. Forensic Med. Pathol. 2:231–237, 1981.

28. Ambach, E., Rabl, W., Unger, C., Weiss, G. The inadequacy of death certificates claiming myocardial infraction without autopsy verification. Forensic Sci. Int. 71:75–76, 1995.

29. Asnaes, S., Frederiksen, V., Fenger, C. The value of the hospital autopsy. a study of causes and modes of death estimated before and after autopsy. Forensic Sci. Int. 21:23–32, 1983.

Chapter 3

Forensic Anthropology and Forensic Pathology

The State of the Art

Eugénia Cunha and Cristina Cattaneo

Summary

This chapter presents a critical analysis of forensic anthropology. An evaluation of the conception of forensic anthropology across European and American countries is attempted. Furthermore, the authors set out to identify the growing fields in which the anthropologist is involved, alone or together with forensic pathologists.

Certification, training requirements, and teaching are rather heterogeneous across the several countries analyzed. Yet, although the forensic anthropologist profile is not easy to achieve, particularly across Europe, the authors were able to identify some efforts—not yet enough, however—toward the uniformization of the most reliable procedures in order to face the increasing and new challenges of forensic anthropology. The authors recognize at least 11 sub-areas in which the forensic anthropologist can be involved, which is a good witness of the exponential growth of this discipline in recent years.

Key Words: Forensic anthropology; forensic pathology; interdisciplinarity; Europe.

1. INTRODUCTION

The main aim of this chapter is twofold: to evaluate whether the concept of forensic anthropology is the same across European and American countries,

From *Forensic Anthropology and Medicine:*
Complementary Sciences From Recovery to Cause of Death
Edited by: A. Schmitt, E. Cunha, and J. Pinheiro © Humana Press Inc., Totowa, NJ

and to identify the growing fields in which the anthropologist is involved, together with forensic pathologists or physicians specialized in legal medicine.

2. WHAT IS FORENSIC ANTHROPOLOGY?
HOW DOES IT COMPLEMENT FORENSIC PATHOLOGY?
WHO IS THE FORENSIC ANTHROPOLOGIST?

What is a forensic anthropologist? Particularly across Europe, this is a very delicate issue, and it may concern experience and training more so than specific academic qualifications, at least at the moment. In Anglo-Saxon countries, namely the United States and the United Kingdom, the forensic anthropologist falls into a defined category, i.e., that of an individual who practices forensic anthropology (FA), this being "the application of physical anthropology to the forensic context." In the United States, the discipline is more organized at least as far as training is concerned, whereas in Europe, the problem remains intact. In the United States, the Physical Anthropology Section, part of the American Academy of Forensic Sciences, has existed since 1971–1972, and has as its main interest the professional profile of the practitioners of FA. In 1977, section members devised a certification procedure [1]. In 1989, it was already recognized that "a revolution in the training of forensic anthropologists" had occurred [2]. The rise and development of FA in the United States is indeed well documented [1,3,4]. Each year, to maintain their status, diplomates in FA are required to summarize the number and types of cases they have reported, which is a good way to track the work being done in the field [1], although regulations may change drastically from state to state. In the United States, several universities offer graduate and postgraduates courses in FA, which, along with the great amount of publications on the topic (entire books included) in particular during the last 5 yr, testify to the growth of this discipline in North America. The reality in Europe is now quite different.

Again, in the United States, for some states, such as Tennessee, there are statistics of FA casework that date back to 1971 [5,6]. For Canada, figures on number of cases are also available [7]. Some European countries, or at least some cities of these countries [8,9], have these types of data as well, but, as far as the authors know, a comparison between different countries was never performed, which precludes an accurate comparison with the American reality.

Finally, whereas in the United States, FA is a fully regulated profession [10], in Europe, as far as the authors know, only in England is FA credibility achieved by means of the Council for the Registration of Forensic Practitioners.

Although the history of FA is out of the scope of the present article (*see* Chapter 1), this brief chapter comments on the situation of FA in Europe with respect to the United States and illustrates the existence of asymmetries.

In Europe, a European workshop on FA has been taught every second year since its first edition in Brest in 1991 (with some cosponsoring by the Smithsonian Institution *[11]*). At present, some courses on this matter are being given by universities in the United Kingdom, the Universities of Dundee *(12)* and Bradford *(13)* perhaps offering the most assertive courses. Although subsequent employment is definitely a problematic issue, Black *(10)* points out that there is already saturation of these courses, with students on waiting lists. In Norway, FA is taught as part of a forensic odontology course *(14)*. In Spain, there are some intensive courses in FA, such as the one of the University of Granada, whereas in Portugal, FA is taught both at the masters and postgraduate levels in forensic medicine and/or forensic sciences. In Italy, only the University of Milan offers postgraduate and masters courses, whereas other universities have organized workshop-type courses. Thus, across Europe, the issue of training is very poor and not homogeneous, and the quality of such training cannot be ascertained. This is certainly an issue to solve.* The other issue is that it is very unlikely that there will be—even when FA will be well known to judges—a large market for individuals specialized only in FA. An imbalance of number of students and job opportunities is already evident.

It is very difficult to perform a crosscountry analysis of the status of FA and anthropologists in Europe, with regard to professionalism, training, and type of work, as has been done for the United States. Only recently have people who work in the field across Europe started discussing, comparing notes, and approaching the issue. Thus, only in recent times has the need for the constitution of a European association where these types of questions are discussed and solved appeared. Hence, the main goals of the recently formed the Forensic Anthropology Society of Europe *(15)*, a subsection of the International Academy of Legal Medicine, are education, harmonization, and certification, along with the promotion of research. The Profile and Training of Forensic Anthropologists in Europe has to be defined in detail. Taking into account that the reality is different from one country to another and that the issue of unidentified cadavers and human remains is almost unknown *(16)*, a call for FA in Europe is mandatory *(9)*.

In the United States, the background of experts on FA is essentially physical anthropology (Krogman, Ubelaker, Galloway, Simmons, and others). This

---

* E. Baccino (one of the authors in this book) had his article, which addressed this issue, published in the *International Journal of Legal Medicine* in November 2005 *(16a)*.

is clearly perceptible through the definition of FA given by Ubelaker: "FA represents the application of knowledge and techniques of human skeletal biology to modern medical legal problems" *(17)*. In Europe, the reality is much more diverse. In Spain, the great majority of individuals practicing FA have a medical formation (Canarias, Granada, San Sebastian, Barcelona). In Portugal, physical anthropology is the basic formation of the majority of experts who deal with cases, with an increasing collaboration between forensic pathology (FP) and FA in the last 5 yr *(18)*. In France, FA cases are mainly dealt with by experts with a medical formation (Montpellier, Toulouse, Marseille). England has the strongest relation between archaeology and FA. Inclusively, FA courses are taught in archaeological departments *(19,20)*. Yet Sue Black, perhaps the best-known FA in the United Kingdom, considers that "FA is clearly still in its infancy in the UK, and I suspect that the next 10 years will see it approach maturity." When analyzing the expansion of this discipline in her country, she says that its origin is difficult to interpret. "Whilst it would of course be most tempting to assume that they have arisen directly from the demands of the court, there is the unfortunate possibility that they are, in part, a symptom of popularity" *(10)*.

In German-speaking countries, the concept of FA has similarities with the American one: "…application of principles of human biology to questions of identification" *(21)*. In Italy, the situation is similar to France, where FA is still a domain of forensic pathologists who have some expertise with human bones in the more favorable cases (Milan, Bari), although in some cities (Milan, Bologna), biologists with anthropology training and physical anthropologists are beginning to approach the field.

In Central and South America, the development of FA presents strong asymmetries. Despite the obvious need of FA expertise, discrepancies do exist. Whereas some countries, such as Argentina and Guatemala, have some of the best-known groups in FA, the Equipo Argentino de Antropologia Forense *(22)* and Fundacion/Equipo de Antropologia Forense de Guatemala *(23)*, respectively, others, such as Brazil, are far from having experts in FA. As far as the authors know, in Brazil, there are almost no offices exclusively assigned to analyze skeletal remains. The progress of FA in Latin America has been described in several reviews *(see also* refs. *24* and *25)*.

One of the obstacles to overcome in Europe is a cultural one. In fact, in many countries there still seems to be a distinct division between experts who work in the forensic scenario, namely forensic pathologists, and those who work in the anthropological context, mainly anthropologists working on archaeological material. The scientific and forensic community has come to realize that there exists a void when human remains are found in the forensic scenario. Most forensic pathologists do not have training or a background in anthropology and osteology, whereas classic anthropologists may not be used to working with human remains still bearing some soft tissue or those found in a modern criminal context. Although the basic element underneath both analyses is the same—the human skeleton—practice/experience with remains from forensic settings is indeed essential. The medicolegal way of thinking is something that comes with experience, and it is quite different from the approach of one who is reconstructing life from an "archaeological" skeleton. The biological information that is sought from the skeleton is the same in both circumstances (sex, age, ancestry, stature, etc.); however, the consequences of the application are not identical. Whereas in a forensic case an error in sex determination could have serious consequences, if the sex of a medieval individual is not correctly determined, the consequences may not be as serious. Moreover, increasingly, FA cases are not exclusively restricted to dry bones. Experience with remains with soft tissues is therefore also required.

Physical anthropologists have always been—if ethnographists, cultural anthropologists, and geneticists who work on human variation are set aside (and even here, the fields superimpose one another)—considered experts in human osteology. Thus, the anthropologist's contribution to anything coming from the forensic scenario "traditionally" deals with aging, sexing, and determination of ancestry, stature, and so forth. In other words, anything similar to what the anthropologist's task is when studying skeletal remains of ancient populations. However, traditional anthropology is not enough for the forensic context. The matter of frontal sinus analysis for identification or identification by bone morphology in general is not approached at all by anthropologists dealing with remains from archaeological contexts. Matching the tears and cuts on the coat, t-shirt, etc., with those seen on the skeleton is obviously another issue out of the scope of those dealing with skeletons hundreds or thousands of years old. It therefore becomes evident that the forensic anthropologist also has to deal with remains that bear soft tissue, such as severely putrefied remains or burned remains, or with skeletal material that bears signs of a violent death. In a way, soft tissues are not a monopoly of the forensic pathologist anymore. This means that the forensic anthropologist needs more thorough training in forensics. Even from a conceptual point of view, approaching similar problems involves acquiring a certain mentality, a *modus pensandi* that is necessary when discussing most probable, possible, or incompatible determination, which is typical of the forensic pathologist. On the other hand, the forensic pathologist, given the extreme potential of osteological analysis, cannot also carry the burden of knowing how to interpret every single sign left on bone material, nor can the forensic pathologist (if untrained in anthropology and osteology) read and interpret the clean bones, perform sexing, aging, pathological studies on such material. Still, in agreement with Black (10), many police officers, coroners, procurator fiscals, and even forensic pathologists have commented on how amazed they are at the amount of information an osteologist can extract from the skeleton. In other words, both quantity and quality of information registered on the bones can only be decodified by experienced forensic anthropologists. Clearly, a fusion has to occur. This is the reason why it is very difficult to categorize—as far as provenance or training is concerned—a forensic anthropologist. It can be an anthropologist who, in some way, has specialized in subdisciplines related to FP, or a pathologist who has specialized in osteology or physical anthropology. However, the best solution is to always have the two working together. True interdisciplinarity is like that. Even if a forensic anthropologist assists in many autopsies, he or she will never be a forensic pathologist as a result of that experience. The opposite situation is also valid: a forensic pathologist with some FA cases performed will not be a forensic anthropologist. Furthermore, FA, as a forensic science, cannot be compared with forensic odontology, toxicology, botany, or entomology. These last examples all have to do with a very restricted aspect of the body or body parts, or with biological phenomena related to other parts of biology or sciences more in general. The anthropologist and pathologist both have to deal with the human body *in toto*: the more soft tissue on it, the more it is the domain of the pathologist, the more skeletonized, decomposed or burned, the more it is the domain of the anthropologist. However, these extremes encompass a large spectrum, full of notions and continuous new information, which, perhaps, will always require the combination of these two figures. A forensic pathologist will always be more at ease with a fresh cadaver, whereas an anthropologist deals mainly with skeletal remains. It should be borne in mind that the same cadaver can show various stages of conservation, which is a very good illustration of the interdisciplinary nature of expertise (*see* Chapter 7).

Judicial requests for solutions of "anthropological" problems from judges are increasing not only in quantity, but also in quality. Yet in this respect, the situation in United States and Europe is quite different. What are the identification methods accepted by the courts? Whereas in North America, it is frequent to see forensic anthropologists give their testimony in court, in the Old World, this happens very rarely. Again, whereas in the United States, the question of admissibility of scientific evidence in what concerns FA is being regulated, since the Daubert case (26–28), European countries lack rules on this matter and on many other FP matters. The FA investigation has to be undertaken with the perspective of being presented to a court. FA should be ready to defend its methodologies whenever required. Subscribing Rogers and Allard: "… the results of FA analyses are of little use if they cannot be admitted into evidence, or, once admitted, cannot be made intelligible and compelling to a jury" *(26)*.

In order to ensure their admissibility in court, in the United States, FA methods and theory must meet the standards set by Daubert *(27,28)*, and in Canada, those of the Mohan ruling *(26,27)*. Yet, in Europe, as far as the authors know, the question of admissibility of scientific evidence in what concerns FA is not regulated. The only exception is the United Kingdom, where, before the existence of Council for the Registration of Forensic Practitioners, the courts had no credible means of refuting the reports of pseudoexperts *(10)*.

As pointed out by Christensen *(27)*, today it is extremely rare for an expert's opinion to be unchallenged in court. For instance, when comparing an antemortem X-ray and postmortem one, an expert has to be objective and precise on how many matching points are required for a positive identification.

Regardless of such problems — which, nonetheless, need to be solved — new frontiers are opening to FA (*see* Chapter 4). Anthropologists deal with biological diversity; therefore, anthropological experts are required for identification of the living with increasing frequency. Once again, who should perform this task — a pathologist, an anthropologist, an odontologist? The best possible answer is maybe all three, individually or together, depending on the case, so long as the expert has proper training and qualifications in the field. This is the main goal toward which growing anthropological societies should strive: education, certification, harmonization, and research in the field.

For this reason, it seems important to summarize briefly the classic and more modern roles of FA in the world of legal medicine.

3. CLASSIC AND MODERN ROLES OF FA WITHIN THE MORE GENERAL CONTEXT OF LEGAL MEDICINE

There are several areas in which the anthropologist is necessary and indispensable in forensic scenarios, particularly those involving the recovery of human material and identification.

3.1. Recovery of Human Remains/Scene of Crime

Scenes of crime in which findings involve human remains can involve the forensic pathologist. However, in several scenarios, the pathologist might not have proper training to retrieve and properly deal with the human remains.

The need for interdisciplinarity in the process of recovering buried victims is obvious *(30)*. In this respect, physical anthropologists are key personnel in the case of skeletonized or partly skeletonized remains and offer an area of expertise that can complement that of the medicolegal staff *(29)*.

This is the case of partly skeletonized remains found "on surface," badly charred bodies, and buried bodies. In the case of quasiskeletal, skeletal, or charred remains found on surface, the person appointed to observe, register, recover, and generally "take care" of the remains must have experience in osteology. Lack of such experience may lead to serious errors, such as nonretrieval of skeletonized remains scattered across the surface by fauna. In order to recover the entire skeleton, it is necessary to be able to perform quickly an inventory of all human bones and know how to identify them. Frequently, body parts that are at or near the scene of crime are not collected because of such lack of preparation. In particular, when dealing with nonadult skeletal remains, very small bone pieces can be misidentified or simply not recognized at all by nonexperts. This implies loss of information. Similar or even more difficult problems are encountered in the case of charred bodies where the specialist has to retrieve all body parts scattered in a car, for example, among other debris. A case where the victim was burned all night in an outdoor oven was one of the first Portuguese cases where the police asked for the collaboration of a forensic anthropologist in order to find and identify *in situ* very small fragments of human remains. Fire is indeed one of the most popular ways to disguise crimes and identity.

In the case of buried remains, these must be exhumed and collected with stratigraphical and archaeological strategies. Most anthropologists have experience in excavation; otherwise, a forensic archaeologist should be called in (another subdiscipline of anthropology). Retrieval and registration of remains without archaeological methodology will lead to loss of body parts, loss of stratigraphical information useful for determining the postmortem interval (PMI), and damage to bones that will lead to difficulties in interpreting bone trauma (*see* Chapter 6).

3.2. Determining PMI (Is It of Forensic Relevance?)

The older human remains are, the more difficult it is to estimate the PMI. Once the remains reach the morgue or the laboratory, the pathologist is left with entomological methods, if soft tissue and larvae are present and very little else for determining PMI. The anthropologist, if it is the case of dry bone, can express an opinion on whether the bone looks archaeological or recent, but nothing more, other than sending the bone for chemical analyses (carbon 14, strontium radioisotopes, etc.). Once again, on-site intervention of a trained anthropologist means being able to verify whether, for example, in the case of commingled skeletal remains found under the road surface, the presence of a high minimum number of individuals could orient toward ancient or historical remains, or indicate which environmental markers (stratigraphy, etc.) may be relevant for PMI determination. The experience of the forensic anthropologist is also essential for the recognition of cemetery remains in a forensic context *(7)*.

This is indeed one of the more difficult questions to be answered by FA because of the virtual absence of methods by which to evaluate the PMI, especially if they are out of the context of their retrieval. Sometimes it is impossible to say whether it is a case from past populations or a forensic case. In Portugal, a case is considered an FA as long as no more than 15 yr have passed from the time of death. In Spain, the number of years is 25. In Italy, remains are considered relevant if they are post-World War II. In other countries, this period reaches 70 yr. The problem is that there are no accurate methods with which to quantify PMI, often making it virtually impossible to differentiate between 15 and 50 yr, for example, which has obvious important implications for legal procedures.

3.3. Determining the Human Origin of Remains

An important percentage of cases submitted to FA analysis concerns animal remains. In the US FBI statistics presented by Ubelaker in 2001 *(4)*, about 25% of the remains analyzed in the institute in a 25-yr period were animal bones.

Most frequently, when bones or body parts are found, it is sometimes evident to nonanthropologists whether they are human. However, in cases of badly burned bones, of fragmented diaphyseal shafts and cranial bones of very small animals, this may not be so evident. A well-trained anthropologist can perform species determination and/or indicate which lab tests may be more useful for this purpose (for example, histological or biomolecular analysis).

3.4. Building the Biological Profile (Putrefied, Burned, Skeletal, Dismembered)

The anthropologist should always work side by side with the pathologist in the case of decomposed unidentified remains. In this case, it is the anthropologist's precise role to determine age, sex, race, height, pathologies, and other anomalies in order to create a biological profile, or, in other words, to generate the osteobiography. Among the "big four" parameters usually included in the biological profile, ancestry is the most problematic (*see* Chapter 12). During the autopsy, after adequate histological, genetic, and toxicological sampling has been performed, the forensic anthropologist can observe

the state of the remains, decide whether it is best to completely clean them
and study the skeleton (sometimes a clean skeleton can provide much more
information than a putrefied body), and be able to give indications on what
samples to take. For example, for aging a burned adult body within which the
pubic symphysis and teeth are no longer preserved, the anthropologist can
suggest alternative methods (e.g., femur slices for histology; *see* Chapter 11).
In the lab, the anthropologist will work at building the biological profile, up
to facial reconstruction.

3.5. Craniofacial Reconstruction

This technique, which can be performed manually or with computer software, is very imprecise and should be used only to stimulate the memory of
observers in order to reach a suspicion of identity. Confronting the public
with an image of the victim's face can help in determining identity, particularly in cases where there is no idea who the victim could be. The latest pro-
gressions in this field are making it possible to obtain more accurate images
(31). This is becoming a very technical and specialized subfield, requiring
the aid of experts in digital images and/or artists.

3.6. Personal Identification of Human Remains

Personal identity often relies on the presence of idiosyncratic features
(5). Observation of distinctive skeletal features—and particularly looking for
them with the pathologist and/or radiologist—may be crucial in identification
(*see* Chapter 15). The triple discrimination between pseudopathology, morphological alteration, and paleopathology is a task for the forensic anthropologist (*see* Chapter 14). Furthermore, the forensic anthropologist should
indicate which skeletal features may be more useful (and thus preserved) for
eventual skeletal identification. Although the true prevalence of the great
majority of the morphological traits are not known, surely a sternal perforation will be more useful for identification purposes than a septal aperture (*see*
Chapter 14). In addition, the anthropologist has to able to describe the effects
of the pathological alterations on the individual lifestyle, such as gait.

Because identification is most of all a comparative process, another legal
issue is to know how many skeletal features, in accordance between ante- and
postmortem record, are enough to decide for a positive identification. This is
not yet regulated in Europe, and, understandably, may be a particularly difficult task.

One of the methods that identification very often relies on is genetic
analysis. In the last decade, identification based on DNA analysis increased

so much that, among the nonexperts, the idea that DNA can solve everything started to take a stand. Although the usefulness of DNA analysis is undeniable, it is worthwhile to keep in mind that it cannot be seen as a solution whenever identification is in question. In effect, as identification is above all a comparative process, it only leads to the victim's identity when there is some other DNA for comparison. One setback for DNA could be degradation, particularly in the case of skeletal remains. Thus, the relation between forensic genetics and FA should also be very close, which is well illustrated by the case of the Twin Towers of the World Trade Center *(29)*.

3.7. Assisting in the Determination of Cause and Manner of Death

In general, wherever bone traumatic injuries are concerned, the presence of a forensic anthropologist should be mandatory. The forensic anthropologist should always give a statement on the distinction between antemortem, perimortem, and postmortem origin. And, as previously stated, the forensic anthropologist's presence at the autopsy table may be essential, even when some soft tissue is present. An interesting example is the case of charred remains. In such cases, at times, the bone is exposed, but charred periosteum may shrivel over bone lesions (firearm injuries, cut marks, etc.) and makes them invisible unless the bone is cleaned. This can be performed at the autopsy table or, if need be, in the lab. Skeletal or partly skeletonized remains and completely charred bone are best studied in the lab. It is important to bear in mind that the responsibility of cause of death assignment is of the forensic pathologist. Therefore, the forensic anthropologist cannot and should not try to replace the forensic pathologist. The job of the forensic anthropologist is to assist the forensic pathologist in this respect, providing key clues/elements that no other specialist can give.

3.8. Mass Disasters

The anthropologist, in the case of mass disasters, can be crucial for many of the reasons stated above, depending on the type of disaster, from recovery of the remains to personal identification and trauma analysis (*see* Chapter 18). The World Trade Center Identification Project is a good example of the usefulness of FA *(29)*.

3.9. Mass Graves and War Crimes

To a greater extent, forensic anthropologists are heavily committed to assist in human rights investigation. In the excavation of the mass grave, the knowledge of the forensic anthropologist is sometimes irreplaceable because most of the forensic pathologists do not have this kind of experience. Identification will be mainly achieved by the anthropologist who can also assist the forensic anthropologist in providing information pertaining to the cause of death and torture methods.

The participation of anthropologists in international human rights investigations between 1990 and 1999 is thoroughly explained in a recent article by Steadman and Haglund *(32)*. Surveying the Argentine Forensic Anthropology Team, the Guatemala Forensic Anthropology Foundation, Physicians for Human Rights, and the UN-sponsored International Criminal Tribunal for the former Yugoslavia concluded that more than 100 anthropologists had investigated about 1300 sites. Examples of exhumations recently investigated are therefore numerous *(33)*.

3.10. The Living: Identifying Living Individuals

More and more cases see anthropologists involved in the identification of the living. These are frequently cases in which two-dimensional images from video surveillance systems (showing robberies, assaults, and so on) are the only element available for identifying a suspect. This is a completely different aspect of FA that deals with human diversity and strives to verify morphological and metric characteristics that make the physionomy of one person distinct from that of another, or other features, such as ear morphology. The difficulty of facial identification is documented by recent literature *(34)*.

3.11. Determining the Age of Individuals for Reasons of Imputability

It is the case of living subjects with no identification documents. Frequently, these people are arrested and declared underage. Anthropological, radiological, and odontological assessment is required for determining the probability whether they are of or underage (14, 18, or 21 yr, depending on crime and country). This involves skeletal and dental radiological assessment once the issue of ancestry has been taken into consideration (*see* Chapter 4).

In recent times, more and more working groups, with the participation of forensic anthropologists, have been established to investigate questions in the examination of living persons *(21,35)*. Subscribing Schwiy-Bochat *(21)*, the interdisciplinary cooperation of forensic physicians with other scientists in the question of age assessment of adolescents is particularly fruitful.

3.12. Determining the Age of Subadults in Photographic Material (Child Pornography)

Once again, pornographic images can be the object of medicolegal/anthropological assessment. According to the country and legislation involved, the question frequently asked is what the age of the child or adolescent is (if, for example, under 10, 14, 16, or 18 yr). This is a novel and very difficult aspect of anthropological application of age estimation because facial and secondary sexual characteristics are extremely variable and do not necessarily represent chronological age *(36)*. Alternatively, there is the need to identify children, even those who have disappeared years before; in these cases, artificial aging of images is necessary, which is generally done with specific software.

4. FINAL COMMENTS

No doubt FA has shown an exponential growth in the last years. This fact justifies a detailed analysis of this irreplaceable medicolegal discipline.

The main aim of this chapter was to evaluate whether the concept of FA is the same in/across European and American countries and to know who the experts practicing FA in those countries are. When this chapter was conceived, one of the aims was to try to achieve the profile of a "forensic anthropology" expert around a part of the world. Is he or she a medical coroner? Is he or she an anthropologist/biologist? Does he or she work together with forensic pathologists? Does he or she really go to the autopsy table? How often? What about aging the living? Who is performing these cases? Quickly, it was realized that it is not yet possible to answer these questions. Although some statistics exist for the United States *(4)* and Canada *(26)*, for instance, these figures for Europe are not yet completely quantifiable.

Nevertheless, some conclusions can still be drawn with the existing knowledge of the reality of FA worldwide. Different backgrounds of FA lead to the application of different methodologies in the assessment of the biological profile of an individual; the need for international standardization of methodologies within the discipline is thus obvious. Efforts in this direction are being done, among others, by the Forensic Anthropology Society of Europe.

The presence of a forensic anthropologist at the autopsy table for specific types of cases is becoming increasingly mandatory. The interdisciplinary nature of this discipline has been obliging to a strong complicity between forensic pathologists and forensic anthropologists. Finally, the fields in which FA has been intervening are clearly in expansion, implying the development of subspecialties inside the discipline.

REFERENCES

1. Ubelaker, D. Skeletons testify: anthropology in forensic science. Yearb. Phys. Anthropol. 39:229–244, 1996.
2. Wienker, C. W., Rhine, J. S. A professional profile of the Physical Section Membership, American Academy of Forensic Sciences. J. Forensic Sci. 34:647–658, 1989.
3. Galloway, A., Simmons, T. L. Education in forensic anthropology: appraisal and outlook. J. Forensic Sci. 42:796–801, 1997.
4. Grisbaum, G. A., Ubelaker, D. H. An Analysis of Forensic Anthropology Cases Submitted to the Smithsonian Institution by the Federal Bureau of Investigation from 1962 to 1994. Smithsonian Contributions to Anthropology, 2001, Vol. 45. Smithsonian Institution Press, Washington, D.C., 2001.
5. Bass, W. M., Driscoll, P. A. Summary of skeletal identification in Tennessee: 1971–1981. J. Forensic Sci. 28:159–168, 1983.
6. Komar, D. Twenty-seven years of forensic anthropology casework in New Mexico. J. Forensic Sci. 48:521–524, 2003.
7. Rogers, T. Recognition of cemetery remains in a forensic context. J. Forensic Sci. 50:5–11, 2005.
8. Cunha, E., Mendonça, M. C. Forensic anthropology in Portugal: the state of knowledge. In: Proceedings American Academy of Forensic Sciences Annual Meeting. 54th Annual Meeting. Atlanta, GA, p. 230, 2002.
9 Cattaneo, C., Baccino, E. A call for forensic anthropology in Europe. Int. J. Legal Med. 116:N1–N2, 2002.
10. Black, S. Forensic anthropology—regulation in the United Kingdom. Sci. Justice 43:187–192, 2003.
11. Ubelaker, D. H. Methodological considerations in the forensic applications of human skeletal biology. In: Katzenberg, M. A., Saunders, S. R., eds., Biological Anthropology of the Human Skeleton. Wiley Liss, New York, NY, pp. 41–67, 2000.
12. What is Forensic Anatomy? University of Dundee, Scotland. Available at http://www.dundee.ac.uk/admissions/newcourses/forensicanth/. Last accessed on Aug. 31, 2005.
13. Forensic Anthropology. University of Bradford, UK. Available at http://www.brad.ac.uk/acad/archsci/depart/pgrad/forensic/PS_FA.ph. Last accessed on Jan. 13, 2006.
14. The 6th International Course in Forensic Odontology—Personal Identification by Dental Methods, 2005. Oslo.
15. Laboratorio di Antropologia e Odontologia Forense, Istituto di Medicina Legale e delle Assicurazioni, Università degli Studi di Milano [in Italian]. Available at http://users.unimi.it/labanof/. Last accessed on Jan. 13, 2006.
16. Cattaneo, C., Ritz-Timme, S., Schutz, H. W. Unidentified cadavers and human remains in the EU. Int. J. Legal Med. 113:N1–N3, 2000.
16a. Baccino, E. Forensic Anthropology Society of Europe (FASE), a subsection ot the IALM, is 1 year old. Int. J. Legal Med. 119:N1, 2005.
17. Ubelaker, D. Latest development in skeletal biology and forensic anthropology. In: Boaz, N. T., Wolfe, L. D., eds., Biological Anthropology: the State of the Sciences. International Institute for Human Evolutionary Research, Bend, OR, pp. 91–106, 1995.

18. Cunha, E., Pinheiro, J., Ribeiro, I. P., Soares, J., Vieira, D. N. Severe traumatic injuries: report of a complex multiple homicide case. Forensic Sci. Int. 136: 164–165, 2003.
19. Hunter, J. Forensic archaeology in Britain. Antiquity 68:758–769, 1994.
20. Black, S. Forensic osteology in the United Kingdom. In: Cox, M., Mays, S., eds., Human Osteology in Archaeology and Forensic Sciences. GMM, London, pp. 491–504, 2000.
21. Schiwy-Bochat, K.-W., Repert, T., Rothschild, M. A. The contribution of forensic medicine to forensic anthropology in German-speaking countries. Forensic Sci. Int. 111:255–258, 2004.
22. Argentine Forensic Anthropology Team, (Equipo Argentino de Antropología Forense, EAAF). Available at www.eaaf.org. Last accessed on Aug. 31, 2005.
23. Guatamalan Forensic Anthropology Team. The Massacres of Rabinal. Available at: http://garnet.acns.fsu.edu/~sss4407/EAFG.
24. Iscan, M. Y., Olivera, H. Forensic anthropology in Latin America. Forensic Sci. Int. 109:15–30, 2000.
25. Iscan, M. Y. Global forensic anthropology in the 21st century. Forensic Sci. Int. 117:1–6, 2001.
26. Rogers, T., Allard, T. T. Expert testimony and positive identification of human remains through cranial suture patterns. J. Forensic Sci. 49:203–207, 2004.
27. Christensen AM. The impact of Daubert: implications for testimony and research in forensic anthropology and the use of frontal sinuses in personal identification. J. Forensic Sci. 49:1–4, 2004.
28. Christensen, C. Testing the reliability of frontal sinuses in positive identification. J. Forensic Sci. 50:18–22, 2005.
29. Budimlija, Z., Mechthild, K., Zelson-Mundorff, A., et al. World Trade Center Human Identification Project: experiences with individual body identification cases. Croat. Med. J. 44:259–263, 2003.
30. Hunter, J., Roberts, C., Martin, A. Studies in Crime: An introduction to Forensic Archaeology. Bradford, London, 1996.
31. Greef, S. V., Willems, G. Three dimensional cranio-facial reconstruction in forensic identification: latest progress and new evidences in the 21st century. J. Forensic Sci. 50:12–17, 2005.
32. Steadman, D. W., Haglund, W. D. The scope of anthropological contributions to human rights investigations. J. Forensic Sci. 50:23–30, 2005.
33. Black, S. M., Vanezis. P. The forensic investigation of mass graves and war crimes. In: Payne-James, P., Busuttil, A., Smock, W., eds., Forensic Medicine: Clinical and Pathological Aspects. Greenwich Medical Media, London, 2003.
34. Fraser, N. L., Yoshino, M., Imaizumi, K., Blackwell, S. A., Thomas, C. D., Clement, J. G. A Japanese computer-assisted facial identification system successfully identifies non-Japanese faces, Forensic Sci. Int. 135:122–128, 2003.
35. Garamendi, P. M., Solano, M. A. Jornadas sobre Determinacion de la edad en menores indocumentados. Donosta. San Sebastián. 4–5 Maio. 2004. Instituto Vasco de Medicina Legal. [In Spanish.]
36. Greil, H., Kahl, H. Assessment of developmental age: cross-sectional analysis of secondary sexual characteristics. Anthropol. Anz. 63:63–75, 2005.

PART II

Aging Living Young Individuals

Chapter 4

Biological vs Legal Age of Living Individuals

Francesco Introna and Carlo P. Campobasso

Summary

The demand of forensic age determination in living individuals deals mostly with juvenile or subadults because in most European countries, the legally relevant age limit ranges between the 14th and 21st year of life. Among the variety of scientific procedures available in age assessment, there is wide agreement that methods based on sexual, skeletal, and dental maturity are suitable. Unfortunately, there are obviously problems with using "age" in a system measuring maturity and therefore, biological age (sexual, dental, or skeletal) does not always correspond to chronological age (legal). None of the modern techniques is both easy to use and practical, as most of them result in a slight over- or underestimation, depending on the applied method, the range of human variation between sex and population, and discrepancies between biological and legal age. The margin of error can be substantial in living individuals, sometimes by as much 2–3 yr either side, or at best, 12 mo, even by combined methods. The physician should use all the available evidence, including multiple maturity indicators, and must approach each case with caution, because the poor correlation between maturity and chronological age represents a fundamental limitation to age-determination practices in forensic settings.

Key Words: Age determination; living individual; skeletal and dental maturity.

1. INTRODUCTION

Age estimation of living individuals is one of the most difficult problems in clinical forensic medicine. It is a prerequisite for personal identification, and

From *Forensic Anthropology and Medicine:*
Complementary Sciences From Recovery to Cause of Death
Edited by: A. Schmitt, E. Cunha, and J. Pinheiro © Humana Press Inc., Totowa, NJ

it is increasingly important in criminal matters. In fact, if doubts arise regarding the age of a person suspected of a crime (i.e., robbery, extortion, fraud, physical assault, arms offences, murder, etc.), forensic age estimation is promptly requested by authorities to ascertain whether the person concerned has reached the age of imputability (criminal responsibility). In most European countries, the legally relevant age limit range is between the 14th and 21st year of life *(1)*. For example, in Italy as well as in France and Germany, the relevant age limit above which a person has legal responsibility is 14 yr, and the age limit of 18 is decisive for establishing whether juvenile delinquency law or general criminal law in force for adults is to be applied.

In Europe, the demand of forensic age determination deals mostly with juvenile or subadult delinquents, but it also deals with illegal young immigrants and refugee children requesting political asylum. The need for accurate techniques for age estimation has never been greater than in last two decades because of the increase in international migration because of recurrent armed conflicts, which has lead to a steady rise of foreign populations in many European countries. Most young immigrants have no valid proof of birth date (legal age); they lack valid identification documents; they also either do not know their age or are suspected of not giving their correct age. For asylum seekers, the refugee's birth might never have been registered or identity documents never issued. In such individuals, age estimation is therefore crucial, and represents one of the main requests made by police and judicial authorities to physicians.

The request may also come from a child's legal representative or from a government agency. In the context of international protection, the United Nations High Commissioner for Refugees (UNHCR) remarks in relation to refugee children that it is often necessary for the asylum country to determine the age of a young person who has, or is claiming, refugee status, because there should be different procedures or programs for refugees who are below a specific age, for example, 14 or 18 yr *(2)*. In such a case, the UNHCR states that children seeking asylum should not be held in detention (section 7.6 of UNHCR guidance), and that children should be given the benefit of the doubt if the exact age is uncertain (section 5.11c of UNHCR guidance). Therefore, when identity documents are not relied on to establish age, authorities usually need not only age calculation mainly for differentiating the juvenile from the adult status, but also in relation to school attendance, social benefits, adoption procedures, employment, and marriage.

For this purpose, physicians such as pediatricians, dentists, or forensic experts are often asked to give their opinion on whether a person is younger or older than 18 yr. The indicators most commonly used in assessing subadult age include somatic, sexual, skeletal, and dental maturity. Among the variety of scientific procedures available in age assessment, there is wide agreement that the following methods are suitable: physical inspection with determination of body measures and signs of sexual maturation, radiographic examination of the left hand and wrist, and examination of the oral cavity by a dentist with evaluation of an orthopantogram *(3)*.

1.1. Physical Inspection

The clinical examination of the living individual is the first step of the aging process, as the visual recognition of somatic maturity is the simplest age estimation method. Pediatricians usually base age assessments in children on constitutional type and physical appearance of sexual maturity indicators.

Physicians commonly use height and weight measurements as primary tools for assessing a child's physical growth in relation to other children of the same gender and age. These anthropometric measures are noninvasive, inexpensive, easy to perform, and are also well related to the general increase in size and length of the whole body *(4)*. During the physical examination, they are commonly recorded with stadiometers and properly calibrated scales. Based on stature and weight, body mass index (BMI) is also easy to obtain because it is defined as weight in kilograms divided by the square of stature (standing height) in meters. BMI was only recently recommended as additional routine measurement of growth, as it is a valuable index of body composition (adiposity) to determine underweight or obesity in the clinical environment by comparison of an individual to age and sex-specific percentiles from a reference population *(5)*.

During the inspection of maturity indicators, the development of an individual's secondary sex characteristics (sexual age) is also used in the age-assessment process, especially at puberty (usually between the ages of 8 and 13 yr; the average age is 11 yr). The appearance of pubic and axillary hair, for example, can reflect progressive stages in the sexual maturation of boys (with the concomitant growth of external genitalia such as penis and scrotum) and girls (with the concomitant breast enlargement and onset of menstruation). Breast, genital, and pubic hair development can be classified for boys and girls, using Tanner's five stages *(6,7)*, which is a sequential process that children go through as they pass into puberty. For example, the onset of puberty in boys is marked by testicular enlargement, and pubic hair usually appears initially on the scrotum and at the base of the penis developing to the adult stage, with a final distribution covering the pubes and the medial surface of the thighs (Table 1). In girls, the first menstrual period can occur during the fourth or fifth Tanner stage, usually at around 12 or 13 yr of age. Once a girl

Table 1
Tanner Staging System for Males

Stage	Pubic hair	Penis	Testicles
I	Preadolescent. No pubic hair (except for a fine peach fuzz).	Penis is in the same proportions as in childhood.	Testicles are in the same proportions as in childhood.
II	Sparse growth of long, slightly darkened, pubic hair at the base of the penis.	Slight enlargement.	Testicles begin to get larger. The scrotum begins to get a reddened and roughened texture.
III	Pubic hair increases its pigmentation and gets coarser and curlier, spreading sparsely over the pubic bone.	Increased length more than width	Increased size with further scrotal enlargement. The scrotum texture becomes more like that of an adult.
IV	Hairs have adult characteristics, but not adult distribution. They cover the base of the penis and begin to grown on the upper part of the scrotum.	Further penile enlargement and increased breadth. The glans, or head, of the penis becomes much more prominent.	Further enlargement. The scrotal skin gets darker in color.
V	Adult distribution with spread to medial thighs.	Adult size and shape.	Adult size and shape.

has reached Tanner stage 5, her breasts are fully formed and her pubic hair is adult in quantity and type, forming the classical upside-down triangle shape common to women (Table 2).

However, the sequence and timing of the particular events that occur during puberty (especially if compared with progressive rise in stature) vary considerably from one person to the next because of differences among sex, populations, and socioeconomic factors (8). The onset of puberty is also extremely variable based on sex: girls may have the first signs of pubertal changes at about the age of 8 or 9 yr and boys at about 9 or 10 yr. Equally, pubertal delay can also take place, and the first signs may be significantly delayed to 14 or 15 yr of age, especially in boys.

Ethnicity and socioeconomic factors (mainly environment and diet) may affect the onset of puberty. Alterations in nutritional status and illness can delay the pubertal changes so that a person may actually be older than the

Table 2
Tanner Staging System for Females

Stage	Pubic hair	Breasts
I	Preadolescent. No pubic hair except for a fine, peach fuzz body hair.	A small, elevated nipple with no significant underlying breast tissue.
II	Sparse growth of long, slightly darkened, downy straight hair, mostly along the labia.	Breast bud. There is elevation of the breast and nipple (papilla) as a small mound with increased areolar diameter.
III	Pubic hair increases its pigmentation and gets coarser and curlier, spreading sparsely over the mons veneris area.	Further enlargement and elevation of the breast and areola (with no separation of their contours), which begins to darken in color.
IV	The hair grows in more densely. Hairs have adult characteristics, but not adult distribution.	Projection of the areola and nipple (papilla) to form secondary mound.
V	Adult distribution with spread to medial thighs.	Nipple elevated, areola contour continuous with breast.

physical appearance leads one to believe. Some nutritional deficiency diseases (such as rickets or iron-deficiency anemia), infectious diseases (such as osteomyelitis, smallpox, brucellosis, and so forth) and congenital disorders (such as Turner's syndrome, which is a gonadal agenesis, or achondroplasia or osteochondrodysplasias, which are abnormalities of cartilage and/or bone development) give rise to disproportionate growth (9). Therefore, it is not possible to give a precise age of an individual based only on physical examination or clinical experience. In the clinical setting, measurement of growth is crucial for detecting and treating illness or disorders of development, not for age estimation.

Several growth charts for height and weight (10), standardized percentile curves of BMI for children and adolescents (11), or charts showing the range of ages during which each pubertal event occurs (12) are available to compare an individual's development pattern with that of a healthy standard group of the same age and sex. These comparisons measure the body's general level of maturation, providing only little information of the individual's age and very poor quantitative data on the accuracy of such assessment. In fact, most growth charts are expressed in centile lines rather than standard deviation scores (13).

Percentile curves represent the distribution of the measurement of interest (e.g., height, weight, BMI) and so, what percentage of children of the same gender and age show the identical pattern of pubertal changes. For example, the 50th percentile line represents the mean value for age, so that 50% of children will be above this point, and 50% will be below it. A child of average height and average timing of pubertal growth spurt would follow the 50th percentile throughout life. Based on this way of expressing a child's developmental level of maturity, pediatricians can determine the percentile cutoff points (e.g., 3rd or 5th, and 95th or 97th centile lines) useful to identify children that are too tall or too short, underweight or overweight, compared with children of the same gender and age from reference normal populations.

Therefore, the physical examination usually gives only a glimpse or, even better, an empirical probability on the chronological age of the individual. It can be useful in adolescence or before 14 yr, but not so much in subadults. In fact, most of the above-mentioned physical events related to puberty have already occurred before the critical age limit of 18 yr, when the request of forensic age determination is usually submitted. Specifically around 18 yr, other different indicators of maturity have been studied to assess an individual's age level, among which dental growth and skeletal development are the most commonly used in young adults. Like bones, teeth progress through maturational stages, undergoing continuous change in size and shape. The developmental changes in bones and teeth are intimately related to those of the reproductive system, which is directly responsible for most of the body's externally discernible changes. Therefore, bones and teeth greatly reflect the functional status of the reproductive system and provide a useful index of the general growth during the adolescent period *(14)*.

The assessment of dental and/or bone maturity by X-rays represents the most objective method among the range of diagnostic procedures available for age estimation, and appears to be also suitable for forensic application in living individuals. Evaluation of ortopantomograms and X-rays of the left hand and wrist is the method of choice widely used by experts for forensic age assessment. Radiographic examination of other segments of the skeleton provides only little additional information to the aging process; it is also not recommended because it involves an unnecessary increase in radiation exposure to the rest of the body *(1)*.

1.2. Dental Age

Dental growth and emergence (tooth eruption) have long been recognized as the most useful criteria for estimating age because dental age can be analyzed both radiologically and through clinical examination. Studying tooth emergence by clinical inspection of the oral cavity is simple and does not require expensive tools or equipment. Younger ages can be assessed visually with greater accuracy because more teeth are undergoing formation, and the intervals between morphological stages are shorter, and therefore, more precise *(15)*. However, all permanent teeth except the third molars have finished their development after the median ages of 15 or 16 yr. In fact, if the third molar crowns are less than half complete, it is virtually certain that the subject is less than 14 yr old *(16)*. Late in adolescence, only the third molars continue to form *(17)*. At this stage, the third molars have completed their crown developments, and the roots are the only dental structure that can be used for age estimation *(18)* up to a median age of about 19–20 yr, when apex closure has taken place *(19)*. In younger adults, the calcification stages of the third molars are the most reliable dental indicators, but in living individuals, they can be examined only by X-rays or ortopantomographs (Fig. 1).

Gleiser and Hunt *(20)* first suggested that an assessment of tooth calcification, rather than emergence, may be more useful for age estimation. Actually, the worldwide reference method of age determination in living individuals remains the Demirjian's system, which classifies eight stages of crown and root formation used to score the third molar development *(21)*. This system is based on a 20-yr study of more than 7000 subjects of French-Canadian origin, aged 2–20 yr. Using Demirjian's eight-grade classification, a study of the American Board of Forensic Odontology (ABFO) reported adequate probabilities of age assessment based on the level of third molar formation, providing regression formulae relative to the medicolegal question of whether an individual is at least 18 yr of age *(17)*. If the third molar root apices are completely closed, and the periodontal ligament has attained a uniform width (stage H of Demirjian's system), there is a high probability (90.1% for white males and 92.2% for white females) that an individual is at least 18 *(16)*. The ABFO study also observed that according to Kullman et al. *(18)* and Levesque et al. *(19)*, maxillary third molars formation was slightly advanced over mandibular third molars, and root formation occurred earlier in males than females. Recent papers have confirmed such findings with respect to the earlier development of third molars in males compared with females, and the same trend of an earlier third molar development in the maxilla compared with the mandible *(22–24)*.

However, several limitations of the Demirjian's system have been recently illustrated, among which the most important are the following: it is based on observations derived from radiographs, the choice of the tooth developmental stage is quite subjective, and age cannot be precisely evaluated after 16 yr *(25)*. Specifically around 18 yr, the different analyses regarding the wisdom

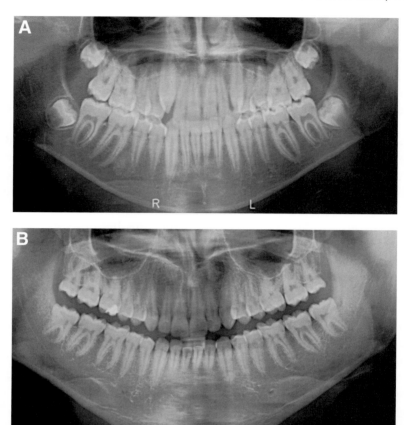

Fig. 1. Ortopantomographs at age of 13 yr, 6 mo **(A)** and at age 17 yr, 10 mo **(B)**.

teeth do not yield precise conclusions *(22,26,27)*. In this matter, the ABFO study also remarks that the third molar is a nonideal developmental marker because it is the most variable tooth in the dentition with regard to size, time of formation, and time of eruption, and it can be congenitally absent, malformed, impacted, or extracted *(17)*.

Thorson and Hagg *(26)* already suggested that the dental development of the third mandibular molar should not be used for estimation of chronological age in individuals because of its very low accuracy. Based on accuracy tests, the authors stated that the 95% confidence interval of the difference between estimated age and true chronological age is quite large, about ±4.5 yr in girls and ±2.8 yr in boys. A more recent article also provides a confidence interval age estimate up 95%, and regression formulae with a standard deviation of 1.49 or 1.50 yr for males and females, respectively *(24)*, which is quite a short difference between age prediction and chronological age. However, it is obvious that most of the studies on wisdom teeth calculate only probabilities for an individual to be above or below a predefined age, such as 18 yr. Actually, the 100% confidence in dental age assessment has been never reached, and no one can make an exact judgment or a certain prediction of age. There is only an empirical probability of an individual being at least 18 as based on stage of third molar formation *(16)*. It is important to note that even before the age of 18, some or all third molars might have reached complete root development *(21,28)*. This indicates, according to Mesotten et al. *(22)*, that linking the completion of root development (closure of apical ends) of one or more third molars to an age over 18 yr is unsatisfactory.

Such remarks should be kept in mind by all experts and investigators involved in forensic age estimation. In the scientific literature, there is quite absolutely unanimity that, based on dental growth, it is impossible to determine exactly whether a young person is younger or older than 18 yr. The result of age estimation is an extrapolation by a probability procedure. Therefore, it is impossible to give a precise age; the only appropriate way is to give an age interval for a specific confidence *(29)*.

A possible option to increase the precision and the accuracy in the dental age-estimation process by root development of the lower third molar could be to use an additional stage of root mineralization in the Demirjian's system *(18)*, or comparing the standard deviation with other skeletal age calculation techniques based on, e.g., hand and wrist bones. In fact, according to Ubelaker *(30)*, it is generally agreed that assessment of age reflects greater accuracy when derived from multiple indicators. The investigator should always use multiple sources when attempting age estimation based on the assessment of dental and skeletal maturity, as they offer superior results to those obtained by single age indicators *(31)*, especially in living individuals.

An extensive literature review of forensic odontology concluded that teeth are better suited for age estimation than bones *(29,32)*. Developing teeth remain a widely used method to assess dental maturity, and the formative stage of the third molar can be certainly considered the only quantitative biological variable available for estimating the age of an individual in his late teens or early 20s *(17)*. However, some authors still assume that skeletal methods are more accurate *(33)*.

1.3. Skeletal Age

The growth of the human skeleton is of major importance for the aging process as the appearance of ossification centers and union of epiphysis relate to a fairly definite sequence and time table that makes skeletal maturity a reliable age indicator according to sex and ethnical differences. For the first three decades of postnatal life, age changes in the bones of the upper and lower extremities are relatively very reliable and may give age estimates within 1–2 yr *(14)*.

Determination of skeletal development is clinically relevant as it provides the only means of assessing rates of maturational change throughout the growing period *(34)*. Skeletal maturity assessment is a common procedure in pediatric radiology, and is frequently requested as part of the evaluation of children who are either too tall or too short for their chronological age. Such assessment can also be useful in the management of children with various endocrinopathies (especially those involving the pituitary gland, thyroid, and gonads) or in children with malformation syndromes, and in planning orthopedic procedures in which the outcome may be influenced by subsequent growth of the child (e.g., surgical management of scoliosis or leg-length discrepancy). In many cases, the decision whether to treat a child with growth hormones depends on the outcome of bone age estimation *(35)*.

One of the best known methods of measuring skeletal maturity in children and young adults is by radiological assessment of hand and wrist bone development. This is a medical procedure often used in forensic settings to provide evidence about a person's chronological age by measuring skeletal maturity. X-rays of the left hand and wrist are usually taken, and their use is strongly recommended by experts because they show enough detail for age estimation (Fig. 2). The hand and wrist region has a large number of ossification centers and can be easily radiographed with minimal radiation exposure to the rest of the body. In fact, an X-ray of the hand and wrist involves a very low dosage of radiation and presents negligible risk of contamination *(8)*.

The Radiographic Atlas of Skeletal Development of the Hand and Wrist made by Greulich and Pyle (G&P) in 1959 *(36)* is the most commonly used bone age standards. The atlas method has the advantage that it is quick and easy to use. A given individual's hand radiograph is compared with the standard films in the atlas, and the closest match is obtained. A well-trained radiologist takes few minutes to determine the bone age from a single hand radiograph.

Standards such as those of G&P were designed to provide clinicians and others with clear definitions of average development, but they do not provide data, however, on the possible range of variation around the mean *(30,37)*.

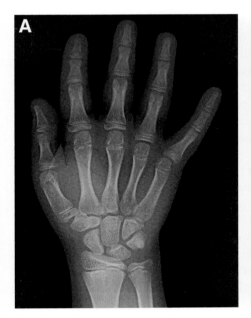
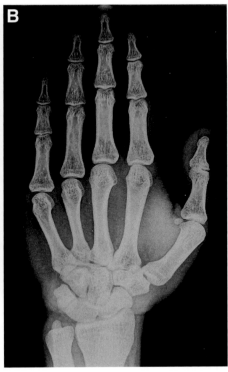

Fig. 2. Hand–wrist X-rays at age 13 yr, 2 mo **(A)** and at age 18 yr, 3 mo **(B)**.

Unfortunately, this method has also some other limitations, as it is less objective and quite imprecise, especially if applied to a modern or different ethnic group. In fact, the atlas was compiled solely from Caucasian children of the upper socioeconomic class who lived in the 1930s. Some authors have demonstrated that the G&P standards must be used with reservations to determine bone age in children of today and of diverse ethnicity, particularly when making clinical decisions requiring accurate skeletal age in black and Hispanic girls and in Asian and Hispanic boys in late childhood and adolescence *(38,39)*. Another recent study found the G&P standards also imprecise for American children of European and African descent born after 1980, concluding that new standards are needed to make clinical decisions that require reliable bone ages and accurately represent a multi-ethnic pediatric population *(40)*.

Following the G&P atlas, several other authors proposed more sophisticated systems for predicting age from carpal and wrist bone appearance and development. A valuable alternative to the G&P atlas method is based on assigning numerical scores to bones, depending on their levels of maturity. Since 1975, Tanner et al. *(41)* improved and extended Acheson's method *(42)*, developing the Tanner and Whitehouse system (TW2), which makes use of eight or nine stages for each of 20 hand and wrist bones. However, because of the presence of many metacarpal and phalangeal bones in the hand and wrist X-ray, the authors promulgated two more separate scores for skeletal maturity, one concerning the carpals only and the other the radius, ulna, and short finger bones (RUS).

The method TW2-RUS seems to be more reliable than the G&P method *(43,44)*, because the standards for bone age derive from research based on a large sample of approx 3000 modern boys and girls. A large-scale comparison of the atlas-matching method of G&P and the bone-by-bone approach of TW2-RUS *(45)* measured greater intraobserver variation for the G&P method than for the TW2 (95% confidence limit, –2.46 to 2.18 vs –1.41 to 1.43, respectively). Furthermore, because the two methods of bone age assessment did not give equivalent estimates, Bull et al. *(45)* suggested that one method only (preferably the TW2) should be used.

The TW2 method seems to be more accurate than the G&P atlas system, but it is also a more rigorous and time-consuming approach. An average time of 7.9 min for TW2 and 1.4 min for G&P assessments has been calculated *(46)*. Furthermore, problems in assigning bone ages by the TW2 method arise from many sources *(47)*, among which the most significant is poor positioning of the hand when the radiograph is taken. This error can alter the radiographic appearance of the epiphysis and makes interpretation unnecessarily difficult.

In particular, several investigators have commented on the variance between radiography and macroscopy in the evaluation of the progress of epiphyseal union *(48)*. In fact, most papers illustrating the development of the centers of ossification are based on radiographic survey data, rather than dry bone. However, because the process of epiphyseal fusion begins in the center and can progress quite far before the external epiphyseal margin is fused, sometimes the epiphysis can radiographically appear completely fused, whereas macroscopically it is only partially fused. Thus, the X-ray would indicate a more advanced stage of union than would the naked eye. Some authors suggest that the radiograph might show union as much as 3 yr earlier than is anatomically apparent *(49)*, but Krogman and Iscan *(50)* argue that the difference is no more than plus or minus 6 mo.

On the other hand, during the process of fusion there is a buildup of compact bone at the epiphyseal plate. This can appear on X-ray as a line of radiodensity, sometimes referred to as a "persistent line of fusion," which remains visible up to several years after the epiphyseal line appears macroscopically to be completely obliterated *(14)*. In such a case, if this radiodense line is interpreted as evidence of recent fusion, the X-ray might indicate a less advanced stage of union than would be osteologically apparent. It is therefore clear that, because currently both macroscopically and radiographically based standards are used in anthropology and medicine to estimate skeletal age, the forensic expert should avoid using standards developed on osteological basis to interpret radiological observations *(48)*.

A concomitant problem in the application of radiographic standards for epiphyseal union is the lack of uniformity in evaluating stages of union. This is also because of the severe limitations in comparability, reproducibility, and verification of the different methods recommended by several scientific groups, each of them using their own protocol. Other sources of error in clinical practice are the lack of consistency in repeat ratings of the same film by one or more observers (intra- and interobserver error) and using the system outside the limits of its design *(47)*. Computerized systems for assessing skeletal maturity have been developed with the aim of reducing many of the inconsistencies associated with radiographic investigations. Computerized bone age estimation has the obvious advantage of saving the radiologist's time because the computer, not the operator, usually rates the bone. The image is digitalized and then represented by a large number of mathematical coefficients. Furthermore, computer estimates are likely to be more reproducible than human estimates because of the automatic recognition of different stages of bone maturation. Based on the TW2-RUS method, the so-called computer-assisted skeletal age scores (CASAS) have been created to increase reliability and validity *(51,52)*. CASAS seems to be more reliable and more valid estimator of skeletal maturity than the manual version of the TW2-RUS method *(53)*.

Among the computer-aided methods to assign skeletal age, worth mentioning is that one developed recently by Niemejer et al. *(54)*, but the most common is certainly the Fels method designed by Roche et al. *(55)*, which uses 98 maturity indicators. Using the Fels method, the radiologist rates the bone, and the recorded grades are entered into a computer that provides the bone age and the standard error. This is the only method, to the best of the authors' knowledge, that provides an estimate of error (possible range of variation around the mean), very useful in forensic settings. Unfortunately, experience with such computer-aided methods (i.e., CASAS) as well with the Fels method is very limited, and the most commonly used methods are still the G&P atlas and the manual version of the TW2-RUS. However, because the assessments made using the G&P atlas are often inaccurate *(56)*, at present, the manual version of the TW2-RUS should be considered the golden standard in forensic settings and the most reliable method of age estimation, in accordance with the considerable changes recently made by the authors *(57)*.

Several medical experts have criticized the reliance on age testing by hand and wrist X-rays and emphasized the inaccuracy of this practice *(58)*. For example, based on a comparison between the TW2 and Fels methods, van Lenthe et al. *(59)* have found no agreement in skeletal ages. Such discrepancies can be ascribed not only to differences in the statistical methods of the scoring system and the scales of maturity, but also to differences in maturation of the reference population. In their atlas, G&P *(36)*, explicitly recognized the discrepancies in chronological and skeletal ages and numerous studies of the bone age standards—such as those based on dental development—have found similar discrepancies. In fact, even if dental and skeletal development have strong relationships with chronological age, the accuracy of this relationship is greatly affected by many factors, among which are sexual and population variability, and also genetic, nutritional, metabolic, environmental, or functional factors. Therefore, skeletal age does not necessarily correspond to chronological age.

2. BIOLOGICAL VS CHRONOLOGICAL AGE

In this matter, the concept of biological age, as opposed to a chronological age, needs to be introduced. According to Baer *(60)*, biological age represents "an aggregate or composite of many discrete development factors," most of them intimately related with each other. It is not feasible to assess all the systems in the body, so most commonly, only certain key indicators of development are used *(8)*, such as somatic, sexual, dental, or skeletal maturity indicators.

Based on the methodological approaches already mentioned, age estimation of a living individual involves establishing the physiological age of the skeleton, constitutional and sexual type, tooth eruption and/or mineralization, and then attempting to correlate them with chronological age. The assumption for age assessment is that sexual, dental, and bone development is unanimously considered representative of the general physical maturity. Unfortunately, chronological age, sexual age, dental age, and skeletal (or bone) age are not necessarily the same in a given individual. Deviation among these four ages is common and well appreciated in medical practice because biological age (sexual, dental, or skeletal) does not always correspond to chronological (legal) age. The main reason for such discrepancies is that assessments of an individual's age measure maturity, not chronological age, which is age measured by the time (years and months).

There are obviously problems with using "age" in a system measuring maturity. A sexual, skeletal, or dental year, unlike a chronological year, is not constant at all stages of development, and maturation levels can differ within and between individuals *(8)*. There is an intimate relationship between chronological age and biological age indicators, but it is neither constant nor linear *(61)*. In fact, a number of physical traits are expressed in terms of age equivalents, and by comparing these, one can determine whether a child is advanced in some areas and slow in others.

For example, the bone age represents an equivalent level of skeletal development rather than a true chronological age *(62)*. Bone age is used to determine skeletal maturity for assessing biological development in clinical and auxological studies. Hand and wrist X-rays were designed mainly to assess delays or advancement in maturation of the bone, knowing the individual's chronological age rather than as a means of testing chronological age. Skeletal age is indeed a person's age measured by matching bone development (as shown by X-rays) with bone development of an average person of known chronological age.

During age-determination practices in forensic settings, physicians often estimate the bone and dental ages, and interpret them as the chronological ages that would have been attained if the individual had been maturing at the same rate as the individuals of identical sex and reference population *(62)*. But the accuracy of the age estimation is greatly influenced by sexual and ethnic variability, and the necessity to use sex- and population-specific standards has been recently emphasized by Schmitt et al. *(61)*, suggesting that national standards should be established and updated regularly if bone age or dental age are to be used to assess development.

The issue of which reference population to use in assessing the adequacy of growth during childhood is crucial in clinical settings as the appropriateness of the reference charts needs to be regularly reviewed. For example, the original Tanner and Whitehouse charts for height and weight *(10)* are actually obsolete because of the well-recognized secular trend toward increasing height at all ages *(63)*. They have been replaced recently by more recent growth charts, such as those developed in the United States by the National Center for Health Statistics, with improved data and statistical procedures *(64)*. British modern growth charts are also available *(65)*, and boys and girls are usually plotted on different charts because their growth rates and patterns differ.

Even if methods elaborated in forensic sciences are most often based on sex- and population-specific standards representing individuals from the major geographical regions of the world, the variability between individuals within the same sex and population usually represents a common source of error in age assessment, often underestimated (66). Variation in the biological aging process has profound effects on age assessment in living individuals as well as at death (61), and sometimes the margin of error in correlating biological age with chronological age is too great to permit accurate forensic conclusions. Remarkable differences (up to 3 yr) between bone age and chronological age have been observed in healthy subjects, probably reflecting the effect of the secular trend toward earlier maturation or alterations in pubertal development (62).

A discrepancy between the chronological age and the bone age can also indicate an atypical skeletal development. For example, Himes (67) demonstrated that chronic malnutrition can delay maturation by 2 or 3 yr. Even poor hygienic conditions can produce a retarding effect of skeletal maturation, demonstrating how environment or socioeconomic status can deeply affect the rate of general growth more than genetic or ethnical factors. In fact, it is well known that there is a genetically determined potential of skeletal maturation that does not depend on ethnicity and is available for exploitation under optimal environmental conditions (i.e., high socioeconomic status), whereas a less favorable environment may lead a significant delay in skeletal maturation (68). Like any other human biological characteristic, dental and bone formation has a regional or large-scale geographic variation, which is (sometimes inappropriately) called "ethnicity."

Ethnic origin, in particular, seems to influence much more tooth mineralization rather than skeletal maturation, as demonstrated by a comparative study of wisdom tooth on three population samples (German, Japanese, and South African). The use of population-specific standards can especially enhance the accuracy of forensic age estimates based on wisdom tooth mineralization (69). On the other hand, a recent investigation on the effects of ethnicity on skeleton and related consequences for forensic age estimations concluded that skeletal maturation takes place in phases that are identically defined for all ethnic groups (68). Time-related differences in passing those stages of skeletal maturation within the relevant age group appear to be unaffected by ethnic identity, but the socioeconomic status of a given population seems to be of decisive importance to the rate of ossification. Thus, the application of X-ray standards to an individual of a socioeconomic status lower than that of the reference population can lead to underestimation of that person's age. The risk of underestimation of age should be underlined in any expert opinion to protect the person.

3. COMBINED METHODS AND STATE OF THE ART

Because the level of reliability and accuracy in age assessment is highly variable between studies, it appears that no stable method exists. None of the modern techniques are both easy to use and practical for forensic practitioner as most of them result in a slight over- or underestimation, depending on the applied method and discrepancies between biological and legal age. Even the most thorough medical tests cannot provide conclusive evidence of a young person's age as they measure maturity, not chronological age. Furthermore, no single maturity indicator of age is ever likely to reflect accurately the many factors that accumulate with chronological age, each of which can contribute valuable information to the age estimate in living as well in dead people *(70)*. Therefore, the investigator should use all the available evidence, including multiple age indicators as multifactor techniques are recommended by many authors *(71)*.

Ubelaker *(30)* sagely suggests that all appropriate techniques must be employed before reaching a decision, to minimize the effects of factors not directly related to the aging process. Special emphasis should be given to age indicators with the highest correlation with chronological age, and any final estimate should express the known variability in the aging process, especially with regard to the sex and population affinity of the individual *(31)*. In this matter, Pfau and Sciulli *(72)* introduced a promising radiographic method for age estimation, using multiple criteria designed mainly for subadults and useful for the formation of age standards for a specific population.

Therefore, sexual changes, bones, and teeth can be actually considered (all together) the only reliable indices in assessing a living individual's age in forensic settings. Comprehensive approaches to age estimation that consider multiple maturity indicators are superior to isolated methods *(73)*, and their success reflects not only the morphological expression of the aging process, but also the technique complexity and the experience of the investigator.

Regarding the combination of procedures for age assessment, a multimedia database is also available. It is the Electronic Encyclopedia on Maxillo-Facial, Dental and Skeletal Development developed by Demirjian *(74)*, which contains almost 4000 digitalized X-rays collected between 1966 and 1981 at the Growth Center of the University of Montreal and divided in two sets: babies (from birth to age 6 yr) and adolescents (from 6 to 17 yr). The encyclopedia, in CD-ROM format, provides an archive of anthropometric and cephalometric data, and dental and skeletal X-rays, which is often of great value as a reference.

The most obvious application of the data contained in the CD-ROM is in comparing observations and measurements obtained from a set of unknown individuals to information obtained from children of known ages *(74)*. The data can also be studied from a statistical point of view by using percentile values. The encyclopedia also includes programs for direct calculation of age, separately for males and females. When searching by age, three different assignments are given to every child: chronological, skeletal, and dental. Skeletal age is calculated by the TW2-RUS methods, whereas dental age is based on the Demirjian's systems. The user can easily move between X-rays and measurements of subjects at a given chronological age, comparing dental and skeletal development to his or her unknown, or move through the dental or skeletal X-rays of a specific individual, comparing his or her unknown to individuals at various chronological ages. By using cross-sectional or longitudinal studies, everyone can appreciate the tremendous variation intrinsic to the human growth process.

According to Ritz-Timme et al. *(75)*, it is surprising how few attempts have been made to find common standardization, calibration, and evaluation procedures for age estimation in living individuals as well in human remains, especially in the beginning of this century, in which quality control has achieved a great importance in all fields of the biomedical sciences. Actually, there are no generally accepted guidelines concerning quality assurance in age estimation. Efforts in this direction are necessary in order to guarantee adequate answers to the important legal and social issue of age estimation in forensic medicine.

In age estimation of living individuals, the only guidelines available are those developed by the international and interdisciplinary Study Group on Forensic Age Estimation *(76)*, constituted in Berlin in March 2000, which currently has 76 members from Germany, Belgium, France, Norway, Spain, and the United States. This is the only official step made by a scientific community for issuing expert opinions in order to standardize the yet rather heterogeneous procedure and to implement quality assurance policies in this area *(3)*. According to recommendations of the Study Group, every expert opinion must comprise three independent parts contributed by forensically experienced physicians of the relevant disciplines (auxology, radiology, and dentistry). These include the physical examination, the X-ray evaluation of the left hand by a radiologist, and a dental examination that records dentition status and evaluates an orthopantogram. An additional X-ray examination or computed tomography scan of the clavicle is also recommended to establish whether a person has reached the age of 21, based on the fusion of the medial epiphysis.

The physical examination determines anthropometric measures, such as stature and weight, along with signs of sexual maturity and identification of any developmental disorders that might affect age-appropriate development; Tanner's sexual maturity rating *(6,7)* is commonly used for this purpose. The mineralization of the third molars is assessed using the information stages described by Demirjian et al. *(21)*, modified in accordance with Mincer et al. *(17)*. Criteria for evaluating left-hand radiographs include the form and size of bone elements and the degree of ossification of epiphyseal cartilages. Radiographic atlas and/or single bone methods such as the G&P *(36)* and TW2 *(41)* techniques are used. The X-ray image is compared with standards of the relevant age and sex, thus, degree of skeletal maturity is determined for selected bones.

The accuracy of the combined method proposed by the Study Group has been evaluated by statistical analysis, concluding that deviation between estimated and true age ranged between ±12 mo in most of the cases *(77)*. These results confirm how difficult is to determine exactly the age of living individual, even based on a combination of techniques using multiple maturity indicators. In this respect, the Study Group has emphasized that the central forensic aspect of an expert report is giving the most probable age of the individual examined and/or the degree of probability that the stated age is the actual age or that the individual's age is higher than the relevant penal age limit. Reference studies on which the age estimation is based have to be necessarily quoted in the final report.

Because in forensic science mere visual estimates are simply unreliable and unacceptable, the use of validated and scientifically based formal methods is crucial for every forensic evaluation *(78)*. The age-assessment procedure developed by the Study Group can be considered a valuable approach to give some objectivity to age-determination practices, even if some remarks can be highlighted. They concern mainly the choice of standards for sexual maturation and for hand and wrist X-rays. For example, Tanner growth charts for height and weight *(10)*, as well the G&P atlas *(36)*, are no longer reliable for use and could be inaccurate because they do not represent a modern multi-ethnic pediatric population. Furthermore, different population-specific standards should be considered or, even better, new reference studies should be developed. With respect to the quality control in forensic age-determination practice, more studies are needed to test the reliability of existing techniques on samples other than those originally used to develop the technique or formulae.

Another statement deals with the radiographic analysis of teeth and bones and therefore the applicability of additional X-rays (such as those recommended for the clavicle): radiography plays a very important role for the inspection of dental maturity and skeletal development and, indeed, it is of invaluable assistance in the age-estimation practice. Nevertheless, a radiograph is, after all, a diagnostic intrusive procedure and must be guided by principles of medical ethics.

Dental X-rays or hand and wrist X-rays involve always a minimal radiation exposure, and precautions must be necessarily taken when radiographs are used, in particular, for pregnant girls. An alternative procedure of skeletal age assessment has been proposed using a less invasive method such as dual-energy X-ray absorptiometry, and a high degree of agreement of bone age assessments based on dual-energy X-ray absorptiometry and radiographic images has been observed (79).

However, regarding the radiographic analysis in the assessment of age, since 1996 the Royal College of Radiologists (80) gave useful advice to its members, arguing strongly that ionizing radiation should be used only in "cases of clinical need." In fact, X-rays should be considered unjustified if requested only to ascertain the alleged chronological age. Otherwise, X-ray examination that is not based on medical indication has to be authorized by an authority order.

With respect to the principles of patient autonomy, welfare, and consent, some other invasive procedures, such as dentine sampling by tooth extraction or biopsy in living individuals, even if strongly recommended based on their high accuracy (75,81), should be also considered unjustified especially if forced against the individual's wishes. It is true that methods for sectioned teeth seem to give more reliable results when compared with methods for intact teeth (78), but this practice can only be considered depending on the circumstances of individual cases (i.e., loss of single tooth), and in adulthood, when the criteria for the aging process, such as the eruption and the development of roots, are not available. In fact, once the adult dentition is fully formed, accurate age assessment by dental means becomes difficult without the removal of a tooth for microscopic analysis.

In order to increase the accuracy of age estimates and to identify age-relevant development disorders, a combination of methods, such as those mentioned previously, is strongly recommended. However, even using a multifactor technique, the authors believe that the margin of error seems too great to permit reasonable conclusions in forensic settings. The poor correlation between maturity and chronological age represents a fundamental limitation to age-determination practices, especially for forensic purposes. Based on such inaccurate estimates, authorities could incarcerate some children in adult detention centers, which are unsafe and inappropriate for minors.

In this respect, in a letter to the Department of Homeland Security, several American leaders in dentistry, medicine, and psychology have recently expressed their strong concern over irresponsible age-determination practices affecting the lives of young immigrants, including asylum seekers (82). In a public comment to American Immigration and Naturalization Servise, Ferraro

(58) also expressed the danger of the current age-determination practice in forensic settings, because of its apparent accuracy that is given an unwarranted scientific legitimacy *(58)*.

4. CONCLUSION

According to Maples *(83)*, age determination is ultimately an art, not a precise science. The margin of error can be substantial in living individuals, sometimes by as much as 2–3 yr either side, or at best, 12 mo, even by using combined methods *(77)*. On the other hand, estimates of age may lose credibility if they are too precise, because many biological variables in humans exist to achieve reliable results, and there are several hazards in any age-estimation method. Even the most thorough medical tests cannot provide conclusive evidence of a young person's age as they measure maturity, not chronological age. Therefore, no age-determination technique would ever be extremely precise and accurate because human development is complex and variable.

In the Guidelines for Paediatricians *(84)*, the Royal College of Paediatrics already focused on how age determination is extremely difficult to do with certainty, and no single approach to this can be relied on. There may be difficulties in determining whether a young person who might be as old as 23 yr could, in fact, be under the age of 18. For young people aged 15–18 yr, it is even less possible to be certain about age.

As there can be a wide margin of error in assessing age; it may be best to word a clinical or forensic judgment in terms of whether a child is probably, likely, possibly or unlikely to be under the age of 14 or 18. According to the Guidelines for Paediatricians *(84)* forms of sentences such as "Her/his age may be in the range *x–y* years," or "He/she is likely to be the age that he/she claims for the following reasons: [give reasons]," may be appropriate. According to recommendations of the Study Group on Forensic Age Estimation, the estimates should necessarily refer to the margin of error or the possible range of variation around the mean associated with that particular method adopted, and reference studies on which the age estimation is based have to be necessarily quoted in the final report. Nevertheless, when the exact age is uncertain, the child should be given the benefit of the doubt.

In conclusion, every investigator must approach each case with caution regarding the discrepancies between biological and legal age, the range of human variation between sex and population, the intervention of pathological conditions, and the appropriate application of standards discussed and presented in this chapter.

REFERENCES

1. Schmeling, A., Olze, A., Reisinger, W., Geserick, G. Age estimation of living people undergoing criminal proceedings. Lancet 358:89–90, 2001.
2. United Nations High Commissioner for Refugees. Guidelines on policies and procedures in dealing with unaccompanied children seeking asylum. United Nations High Commissioner for Refugees, Geneva, February 1997.
3. Schmeling, A., Olze, A., Reisinger, W., Geserick, G. Forensic age estimation of living people undergoing criminal proceedings. Forensic Sci. Int. 144:243–245, 2004.
4. Vaughan III, C., Litt, I. F. Developmental pediatrics: assessment of growth and development. In: Behrman, R. E., Vaughan III, C., eds., Nelson Textbook of Pediatrics, 13th Ed., WB Saunders, Philadelphia, PA, pp. 24–33, 1987.
5. Pietrobelli, A., Faith, M. S., Allison, D. B., Gallagher, D., Chiumello, G., Heymsfield, S. B. Body mass index as a measure of adiposity among children and adolescents: a validation study. J. Pediatr. 132:204–210, 1998.
6. Marshall, W. A., Tanner, J. M. Variations in pattern of pubertal changes in girls. Arch. Dis. Child. 44:291–303, 1969.
7. Marshall, W. A., Tanner, J. M. Variations in pattern of pubertal changes in boys. Arch. Dis. Child. 45:13–23, 1970.
8. Feik, S. A., Glover, J. E. Growth of children's faces. In: Clement, J. G., Ranson, D. L., Ranson, D., eds., Craniofacial Identification in Forensic Medicine. Arnold, London, pp. 203–224, 1998.
9. Iscan, M. Y., Kennedy, K. A. R. Reconstruction of life from the skeleton. Liss, New York, pp. 109–127; 191–200, 201–222, 1989.
10. Tanner, J. M., Whitehouse, R. H. Clinical longitudinal standards for height, weight, height velocity and weight velocity and stages of puberty. Arch. Dis. Child. 51: 170–179, 1976.
11. Hammer, L. D., Kraemer, H. C., Wilson, D. M., Ritter, P. L., Dornbusch, S. M. Standardized percentile curves of body-mass index for children and adolescents. Am. J. Dis. Child. 145:259–263, 1991.
12. Valadian, I., Porter D. Physical Growth and Development from Conception to Maturity. Little Brown, Boston, MA, 1977.
13. Wright, C. M., Booth, I. W., Buckler, J. M. H., et al. Growth reference charts for use in the United Kingdom. Arch. Dis. Child. 86:11–14, 2002.
14. Krogman, W. M., Iscan, M. Y. The Human Skeleton in Forensic Medicine. Charles C. Thomas Publisher, Springfield, IL, pp. 50–102, 1986.
15. Hagg, U., Matsson, L. Dental maturity as an indicator of chronologic age. The accuracy and precision of three methods. Eur. J. Orthod. 7:25–34, 1985.
16. Mincer, H. H., Harris, E. F., Berryman, H. E. Molar development as an estimator of chronologic age. In: Bowers, C. M., Bell, G. L., eds., Manual of Forensic Odontology, 3rd Ed. American Society of Forensic Odontology, Saratoga Springs, NY, 86–89, 1997.
17. Mincer, H. H., Harris, E. F., Berryman, H. E. The ABFO study of third molar development and the use as an estimator of chronological age. J. Forensic Sci. 38:379–390, 1993.

18. Kullman, L., Johanson, G., Akesson, L. Root development of the lower third molar and its relation to chronological age. Swed. Dent. J. 16:161–167, 1992.
19. Levesque, G.-Y., Demirjian, A., Tanguay, R. Sexual dimorphism in the development, emergence and agenesis of the mandibular third molar. J. Dent. Res. 60:1735–1741, 1981.
20. Gleiser, I., Hunt, Jr., E. E. The permanent mandibular first molar: its calcification, eruption and decay. Am. J. Phys. Anth. 13:253–281, 1955.
21. Demirjian, A., Goldstein, H., Tanner, J. M. A new system of dental age assessment. Hum. Biol. 45:211–227, 1973.
22. Mesotten, K., Gunst, K., Carbonez, A., Willems, G. Dental age estimation and third molars: a preliminary study. Forensic Sci. Int. 129:110–115, 2002.
23. Solari, A., Abramovitch, K. The accuracy and precision of third molar development as an indicator of chronological age in Hispanics. J. Forensic Sci. 47:531–535, 2002.
24. Gunst, K., Mesotten, K., Carbonez, A., Willems, G. Third molar root development in relation to chronological age: a large sample sized retrospective study. Forensic Sci. Int. 136:52–57, 2003.
25. Foti, B., Layls, L,, Adalian, P., et al. New forensic approach to age determination in children based on tooth eruption. Forensic Sci. Int. 132:49–56, 2003.
26. Thorson. J., Hagg, U. The accuracy and precision of the mandibular molar as an indicator of chronological age. Swed. Dent. J. 15:15–22, 1991.
27. Kullman, L. Accuracy of two dental and one skeletal age estimation method in Swedish adolescents. Forensic Sci. Int. 75:225–236, 1995.
28. Tanner, J. M. Physical growth and development. In: Forfar, J. O., Arnell, C. C. eds., Textbook of Pediatrics, 2nd Ed. Churchill Livingstone, Edinburgh, pp. 249–303, 1978.
29. Liversidge, H. M., Herdeg, B., Rosing, F. W. Dental age estimation of non-adults: a review of methods and principals. In: Alt, K. W., Rosing, F. W., Teschler-Nicola, M., eds., Dental Anthropology. Fundamentals, Limits and Prospects. Springer, Vienna, pp. 420–422, 1998.
30. Ubelaker, D. H. The estimation of age at death from immature human bone. In: Iscan, M. Y. Ed., Age Markers in the Human Skeleton. Charles C. Thomas, Springfield, IL, pp. 55–70, 1989.
31. Lovejoy, C. O., Meindl, R. S., Mensforth, R. P., Barton, T. J. Multifactorial determination of skeletal age at death: a method and blind tests of its accuracy. Am. J. Phys. Anthropol., 68:1–14, 1985.
32. Rösing, F. W., Kvaal, S. I. Dental age in adults: a review of estimation methods. In: Alt, K. W., Rosing, F. W., Teschler-Nicola, M. eds., Dental Anthropology. Fundamentals, Limits and Prospects. Springer, Vienna, pp. 443–468, 1998.
33. Helm, S. Relationship between dental and skeletal maturation in Danish schoolchildren. Scand. J. Dent. Res. 98:313–317, 1990.
34. Cox, L. A. The biology of bone maturation and ageing. Acta Paediatr. 423:S107–S108, 1997.
35. Zerin, J. M., Hernandez RJ. Approach to skeletal maturation. Hand Clin. 7:53–62, 1991.

36. Greulich, W. W., Pyle, S. I. Radiographic Atlas of Skeletal Development of the Hand and Wrist, 2nd Ed. Stanford University Press, Stanford, CA, pp. 9–13, 1959.
37. Ubelaker, D. H. Estimating age at death from immature human skeletons: an overview. J. Forensic Sci. 32:1254–1263, 1987.
38. Loder, R. T., Estle, D. T., Morrison, K., et al. Applicability of the Greulich and Pyle skeletal age standards to black and white children of today. Am. J. Dis. Child. 147:1329–1333, 1993.
39. Ontell, F. K., Ivanovic, M., Ablin, D. S., Barlow, T. W. Bone age in children of diverse ethnicity. Am. J. Roentgenol. 167:1395–1398, 1996.
40. Mora, S., Boechat, M. I., Pietka, E., Huang, H. K., Gilsanz, V. Skeletal age determinations in children of European and African descent: applicability of the Greulich and Pyle standards. Pediatr. Res. 50:624–628, 2001.
41. Tanner, J. M., Whitehouse, R. H., Marshall, W. A., Healy, M. J. R., Goldstein, H. Assessment of skeletal maturity and prediction of adult height (TW2 method). Academic, London, 1975.
42. Acheson, R. M. A method of assessing skeletal maturity from radiographs. A report from Oxford Child Health Survey. J Anat. 88:498–515, 1954.
43. Roche, A. F., Johnson, J. M. A comparison between methods of calculating skeletal age (Greulich-Pyle). Am. J. Phys. Anthropol. 30:221–230, 1969.
44. Roche, A. F., Davila, G. H. The reliability of assessments of the maturity of individual hand-wrist bones. Hum. Biol. 48:585–590, 1976.
45. Bull, R. K., Edwards, P. D., Kemp, P. M., Fry, S., Hughes, I. A. Bone age assessment: a large scale comparison of the Greulich and Pyle, and Tanner and Whitehouse (TW2) methods. Arch. Dis. Child. 81:172–173, 1999.
46. King, D. G., Stevenson, D. M., O'Sullivan, M. P., et al. Reproducibility of bone ages when performed by radiology registrars: an audit of Tanner and Whitehouse II versus Greulich and Pyle methods. Br. J. Radiol. 67:848–851, 1994.
47. Cox, L. A. Tanner-Whitehouse method of assessing skeletal maturity: problems and common errors. Horm. Res, 45:53–55, 1996.
48. Sorg, M. H., Andrews, R. P., Iscan, M. Y. Radiographic aging of the adult. In: Iscan, M. Y., Ed., Age Markers in the Human Skeleton. Charles C. Thomas, Springfield, IL, pp. 169–193, 1989.
49. Drennen, M. R., Keen, J. A. Identity. In: Gordon, I., Turner, R., Price, T. W., eds., Medical Jurisprudence. Livingston, Edinburgh, pp. 336–372, 1953.
50. Krogman, W. M., Iscan, M. Y. The human skeleton in forensic medicine. Charles C. Thomas Publisher, Springfield, IL, 458–479, 1986.
51. Tanner, J. M., Gibbons, R. D. Automatic bone age measurement using computerized image analysis. J Pedriatr. Endocrinol. 7:141–145, 1994.
52. Tanner, J. M., Gibbons, R. D. A computerized image analysis system for estimating Tanner-Whitehouse 2 bone age. Horm. Res. 42:282–287, 1994.
53. Frisch, H., Riedl, S., Waldhor, T. Computer-aided estimation of skeletal age and comparison with bone age evaluations by the method of Greulich-Pyle and Tanner-Whitehouse. Pediatr. Radiol. 26:226–231, 1996.
54. Niemeijer, M., van Ginneken, B., Maas, C., Beek, F. J. A., Viergever, M. A. Assessing the skeletal age from a hand radiograph: automating the Tanner-Whitehouse

method. In: Sonka, M., Fitzpatrick, J. M. eds., Medical Imaging 2003: Image Processing. SPIE, pp. 1197–1205, 2003.

55. Roche, A. F., Chumlea, W. C., Thissen, D. Assessing the skeletal maturity of the hand-wrist: FELS method. Springfield, IL, Charles C. Thomas Publisher, 1988.
56. Gilli, G. The assessment of skeletal maturation. Horm. Res. 45:45–52, 1996.
57. Tanner, J. M., Healy, M. J. R., Goldstein, H., Cameron, N. Assessment of skeletal maturity and prediction of adult height (TW3 method). Saunders, 2001.
58. Ferraro, N. F. Comment to the Immigration and Naturalization Service (INS) regarding determination of chronological age using bone age and dental age standards. Public comment on proposed Rule at 64 FR 39759 (INS No. 1906-98) In: From Persecution to Prison: The Health Consequences of Detention for Asylum Seekers. Physicians for Human Rights (PHR), June 2003. Also available on the PHR website at http://www.phrusa.org/campaigns/asylum_network/detention_execSummary/detention_pdf.pdf. Last accessed on Feb. 15, 2006.
59. Van Lenthe, F. J., Kemper, H. C., van Mechelen, W. Skeletal maturation in adolescence: a comparison between the Tanner-Whitehouse II and the Fels method. Eur. J. Pediatr. 157:798–801, 1998.
60. Baer, M. J. Growth and maturation. An introduction to physical development. Doyle, Cambridge, MA, 1977.
61. Schmitt, A., Murail, P., Cunha, E., Rougé, D. Variability of the pattern of aging on the human skeleton: evidence from bone indicators and implications on age at death estimation. J. Forensic Sci. 47:1203–1209, 2002.
62. Johnston, F. E., Zimmer, L. O. Assessment of growth and age in the immature skeleton. In: Iscan, M. Y., Kennedy, K. A. R., eds., Reconstruction of Life from the Skeleton. Liss, New York, NY, pp. 11–40, 1989.
63. Rona, R., Chinn, S. The national study of health and growth. Oxford University Press, Oxford, 1999.
64. Kuczmarski, R. J., Ogden, C. L., Guo, S. S., et al. CDC growth charts for the United States: methods and development. Vital Health Stat. 11:1–190, 2002.
65. Cameron, N. British growth charts for height and weight with recommendations concerning their use in auxological assessment. Ann. Hum. Biol. 29:1–10, 2002.
66. Ubelaker, D. H. Methodological consideration in the forensic applications of human skeletal biology. In: Katzenberg, M. A., Saunders, S. R. eds., Biological Anthropology of the Human Skeleton. Wiley-Liss, New York, NY, pp. 41–67, 2000.
67. Himes, J. H. Bone growth and development in protein-calorie malnutrition. World Rev. Nutr. Diet. 28:143–187, 1978.
68. Schmeling, A., Reisinger, W., Loreck, D., Vendura, K., Markus, W., Geserick, G. Effects of ethnicity on skeletal maturation: consequences for forensic age estimations. Int. J. Legal Med. 113:253–58, 2000.
69. Olze, A., Schmeling, A., Taniguchi, M., et al. Forensic age estimation in living subjects: the ethnic factor in wisdom tooth mineralization. Int. J. Legal Med. 118:170–173, 2004.
70. Meindl, R. S., Lovejoy, C. O. Ectocranial suture closure: a revised method for the determination of skeletal age at death based on the lateral-anterior sutures. Am. J. Phys. Anthropol. 68:57–66, 1985.

71. Bedford, M. E., Russel, K. F., Lovejoy, C. O., et al. Test of the multifactorial aging method using skeleton with known age-at-death from the Grant collection. Am. J. Phys. Anthropol. 91:287–297, 1993.
72. Pfau, R. O., Sciulli, P. W. A method for establishing the age of subadults. J. Forensic Sci. 39:165–176, 1994.
73. Baccino, E., Ubelaker, D. H., Hayek, L.-A., Zerilli, A. Evaluation of seven methods of estimating age at death from mature human skeletal remains. J. Forensic Sci. 44:931–936, 1999.
74. Reichs, K. J., Demirjian, A. A multimedia tool for the assessment of age in immature remains: the electronic encyclopedia for maxillo-facial, dental and skeletal development. In: Reichs, K. J., Ed., Forensic Osteology. Advances in the Identification of Human Remains. Charles C. Thomas Publisher, Springfield, IL, pp. 253–267, 1998.
75. Ritz-Timme, S., Cattaneo, C., Collins, M. J., et al. Age estimation: the state of the art in relation to the specific demands of forensic practise. Int. J. Legal Med. 113: 129–136, 2000.
76. http://www.charite.de/rechtsmedizin/agfad/empfehlungen1.html#Englisch. Last accessed on Feb. 15, 2006.
77. Schmeling, A., Olze, A., Reisinger, W., Konig, M., Geserick, G. Statistical analysis and verification of forensic age estimation of living persons in the Institute of Legal Medicine of the Berlin University Hospital Charitè. Legal Med. 5:S367–S371, 2003.
78. Soomer, H., Ranta, H., Lincoln, M. J., Penttila, A., Leibur, E. Reliability and validity of eight dental age. Estimation methods for adults. J. Forensic Sci. 48:149–152, 2003.
79. Pludowski, P., Lebiedowski, M., Lorenc, R. S. Evaluation of the possibility to assess bone age on the basis of DXA derived hand scans—preliminary results. Osteoporos Int. 15:317–322, 2004.
80. Watt, I., Faculty of Clinical radiology. Letter ref. BFCR 9 to all Home Clinical radiology Fellows and Members, 1996.
81. Ritz, S., Stock, R., Schutz, H. W., Kaatsch, H.-J. Age estimation in biopsy specimens of dentin. Int. J. Legal Med. 108:135–139, 1995.
82. Letter from American Leaders in Dentistry, Medicine, and Psychology Expressing Concern Over Irresponsible Age Determination Practices Affecting the Lives of Young Immigrants, Including Asylum Seekers to the Department of Homeland Security. Available on the Physicians for Human Rights website at http://www.phrusa.org/campaigns/asylum_network/pdf/age-testingletter.pdf. Last accessed on Feb. 15, 2006.
83. Maples, W. R. The practical application of age-estimation techniques. In: Iscan, M. Y., Ed., Age Markers in the Human Skeleton. Charles C. Thomas Publishers, Springfield, IL, pp. 319–324, 1989.
84. Levenson, R., Sharma, A. The health of refugee children. Guidelines for Paediatricians. Royal College of Paediatrics and Child Health, London, 1999.

PART III

Pathophysiology of Death
and Forensic Investigation:
From Recovery to Cause of Death

Chapter 5

Decay Process of a Cadaver

João Pinheiro

Summary

Because forensic anthropologists and pathologists can be confronted in their professional practices with bodies or mortal remains in different states of preservation and/or decay, it is essential for this book to have a chapter that fully documents the pathway of a body from its death until disintegration.

The different ways a corpse can progress from putrefaction directly (or not) to skeletonization, passing through conservation processes such as saponification or mummification are presented here, always taking into account the forensic relevance of each stage, the time and conditions needed, as well as the duration. Full, illustrated examples of cases that have contributed to solve forensic questions are provided. Factors that might influence the speed of putrefaction and the interrelations—through chemical reactions between these processes—are also debated.

Key Words: Decay; decomposition; putrefaction; saponification; adipocere; mummification; skeletonization; disarticulation; forensic; autopsies.

1. Introduction

It is common for forensic anthropologists and pathologists to be confronted in their professional practice with bodies or human remains states of preservation and/or decay that are not entirely to their liking, such states being outside their knowledge and experience. The forensic pathologist generally feels more at ease with a fresh body, whereas the forensic anthropologist would certainly prefer to work with dry bones. Ideally, the forensic anthropologist

From *Forensic Anthropology and Medicine:*
Complementary Sciences From Recovery to Cause of Death
Edited by: A. Schmitt, E. Cunha, and J. Pinheiro © Humana Press Inc., Totowa, NJ

should always be called whenever a body appears whose morphological characteristics do not permit any identification. Such cases are usually in an advanced state of decay: with adipocere, mummified, carbonized, skeletonized, or with a mixture of all of these. Indeed, the same cadaver may reveal various states of preservation at the same time. This fact is closely connected to the different transformations that may take place in a body from the moment of death to skeletonization, upon the action of various extrinsic and intrinsic factors, which are analyzed here.

For this reason, it is fundamental that the pathologist has prior knowledge of the various alterations that take place postmortem (the object of the study of forensics called taphonomy). These alterations particularly affect the soft tissues, and are decisive not only for the time taken for skeletonization to occur, but also for the state of preservation of the cadaver *(1)*. Between a fresh cadaver and a heap of loose bones, there are a series of stages of decomposition and/or preservation that may occur when the environmental conditions are right. Various authors have drawn attention to the need to understand this process *(2,3)*, whereas some of the definitions of forensic anthropology itself, such as the one of Bass *(4)*, presuppose the existence of cases other than those skeletonized: "…the science that focuses principally on the identification of remains that are *more or less skeletonized*, in the legal context."

This journey along the taphonomic process will certainly be useful in its earlier stages for anthropologists that are not used to working with almost-fresh cadavers, and in the final phase (skeletonization) for pathologists, who are normally not too fond of working with bones.

2. DECOMPOSITION

The process by means of which a cadaver becomes a skeleton, through the destruction of the soft tissue, is quite complex. In discussing the decomposition process, it is important to remember that, as with everything in biology, the exception is the rule, or rather, that there are no two individuals alike, nor any two decomposition processes alike. This is why this stage can be difficult.

The decomposition of a body is a mixed process that varies from cellular autolysis by endogenous chemical destruction to tissue autolysis, by either the release of enzymes or external processes, resulting from the bacteria and fungus in the intestines or from outside *(5)*. Predators, ranging from insects to mammals, participate in the process and may accelerate it. It can therefore be said, with Di Maio *(6)*, that decomposition involves autolysis (the destruction of cells and organs by an aseptic chemical process) and putrefaction (because of bacteria and fermentation). Thus, whereas common sense understands decomposition to be synonymous with putrefaction, in the forensic context, it has a much broader meaning, covering all stages from the moment of death to the dissolution of all body parts.

It is a process that varies greatly from body to body, environment to environment, according to whether the body is clothed or naked, the circumstances of the death and the place where the body is found, the climate, and so forth. For example, it is known that putrefaction occurs much faster in bodies that are left in the open air than those immersed in water, whereas buried bodies decay at a much slower rate (7–9). In these cases, factors such as the length of time before the body was buried (thus allowing putrefaction to begin), the temperature at the site, the presence or absence of oxygen, the depth of the body, topography of the soil (rather than its composition), and the type of coffin used, considerably affect the speed of decomposition (6). However, whereas many exhumations have little to offer to certain investigations, this should not devalue their importance. Indeed, this can never be anticipated, because there are cases in which bodies are in truly surprising states of conservation. In an autopsy performed by the author, it was possible, some months after the burial, to undertake a detailed examination, entirely unexpectedly, of a spontaneous brain hemorrhage in a body that had been buried in winter in an area of harsh climate (atmospheric temperatures between –3 and 10°C).

Decomposition may also vary within the same cadaver, with some parts of the body showing adipocere, other parts mummified, and still others only putrefied (Fig. 1). This will depend on the different "microenvironments" that develop around them, in accordance with the place where they are found. There are also various possible interconnections between these states, which makes it difficult to estimate the date of death.

The calculation of the postmortem interval (PMI), one of the most controversial and difficult problems in legal medicine, becomes more acute in cases of decomposition. Excluding the precious assistance provided by forensic entomology (a separate discipline that is not dealt with here), various methods have been used to calculate this interval, while of course taking into account the subjective nature of the individual assessment. Prieto (9) lists the evaluation of biomarkers like lipids, nitrogen, amino acid content, neurotransmitters, decompositional byproducts, persistence of blood remnants in bone tissue; extent of DNA deterioration; changes sustained by microanatomical skeletal structure; and carbon 14. Others have tried to study the variations of factors that influence decomposition in certain cases, either prospectively (through the formation of adipocere [10,11]) or retrospectively (by analyzing cases that have already been solved in order to study particularly extrinsic factors that affect it [9,12]).

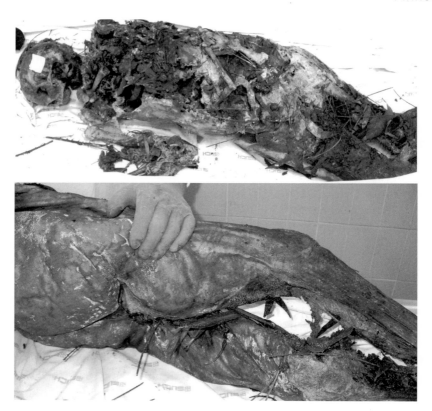

Fig. 1. Coexistence of three states of decomposition in the same body: skeletonization of the head, adipocere in the trunk organs, and mummification of the limbs. Note skin's leathery appearance. The body belongs to a 93-yr-old woman found facedown in the countryside, whose positive identification was achieved. Cause of death was ascertained.

In all cases, and despite the relevance of some of these methods, the establishment of PMI continues, for most pathologists, to be based on individual analysis and experience obtained in similar cases. And, whereas it is legitimate to suggest a date for past populations with some margin of variation, it is always very difficult to risk a prognosis in forensic cases, because there are so many factors involved, and the range of variation is so broad. This is supported by a number of authors *(8,10–13)*, who, because of the multiplicity of factors involved, find it impossible to attribute a credible time interval for each of the stages of decomposition.

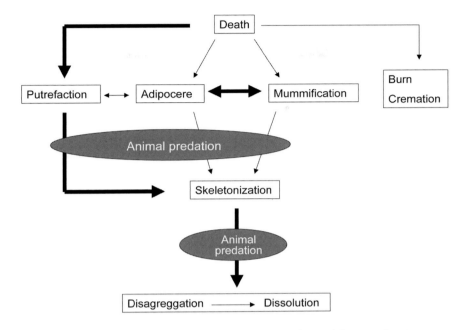

Fig. 2. Steps of body decomposition. (Adapted from ref. 5.)

What can be done, of course, when required for a particular decomposition process, is to indicate the time suggested in the literature and validated by experience as necessary for each of the processes to take place, and from this, it is possible to get an idea of the PMI.

After death, most bodies that have not been embalmed will start putrefying quickly and will liquefy in some time, leaving only the skeleton (Fig. 2). Others, however, may pass through some of the preservation processes mentioned previously (mummification, saponification), interchangeable among themselves, which will lead eventually to skeletonization. A skeletonized body will tend to disintegrate, or alternatively, to fossilize, a process that may take millions of years. Figure 2 shows this process of decomposition, which will be discussed, as far as disaggregation or fossilization is concerned.

2.1. Putrefaction

Putrefaction is usually the first stage of decomposition, although it is not always found, and consists of the gradual dissolution of the tissues to gases, liquids, and salts *(7)*. Not only is it the subject of numerous publications, it is also covered in any book about legal medicine and forensic pathology.

Many authors distinguish phases and stages in the putrefaction process, some of which are based on the study of the decomposition of animal carcasses. For example, Shean et al. *(14)* distinguish 4 phases (decomposition of the soft tissue, exposure of bone, remains only with connective tissue, and bone only) that are broken down into 15 stages, whereas Galloway et al. *(15)* distinguish 5 phases and 21 stages, to cite only some. Others describe these stages with great temporal precision, which, although revealing great erudition and being very successful in lessons or lectures, are inadequate for practical application given the enormous variability of the development of this process. These discrepancies between suggested periods and phases of decomposition, along with the study of animals, naturally limit the value of these findings. In the author's opinion, what is much more important than knowing the stage of putrefaction, or how long it has taken to get there, is the ability to recognize the elements that characterize clearly and objectively the stage of putrefaction, and the artifacts that this may induce, and to know its potential and limits in terms of thanatological research.

Therefore, described here chronologically are the alterations undergone by a body after the death, in a place with temperate weather. It should be emphasized that the times mentioned are merely indications and in no way exact because some of the characteristics described may appear considerably earlier or later than suggested.

2.1.1. FIRST WEEK

One of the earliest signs of putrefaction is the discoloration of the lower abdominal wall in the right iliac fossa because of the proximity of the cecum to the surface. Intestinal bacteria break down the hemoglobin into sulfohemoglobin and other colored pigments (the "green abdominal stain," as it is known in some countries), which extends from the right iliac fossa to the whole of the abdomen and thorax (Fig. 3). These bacteria are also responsible for the formation of gases, provoking edema of the face and neck. The gases released in this process (sulfuretted hydrogen, phosphoretted hydrogen, methane, carbon dioxide, ammonia and hydrogen *(7)*, and some mercaptans) are responsible for the unpleasant odor that is characteristic of these bodies. Other effects produced by gases include a marked increase in the volume of the abdomen, which is under tension, and of the scrotum and penis, which may gain extraordinary dimensions. The face and neck also increase greatly, with protrusion of the eyes and tongue, making identification difficult.

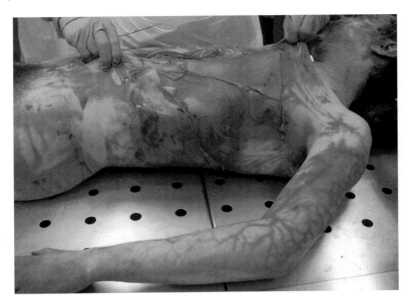

Fig. 3. The colors of putrefaction: abdominal green, which had begun in the right inguinal region; red marbling, typically on the lateral part of the trunk, shoulders, and upper limbs; reddish, purplish of the putrefactive phlyctenae. Note the skin slippage. (*See* ebook for color version of this figure.)

The phenomenon known as "marbling" in Anglo-Saxon literature (or Brouardel's "posthumous circulation," as it is better known in the Latin countries), which results from the colonization of the venous system by intestinal bacteria that hemolyze the blood, is very characteristically found at this time. It appears on the thighs and sidewalls of the abdomen, chest, and shoulders (*see* Fig. 3), first with a reddish color and, later, green.

Skin blisters containing reddish purplish serous liquid erupt in the sloping regions (*see* Figs. 3 and 9). These should be distinguished from the phlyctenae that result from burns; phlyctenae containing a serous liquid are of course characteristic of second-degree burns, but they are usually surrounded by an erythematous ring, something that is not found in putrefactive blisters.

The epidermis becomes fragile and tears easily, which means that it may come off in large areas, leaving the red dermis visible, similar to what happens with first- and second-degree burns (Fig. 4). Such patches may also be caused by the bursting of the phlyctenae, when these are large and contain liquid under pressure. The skin may also come off on the fingertips, which, of course, hinders the taking of fingerprints.

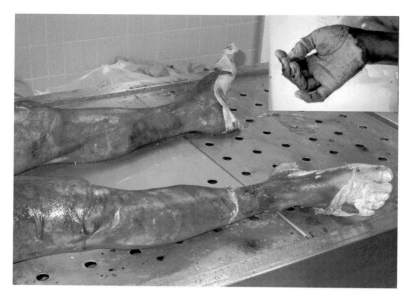

Fig. 4. Skin slippage, leaving the dermis visible. For the inexperienced, this can be confused with second-degree burns. On both hands and feet, and like burns or drowning, the skin can be removed like a glove. Fingerprints will then be difficult to obtain.

In hairy areas, hairs will come off at the slightest pressure. This phase of putrefaction may also provide some curious aspects, such as the "gloves" made of skin on the hands (*see* Fig. 4), or the use of the hair by birds for nest building *(6)*.

2.1.2. SECOND AND THIRD WEEKS

The increase of pressure on the abdomen produced by putrefactive gases leads to the ejection of feces and urine, and there have been cases described of uterine prolapse, and even of a postmortem birth *(5,7)*. This pressure also leads to the expulsion of liquids from any orifice, particularly in the early stages, from the mouth and nostrils. As this liquid is often bloody, it can lead to complications for differential diagnosis because inexperienced pathologists may confuse these cases with cases of violent death (Fig. 5). Tracheobronchial foam may also be produced by the same mechanism that creates a mixture of air with the tracheobronchial liquids. Internally, small gas bubbles are frequently found in the soft viscera, giving these organs a "foamy" appearance.

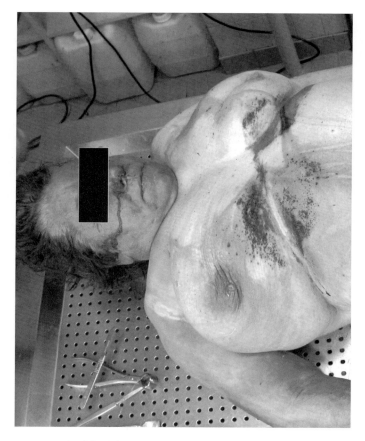

Fig. 5. Purging of a bloody liquid from nostrils because of the gaseous dilatation of the abdomen. Note the abrasions under the breasts, which could be erroneously considered antemortem, but were produced, in fact, by skin pressure with postmortem exsiccation.

2.1.3. FOLLOWING WEEKS

The green color gradually darkens to black, making identification even more difficult. The association of this with edema and the formation of gas in the head lead to an increase in its size and the flattening of anatomical prominences, causing an "africanization" of features, known in some places as "blackman's head" (Fig. 6). This phenomenon may arise, however, much earlier. The swelling of the face, in fact, begins immediately in the first week, depending on environmental conditions, and is accompanied by protrusion of the tongue between the dental arches.

Fig. 6. Stage of advanced putrefaction with gaseous bloating and larval infestation, causing obvious problems in the identification of the victims.

The cadaver in this state gives the impression of being a very heavy individual. However, this is a false impression because it is effectively the volume that is increased and not the weight, which may even be reduced because of the presence of the gases *(6)*.

This phase coincides with infestation by maggots, which dig holes and pathways in the skin and tissues, opening up routes for other bacteria from the environment (Fig. 7). The combined action of the proteolytic enzymes of the maggots and the voracious appetite of other predators greatly accelerates putrefaction at this stage.

2.1.3.1. Organs

Internal decomposition takes place at a slower pace, and it is sometimes surprising how many diagnostic elements may be collected from a cadaver whose state of putrefaction appears to have little to reveal. It is commonplace to say that *putrefaction is the greatest enemy of the pathologist*. However, this unquestionable truth is often counteracted by fortunate exceptions, which justifies using all the rigor and detail normally demanded by a standard autopsy for these cadavers as well. The frequently given excuse that there is no point in taking the necropsy or dissection much further because the putrefied

Fig. 7. Maggots digging holes and sinuses via proteolytic enzymes, opening the access to external bacteria that will speed up the putrefaction process.

body has little forensic value, is largely the result of the chronic laziness of some professionals.

The proliferation of microbes leads the internal organs and internal vessels to acquire a winey purplish hue, although some organs, such as the liver or stomach, may more commonly be a dark brownish green.

Putrefaction takes place at this level at different speeds:

1. The intestines, suprarenal glands, and spleen may putrefy in hours.
2. The encephalon discolors, becoming grayish pink and liquefies in about 1 mo (Fig. 8); signs of brain disease disappear (e.g., meningeal hemorrhages, tumors).
3. The heart is moderately resistant. The coronary arteries remain visible for many months, allowing the diagnosis of valve and coronary disorders, and coronary thromboses in necropsies that seem doomed to failure, a circumstance that is well known among pathologists that work daily in the autopsy rooms.
4. Kidneys, lungs, and bladder are also resistant (Fig. 8).
5. The prostate and uterus are the least vulnerable.

The capsules of the kidney, spleen, and liver resist putrefaction more than their respective parenchymas, and these organs transform into sacs

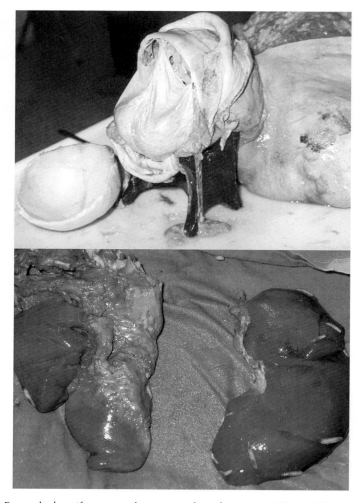

Fig. 8. Encephalon (from another case) discolors (grayish) and liquefies in 15 d to 1 mo, depending on the conditions involved. However, heart, lungs, and (especially) kidneys moderately resist putrefaction. These belong to the body of a girl in adipocere, buried in soil for approx 2.5 mo (the same as in Fig. 11).

containing a pasty liquid, winey red in color, which will later burst, making it then impossible to recognize the organs.

These different rates of decay of the organs may be proportional to the amount of muscular and conjunctive tissue they contain, according to some authors, cited by Gordon et al. *(7)*.

2.1.4. LATER ALTERATIONS (MONTHS)

The viscera and soft tissues disintegrate, whereas organs such as the uterus, heart, and prostate last longer, as do tendon tissues and ligaments attached to the bones.

The body will then finally enter into the phase of skeletonization, depending on the place where it is found and the season of the year. Some fragments of skin, protected by clothing or that come between the body and the support surface, may remain preserved, mummified, or with adipocere (*see* Fig. 1).

2.1.5. PUTREFACTION OF A BODY EXPOSED TO THE AIR

The rate at which a body decomposes is extremely variable. In the author's experience, for the bodies of patients who have died in the hospital in the summer and are not refrigerated (Portugal has a temperate, Mediterranean climate), a single afternoon is enough for the process to start. In fact, the earlier it starts, the faster it will be.

Various factors influence the speed of putrefaction: the atmospheric temperature and humidity level *(10)*, the movement of air, state of hydration of the tissues and nutritional state of the victim, age, and respective cause of death *(5,7)*. Thus, low temperatures, which inhibit the growth of bacteria, retard the process considerably. The optimum temperature for the activation of bacteria responsible for putrefaction is 37.5°C *(7)*. In a simultaneous double homicide autopsied by the author, the effect of temperature on the rate of putrefaction in each of the corpses found at home was clearly perceptible (Fig. 9). Exposure to warm humid air, and the movement of this, also accelerates putrefaction *(7)*.

In tissues that are greatly hydrated, with a higher liquid content, such as occurs in cases of deaths through chronic congestive heart failure, putrefaction is faster. Victims who are dehydrated or who had suffered from vomiting and diarrhea resist much longer.

The process is faster in children than in adults and also in more obese people than in thinner individuals *(6,7)*. However, newborn infants show some resistance to the start of the process.

Di Maio *(7)* claims that bodies wearing heavy clothes putrefy more quickly than those that are more lightly dressed, whereas other authors stress that a clothed body decomposes less quickly than a naked one *(15)*. It is also necessary to take into account the kind of fiber that is used in the clothing, whether natural or synthetic.

Of course, someone who dies of septicemia or from some acute infection will already contain a proliferation of bacteria, which means that the

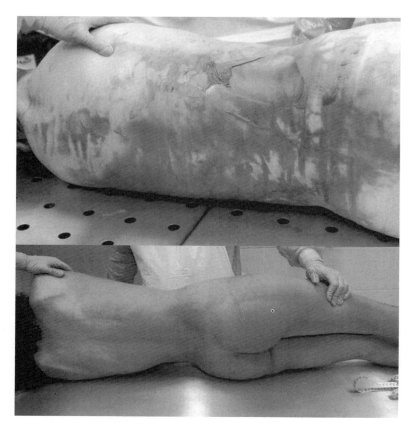

Fig. 9. Different stages of putrefaction observed in two bodies, both shot at home and recovered 3 d after the crime, on a moderate winter day. The man on the top had a heater working near him; the girl lay on the floor of her bedroom, without any source of heating.

process will be significantly accelerated. This acceleration will be greater in the trunk than in the limbs, certainly for the same reason (that is, the absence of bacteria in the muscular tissue of the limbs, as opposed to the abundance in the organs of the trunk, especially the abdomen).

The presence of traumatic lesions caused by a blunt instrument or firearm may also affect the speed of decomposition *(15)*, in that they open up holes through which air and insects may enter. Flies, however, tend to prefer the natural openings.

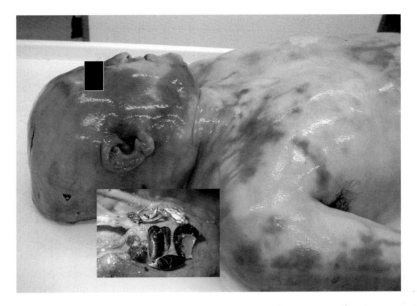

Fig. 10. Decomposition in water showing the first signs of adipocere in a victim drowned in the central Atlantic Ocean for 8 d: a white, waxy appearance, complete slippage, without hair. Note the little injuries on the posterior head, without bloody infiltration, meaning a postmortem lesion by teeth of marine predators. The detail shows the colonization of the larynx by known comestible marine predators: mussels, goose barnacles, crabs.

2.1.6. DECOMPOSITION OF AN IMMERSED BODY

As has already been mentioned, decomposition is slower in water than for a body exposed to the air, because of both the lower temperatures and degree of protection that the water offers from insects and predatory mammals. However, one should not forget that there are also sea and bird predators whose action, in exposing areas of adipose tissue to the water, also promotes adipocere (Fig. 10).

Normally, a body floats head down because the head does not develop gas formation as easily as the abdomen or thorax, which causes fluids to gravitate to the head. This means that putrefaction is more visible on the face and front of the neck, making identification more difficult. The appearance is also significantly different from a putrefied body because it is frequently associated with saponification, with a general peeling of the skin, and accentuated white coloring (*see* Fig. 10). Bodies acquire a waxy white

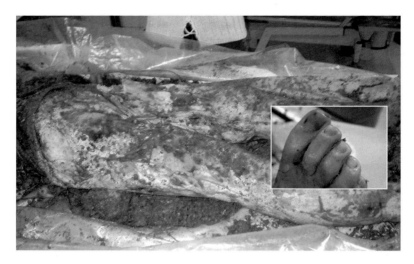

Fig. 11. Buried corpses decay at much slower rate than immersed or air exposed bodies. Observe the excellent preservation of the body of a girl, after 2.5 mo of burying, conserved in adipocere. Note the unexpected detail of the toes.

hue, and the appearance of the head without hair makes it difficult to identify; indeed, some professionals have been ill advisedly led to believe that such cases had been subjected to oncological therapies. Because of the putrefactive process, the bodies float continuously, even when they have been attached with stones for example, to make them sink to the bottom (*see* Fig. 12).

Putrefaction is also faster in warmer stagnant waters that contain decomposing organic matter, such as industrial effluents, and so forth. It is also faster in fresh water than in saltwater *(7)*. Some authors *(5,8)* contest this last point, however, on the grounds that bacterial colonization results much more from bacteria in the digestive tract and airways of the victim than from the aquatic flora. Finally, as soon as the body has been removed from the water, putrefaction accelerates considerably.

2.1.7. DECOMPOSITION AFTER BURIAL

It has been demonstrated that this is the process in which putrefaction advances least, in relation to bodies left in the open air or in the water (Fig. 11). For this reason, in some Brazilian states with scarce resources where there are no conditions of refrigeration, the medicolegal services bury the bodies in order to prevent them from decaying, exhuming them some days later when the autopsy may be carried out. Thus, the soil functions as a kind of primitive refrigeration chamber.

This slower rate of decomposition is for obvious reasons: the absence of air, inaccessibility to predators, and low temperature. The time taken before burial also affects the whole process. If putrefaction had not yet begun, the body will remain in a better state of preservation than if the process had already gotten underway.

The kind of soil and depth at which a body is buried are also factors to be taken into account. The process is faster in damp, porous soils and in bodies that are buried near the surface *(5,7,8)*. The topography of the land is, however, more important than the type of terrain. If the body is buried in a valley or below the water table, the action of water will also be felt *(5,8)*.

Bodies buried deeply in coffins decompose more slowly that when they are in shallow graves—the temperatures are lower, there is less air, and they are less affected by water *(5,7,8)*. The type of coffin also influences the decomposition process. Laminated wooden coffins rot quickly, whereas those made of zinc or lead offer better protection.

2.2. Adipocere

The formation of adipocere is a natural preservation process that has been known for centuries. Its name, attributed to Fourcroy in 1789, comes from the combination of the Latin *adipo-* (fat) and *cera* (wax) *(5)*. This process, which some wrongly consider as a part of putrefaction *(6,7)*, is known as *saponification*.

It is a variable and irregular process, only occasionally involving the whole body, which results from the hydrolysis and hydrogenation of the adipose tissue. This produces a waxy, fatty substance that is brittle; in color, it is yellowish off-white (*see* Figs. 11 and 12), although when stained by decayed matter or blood, may acquire reddish, grayish, or gray-green tones (*see* Fig. 10). It also gives off a characteristic "earthy, cheesy, and ammoniacal" odor, which may be recognized by dogs trained to discover human remains *(11)*.

Despite some points that are controversial and unclear, the biochemical sequence of the formation of adipocere is, today, largely well established. The process begins immediately after death *(10,11)*, with the hydrolysis (mediated by enzymes) of the triglycerides, which cleave the fatty acids from the glycerol molecules, giving rise to a mixture of unsaturated (palmitoleic acid, oleic acid, linoleic acid) and saturated (myristic acid, palmitic acid, stearic acid) fatty acids *(16)*. As the process advances, the quantity of fatty acids increases, and the triglycerides diminish until they disappear completely *(11)*. When there are sufficient enzymes and water, decomposition will continue

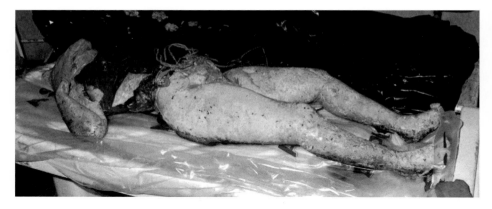

Fig. 12. Saponified body of a woman (both women and children are more likely to saponify) attached to stones to sink in a domestic well (suicide). Note the discoloration and the fat appearance of the skin.

with the hydrogenization of unsaturated fatty acids into saturated, after which the process is considered complete and stable. However, during hydrolysis and hydrogenization, some other products are formed. Free fatty acids may attach to sodium and potassium ions of the interstitial liquid and cellular water, and later, to calcium ions, forming fatty acid salts. The subsequent action of some microorganisms leads to the formation of 10-hydroxy fatty acids—the most common of which is 10-hydroxy stearic *(11,16,17)*—and, according to Takatori *(17)* of 10-oxo fatty acids. This author has shown that bacteria, such as *Pseudomonas, Staphylococcus aureus*, and *Clostridium perfringens*, produce 10-hydroxystearic acid from oleic acid, whereas *Micrococcus luteus* produces oxo fatty acids *(17)*. These acids, and their respective soaps, as well as participating in the formation of adipocere, also help to stabilize it. This stability may be attributed to the action of ionic, covalent, hydrogen bonds between the carboxyl terminal of the fatty acids and the hydroxyl groups *(16)*. These substances and glycerol form a matrix with fiber residues, nerves, and muscles, which gives a degree of solidity to the saponified mixture *(5)*.

At the moment of death, the body's fatty acid content is 1%, but with adipocere, in the first month, it goes up to 20%, and at 3 mo is 70% *(5)*. It is thought that the process is only superficial and therefore does not involve the viscera *(7)*. However, whereas subcutaneous fat is the most affected, internal structures containing adipose tissue, such as the mesentery, epiploon (omentum), perirenal fat, or organs with pathological processes involving a lipidic metabolism, may also be involved.

2.2.1. CONDITIONS

Saponification requires some heat, necessary for the development of the microbes referred to in the previous subheading, as well as water, which may be exogenous or from the organism itself *(1,5)*. For this reason, it generally appears in damp environments *(5)* in bodies immersed in cold water with a low oxygen content *(1,10)*. Pfeiffer *(16)* associates the persistence of adipocere to the presence of Gram-negative microorganisms, which are known to develop in anaerobic environments.

However, saponification is also found — much more often than is thought — in tombs, crypts, and graves, even dry ones, in a few days; the water from the organism is enough to set in motion the chemical transformations necessary for the process. Adipocere benefits from a process of self-promotion, because it inhibits putrefaction, increasing acidity and dehydration, thus reducing the growth and spread of putrefactive organisms.

Women (*see* Fig. 8) and children are much more likely to undergo this preservation process because they have a greater fat content. For the same reasons, the parts of the body that tend most to saponification are the cheeks, eye sockets, chest, abdominal wall, and buttocks.

2.2.2. CHRONOLOGY

Adipocere may last for decades, even centuries. It can form between 3 and 12 mo *(5–7,11,10,18)*, although this is variable; the first signs may be visible as early as the third week after death *(5,11,10,19)* or even earlier (8 d), as was the case of a victim of drowning in the central Atlantic Ocean (Portuguese coast) autopsied by the author,* where atmospheric temperatures ranged from 16 to 30°C (average of 20°C), and the average of sea water temperature was 18°C (*see* Fig. 10).

Studies carried out in the area of marine taphonomy cited by Kahana *(12)* consider that, in cold waters (4°C), some 12–18 mo are required for saponification, whereas in waters of between 15 and 22°C, only 2–3 mo are needed; very high temperatures are necessary for the process to be evident in 1–3 wk. However, other reports are highly contradictory. The same author reports bodies recovered from a wreck of a Belgian ship in the China Sea, saponified at 38 d in water temperatures of between 10 and 12°C, among other discrepancies. It should be emphasized that in the same sample, three bodies were

---

* During the period this body was submersed, weather was similar, with the exception of a day when meteorological conditions had suffered a sudden change, with an increase of both atmospheric temperature (to 35°C) and the temperature of the sea water, which ranged from 19 to 36°C.

found later (after 433 d) with adipocere, but with some parts skeletonized. Studies of controlled decomposition in samples of pig carcasses *(11)* in shallow graves have shown that there is no correlation between stages of saponification and the period of decomposition, which once more confirms the variability of the whole process and the probable intervention of other factors as yet unstudied, such as temperature, humidity, pH, clothing, and soil type.

These findings reinforce the idea that has been argued consistently in this text as to the lack of confidence in estimates of PMI based on states of decomposition of the body.

The decay of the adipocere is not completely clarified because it has been alleged that soil microbiota including bacteria, fungus, and algae may play a role in this decomposition. Pfeiffer *(16)* suggests that the maintenance of adipocere is associated with the development of Gram-negatives in a slightly anaerobic environment, and that its decay has to do with exposure to conditions of aerobiosis and to the presence of Gram-positive bacteria. This fact has been confirmed for many by practical experience, because a saponified body that has been removed from its environment for autopsy starts to decay much more rapidly than it did before its removal.

2.2.3. FORENSIC VALUE

The medicolegal interest of saponification lies not only in the possibilities it offers for identification because it conserves some bodily forms, but also in determining the cause of death. It is, however, rare for a body conserved only through adipocere to be recognized by the face, given the physiognomic distortions that are common despite preservation (*see* Fig. 10).

In Portugal, an eminently maritime country, it is curious to note that the majority of saponified bodies come from domestic wells because of either suicide (a very common method in the elderly rural population) (*see* Fig. 12) or accidental falls. This state of conservation of the body often permits medicolegal determination of the cause of death. For this purpose, saponification may be very important, particularly in situations of death by firearm because the preserved fatty organs may reveal the bullet's trajectory (Fig. 13). The author performed an autopsy on a victim of the Balkan War of the 1990s in Kosovo, where it was possible to reconstruct approximately the paths of two projectiles in a body that was completely saponified, but where the organs were difficult to distinguish.

Lakes, rivers, seas, and wells are also often used to hide murder victims, for which reason great attention should be paid to bodies recovered from water; one should not, as so many experts unfortunately do, leap to the easy conclusion of death by drowning. *A body recovered from the water may have died of*

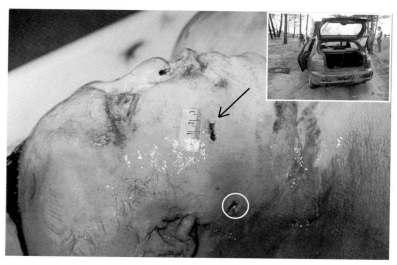

Fig. 13. A saponified head of a homicide victim, found closed inside the back of his car, sunk in a lake to hide the body. The author could recover the four bullets and determine its pathway. Two of the shots penetrated the body through the same hole seen on the face (arrow). Another entrance hole can be noted below the ear (circle). Note the preserved aspect of the face that could lead, but with some difficulty, to a positive identification. (*See* Fig. 3, Chapter 7 to observe the X-ray.)

anything, even drowning. Among many examples present in the literature, Dix *(19)* tells of four separate cases of homicides, accidentally collected from Lake Missouri, all saponified.

2.3. Mummification

This is a process of natural or artificial conservation, which consists of the dehydration and *exsiccation* (the process of drying up) of tissues. It may be partial and coexist with other forms of conservation and/or putrefaction (*see* Fig. 1). It extends more easily to the whole body than other processes, such as saponification *(8)*.

It is characterized by dryness and brittle, torn skin on the prominences (cheeks, forehead, sides of the back, and hips), generally brown in color, though coexisting with white, green, or black zones because of colonization by fungus (*see* Fig. 1), just as leather jackets look after they have been left for some time in a musty wardrobe and start to become mildewed.

As for the internal organs, the process varies in relation to the time since death, and they may be partially mummified, putrefied, with adipocere, or even absent. Radanov et al. *(20)* describe an extreme and unique case of the natural mummification of a brain, which was surprising, taking into account the softness of brain tissue, as well its fatty composition. The body had come from a mass grave with 39 other bodies and had been buried for 40–50 yr, at a shallow depth in a stony terrain, exposed to sunlight.

It is common for there to be slight adipocere in mummified bodies. Indeed, there is a close interconnection between these two processes; the use of the water from the body for hydrolysis of fats contributes also to the exsiccation of tissues *(5,8)*. This relationship is extendable to the biochemical level, as has been demonstrated by Makristathis et al. *(21)*, who detected in mummies the same constituents of saponification: palmitic, oleic, and 10-hydroxystearic acid, among other substances.

2.3.1. CONDITIONS

As is to be expected, mummification is found in dry, ventilated environments *(1,5)* and generally, though not always, in warm places where the body loses fluids through evaporation *(5,6)*: closed rooms, attics, wardrobes and pantries, barns, stairwells, and so on. More extensive and complete mummification occurs in desert environments; indeed, this preservation process was practiced by the ancient Egyptians, who added spices and herbs to the heat *(1,5,8)*.

Mummification also takes place in icy environments, not only because of the dryness of the air, but also because of the low growth of bacteria at such temperatures. A frozen mummy approx 5000 yr old (known as the Tyrolean Iceman) discovered in the Alps in 1991 has become famous as a veritable star of anthropology, like others from Peru that are also thousands of years old *(21)*. The former, however, raises the question of knowing whether mummification, which is by definition related to exposure to dry air, may take place in the snow. Ambach and Ambach *(22)* justify this from a physical point of view, given that evaporation may occur from a frozen body through a superficial covering of snow (porous and air-permeable), if the weather conditions establish a water vapor pressure gradient between the snow layers.

Makristathis et al. *(21)* compared the composition of the fat of mummified bodies from different parts of the world: the Tyrolean Iceman; two bodies found in alpine glaciers near to this; a body that had been immersed for 50 yr in an Austrian mountain lake; two bodies buried in the permafrost of Siberia; two Peruvian mummies, one from the Andes (500 yr old) and one from the Peruvian desert (1000 yr old); and three fresh bodies as a control. The composition of fatty acids was very similar between the samples of fresh bodies and those from the dry mummification of Peru, in which no significant concentrations of 10-hydroxystearic acid were found, with oleic acid predominating. These were also the best preserved bodies. In addition, all those conserved in ice or in contact with water showed a high concentration of 10-hydroxystearic acid, suggesting the association of this acid with conditions of conservation in water. The Tyrolean Iceman was situated somewhere between the mummies conserved dry and those from the ice, and was in a much better state of preservation than many more recent bodies, only tens of years old, also from glaciers. This can be explained by the rapid initial desiccation caused by the cold mountain winds, followed by a burial in ice with periods in water.

Dehydration before death may also favor this process. Indeed, this is similar to an ancient Japanese practice of natural self-mummification, according to which bonzes (Buddhist monks), nearing the end of their lives, would progressively reduce their solid food intake, then the liquid, so that they were practically desiccated at the moment of death. They were buried, and then exhumed 3 yr later, when they were found to be already mummified, without any other kind of intervention *(23)*.

2.3.2. CHRONOLOGY

The time necessary for mummification to take place is not well documented because of the long periods that usually occur before the body is discovered. It certainly takes some weeks *(5,7,8)* and, in the early stages, is mixed with putrefactive alterations, especially in the internal organs. In the deserts of Arizona, corpses exposed to the air require between 11 d and 1 mo to mummify *(15)*. After they are dry, they may last years, even centuries *(5,7,8)*.

The action of predators *(see* Fig. 2) in this phase may accelerate the disintegration of the exsiccated tissues, which are fragile and brittle; fragments of parchment-like skin, tendons, and ligaments attached to the bones may remain for much longer, however.

2.3.3. FORENSIC VALUE

Mummification can have significant medicolegal relevance for the two great objectives of forensic anthropology, identification of the body and establishing cause of death. Concerning the former, mummies are often found in a surprising state of preservation (Fig. 14), and it is usually much easier to investigate the victim's identity in these situations than with adipocere. Concerning the latter, large lesions may be preserved. However, the detection of ecchymosis or wounds may be made difficult or impossible because of discoloration, artifacts, and the action of fungus.

Cadavers in this state are sometimes the victims of homicides that have been left in a place propitious to mummification. It can also be found in cases of natural death of people that live alone. It is a very common process in

Fig. 14. The hands of a clerical mummified in a crypt (18th century). The perfection of the details is surprising.

fetuses or newborn infants, who mummify much more rapidly and completely, often because of the types of graves or ventilated domestic locations where they are deposited (Fig. 15).

Autopsies in these cases require particular dexterity because the skin, which is brittle and disintegrates easily, is difficult to dissect. Some methods of softening the tissues to permit better observation and histological study *(5)* have been described; one of these involves the use of a solution of 20% poly-ethylene glycol, with controlled pH of 8.0 and the addition of 1% Stericol to inhibit the growth of bacteria and fungus *(24)*.

2.4. Skeletonization

As the name suggests, this consists of the removal of all soft tissue from the bone, and is the field *par excellence* of the forensic anthropologist.

A body that has been reduced merely to its bones may be, however, present in its totality, thus constituting a complete skeleton (Fig. 16). Differ-ent states of preservation may nonetheless coexist, as mentioned previously, of which one may be skeletonization, which will be, in this case, partial. When this happens, the classic scenario is skeletonization of the cranium (which has the least soft tissues), mummification of the extremities, and saponification of the back *(see* Fig. 1). The natural and most frequent tendency, if conditions are propitious, is for complete skeletonization.

In the certain (and very frequent) case of a group of bones (Fig. 17)— sometimes already eroded, found in a church cemetery, obviously in a phase subsequent to skeletonization, when the bones are completely disarticulated and fragmented—it seems incorrect to designate this as a skeleton or body in

Fig. 15. A mummified fetus of approx 28 wk found in a crypt after rebuilding a cemetery. The attachment of the umbilical cord suggests a probable live-born infant.

Fig. 16. A complete skeletonized body at the autopsy room after the inventory.

Fig. 17. Ossuary (and not a skeletonized body) containing more than one individual.

skeletonization. The term *ossuary*, frequently used in forensic practice, would seem to be more suitable. It should be noted that these piles may include bones that have been disturbed and mixed up, and therefore belong to different individuals; this naturally requires specific methods of analysis *(25)*.

2.4.1. CONDITIONS

The time required for a body to become a skeleton is very variable because skeletonization is a complex phenomenon involving the intervention of multiple factors. Many studies have been carried out (often based on the decomposition of animals) to assess the influence of each of the taphonomic variables *(26)* on the preservation of the body and to quantify the average time taken for each phase of decomposition of the cadaver *(15,27,28)*. Recall that the higher the temperature and humidity, the greater the rate of decomposition and skeletonization, and that it is also important whether or not the body is buried, among many other factors already described in relation to general decomposition. Clark et al. *(1)* point out that a body buried in a warm environment may skeletonize as quickly as a body exposed to the air in a temperate environment, always depending on factors like the depth at which it is found, soil type, and so on.

As was mentioned with regard to mummification, the ligaments and some tendons are the soft tissues that most resist leaving the bone. Skin, soft tissues, and organs are lost much earlier. Disarticulation consists in the disappearance of the soft tissues, which, in living beings, hold bones together within a joint *(3)*. Thus, even when each bone is in the right place, the skeleton is considered disarticulated whenever the soft tissues do not join the bones together.

Disarticulation is very common in skeletonization and, in unburied bodies, takes place in a cephalic–caudal direction, and from the center to the periphery, that is to say, the head (without the jaw) usually separates first from the spine and then, the other limbs *(29)*. Dirkmaat and Sienickis *(30)* have proposed the following sequence for human disarticulation in bodies exposed to the air: first the head, because of the accessibility of its cavities to insects, followed by the sternum and clavicle; the upper limbs decompose much faster than the lower ones; the pelvis separates much later than the trunk, and the ribs do so in different degrees; the feet, often in socks and shoes, last much longer than the rest. The vertebral column, although exposed early, is one of the last to break up because of the strong costovertebral and intervertebral ligaments. Unprotected hands and feet are, however, the first to disarticulate, sometimes even before the head separates *(3)*. For bodies that have come out of water, Haglund *(31)* established that the areas that lose their soft tissues first, leaving the bones visible, are those covered by soft layers of tissue like the head, hands, and front of legs. Disarticulation begins with the bones of the hand and wrists, bones of the feet and ankles, jaw, and cranium. Finally, the legs and arms separate.

2.4.2. Chronology

The skeletonization process varies greatly in accordance with the place where the body is found (in the open air, it is much faster than in an enclosed environment) and the season of the year (the autumn conserves better than the peak of summer). Various authors *(6,27,32)* have documented that, in a warm, damp environment, complete skeletonization may occur between 1 and 2 wk. The author performed an autopsy on a homicide victim that had skeletonized completely in 15 d at home *(33)*. The most extreme case is reported by Clark et al. *(1)*, in which skeletonization occurred in 3 d in a very humid environment where there was great insect activity; at the other extreme, there are cases of freezing that may take thousands of years. Knight *(5)* estimates, however, that in temperate climates, a period of 12–18 mo is normal for skeletonization with tendons, periosteum, and ligaments present, and around 3 yr for a "clean" skeleton.

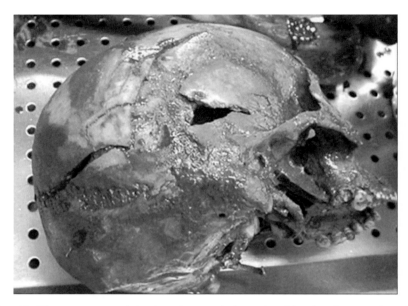

Fig. 18. Blunt trauma of the head on a skeletonized body of a murder victim, hidden in a ditch for 5 yr. With only the bones, the forensic pathologist and anthropologist arrive to the presumable cause of death.

The bone gradually wears away in the meantime, with fractures, decalcification, and dissolution because of the combined action of various factors, such as acidic soils and water, in a process that begins, for some authors *(15)*, after 9 mo of exposure. After the complete separation of the bony parts, this disaggregation accelerates markedly, until the body may even disappear completely.

2.4.3. FORENSIC VALUE

Despite being the most impoverished stage of decomposition from the point of view of legal medicine, skeletonization is undoubtedly an important, and sometimes unique, source of information for determination of violent death by firearms, or blunt or sharp instruments. Furthermore, there are a number of examples that demonstrate the relevance of skeletons for the identification process.

The author's experience includes the case of a skeletonized body found in a ditch at the person's home, after being hidden 5 yr, killed with a blunt instrument (Fig. 18). In another situation in which the author participated concerning a multiple murder in an African country, it was possible, based on a multidisciplinary study of the mostly skeletonized remains, to solve questions of identification and to determine the cause of death, which the case had raised *(34)*.

Finally, it is in this state of skeletonization that most victims of political genocide and/or crimes against humanity across the world are found, such as in the Balkans, East Timor, Latin America, Africa, and Iraq. The International Criminal Tribunal for the former Yugoslavia, in the trial at The Hague of those presumed responsible for the abuse of human rights in the Balkan conflicts, made use of this kind of expertise in decomposed bodies. The investigations were carried out by multidisciplinary teams under the auspices of the United Nations, which included forensic pathologists and anthropologists from around the world, some from organizations like the Equipo Argentino de Antropologia Forense or Physicians for Human Rights, which have proven essential for the demonstration of these crimes. These missions have truly galvanized this common adventure of forensic pathology and forensic anthropology—well documented in an article by Steadman *(2)*—which has not only efficiently resolved questions that were raised, but has also established some highly stimulating challenges for the future, permitting a more effective administration of justice and thus, the pacific cohabitation of peoples in a happier, healthier, and less violent world.

3. CONCLUSION

At the end of this chapter, the hope is to have given a perspective of the main alterations a human body might suffer until it is found or even completely disappears. Forensic anthropologists as well as forensic pathologists must be familiarized with these processes in order to be prepared to get involved as experts in cases for which they are called. Nobody ever knows in which state a cadaver will be presented. Thus, it is good practice that immediate and midputrefaction is not an unknown matter for forensic anthropologists. In the same way, forensic pathologists should also know how to deal with bare bones.

Interdisciplinarity is then essential. Referred everywhere *(2,33,35–37)* and permanently requested, it will be the issue of Chapter 7, and mentioned often in other chapters of this book.

This type of multidisciplinary experience has been conducted in Portugal in the last 5 yr, using the knowledge of these concepts and processes, with significant success both in terms of civil purposes and even for the administration of the justice regarding the penal law. An example of the first is, among some cases of successful identification and distinction between more than an individual in cemeteries graves, the identification of an old female (who disappeared after a family quarrel and was found decapitated in a river) partially by personal belongings, but confirmed trough exuberant pathological vascular disorders of the leg bones *(38)*. Concerning criminal justice, the author and forensic anthropologist Eugénia Cunha (two coeditors of this book) performed some successful cases on victims of homicides already presented *(33,34)*.

This spirit, embodied by the whole philosophy of this book, must be kept and developed, not only in the international situations in which forensic professionals can be asked to participate, but also in routine cases in each country, as is shown, in Chapter 7.

REFERENCES

1. Clark, M. A., Worrell, M. B., Pless, J. E. Postmortem changes in soft tissues. In: Haglund, W. D., Sorg, M. H., eds., Forensic Taphonomy: the Postmortem Fate of Human Remains. CRC Press, Boca Raton, FL, pp. 156–164, 1997.
2. Steadman, D. W., Haglund, W. D. The SCOPE of anthropological contributions to human rights investigations. J. Forensic Sci. 50:1–8, 2005.
3. Rocksandic, M. Position of skeletal remains as a key to understanding mortuary behavior. In: Haglund, W. D., Sorg, M. H., eds., Advances in Forensic Taphonomy: Method, Theory and Archaeological Perspectives. CRC, Boca Raton, FL, pp. 99–113, 2002.
4. Bass, W. M. Anthropology. In: Siegel, J. A., Saukko, P. J., Knupfer, G. C., eds., Encyclopedia of Forensic Sciences, Vol. 1. Academic, San Diego, CA, pp. 194–284, 2000.
5. Knight, B. Forensic Pathology, 2nd Ed. Arnold, London, pp. 51–94, 1996.
6. Di Maio, V. J., Di Maio, D. Forensic Pathology, 2nd Ed. CRC Press, Boca Raton, FL, pp. 21–41, 2001.
7. Gordon, I., Shapiro, H. A., Berson, S. D. Forensic Medicine: a Guide to Principles, 3rd Ed. Churchill Livingstone, Edinburgh, pp. 1–62, 1988.
8. Saukko, P., Knight, B. Knight's Forensic Pathology, 3rd Ed. Arnold, London, pp. 52–97, 2004.
9. Prieto, J. L., Magaña, C., Ubelaker, D. H. Interpretation of postmortem change in cadavers in Spain. J. Forensic Sci. 49:918–923, 2004.
10. Yan, F., McNally, R., Kontanis, E. J., Sadik, O. A. Preliminary quantitative investigation of postmortem adipocere formation. J. Forensic Sci. 46:609–614, 2001.
11. Forbes, S. L., Stuart, B. H., Dadour, I. R., Dent, B. B. A preliminary investigation of the stages of adipocere formation. J. Forensic Sci. 49:1–9, 2004.
12. Kahana, T., Almog, J., Levy, J., Shmeltzer, E., Spier, Y., Hiss, J. Marine taphonomy: adipocere formation in a series of bodies recovered from a single shipwreck. J. Forensic Sci. 44:897–901, 1999.
13. Micozzi, M. S. Postmortem Change in Human and Animal Remains: a Systematic Approach. Charles C. Thomas, Springfield, IL, 1991.

14. Shean, B. S., Messinger, L., Papworth, M. Observations of differential decomposition on sun exposed v. shaded pig carrion in coastal Washington State. J. Forensic Sci. 38:938–949, 1993.
15. Galloway, A., Birkby, W. H., Jones, A. M., Henry, T. E., Parks, B. O. Decay rates of human remains in an arid environment. J. Forensic Sci. 34:607–616, 1989.
16. Pfeiffer, S., Milne, S., Stevenson, R. M. The natural decomposition of adipocere. J. Forensic Sci. 43:368–370, 1998.
17. Takatory, T. Investigations on the mechanism of adipocere formation and its relation to other biochemical reactions. Forensic Sci. Int. 80:49–61, 1996.
18. Mellen, P. F. M., Lowry, M. A., Micozzi, M. S. Experimental observations on adipocere formation. J. Forensic Sci. 38:91–93, 1993.
19. Dix, J. D. Missouri's lakes and the disposal of homicide victims. J. Forensic Sci. 32:806–809, 1987.
20. Radanov, S., Stoev, S., Davidov, M., Nachev, S., Stanchev, N., Kirova, E. A unique case of naturally occurring mummification of human brain tissue. Int. J. Legal Med. 105:173–175, 1992.
21. Makristathis, A., Scharzmeier, J., Mader, R. M., et al. Fatty acid composition and preservation of the Tyrolean Iceman and other mummies. J. Lipid Res. 43:2056–2061, 2002
22. Ambach E, Ambach W. Is mummification possible in snow? Forensic Sci. Int. 54:191–192, 1992.
23. Hedouin, V., Laurier, E., Courtin, P., Gosset, D., Muller, P. H. Un cas de momification naturelle [in French]. J. Med. Legale Droit Med. 19:43–45, 1993.
24. Garrett, G., Green, M. A., Murray, L. A. Technical method—rapid softening of adipocerous bodies. Med. Sci. Law 28:98–99, 1988.
25. Ubelaker D. Approaches to the study of commingling in human skeletal remains. In: Haglund, W. D., Sorg, M. H., eds., Advances in Forensic Taphonomy: Method, Theory and Archaeological Perspectives. CRC Press, Boca Raton, FL, pp. 331–351, 2002.
26. Henderson, J. Factors determining the state of preservation of human remains. In: Boddington, A., Garland, A. N., Janaway, R. C., eds., Death, Decay and Reconstruction: Approaches to Archaeology and Forensic Science. Manchester University Press, Manchester, pp. 42–53, 1997.
27. Mann, R. W., Bass, W. M., Meadows, L. Time since death and decomposition of the human body: variables and observations in case and experimental field studies. J. Forensic Sci. 35:103–111, 1990.
28. Sledzik P. Forensic taphonomy: postmortem decomposition and decay. In: Reichs, K, ed., Forensic Osteology: Advances in the Identification of Human Remains. Charles C. Thomas, Springfield IL, pp. 109–119, 1998.
29. Rodriguez, W. C., Bass, W. M. Decomposition of buried bodies and methods that may aid in their location. J. Forensic Sci. 30:836–852, 1985.
30. Dirkmaat, D. C., Sienicki, L. A. Taphonomy in the northeast woodlands: four cases from western Pennsylvania. Proceedings of the 47th Annual Meeting of the American Academy of Forensic Sciences, Seattle, Washington. 1:10, 1998.

31. Haglund, W. D. Disappearance of soft tissue and the disarticulation of human remains from aqueous environments. J. Forensic Sci. 38:806–815, 1993.
32. Galloway, A. The process of decomposition: a model from Arizona-Sonoran Desert. In: Haglund, W. D., Sorg, M. H., eds., Forensic Taphonomy: the Postmortem Fate of Human Remains. CRC Press, Boca Raton, FL, pp. 139–150, 1997.
33. Cunha, E., Pinheiro, J., Corte Real, F. Two Portuguese homicide cases: the importance of interdisciplinarity in forensic anthropology. ERES (Arqueología y Bioantropología) 15:65–72, 2005.
34. Cunha, E., Pinheiro, J., Ribeiro, I. P., Soares, J., Vieira, D. N. Severe traumatic injuries: report of a complex multiple homicide case. Forensic Sci. Int. 136:164–165, 2003.
35. Symes, S. A., Woytash, J. J., Kroman, A. M., Wilson, A. C. Perimortem bone fracture distinguished from postmortem fire trauma: a case study with mixed signals. Proceedings of the 54th American Academy of Forensic Sciences, Vol. 11. New Orleans, LA, 300, 2005.
37. Verano, J. Serial murder with dismemberment of victims in an attempt to hinder identification: a case resolved trough multidisciplinary collaboration. Proceedings of the 54th American Academy of Forensic Sciences, Vol. 11. New Orleans, LA, 329, 2005.
38. Pinheiro, J., Cunha, E., Cordeiro, C., Vieira, D. N. Bridging the gap between forensic anthropology and osteoarchaeology—a case of vascular pathology. Int. J. Osteoarchaeol. 14:137–144, 2004.

Chapter 6

Understanding the Circumstances of Decomposition When the Body Is Skeletonized

Henri Duday and Mark Guillon

Summary

When a skeletonized body is found, the presence of an anthropologist is required to understand the circumstances of which the human remains reached the situation in which they are discovered. For this purpose, archaeological anthropology (called *field archaeology*) and forensic anthropology share the same techniques. This chapter aims to advise as to what should be done and registered precisely on the field when bone remains are exhumed or found on the surface of the ground. It also describes in detail the osteological observations that enable determination of whether it is a primary or a secondary deposit, and to restitute the cadaver environment. This methodological approach is enlarged to include multiple deposits. Although this discipline has mostly been developed in the archaeological funerary context, it provides valuable analysis tools when human bones are involved.

Key Words: Forensic anthropology; field anthropology; taphonomy; primary deposit; secondary deposit.

1. INTRODUCTION

The objectives of archaeological anthropology and forensic anthropology are fundamentally different. The first field studies mortuary gestures,

From *Forensic Anthropology and Medicine:*
Complementary Sciences From Recovery to Cause of Death
Edited by: A. Schmitt, E. Cunha, and J. Pinheiro © Humana Press Inc., Totowa, NJ

whereas the second's aim is to identify unfunerary but intentional gestures, and studies human remains from accidents.

However, archaeological and forensic anthropologies share many techniques, and for both of them, the field part is essential; thus, an important part of the possibilities of interpretation depends on the quality of field recordings. However, cultural research backgrounds are different. On the forensic side, the cultural background is all the listed criminal gestures and the data recorded on accident sites (from the individual accident to the mass disaster) that matters; on the archaeological side, the cultural background is built from the historical and archaeological knowledge of the studied community.

In France and in all countries where preservation, survey, and systematic studies have been developed for buried patrimony, interpretative thought in archaeology has given preference to settlement sites. The study of gravesites did not benefit immediately from of the technical progress of the field and recording methods. This is paradoxical, because as Binford has already written in a chapter introduction (in which the data came from Anglo-Saxon literature between 1886 and 1964): "Human burials are one of the most frequently encountered classes of cultural feature observed by archaeologists" *(1)*. In his book, the author regrets that there was not a specific approach to graves in archaeological study. The sentence above indicates that Binford deplored the lack of precision and therefore, the weak point in exploiting funerary data, just as the authors deplored in France the same deficiency in European excavations or large-scale foreign digs; this was until the late 1970s, when a few researchers, including one of the authors (H. Duday) began to formalize tools for fieldwork.

One can also criticize the fact that anthropological studies have too long been only biometric and physical approaches, and this even for funerary sites. On the forensic side, it is interesting to notice that the anthropologist taking part in an inquiry has long been confined to laboratory work. This becomes apparent in Stewart's 1979 book *Essentials of Forensic Anthropology*, which is a study of bones, of course, but essentially out of its field context: identification, sex, age at death, race, and stature *(2)*. This important work had the great advantage of rewriting numerous techniques spread through various publications and making them available for anthropologists, but Stewart was not convinced of the necessity for an anthropologist in the field for human surface remains except in particular cases, for instance, regarding burned remains, for which he recommends archaeological knowledge (ref. *2*, pp. 30–31). Stewart was preceded in 1963 by Brothwell's *Digging up Bones*, published by the British Museum for the archaeological researchers, where the author wrote, "Bones are commonly an embarrassment to archaeologists, even though the skeleton offers a no less fruitful subject of enquiry than ceramics, metals, architecture or any other field of historical or prehistoric study" *(3)*. At the same time in France, Leroi-Gourhan, Bailloud, and Brézillon *(4)* were publishing the excavation of the Mournouards collective grave discovered in the Marne County during the summer of 1960; in the South of France, Courtin pointed out in his doctoral thesis, the importance of graves in the study of human Neolithic communities in Provence *(5)*. Thus, the 1960s marked a turning point for funerary archaeology on both sides of the Atlantic that would have consequence on recovery methods for both fields.

The archaeologists, before the forensic scientists, realized their field activities were destructive toward the subject of their studies, and that the information from the site had to be as precise as possible. Thus, techniques have been developed in this purpose by the archaeoanthropologists to record exactly the position of human remains in the three dimensions of space and in their anatomical relation with the other bones.

When the archaeologist arrives on the field, the archaeologist should not wonder what is important and what is not; in an ideal situation the archaeologist should work without *a priori*. The archaeoanthropologist should arrive on the funerary structure without any personal cultural background, because he or she could be caught out by an unexpected variation that could be overlooked if the digging is rushed; for instance, human bones are not evidence for funerary context, even though most human remains discovered in archaeological context are part of a grave. Therefore, the ideal is a complete recording from the outset. Thus, it is in this exact state of mind that a forensic anthropologist must be every time a new case is begun. In fact, both archaeological and forensic researchers are influenced by their professional education, and this must be an advantage, not a disadvantage.

The progress of the last 20 yr has allowed consideration of human bones as important as any other kind of remains; one of the most positive consequences has been to bring to the forefront the absolute necessity of very precise field recordings. Observation, recording, and studying of the spatial organization of the remains are essential steps of fieldwork. For both scientific contexts, the field period is primordial, and further possibilities of interpretation depend on the quality of recordings.

The anthropologists, like the archaeologists, became aware that they only had access to the final state of the funerary structure on which they were working, and that all the processes—human and nonhuman—that led to this final state were to be understood as far as was possible *(6–9)*. This leads to the archaeological hypotheses that will participate in the construction of a real anthropology of death. With forensic as with funerary anthropology, the process leading to the state of the corpse (or the corpses) on discovery is the result of two events:

1. The original characteristics of the deposit.
2. The chance modifications that shall be referred to here as "taphonomy."

They can be caused by human (posterior digging of a trench, a grave) or nonhuman agents; among the latter, the authors want to place emphasis on gravity and on external factors (burrowing animals, roots, collapse, flowing, etc.).

Before going into detail, the authors would like to point out the fact that the status of forensic anthropologist does not exist in France; the Anglo-Saxon world is ahead in this matter, through the existence of a real body of scientists in this field, with complete teaching courses in England and the United States.

2. TECHNICAL PROGRESS IN FIELD OPERATIONS

First of all, it is important to differentiate between two situations according to when the team arrives in the field and whether the bones are buried or on the surface of the ground (in other words, directly accessible). In both fields, forensic and archaeological, the two situations can materialize. From now on in this chapter, the word *excavation* will be used equally for both contexts, whatever the location of the human remains might be.

When a corpse has been buried, useful information will be provided by the locating of the hole, the characteristics of the pit, and perhaps the presence of a container. This process will be the same for both forensic and archaeological anthropologists. There are the usual archaeological techniques that are used as a first step to "delineate the horizontal outline of the burial feature," as Dirkmaat and Adovasio rightly emphasize *(10)*, and the carrying out of map making before the excavation itself. The recommendation by many researchers of archaeological methods in the context of forensic inquiries testifies well to the evolution evoked in the Introduction: forensic teams ask for more precision during the field phase.

When the digging is revealed, sediment is removed up to the bones' highest level or other remains* associated with bones. The filling dynamics of the pit (immediate or shifted forward in time, fast or progressive, human or natural) can only be understood by the observation of the sedimentary and stratigraphic units that characterize the infilling. The best way of excavating skeletons is characterized by a double preoccupation. On one side, the bones

* The word *remains* will be used in both contexts.

must be cleared as much as possible, and on the other, they must be all left exactly in position (even the smallest and the most fragile ones), until the recording.

As soon as the bones have been cleared, the field conditions become identical to those when remains are on the surface, and the two processes are then the same. Each cleaning phase is followed by a plan view (photography and/or drawing both with scale; *see* Chapter 3) and by a recovery phase with documentation (for details, *see* ref. *10*). The number of clearing phases depends on the number of corpses. Superimposition of bodies and their more or less important commingled state make the excavation more complex. For an individual deposition, the complexity depends on the position of the corpse and on the superimposition it involves. If the cadaver is lying on its back, excavation will be quite simple, except for the neck area, where it will be necessary to record the superior cervical vertebrae after removing the skull (*see* further in the text). If the corpse lies on its side in a more or less contracted position, there will be many superimpositions (thorax, long bones of the limbs, extremity bones, and so on), and the digging requires several stages.

Then comes the recording phase, its purpose to keep the registration of each bone's position in the three dimensions and, as well, the position of other remains from the cadaver, such as prostheses, dentures, and calculus. The relation between and among bones themselves, and between the bones and the other elements of the deposit (the infilling, if there is one, the surrounding architecture, all artifacts, injuring elements, bullets, and so forth) must also be precisely registered.

The recording process begins with setting up a topographic locating system. Considering the whole site, a grid system is normally used, and the square size depends on the surface of the site. Triangulation can be used with the three-point system or with the adjacent triangle system (very useful in water with bad visibility), or electronic recording by theodolite. Whatever technique is used, it will always be necessary to place the site in geographical coordinates including altitude, a global positioning system being very useful in this case. It is often interesting to put up an internal topographic system for each deposit, especially if it is a rather small deposit (i.e., individual): small grid system or orthonormal system; these grids will have to be placed in the whole site system.

At this stage of the field process comes what shall be called the "graphic recording, photography, and/or drawings."

Photographs (or drawings) must be taken immediately after each stage of clearing (Fig. 1), and if the bones are on the surface, it must be the first step. If possible, zenithal views should be used at the human focal length

A

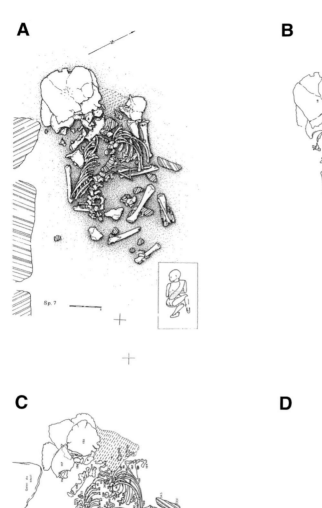

Sp. 7

B

C

D

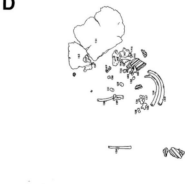

(around 50 mm for 135 format); very little distortion will then appear, and it will be possible to use the photographs as an exact registration document, even to measure distances (that is why it is so important to place a scale on the pictures, with a "North" arrow). If it is impossible to take vertical views (i.e., with a very low ceiling in a cellar or a cave), it will still be possible to use a rectification program afterward, but however powerful it is, its use will have a limit—if one bone is hidden by another, it will never become visible. The zenithal photographs must be completed by perspective views that give a better perception of the volumes; in some cases views level with the ground will be useful (Fig. 2). The most rigorous way for considering the vertical dimension is the photometric recording technique, but it is very expensive and of course cannot be used in every case. In any case, many detailed photographs should be taken. The progress of digital photography and the low price of the equipment allow its use in all cases, which gives immediate availability of the photographs and makes the creation of computer archives very easy. The rapid increase in the pixels allows zooms and enlargements without loss of definition; many details can then become clearer or can even be discovered on the screen.

The graphic recording can also be done by drawing on graduated paper, in a scale that changes according to the structure and the precision wanted: 1:5 is the best scale for an adult skeleton (1:10 can be used, but never less); for a young child or a baby, one should use a 1:2 scale or even a 1:1 scale. The drawing technique records precisely the position of the remains, and it gives time for thought before removing the bones, but it has to be completed with photographs. The data must be recorded in such way to be able to place drawings and photograph in the general map of the site; thus, each document must hold the information that permits it to be placed in the general topographic system. It is then possible to superimpose the consecutive vertical drawings and to rebuild a synthetic view of the site.

For the removing phase, the operator must have at his or her instant disposal a graphic document on which the inventory numbers will be transferred, along with the depth marks and all useful information (for instance the limit of each stratigraphic unit). Drawing on graduated paper gives the

Fig. 1. (opposite page) Map drawing of the neonate's grave, no. 7, discovered in the Roman pottery workshop at Sallèles d'Aude (Aude, France), with restitution of the original position of the body (**A**). This synthetic drawing has been obtained by the superposition of the three successive drawings of the three excavation levels (**B–D**). (Drawing by H. Duday. Excavation by H. Duday and F. Laubenheimer.)

Fig. 2. Ground-level photography (toward the west) of grave no. 141 of the abbey church of Ardenne in Normandy (Caen, France, 17–18th centuries). The coffin was still empty at the time of the excavation. (Photography by D. Corde and M. Guillon. © by the Institut National de Recherches Archéologiques Préventives, France.)

advantage of being available immediately. Of course, digital photos are now often used, which makes it necessary to have a computer and a printer in the field.

The identification of the remains should be done in the field when the bone is removed and then checked in the laboratory. Field documentation must then mention the anatomical identification of the piece, its preservation state, whether it is from the left or right (for the nonaxial skeleton), its slant, its orientation, and its appearing view (facing the zenith). Some of this information might appear clearly on the drawings or in the pictures, and there is no need to repeat the information on the field sheets. It is important to record height and depth data on the graphic documents or on the sheets. This recording uses different leveling systems (manual or laser theodolite, water level, or three-strings aim system), and must be done in a homogeneous manner, as the reference level must be the same for every removal process. The dataset must be clear for any person who will use it later, even a long time after the digging if there is no possibility of consulting anyone who was in the field at the time. Concerning the depth measures, the most useful ones are the ones underneath the bone registered at its removal; they allow discussion of the interaction between the corpse in decay and its support. The superior depth marks only give information on the relation between the corpse and the elements immediately above (for instance, the sediment filling the pit); however, the superior marks are necessary when several corpses are involved, with the question of contact between the dead or presence of sediment between the corpses (*see* Heading 5 addressing multiple deposits). If the bones are not in a horizontal position, it is important to register depth at each extremity.

After this field procedure and the study of the documentation, the interpretative phase is a dynamic process; its objective is the reconstruction of the circumstances that led to the organization of the remains as they are discovered. This process can be applied to any type of deposit where human remains are involved. Forensic science, murder, and accident scenes can be approached with this field method; for archaeology, there is no chronological or geographical specificity; for both contexts, methodological adaptations are dictated by technical constraints.

At this point in the presentation, the decay modalities of the corpses must be discussed, and the discussion shall begin with the simplest situation: with the presence of a unique cadaver that has not been removed from its original place of deposit; thus, there is an individual primary deposition. Before considering this context, the idea of intentionality in the deposit must be addressed. It can be obvious in certain cases, for example, if a pit dug to contain the corpse is discovered. However, it can be very difficult to prove intentionality, and in this case, it is necessary to study the field data to bring it to the forefront. Finally, if the accidental context is not in doubt, intentionality can be dismissed. The accidental origin of the presence of human remains appears more often in the forensic context, but it is not absent from the archaeological context and has sometimes been encountered. As stated on p. 119, the presence of human bones in an archaeological context is not proof of a grave; certain intentional deposits do not come from a funerary situation *(9)*.

3. INDIVIDUAL PRIMARY DEPOSITION

Primary deposition is defined as the deposit of a "fresh" cadaver in the site where the decay will take place. In fact, the physicochemical process of putrefaction starts immediately after death, and even sometimes before (e.g., gangrene, necrosis). However, the topic here will be the phenomenon of decay in a sufficiently advanced stage to provoke dislocation of at least some parts of the skeleton. The anatomical integrity of the body is preserved, or at

least its external general aspect; the corpse was deposited soon after death,*
exactly where it had been discovered.

3.1. Demonstration of the Primary State of the Deposit

3.1.1. THE ANATOMICAL CONNECTIONS: LABILE AND PERSISTENT ARTICULATIONS

The evidence for a primary deposit lies principally on the observation of
the anatomical connections. Indeed, one must prove that when the body was
deposited, the organic structures assuming the joint's maintenance (skin, tendons, capsules, and ligaments) were still present and strong enough to avoid
the dislocation of two contiguous bones. In a fresh cadaver, all the bones are
naturally in a reciprocal disposition according to the architecture of the human
skeleton; the anthropologist then has a reference from which to work. In the
case of a buried corpse, the anatomical relations will be maintained as the
decay takes place in an enclosed space (in archaeology this will be a grave).[†]

Regarding the argument about the maintenance of the reciprocal disposition of the bones, the most pertinent indications concern the articulations
that give way first: the labile connections. Their preservation demonstrates
implicitly the integrity of the cadaver, which would not be shown by the connection of joints resisting longer to the decay processes: the persistent articulations.[§] The time for the integrity of a particular articulation to disappear
completely and the order in which the joints leave the bones free depends on
the treatment (funerary or not) reserved for the body and on the environment
around the corpse. Between the almost immediate and complete destruction
(incineration in a modern crematorium, corpses abandoned to big predators,
such as hyenas, etc.) and perfect preservation during several millennia, which
can be observed in certain cases of mummification (by the cold, the dryness,

---

* It is not always the case that a fresh cadaver is indicative of a recent death. A good
  example is the case of a very cold winter when the ground is frozen, which makes
  it impossible to dig a grave; therefore, the corpse is kept in the snow until milder
  weather allows the inhumation, when at the same time, the decay process restarts.
  Thus, what is important is not the time between death and funeral, but the state of
  the corpse at the time of the deposit.

[†] It will be shown that the presence of a container can lead to a much more complex
  situation.

[§] The word *labile*, which comes from biology and physics, means "what can be
  easily, rapidly destroyed;" the authors chose to use the word *persistent*, with an
  concept of time, rather than *resistant*, which could create a confusion with the idea
  of mechanic resistance *(9,11)*.

the salinity, the acidity of peat bogs, or by a postmortem treatment), all inter-mediaries can be considered. Thus, it is impossible to draw up a type list for all situations.

The time necessary for a fresh cadaver to become dry is very different between buried and surface deposition. For surface remains, the studies led by Bass *(12,13)* establish a chronology from the first day of deposition to several years. Galloway classifies the decay stages in 5 categories (*see* ref. *12*, Table 1). Experimentation on animal remains have allowed following of the evolution of abandoned bones to weathering. For example, Behrensmeyer *(14)* worked on mammalian bones in Kenya and established six stages, from fresh bones with presence of soft tissue (stage 0) to "bone mechanically fall-ing apart into pieces, very fragile" (stage 6). For the fresh cadaver that lies on the ground, the decay does not affect all the body at the same speed; for example, the part of the corpse in contact with the ground decomposes faster than the rest of it *(15)*.

For a buried corpse (thus protected from carnivores and omnivores), in tempered weather, the time that is necessary for the natural dislocation of the articulations is never less than several weeks, and this gives a limit between primary and secondary deposits. It is important, for this question of limit, to be more precise for this period by going on with the actual researching into the taphonomy of human and animal remains *(16,17)*. Interesting results come from experimentation, but is not the only source. In some cases, archaeologi-cal data can be considered, such as identified graves and/or historical sources. Generally, labile articulations concern rather small bones (cervical vertebrae, hands, distal part of the feet) or fragile joints (scapula-thorax*), which will need very careful digging. On the contrary, persistent articulations join bones with an important biomechanical restrain that involves thick strong ligaments, articulations between atlas and occipital bone, lumbar vertebrae, the sacro-iliac joint, knees, ankle, and tarsals; they are all voluminous and/or solid bones, so it is easier to examine their assembly. Thus, unfortunately, the most visible connections are at the same time the less demonstrative. Particular attention must be paid to the hip articulation. The authors are now sure that it is a labile articulation, and this can be easily be explained by the thinness of the liga-ments; indeed, they are only a thickening of the articulation capsule. The cohesion is provided by powerful muscles (which rapidly decompose after death), and also by the fact that the femora head and the acetabulum fit very closely, one into the other; this congruence, because of the form of the bones

---

* This relation is assimilable to a joint in a anatomical sense.

in contact, is naturally maintained after soft parts have disappeared, so that the hip often remains connected despite being a labile joint.

If preservation of the anatomical connection involving labile articulations is necessary to demonstrate a primary interment or deposit, the opposite argument has no validity; the presence of dislocations, even numerous and important, do not exclude the primary characteristic of the deposit. In other words, evident disorder in the organization of the bones does not mean that they have been handled or moved after death. As an example, imagine that a cadaver has been laid on a light wooden platform, above the floor, in a closed room. The putrefaction will leave the skeleton in connection on its support, until this decomposes as well. This endogenous perturbation—which here means the perturbation appearing in the whole structure around the corpse, in this case the wooden bed's decomposition—will probably leave no anatomical connection if it appears late enough, even though it is sure to be in a primary context, with no disturbance.* The lack of anatomical connections does not mean that it is not a primary deposit. For this to be significant, it must be proven that it is not imputable either to the intrinsic evolution of the deposit or to a perturbation of extrinsic origin, which can be very difficult to establish. This is a fundamental element of the thought process in forensic and funerary anthropology. One must not conclude observing a secondary deposit from disturbed bones without connections; that would be forgetting the most universal taphonomic factor, the law of gravity.

3.1.2. THE FLUIDS OF DECAY AND THE DIAGENESIS OF THE CORPSE ENVIRONMENT

The putrefaction of the cadaver releases organic fluids that will infiltrate the sediment around, and particularly, underneath the corpse. The characteristics of this sediment will change, and it is sometimes possible to detect these changes. In this way, in the case of a deposit in a pit, the enrichment in organic matter has a trophic action on the earthworms, and they will concentrate around the putrescent body. The worms can leave many calcareous spherules that will be detected in the sediment. In addition, earthworms and necrophagous insects attract many predators (insectivores, such as moles, shrews, batrachians, and reptiles) and one might find their bones near the corpse. Some terrestrial gastropods also feed on these invertebrates; for example, *Testacella*, a specific predator of the earthworm, is a carnivorous

---

* The word *disturbance* here means exogenous perturbation, again, in reference to the complete structure around the body. The universal gravitation is thus not to be considered.

slug that carries a vestigial shell on its tail and lays calcified eggs. If such eggs are found near human remains, this shows that earthworms have been particularly active in the pit, and it leads to the conclusion of a primary deposit. If the decomposition had taken place elsewhere than the final grave, dry bones brought in the pit would not have provoked such a rush of necrophagous animals.

It is sometimes even possible to demonstrate the chemical action of decay fluids on geological substratum. This is the case at the collective grave of Villedubert (Aude, France), where the authors demonstrated that the calcareous pebbles from an alluvial terrace of the Aude River had been attacked by phosphoric acid from the corpses. Crystals of calcium phosphates formed inside the cleavage layers resulting from their superficial alteration *(18)*. The same phenomenon has been observed in a collective grave from Normandy (France), on the paving of the funerary chamber *(19)*.

3.1.3. BONE DISPLACEMENT INSIDE THE CORPSE DURING DECOMPOSITION

Inside the entity represented by the fresh cadaver itself, gravity acts on bones in the original volume of the body; the disappearance of the soft parts gives empty spaces within which the bones can move as soon as the tendons and the ligaments have also given way. These movements vary considerably according to the original position of the body, but it seemed important to present here some of those most frequently observed.

1. *The flattening of he rib cage.* For a standing individual, the ribs are not horizontal but oblique, down, and forward (anterodistal direction); this obliqueness can be observed on a fresh cadaver and will increase after the rupture of the links between ribs, ribs and sternum, and ribs and vertebrae; the result will be a significant decrease of the thoracic volume. After field observations, it seems that the last articulations to give way are between ribs and vertebral transverse processes, so that the lowering of the rib shaft is followed by an ascent of the head, which then rises to halfway up the vertebra, just above. In the field, mistakes can occur because of this movement. When removing the ribs, one usually refers to the vertebral rank, but should in fact only refer to the transverse processes–rib relation; however, this articulation can be difficult to record when the corpse is lying on its back, and the observer usually records the articulation between the vertebral body and the rib's head, which, as was just illustrated, is systematically wrong on the dry skeleton.

   The subsidence of the ribs and the disappearance of the viscera are followed by the fall of the sternum (particularly the blade, the corpus sterni) and of any artifacts or bones eventually situated against the anterior face of the thorax or the abdomen. That can be clothing artifacts or bones of the hands, for example (it is frequent to discover carpals and metacarpals scattered in the abdomen, on both sides of the vertebral bodies).

When a corpse is lying on one side, the ribs in contact with the bottom of the pit (or simply with the ground, if the body in on the surface) are "stuck" between the ground and the bones above them. Thus, the increase of the obliquity will only affect the other side, which is free with, consequently, a shifting between the right and left heads for each pair of ribs.

When a body is lying flat on its stomach, there is little difference with what has just been described; however, the fall of the sacrum is usually observed and, after the proximal plunging down of the os coxae's ilium, the highest part of the skeleton will be the ischia. For the archaeologists, particularly in the Christian world, it is more the unusual position of the burial deposit that is surprising than the very different behavior of the bones.

The partial dislocation of the vertebral column, when excavated, it is often divided in segments of several vertebrae in strict connection (generally from two to six); between those segments, one can observe a dislocation provoked by rotation, translation, or angulations. These disarticulations appear as soon as an asymmetry is present in the biomechanical constraints affecting the spine; when the decomposition leads to the rupture of ligaments on an intervertebral segment, a slight displacement occurs and the underlying segments, as well as the one just above, are no longer subject to the dislocation forces; the vertebrae inside each segment will then stay in perfect connection until a new rupture and a new dislocation caused by other constraints appears.

2. *The collapse of the pelvis.* The sacrum is driven in between the two iliac bones like a wedge with an anterior base; the destruction of the sacroiliac ligaments is followed by a forward movement of the sacrum into the free volume given by the putrefaction of the pelvic viscera. If a body is laid on its side, the highest hip bone will fall inside the pelvis as well; on the contrary, for an extended supine corpse, the displacement is less important. Both pelvic bones will fall slightly backward, in the direction of the space that appears when the gluteal muscles decompose.

Thus, even if archaeological publications do not write much about it, there are very often differences between the original organization of the skeleton and what is observed during excavation. The dislocations described here follow rather simple and logical rules that are dictated on one hand, by the chronology of the articulations' destruction, and on the other hand, by the gravity law, which acts in variable ways according to the position of the cadaver. To a certain extent, it is instead the complete lack of perturbation that can bring significant information on the body treatment. However, the fact that displacements happen is not dependent on the labile or persistent characteristics of the joints. It has just been described that the fact that the lumbar vertebrae and the sacroiliac articulation are perturbed in most cases even though they are among the most persistent joints of the skeleton. These articulations give way very late, but they always do (excepted in mummification), and as the bones involved are then thrown off balance by the disappearance of the soft parts, they can move under the effect of gravity. To affirm that there is a primary deposit, it is thus not necessary to observe the preservation of all the anatomical connections, which very rarely happens. Even if the site is not perturbed, it is sufficient to observe the maintenance of the labile connections or, as is seen, to obtain other evidences if all the anatomical relations have disappeared like the presence of the decay fluids or of the necrophagous animals.

3.2. The Original Position of the Corpse

The restitution of the original position of the cadaver is one of the most important pieces of information one can get from the field recordings. In the case of foible disturbing, it is simple to understand the original organization of the bones. The question is much more complex for the extremity bones (especially for the hands) or, as well, for young children's remains for which analysis requires advanced anatomical knowledge and a very detailed excavation. This analysis must take into account the natural movements that the authors emphasized before, and on various phenomena during decay: the flattening of the rib cage, the distension of the abdomen—sometimes its expansion and collapse.

Therefore, the discovered position of the forearms can be different from the deposit position if they were placed on the thorax or the abdomen. Indeed, when bones are on a part of the trunk that will flatten during the decay, they will probably slip toward the underlying "neoformed" empty space. For an extended supine cadaver, it will be the case for the forearm if it is placed in front of the trunk or, if the corpse is lying on its side, for the whole forelimb placed on top.

Another example is given by the rotation of the head. For a grave, this rotation can indeed be a consequence of funerary practice with an intentional orientation of the direction of sight, and then the archaeologists must discuss this position. However, this rotation can also be the result of gravity on the skull, which can cause a loss of equilibrium after the decay of the ligaments of the neck, for instance, when the occipital bone lays on a flat surface.

On the subject in vivo and then on the fresh cadaver the rotation of the head involves the entire cervical column *(20)*; however, the amplitude of the movement is much larger for the two first vertebrae than for the underlying cervical articulations all together. During decomposition, the initial disconnection involves, in most cases, the axis and the third cervical vertebra; sometimes it involves the relation between atlas and axis or the third and fourth cervical vertebrae *(see* Fig. 2), even the fourth and the fifth. It is then crucial to observe the respective position of the superior cervical vertebrae. The preserved connection and continuity between them, with a degree of rotation in conformity with the biomechanical laws at each level, will testify to a real rotation of the head. On the contrary, a disconnection only limited to one intervertebral level that has greater amplitude than is allowed by the morphology of the neck (bones and ligaments) will testify to a deferred rotation because of the action of taphonomic processes. It seems thus essential to record in detail this anatomical region after having removed the cranium and the mandible when they mask the upper part of the cervical column; otherwise, the typologies, in both contexts, will be classified in the same way despite the fact that the initial positions were different. It is sometimes possible to reconstruct some of the missing elements, necessary for the discussion, by studying very carefully the field sheets, but in most cases, the attempt is fruitless, because drawings and photographs are taken with the cranium and mandible that mask the cervical vertebrae; so, the authors insist that they are recorded separately.

In the same situation, one can resort to the reciprocal position of the cranium and the mandible. When the second one has tipped up right, left, or forward and the first one in another direction, there is a high probability that this dislocation had to have appeared during the decomposition. However, it seems that the decay of the temporomandibular joint* and ligaments take place sometimes before the decay of the vertebral column's maintaining structures, sometimes after. In the first case, there is first a dislocation between the cranium and mandible; in the second case, they can both move while staying more or less connected one to the other, even though the head was originally in an axial position.

Apart from these considerations, one must be aware of the limits of this approach. The detailed recording of the osteological field observations allows, in many cases, to state the original position of the body, but one must consider whether the characteristics of the deposit brought to the fore have to do with a rite or a practice, in the sense of gesture, or if these characteristics are because of a random factors. Considering the position of the corpse, or of parts of the corpse, one must not always look for a symbolic codified sense, whether it would be for a community or for a murderer. To set apart the significant elements from the anecdotal ones, the anthropologist must research

---

* The presence of a meniscus gives considerable fragility to this articulation as soon as it is decayed; in this case and when the mouth is opened, the mandibular condyles are not engaged in the glenoid fossa of the temporal but are opposite a convex surface, the articular eminence of the temporal (tuberculum articulare).

in both archaeological and forensic publications and reports, to see whether the observations and conclusions on a particular case can be applied to other cases related to an equivalent context (criminal, accidental, cultural, or chronological).* It is only the recurrence of facts that can prove the intentionality. Interpreting an isolated case as a ritual attitude, as one can often read, is not acceptable. The fact that the skeleton and its surroundings have been very well excavated and recorded with great attention to detail does not confer to this discovery a higher ritualized or worshipful meaning. In forensic and archaeological anthropology, man can (and must) record very precisely a complete casual case.

3.3. Field Anthropology in Search of Its References: Decay and Reconstruction[†]

The order in which the articulations decompose forms one of the essential bases of thought. In Western Europe, there are few detailed studies on this particular point and on the speed of decay according to the environment, and some are old works *(25)*. It is easy to understand that for ethical reasons and for the sensibilities of the current populations, experimentation can only proceed under very close control of the protocol and its possible applications; the European laws are very strict concerning this point. In the United States, such experiments have recently been developed, with ethical and scientific rigor, led by Bass *(12,26,27)*, among others, after years of research, less taken over at that time by the scientific community. One of the first was the *Field Handbook of Human Skeleton*, edited by Spier in 1962 *(28)*, in which Bass writes the chapter on "The Excavation of Human Remains." Recently, the forensic researchers realized the need to build a corpus, but the number of cases and synthesis works are much less numerous than in funerary anthropology. Of course, one must not hope to obtain an exhaustive catalog of all the possible situations, and the authors' recent work on children's graves show the complexity of the argument about the restitution of the position of the corpse and the many possibilities according to the container, transportation and, more widely, the taphonomic events *(29–31)*.

Thus, for an important part, the authors must rely on the multiplication of archaeological observations to establish a corpus of references. At every

---

* This researching of significant elements is easier in the case of a cemetery excavation, as the recurrent nature of the observations can be checked inside the site one is studying; this approach has been applied by one of the authors (M. Guillon) on the medieval cemetery of Tournedos *(21–24)*.
[†] In reference to Boddington et al. *(6)*.

possible occasion, one must know how to record on the field to supply the corpus with data. Together with their American colleagues, the authors insist on the necessity to build this corpus with the data from archaeology and from forensic science *(7,9,11,13,16,22,26,31–39)*. The increasing investment of the anthropologists in postconflict inquiries will bring (unfortunately!) its contribution to the corpus *(40)*, with an ethical thought that will lead to a rethinking of some international texts. Steadman and Haglund insist on the fact that considering the time needed for the penal and judicial processes, corpses are generally in the skeletal state when the anthropologists begin their work in the field.

Leaving the theoretical scope, the authors would like to illustrate this point of the development with an archaeological example. A human skeleton discovered in a level dated from the 6th century BCE, near the old town of Lattes (now Hérault, France). These remains were found 1.5 m under the phreatic level; in fact, it is more likely an antique forensic case, a kind of "news in brief" (drowning, accident) than a burial. The body, that of an old woman, was lying on its stomach, and most of the articulations were strictly preserved in connection, particularly the hands, completely connected, including the sesamoid bones (Fig. 3); it is obvious that decomposition took place exactly where the skeleton was discovered. However, fieldwork brought to the forefront several paradoxical disconnections. The cranium was not in the continuation of the cervical column, which shows an interruption above the fourth cervical vertebra; the atlas, appearing by its lateral right face,* was stuck closely to the occipital's inferior side, very close to the second and third cervical vertebrae, which appear, however, by their superior face; the skull, like the atlas, appeared by its anterolateral right face. The left rib cage showed modifications from original organization: some ribs were dissociated, the fourth and the fifth ones having moved to the back of the vertebral column. The left shoulder moved up at the level of the fourth cervical vertebra, but the clavicle, the scapula, and the humerus' head stayed in strict connection; the left elbow was globally preserved, but the olecranon was in front of the distal extremity of the humerus. Finally, the bones of the left hand were in perfect anatomical relation, even though a hiatus of 7 cm was registered between the proximal carpal row and the distal extremity of the forearm.

---

* The face (or view) of appearance is the zenithal view of the bone. It can be composed of one (e.g., anterior face), two (e.g., anterosuperior face), or three sides (e.g., anterosuperolateral right face); after its orientation has been recorded, it will be possible to replace the bone in the three dimensions of space on the drawing or the photograph.

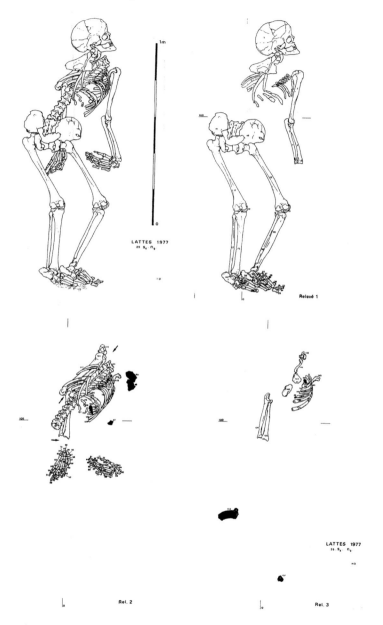

Fig. 3. Plan view (synthesis and successive drawings) of the skeleton of a female discovered in a level dated from the 6th century BCE, Lattes (Hérault, France); details in the text of the drawing. (Drawing by H. Duday. Excavation by H. Duday and H. Prades.)

These displacements are probably related to a ground movement that occurred in a water-saturated environment, with an attraction effect toward the left side of the cervical anatomical region; this attraction provoked the toppling over of the skull and the moving up of the left shoulder. On one side, it is very difficult to estimate the time between death and these movements, considering the particular kind of the environment where the corpse was preserved. On the other, it is possible to assert that some of the ligaments still held bones together: mandible/cranium/atlas, clavicle/scapula/ humerus, and third/fourth cervical vertebrae. At the same time, other ligaments were giving way so that the bones were able to move, with anomalies in their respective position or orientation: atlas/axis, elbow. Finally, some ligaments had been completely destroyed, and this explains the clear dislocation between the third and the fourth cervical vertebrae or the disconnection of the wrist: When the left upper limb moved up, nothing was left of the elements joining the forearm and the hand so that the latter stayed in its original position. One can understand the importance of such a discovery concerning the chronology of the destruction of the different joints. One can parallel these results with the works from W. D. Haglund and M. H. Sorg on the "Human Remains in Water Environment" *(41)*, with differences in the humid environment; these authors propose a chronology of the joint releases for a corpse in an aqueous environment.

Until recently, field archaeology had no real experimental basis, so this discipline has to establish the base of its own thought at the same time that it contributes toward the comprehension of the funerary sites and of the forensic scenes where human remains are involved. Thus, the field is the laboratory, and the excavation is the experiment. It is very important for the forensic scientists and the archaeologists who manage the investigations to be conscious of the responsibility they have. In some forensic cases, the investigations (and sometimes the confessions) lead to a complete knowledge of the circumstances and the sequence of events. A recorded observation can be of minor importance for the comprehension of the site but of major importance for the understanding of the decay processes, and thus, for the interpretation of other cases. A very good example of this "experimental field anthropology" is the recent discovery and study of a funerary pit in which 21 French soldiers and officers who died on the front on September 22, 1914, were buried (ref. *42*; Fig. 4). This well illustrates the complementarities between, on one hand, a real experimentation with practical and ethical limits and, on the other hand, the contribution of the corpus established on both archaeological and forensic field context.

Fig. 4. Vertical view of the pit containing 21 French soldiers and officers who died on the front on September 22, 1914, at Saint-Rémi-la-Calonne (Meuse, France). This excavation (which had not been done for archaeological reasons, but for the identification of the soldiers and the reconstitution of what happened in 1914) led to an important advancement for taphonomic references (Photography H. Paitier. © by the Institut National de Recherches Archéologiques Préventives, France. Excavation by F. Adam and F. Boura.)

3.4. Contribution of the Osteological Observations to the Restitution of the Cadaver Environment

Field archaeological data must allow the determination of the environment in which decay took place. It will then be possible to deduce the characteristics of the space surrounding the corpse and eventually, the kind of container, even if it has not left any trace.

3.4.1. THE DECAY OF THE CORPSE IN AN EMPTY SPACE

In some cases, decay in an empty space is obvious; this can be because of architectural specificities, for instance, a hermetic coffin still empty of sediment at the moment of its discovery (*see* Fig. 2), or because the skeleton lying on the surface of the ground. It is then sufficient to disprove the hypothesis of a buried corpse that would have been later brought out by human actions or natural factors.

The argumentation is much more delicate if, when discovered, the remains are surrounded with sediment. The following reasoning is to be applied. The destruction of the articulation structures progressively leaves the bones free; then, they become mobile, and if the decomposition takes place in an empty space, some bones possibly go out of the initial volume of the cadaver, under the action of gravity or another factor. The cadaver and its close environment can be assimilated to two compartments. The first one is the body itself with its inside space, and the second is the whole space outside the corpse; the two compartments are separated by the cutaneous envelop, the skin. The outside compartment can be open, in the case of a body lying on the ground, or closed, in the case of a buried corpse. The delimited space can be single (a pit, a chamber) or can be itself partitioned, for instance, a coffin in a pit that makes two compartments outside the corpse. This dual system makes it possible to argue about the chronology of the filling, when it occurs, of these different compartments; reality may not be as simple as this outline, but it provides a canvas of thought for the study of decay spaces from which it is possible to consider much more complex situations.

For the observation to be significant, one must eliminate the possibility of external intervention that would have opened a new compartment, that is to say, an empty space in a structure originally filled (for example, this new opening could be a burrow, a new pit, and so on).

When they are because of gravity, the movements of the bones depend here as well on the original position of the body. The only bones capable of falling in the outside volume of the corpse are the ones left off balance by decay of soft parts, in disequilibrium. As certain positions appear quite often, some modalities will be regularly observed, which are worth explanation:

1. When the subject lies supine, the opening of the pelvis can go as far as the flattening of the os coxae and the complete dislocation of the pubic symphysis. Then the os coxae pushes away the femora heads engaged in the acetabular fossae and provokes the lateral rotation of the femurs, with the fall of the patellae outside the knees. It is the case for the right patella of the grave 141 from Ardenne's Abbey church (Normandy, France), although the left one stayed in position (*see* Fig. 2) because the rotation of the left femur has been prevented by the side of the coffin. This external fall of the patellae is very easy to observe and is a good evidence of empty space. Moreover, this element can be observed on the field drawings or photographs, if it is sure that the patellae has not been displaced during the excavation.
2. When the corpse is lying on its side, one of the scapulae and/or one of the os coxae will be on edge and can then fall backward.

Fig. 5. Grave no. 369 of the medieval cemetery of Tournedos (Normandy, France). The fall of the south board of the coffin pushed in the right scapula and humerus, as well as the right os coxae and the bones of the face. (Photography by F. Carré and M. Guillon. © by the Direction Régionale des Affaires Culturelles, Haute-Normandie France.)

One of authors (H. Duday) has seen graves in which the sacrum, the sternum, several vertebrae, and sometimes the cranium had been displaced a considerable distance; the fact that these bones are the ones with the smallest mass suggests a cause other than gravity. In fact, it has been possible to show that these graves had probably been watered by a rise of the phreatic slick, so the bones have floated. Whatever the reason, it is clear that such displacements can only happen in empty space.

Other movements are because of the collapse of the ceiling or the sides of the container; it is the case in the grave 369 from the medieval cemetery of Tournedos (now Normandy, France), in which the fall of the south board of the coffin has pushed in the right scapula, humerus, and os coxae (Fig. 5; ref. *22*).

3.4.2. ORIGINAL EMPTY SPACE/SECONDARY EMPTY SPACE

It is important to distinguish the original empty spaces, which characterize the deposit at the moment of its creation, from what the authors call the secondary empty spaces. The latter appear in the external compartment of the body after a rather long time; they are the result of the disappearance of architectural elements in perishable material whose decomposition is slower than the cadaver's. There are two possibilities: the secondary empty space is a new formation or the bones have a new access to an empty volume; so, bones already separated by decay can then slip in a cavity that was not there, or existed but was inaccessible. This gives paradoxical movements that are often difficult to interpret.

An example is given by the deterioration and the disappearance of a support that raised the head (e.g., fabric cushion, wooden headrest), which will lead to the characteristic result of a complete dislocation of the cranium, usually followed by the atlas, of the mandible and of the upper cervical vertebrae. These disconnections are signs easy to recognize and interpret; it is then desirable for these signs to be taken into account in the forensic and the archaeological typologies, as they concern an element that accompanies the body, an element that has indeed completely disappeared but the existence or the absence of which can be proved by field anthropology.

3.4.3. DECAY IN A FILLED SPACE

The thought process has the same basis and principles as for an empty space, but the reasoning is exactly opposite. When a bone, released by the decay of the soft parts, is in a position of disequilibrium in relation to the external volume of the cadaver, it should fall into this volume; if the displacement does not appear, this means that the volume is not an empty space (Fig. 6). This negative statement comes to demonstrate the existence of a wall effect, the French *effet de paroi*, defined *(11)* by the fact that an element is maintained in an unsteady position (in other words, in a situation of disequilibrium) by a structure that prevents its fall.* At this point, the reasoning focuses on the nature of this structure. It can simply be the limit of a pit or of a chamber (funerary or not), or a perishable partition, for instance, the lateral board of a container; this structure retaining the bones can also be the sediment used to fill the pit as soon as the corpse has been deposited, or at least before the disconnections. The discrimination between all these possibilities is built on general archaeological methods and not on osteological observations: definition of the stratigraphic units between containing structures and filling, locating of coffin nails, ligneous residue. The use of archaeological methods in a forensic context is of the utmost importance *(10)*.

The characterization of the decay environment is thus based on the relation between the different parts of the skeleton and the external volume of the corpse. However, important information can be given by another phenomenon, next to be described.

---

* There is another meaning in French for *effet de paroi*: set of remains stood up and/or lined up along a limit and parallel to it *(43)*; here, it shall be called the "linear delimitation effect."

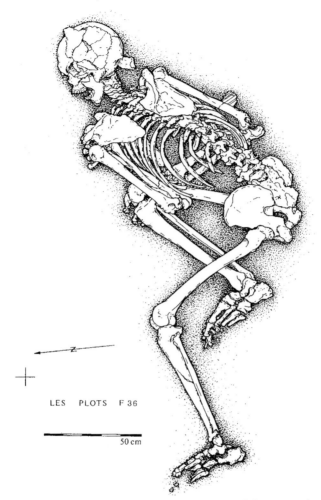

LES PLOTS F 36

50 cm

Fig. 6. Grave from the middle Neolithic period of the site of Berriac (Aude, France) in a silo. The corpse is lying on its stomach. The right hand closes on the right knee so the distal phalanges appear in front of the knee, vertically in the ground; after the disappearance of the interphalanges ligaments, which are known to be very labile, the bones are in a disequilibrium situation in relation to the external volume of the cadaver. These phalanges should have fallen in this external space; their maintaining the original position brings evidence for a "wall effect" (in French *effet de paroi*; *see* Subheading 3.4.2.), which is a filling effect. This zone is far from the pit walls, and as there is no evidence of limit on the left side of the corpse, it is probable that this effect is caused by the immediate filling of the grave (it is in the authors' typology, a "filled soil" grave). (Drawing by H. Duday. Excavation by H. Duday and J. Vaquer.)

3.5. *Filling of the Interior Volume of the Corpse*

It is surprising to notice how much archaeological literature overlooks an essential taphonomic event: the filling of the volume formed by the decay of the soft parts. For buried corpses, the main difference between the moment of the deposit and the moment of the excavation is that muscles, viscera, and fat parts have been replaced by interstitial sediment, except if there is a hermitic container that lasts until the discovery.

3.5.1. PROGRESSIVE FILLING VS DELAYED FILLING

The decay of soft parts forms empty spaces in which the bones can fall by gravity, as soon as they have been released by the ligaments. The authors evoked this phenomenon before, to explain the differences between the original position of the body and the one discovered at the moment of the excavation. These movements possibly appeared only because of the existence of those empty spaces inside the original volume of the corpse; their filling with sediment that prevented any further displacement did not immediately follow the disappearance of the soft parts. On the contrary, if bones have been maintained in their initial position, even though they were in disequilibrium inside the body's volume, the conclusion is a progressive filling. The surrounding sediment replaced the perishable elements of the cadaver as they were disappearing (Fig. 7). In all the cases the authors have worked on, the sediment was mobile (sand, ashes, clay) and percolated by gravitation, an event that can be called the "hourglass effect." This phenomenon can only occur if the sediment is in direct contact with the corpse and when it is observed, it is indirect but certain evidence that the body has been buried in "full soil" (the French *pleine terre*).

3.5.2. FILLING IN OF THE VOLUME FORMED BY THE DECAY OF SOFT PARTS

Various mechanisms are involved in the filling of the interior volume of the cadaver: the collapse by gravity of the sediment above the corpse; the distension of the soil by expansion of clay; and above all, the action of biological agents, among which earthworms play an important part—the enrichment of the soil in organic material in a state of putrefaction attracts a great number of them, and their evacuations accumulate near and inside the cadaver. The knowledge of such phenomena is essential in field anthropology: the "black" or "organic" soil of a filling is not necessarily the result of human action; it can simply show where the activity of worms has been the most intense, and so care should be taken concerning the digging limits of pits or

Fig. 7. Grave nos. 151 and 139 of the abbey church of Ardenne in Normandy (Caen, France). On the left, grave no. 151, the decay occurred in filled space; one can notice the bones in a disequilibrium position away from the walls of the pit and that part of the volume of the rib cage has been preserved, which is impossible in empty space. Notice the clavicles forming a closed angle because of the constriction on the shoulders (*see* Subheading 3.5.2. for details). On the right, grave no. 139, a lead coffin in a wooden coffin; the digging of the pit for grave no. 139 has destroyed a part of grave no. 151, and the gravediggers have removed the left humerus and part of the left foot, without perturbations of the rest of the skeleton. It can be sure that the bones were in a dry state and that the digging was done carefully. (Drawing by M. Guillon. Photography by D. Corde and M. Guillon. © by the Institut National de Recherches Archéologiques Préventives France.)

graves. This observation is verified by the fact that, in a pit, the sediment underneath the skeleton is as black or organic as the one above it. However, this must be precisely recorded to make sure there was not any structure under the body that could have enriched the sediment in organic material, for example, a wooden board.

3.6. Action of the Container on the Organization of the Human Remains: Evidence of Restraining Effects

The shape of the container itself influences the position of the body and conditions as well its taphonomic evolution. A few examples are given, well known in archaeology but not as well in the forensic context, which sometimes led to wrong interpretations.

When the decedent lies in filled ground in a contracted attitude, the peripheral pressure of the sediment can imply the progressive closing of the intersegmental angles, the flexion's degree increasing with the liquefaction of the muscles. The discovery of a hypercontracted skeleton, with the parallel long bones touching each other (Fig. 8) does not mean that the flesh of the cadaver has been removed postmortem or that the body was placed in a tight bag.

Another case is the phenomenon of transversal compression, when the corpse lies on its back in a narrow container (a tight shroud but also a narrow pit, a narrow coffin or a hole in a V form):

1. For the shoulders, this constriction leads to the "verticalization" of the clavicles, their lateral extremity being raised and thrown in an anterior direction because of the narrowness of the container. At the same time, the humeri are submitted to a medial rotation that makes them appear with their lateral face, even their posterolateral face* and the scapulae, in a very oblique position, show an anterolateral face.† On the contrary, the medial extremities of the clavicles are driven down-

---

* If the forearm is in front of the thorax or the abdomen, the medial rotation of the arm (humerus) will be exaggerated by the collapse of the trunk, which is bound to the flattening of the rib cage and the disappearance of the viscera; the radius and the ulna come down until in contact with the vertebrae, and the humerus will then have a paradoxical anatomical orientation, appearing by its posterior face, its head turned outside, losing its strict connection with the glenoid cavity of the scapula.

† This obliquity has to be recorded with the depth measurements of the lateral and medial borders of the bone; however, if these data have not be registered, one can analyze the position of the scapulae on the drawings or the photographs from the field: if the bones are very oblique, or nearly on their medial edge, the coracoid process will seem to be inside (*see* Fig. 7, left scapula) instead of in front (*see* Fig. 7, right scapula) of the glenoid cavity.

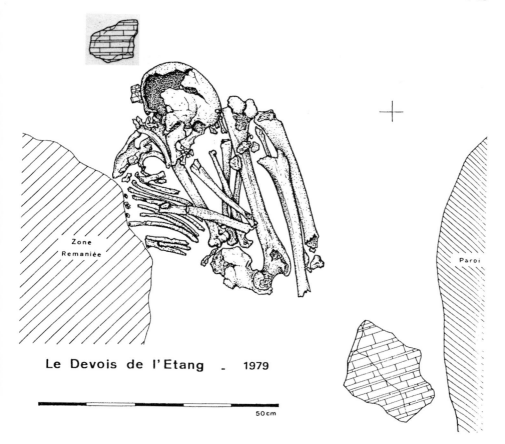

Le Devois de l'Etang _ 1979

50 cm

Fig. 8. One of the chalcolithic graves from the hypogeous of Devois de l'Etang at Tresques (Gard, France). The corpse lies on its left side; the hypercontracted aspect of the skeleton is, in part, caused by the closing of the intersegmental angles—under the peripheral pressure of the sediment, the long limb bones come in contact with each other as the muscles decompose. (Drawing by H. Duday. Excavation by A. Colomer, J. Coularou, H. Duday, X. Gutherz, and A. Raux.)

ward by the manubrium, which generally follows the movement of the first ribs during the flattening of the rib cage. Thus, the clavicle has a tendency to become parallel to the vertebral column because of the two phenomena just described (*see* Fig. 7).

2. For the pelvis, a comparable effect can prevent the flattening of the os coxae; this may be considered like a "wall effect," which can be the result of the presence of the sediment (*see* Fig. 7) or to a board, so this phenomenon can happen in filled or empty space decomposition.

3. If the bottom of the pit is overdug with a sort of gutter, one can observe an elevation of the head and the feet (if the gutter is shorter than the pit). In every case, the discussion needs the study of the depth of all the bones involved. That is why the recording of data in field anthropology includes many measurements of depth marks, on azimuthally view (the appearance face), but also under the bones. It is sometimes necessary, as is seen for the scapula, to record several marks for a single bone, to be able to restore the exact shape of the surface on which the corpse has been deposited.

3.7. Contradiction Between the Taphonomic Analysis and the Evidence of a Container

A fairly common situation brings evidence for decomposition of the corpse in a filled space and at the same time, evidence for the presence of a container or an architecture that has surely made an empty space. The paradox lies in the order of disappearance of the separations and the partitions between the compartments, for example, the fast deterioration of the boards of a wooden container, before the decay of the muscles and ligaments maintaining the bones in connection. A good illustration is given by the grave of a monk, dug in the ground of the Abbey church of Ardenne (Normandy, France) (Fig. 9). The evidence of a coffin has been found, its walls are visible in the section; however, the perfect connection of the bones of the feet, and particularly, their position in unstable disequilibrium far above the bottom of the coffin, bring to the forefront that the filling has appeared faster than the release of the ligaments and tendons of the feet. These phenomena of paradoxical chronology allow the consideration of the nature of the container and the establishment of a hypothesis on the fragility of the material or the bad quality of board assembly.

4. SECONDARY DEPOSIT OF HUMAN REMAINS

First, the word *secondary* characterizes in this text the bone deposit in a technique point of view, without any reference to the thought that led to its constitution. The bones excavated are no longer in the location on the spot where decomposition took place.

In the double context, forensic science and archaeology, the authors must distinguish between *secondary deposit* and *secondary grave*. In the case of secondary deposit, dry bones are brought to the spot where they have been discovered; however, in some situations, the reintervention can occur at a time when a few ligaments from persistent joints still subsist. A secondary grave is defined by social anthropologists as the result of double funeral ceremony; as in the first case, connections can subsist if all the soft parts have

Fig. 9. Grave no. 145 of the abbey church of Ardenne in Normandy (Caen, France). **(A,B)** The evidence of a coffin is proved by its walls, visible in the section; however, the perfect connection of the bones of the feet, and particularly their position in unstable disequilibrium far above the bottom of the coffin, brings to the forefront that the filling occurred faster than the release of the ligaments and tendons of the feet. These paradoxical chronology phenomena raise questions as to the construction of the container and the developing hypothesis on the fragility of the material or the bad quality of board assembling. (Drawing by M. Guillon. Photography by D. Corde and M. Guillon. © by the Institut National de Recherches Archólogiques Préventives France.)

not decomposed when the remains have been transferred in the definitive grave. There are examples where the subsistence of articulations concerns not only the persistent ones but also the labile joints, and are so numerous that the archaeological interpretation, without any historical or ethnological reference, should lead to a primary deposit. A particularly demonstrative example is given by D. Ubelaker *(44)* about funerary pits of Potomac River Indians,* dating from the 16th and 17th centuries. The historical data show that they are real secondary graves, collective and simultaneous, formed in very regular intervals of time, and this independent of the state of decomposition of each corpse. In such a case, the corpse of the subjects who died most recently could have been well connected, which would give, at the time of the excavation, the impression of primary deposits.

Secondary deposits have often been described in literature on the basis of arguments that deserve to be discussed and this in both contexts:

1. Traces of carving have often been considered as a proof of flesh removal from bones, but the problem is that the same traces have been used to propose hypothesis of cannibalism or of "surgery" gestures. The argument must be supported and criticized to have a real signification.

2. The incomplete nature of certain skeletons is sometimes explained by a voluntary choice of bones that would be put in the definitive grave, and explained also by the forgetting, the loss, or the destruction of small bones on the decay area or during transport. This hypothesis certainly has a value, on condition, however, that one can eliminate destruction because of taphonomic reasons (differential bone preservation), to disappearance in desiccation cracks, in inaccessible crevices, or to careless excavation. The same reasoning must be applied on crime scenes, the purpose being to establish the intentionality of the incomplete deposit. During the research of human bodies, it is then imperative to use the meticulous methods described previously in this chapter. (One has too often seen a Caterpillar™ digging the ground in search of murder victims! What is left of the evidence?)

3. An apparent disorder in the disposal of the human remains (according to the original anatomical organization) does not necessarily correspond to a secondary deposit (*see* the above case of the corpse on a wooden bed in a closed room). To prove it, one must show, if it is possible, that the perturbations are of human origin, and that one can eliminate all other source of perturbation.

In both contexts, the determination of secondary deposit often lies on negative evidence. This is why certainties are rare, less often than for primary deposits for which identification relies on positive observations: preservation

---

* Algonquian-speaking Conoy or Pistcataway *(44)*.

of labile articulation, diagenesis of the environment in relation with the fluids of decay. For these deposits in two stages, it is necessary to prove intentional behavior to disprove any ulterior intervention that would not have been scheduled. An archaeological example is given by the use, during several centuries, of a cemetery that implicates accidental intersecting between graves, the more recent grave destroying a part of the older one, and the consequence being the displacement of some of its dry bones.*

What the anthropologists are able to specify is the state of decay that the corpse had reached when its remains have been moved. Considering the lack of other data, nothing in archaeology permits the understanding of the motivation of the displacement, not even the sense conferred to it. Gesture is only the material manifestation of an intention, of a ritual, and to the authors, gesture is often the only information available. In forensic science, the thought, hidden or not, behind the act, is the real question; however, in most cases, one can be sure that digging a hole and reaching human remains for the second time cannot be because of chance.

These archaeological examples must strengthen the forensic anthropologists and their colleagues in a field approach without any apriorism; the scientist's thought has to be sustained by the field documentation and the interpretative phase must be completely separated from the recording phase.

From a technical point of view, and this concerns both forensic and archaeological anthropologists, if the corpse is buried, the intentional removal of bones after decay needs a reopening of the pit. In the case of empty space, and if it is still empty, perturbations can occur among the bones left in the structure, and they depend much on the state of decay at that moment. For a group, or in a forensic case for an individual, the removed bones can represent relics, but they can also have been reburied in another place so that remains of the same subject are at the same time in a primary deposit that became incomplete and in a secondary partial deposit (a very good example is given by Vigneron [45] on Tahiti Island).

It is important to insist on the fact that, except in the accidental context, intentionality is at the start of every behavior, funerary or murderous, which

---

* These bones are not generally treated as neutral remains; they are often the subject of a secondary deposit in an ossuary or in a common grave. This respectful *a posteriori* management must not be considered as characteristic of the period in which the concerned individuals were living; it gives information on the mentality of the gravediggers who have executed these gestures and eventually on the religious thought of the population they belong to. Absolute dating given by the displaced bones has nothing to do with the date of reburial.

is in most cases easy to prove. Much more difficult to prove is the continuation of intentionality in the constitution of the second deposit. The programming of the operations can sometimes be demonstrated, there is then a real step in two stages. Obviously, in each context, neither the intention nor the schedule is the same. In the funerary context, it is programmed to displace the bones, or some of the bones, after decay; this is the double funeral. In the criminal context, it is very rare to see the programming of removing dry bones, even if in some cases it is done to hide them somewhere else, but it was not anticipated. The motivation of the thought processes is not the topic here; it is the identification of the gesture that is the work of the anthropologist.

5. MULTIPLE COLLECTIVE DEPOSITS

Until now, the authors have only dealt with individual depositions. The interpretation on deposit modalities becomes trickier when several corpses are involved and gathered in a limited space. However, even if the excavation and the interpretation are more complex, the analysis tools remain almost the same as what have just been described. However, some cases require specific methods.

5.1. Internal Chronology of the Primary Multiple Deposits

To the problem of individual primary deposit has to be added here the problem of the relative chronology of the deposits; in other words, the successive arrival of the cadavers and the eventual perturbations. The osteological data are in this context of great help, and field anthropology is the only method when time between two deposits is shorter than the possible measurements of the usual dating methods, absolute (carbon 14) or relative (artifacts, stratigraphy). In the case where the constitution of the whole deposit took a long time, one should observe perturbations because of the "arrival" of each new corpse that is in direct contact with dry bones. On the contrary, if all the corpses were deposited at the same time, this kind of displacement will not be observed. (Fig. 10, *see* text of the photographs for detailed example). Here again, the labile articulations are more pertinent than the persistent ones, and this is what the examples show very well with the reasoning on the bones of the wrists and hands. At the same time, the limits of this osteological evidence research appear. It is impossible to differentiate the deposits (successive or simultaneous) when the time between them is shorter than the time necessary for the dislocation of the more labile articulations.

In some situations, a human group can be confronted by a large-scale mortality crisis, leading to a large number of cadavers at the same time (geno-

Fig. 10. Double grave no. 1423 of the medieval cemetery of Tournedos (Normandy, France, 7–14th centuries) of a man (left) and a woman (right). The right hand of the man is on the women's right elbow, and her left hand is on the man's left elbow; this proves that the deposits of the two bodies had been done at the same time, and both cadavers were in a fresh state. (Photography by F. Carré and M. Guillon. © the Direction Régionale des Affaires Culturelles Haute-Normandie, France.)

cide, war crimes, epidemics, natural disaster), resulting in the necessity to dig mass graves (*see* Fig. 4). In these structures, bone displacements can be observed because of the synchronous putrefaction of the piled up cadavers. When decomposing, the soft parts of the underlying corpses leave empty spaces that, on one side, provoke subsidence effects, and on the other, attract the dislocated bones from above.

5.2. Collective Deposits and the Contribution of the Second Rate Osteological Links

Until now, the fundamental reference has been the anatomical connection. The authors tried to understand the conditions that permit the preservation of the relations between bones (and then, get the information about the position of the body) or, on the contrary, to explain the phenomenon that led to their dislocation. This approach presupposes that it is possible to identify each skeleton, or at least part of them, whatever the complexity of the site; this is true as soon as a connection is observed, because it only exists between bones of a single individual. The authors propose to call anatomic connection "first-rate link;" this kind of relation can be observed immediately on the field.

In archaeology, certain funerary sites seem to be enormous piling of bones regrouping dozens, sometimes hundreds of individuals (Fig. 11). In these collective graves, numerous in Western Europe during the second half of the Neolithic period, human remains are, in most cases, dislocated and sometimes extremely broken up (Fig. 11); the connections (first-rate links) concern only a very small part of the deposit and cannot be used as the usual "comprehension key." This kind of deposit has been observed in genocide contexts, and it is important to understand how it has been constituted. In these complex contexts, it is still necessary to identify, as much as possible, the bones belonging to the same subject. As one cannot rely on anatomical connections, one must use other techniques from the laboratory studies, on the bones, and on the maps; this is the researching of the second-rate links:

1. Link by assembling fragments of the same bone.
2. Link by articular contiguity. Some joints have a complex morphology that allows recognition of the bones of the same subject articulating together, for instance, the head joints and the sacroiliac joint.
3. Link by age at death (same stage of maturation).
4. Link by pathological identification.
5. Last, but probably the most important, link by pairing. Even if no skeleton is perfectly symmetrical (laterality effect), a right bone of an individual will resemble more his left bone than to the left bone of another individual.

Fig. 11. General view of the chalcolithic funerary level from the Dolmen des Peirières at Villedubert (Aude, France). This picture gives a significant example of the density and the complexity one can observe in collective graves from the Neolithic period. Note the important fragmentation of the bones. (Photography and excavation H. Duday.)

All these different links have to be related to the exact position of the pieces on the site, so the authors emphasize again the necessity of very precise drawings and/or photographs. Every bone and fragment of bone has to be recorded, as one never knows in advance which remains are going to be important for the comprehension of the structure.

6. Conclusions and Perspectives

Field anthropology, the French *anthropologie de terrain*, appears as an essential approach in the two applications developed in this chapter, forensic science and funerary archaeology. It allows clarification, even to reconstitute the circumstances of body deposition and of gestures practiced on the corpses. Field anthropology brings to the forefront the nature of the space of decay and the characteristics of the container, if there is one, these elements being closely interwoven. This discipline and its techniques are determining analysis tools every time human bones are involved.

The archaeological side participates in the analysis of the funerary sites, with a study of the mortuary practices and of the internal chronology of the deposits; it appears currently to be the privileged means of funerary archaeology. Responsible for its own methods and perspective, this discipline must define the type of observation necessary to lead to the resolution of the numerous problems raised by the interpretation of excavated structures. The strategies of field activities, especially in salvage archaeology, must not be defined without these considerations.

The forensic side of field anthropology contributes toward understanding the circumstances of which the human remains have reached the situation in which they are discovered. The precision of the field methods allows us to neglect as little information as possible and to come back to the recordings as often as necessary.

For the two disciplines, the multiplication of the observations sustains a constantly enriched corpus. The reasoning on the modality of the corpse's deposit, the environment of decay of the cadavers, and the characteristics of the containers must be supplied by funerary archaeology, forensic cases, and the current American experimentation. It is essential to acknowledge the role of field anthropologists, a role that extends much farther than the field stage, and to acknowledge as well this growing body of researchers so that it can work in both investigation fields. For Europe, it seems important to emphasize the necessity of developing the contribution of the anthropologists to the research in forensic science; the entire scientific community concerned with the study of human remains in archaeological and forensic contexts could benefit immensely from this contribution.

REFERENCES

1. Binford, L. R. Mortuary practices: their study and their potential. In: Binford, L. R., ed., An Archeological Perspective. Seminar, New York, NY, pp. 208–243, 1972.
2. Stewart, T. D. Essentials of forensic anthropology. Especially as developed in the United States. Charles C. Thomas, Springfield, IL, 1979.
3. Brothwell, D. R. Digging up Bones. British Museum, London, 1967.
4. Leroi-Gourhan A., Bailloud G., Brézillon M. L'hypogée II des Mournouards, Mesnil-sur-Oger, Marne [in French]. Gallia Préhistoire 5:23–133, 1962.
5. Courtin, J. Le Néolithique de la Provence [in French]. Mémoire de la Société Préhistorique Française, Klincksieck, Lille, 1974.
6. Boddington. A., Garland A. N., Janaway R. C. Death Decay and Reconstruction: Approaches to Archaeology and Forensic Science. Manchester University Press, London, 1987.
7. Crubézy É., Duday H., Sellier P., Tillier, A.-M. Anthropologie et Archéologie: dialogue sur les ensembles funéraires. Réunion de Bordeaux, 15–16 juin 1990

[in French]. Bulletins et Mémoires de la Société d'Anthropologie de Paris, 1990.

8. Castex D., Courtaud P., Sellier P., Duday H., Bruzek, J. Les ensembles funéraires. Du terrain à l'interprétation, actes du colloque "Méthodes d'étude des sépultures" [in French]. Groupe de Recherche 742 du CNRS, Bull. Mem. Soc Anthropol. Paris. 3–4:237–244, 1996.

9. Duday H. L'archéothanatologie ou l'archéologie de la mort. In: Vandermeersch, B., Dutour, O., Hublin, J.-J., eds., Objets et Méthodes en Paléoanthropologie, Comité des Travaux Historiques et Scientifiques [in French]. CNRS, Paris, 2005.

10. Dirkmaat, D. C., Adovasio, J. M. The role of archaeology in the recovery and interpretation of human remains from an outdoor forensic setting. In: Haglund, W. D., Sorg, M. H., eds., Forensic Taphonomy: the Postmortem Fate of Human Remains. CRC Press, Boca Raton, FL, pp. 39–64, 1997.

11. Duday, H. Anthropologie "de terrain", archéologie de la mort. La mort, passé, présent, conditionnel, colloque du groupe vendéen d'études préhistoriques [in French]. La Roche-sur-Yon, pp. 33–58, 1995.

12. Bass, W. M. Outdoor decomposition rates in Tennessee. In: Haglund, W. D., Sorg, M. H., eds., Forensic Taphonomy: the Postmortem Fate of Human Remains. CRC Press, Boca Raton, FL, pp. 181–186, 1997.

12. Galloway, A. The process of decomposition: a model from the Arizona-Sonoran desert. In: Haglund, W. D., Sorg, M. H., eds., Forensic Taphonomy: The Postmortem Fate of Human Remains. CRC Press, Boca Raton, FL, pp. 139–150, 1997.

13. Bass, W. M., Jefferson, J. La ferme des morts Press. Le Cherche Midi, Paris, 2004.

14. Behrensmeyer, A. K. Taphonomic and Ecological Information from Bone Weathering, Paleobiology 4, pp. 4:150–162, 1978.

15. Miccozzi, M. S. Frozen environments and soft tissue preservation. In: Haglund, W. D., Sorg, M. H., eds., Forensic Taphonomy: the Postmortem Fate of Human Remains. CRC Press, Boca Raton, FL, pp. 171–180, 1997.

16. Haglund, W. D., Sorg, M. H., eds., Forensic Taphonomy: The Postmortem Fate of Human Remains. CRC Press, Boca Raton, FL, 1997.

17. Hunter, J., Cox, M., Cheetham, P. Forensic Archaeology, Bournemouth, 2005.

18. Bechtel, F., Duday, H., Platel, N., Raffaillac-Desfosses, C. Unpublished report from excavation, in press, 2001.

19. Billard, C., Guillon, M,. Verron, G., eds., Les Sépultures Collectives de la Boucle du Vaudreuil (Eure, France), in press, 2007.

20. Kapandji, I. A. Physiologie articulaire. Schémas commentés de mécanique humaine. Tome 3 : tronc et rachis [in French]. Maloine, Paris, 1975.

21. Guillon, M. Fouiller, dessiner et démonter avec précision plus de 1000 tombes en 12 mois? L'exemple du cimetière médiéval de Tournedos-sur-Seine [in French]. Bull. Mem. Soc. Anthropol. Paris 3–4:61–66, 1990.

22. Guillon, M. Anthropologie de terrain et paléodémographie: études méthodologiques sur les grands ensembles funéraires; applications au cimetière médiéval de Tournedos-Portejoie (Eure) [in French]. Ph.D. Thesis, University of Bordeaux I, 1997.

23. Carré, F., Guillon, M. Habitat et nécropole de Portejoie: le site de Tournedos/Val de Reuil (Eure), VIIe-XIVe s. In: Lorren, C., Périn, P., eds., L'habitat Rural du Haut

Moyen-Âge (France, Pays-Bas, Danemark et Grande-Bretagne). Actes des XIVe Journées Internationales d'Archéologie Mérovingienne. Mémoires de l'Association Française d'Archéologie Mérovingienne VI [in French]. Musée des Antiquités de la Seine-Maritime, Rouen. pp. 145–158, 1995.

24. Carré, F., Guillon, M. Méthodes d'approche chronologique d'un cimetière rural des VIIe-XIVe siècles: le site de Portejoie (Tournedos-sur-Seine, Eure). In: Delestre, X., Périn, P., eds., La Datation des Structures et des Objets du Haut Moyen-Âge: Méthodes et Résultats. Actes des XVe Journées Internationales d'Archéologie Mérovingienne, Rouen du 4 au 6 Février 1994, Mémoires de l'Association Française d'Archéologie Mérovingienne VII [in French]. Musée des Antiquités de la Seine-Maritime, Rouen. pp. 93–98, 1998.

25. Orfila, M., Lesueur, M. O. Traité des Exhumations Juridiques, et Considérations sur les Changements Physiques que les Cadavres Éprouvent en se Pourrissant dans la Terre, dans l'eau, dans les Fosses d'Aisance et dans le Fumier, 2 vols. [in French]. Béchet Jeune, Paris, 1831.

26. Bass, W. M. Time interval since death: a difficult decision. In: Rathbun, T. A., Buikstra, J. E., eds., Human Identification: Case Studies in Forensic Anthropology. Charles C. Thomas, Springfield, IL, pp. 136–142, 1984.

27. Rodriguez, W. C., Bass, W. M. Decomposition of buried bodies and methods that may aid in their location. J. Forensic Sci. 30:836–852, 1985.

28. Spier, R. F. G. Field Handbook of Human Skeleton. Missouri Archaeological Society, Colombia, MO, 1962.

29. Duday, H., Laubenheimer, F., Tillier, A.-M. Nouveau-nés et nourrissons gallo-romains. Centre de Recherches d'Histoire Ancienne, série Amphore 3 [in French]. Ann. Sci. Univ. Besancon Med. 144:563, 1995.

30. Guillon, M., Sellier, P., Pecqueur, L., Creveuil, S., Durand, R. La mort antique, médiévale et moderne en Île-de-France. In: Tabeaud, M., ed., La Mort en Île-de-France [in French]. Publications de la Sorbonne, Paris, pp. 84–100, 2001.

31. Guillon M. Représentativité des échantillons archéologiques lors de la fouille des gisements funéraires. In: Baray, L., ed., Archéologie des Pratiques Funéraires, Approche Critique de la Fouille des Sépultures [in French]. Mémoires du Mont Beuvray. pp. 93–112, 2004.

32. Krogman, W. N., Iscan M. Y. The Human Skeleton in Forensic Medicine. Charles C. Thomas, Springfield, IL, 1986.

33. Saunders, S. R., Katzenberg, M. A. Biological Anthropology of the Human Skeleton. Wiley-Liss, New York, NY, 2000.

34. Saunders, S. R., Katzenberg, M. A Skeletal Biology of Past People: Research Methods. Wiley-Liss, New York, NY, 1992.

35. Bass, W. M. The excavation of human remains. In: Spier, R. F. G., ed., Field Handbook of Human Skeleton. Missouri Archaeological Society, Colombia, MO, pp. 39–51, 1962.

35. Haglund, W. D., Sorg, M. H., eds., Advances in Forensic Taphonomy: Method, Theory, Archaeological Perspectives. CRC Press, Boca Raton, FL, 2002.

37. Nilsson Stutz, L. Embodied Rituals and Ritualized Bodies: Tracing Ritual Practices in Late Mesolithic Burials (Acta Archaeol Lundensia, 46) Almqvist and Wiksell, Copenhagen, 2003.

38. Duday, H. Archéologie funéraire et anthropologie. Application des relevés et de l'étude ostéologique à l'interprétation de quelques sépultures pré et protohistoriques du Midi de la France [in French]. Cahiers Anthropol. 1:55–101, 1978.
39. Duday, H. Observations ostéologiques et décomposition du cadavre: sépultures colmatées ou en espace vide. Rev Archeol Centre France 29:193–196, 1990.
40. Steadman, D. W., Haglund, W. D. The scope of anthropological contributions to human rights investigations. J. Forensic Sci. 50:1, 2005.
41. Haglund, W. D., Sorg, M. H. Human remains in water environments. In: Haglund, W. D., Sorg, M. H., eds., Advances in Forensic Taphonomy: Method, Theory, Archaeological Perspectives. CRC Press, Boca Raton, FL, pp. 201–218, 2002.
42. Boura, F., Adam, F., Duday, H., Hervet, P., Piechaud, S. Fouille archéologique d'une sépulture militaire de 1914: la sépulture collective de Saint-Rémy-la-Calonne (Meuse) [in French]. Nouvelles Archeol. 48/49 :56–70, 1992.
43. Leroi-Gourhan, A. Dictionnaire de la Préhistoire. Presses Universitaire de France, Paris, 1988.
44. Ubelaker, D. H. Reconstruction of Demographic Profiles from Ossuary Skeletal Samples. A Case Study from the Tidewater Potomac. Smithsonian Contribution to Anthropology, no. 18. Smithsonian Institution Press, Washington, D.C., 1974.
45. Vigneron, E. Recherches sur l'histoire des attitudes devant la mort en Polynésie française. Ph.D. Thesis, Toulouse, Ecole des Hautes Etudes en Sciences Sociales, 1985.

Chapter 7

Forensic Investigation of Corpses in Various States of Decomposition

A Multidisciplinary Approach

João Pinheiro and Eugénia Cunha

Summary

A cadaver may become the object of study for various reasons, and as such, may be situated anywhere between two different but complementary scientific areas: forensic pathology and forensic anthropology. The aim of this chapter is to explain precisely how to deal with the bodies in various states of decomposition, when and why the diverse specialists should intervene, and to provide useful tools for their study.

This chapter is meant to be a practical approach to this multidisciplinary expertise, which is inspired by the model implemented on victims of genocide and crimes against humanity. From the constitution of the team and the necessary equipment until the procedures before, during, and after the autopsy, the methodology based on the forensic investigation of corpses is carefully explained, systematically and widely illustrated. Preparation of remains, identification and separation of body parts, disarticulation, washing and removal of soft tissue, reconstruction and assembling, inventory, and the forensic examination are parts of this work.

Key Words: Decomposition; human remains; diverse states of decomposition; multidisciplinary; preservation; putrefaction; mummification; adipocere; saponification.

From *Forensic Anthropology and Medicine:*
Complementary Sciences From Recovery to Cause of Death
Edited by: A. Schmitt, E. Cunha, and J. Pinheiro © Humana Press Inc., Totowa, NJ

1. INTRODUCTION

During the last decade, multidisciplinary research involving profession-als from various areas but centered on a core of forensic pathologists and anthropologists has developed in the wake of investigations into genocides, crimes against humanity, and mass disasters (refs. *1–10* and Chapters 17 and 18), and it could be supposed that such partnerships are only necessary in those cases. This, however, is not the case. This kind of joint work may also be needed in many other routine situations faced by any legal medicine insti-tute or department. Despite the fact that exhumed murder victims account for only a small minority of all homicides—9% in the United Kingdom *(3)* and 1.38% over a period of 10 yr in the United States *(2)*—the investigation of these cases makes use of multiple police resources and is often very difficult, requiring considerable research and study. Everyone will remember the serial killers in the United Kingdom and the shocking case in Belgium involving children, in which the difficulties experienced by the investigating teams attracted enormous (and uncomfortable) media coverage, leading to great social agitation. There are also many other situations that may generate investiga-tions of this type, such as the disappearance of old people, suicides in wells, cases of accidental drowning, or simply natural deaths that take place at home, but a long time passes before the body is found.

A cadaver may become the object of study for various reasons, and as such, may be situated anywhere between two different but complementary scientific areas, namely forensic medicine (a multiprofessional specialty, although with a markedly medical character, that serves the application of jus-tice; *see* Chapter 2) and forensic anthropology (or, when this is not formally recognized—as is the case in many countries—anthropology of past popula-tions/osteoarchaeology, as its precursor, or at least the area from which most of its professionals came; *see* Chapter 1). Collaboration between these two scien-tific areas underlined in the literature *(3)* has been very advantageous in routine cases in the legal medicine departments, not only with regard to obtaining a positive identification of victims *(11)*, but also in determining cause of death *(12–17)*. Some European Union work groups have already debated this matter, extending it from war crimes to the recovery of the body of an individual victim of murder, and some guidelines have been suggested *(3)*.

A cadaver can raise a number of questions, which can be answered by examination. In addition, cadavers may be found in many different situations (in gardens, buildings, ruins, secluded spots, garages, cars, under water, in single or multiple/mass graves, and so on) and states (complete individuals or only parts, naked, or covered). They may also be found in different stages of

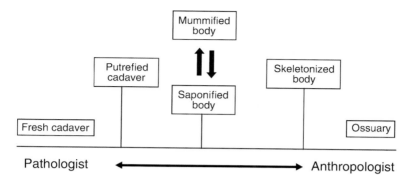

Fig. 1. Moment of intervention of the forensic pathologist and anthropologist.

decomposition, as has already been explained in Chapter 5. This is why a partnership is necessary between the forensic pathologist and anthropologist, whose moment of intervention is shown in Fig. 1: a line functioning as a spectrum, which relates the phases of decomposition of the body with the moment of intervention of each professional.

At one end of this line is the domain of legal medicine, where the forensic pathologist acts. Through training and daily practice, the pathologist naturally prefers a fresh body, i.e., one that has not yet been subjected to the processes of putrefaction and/or conservation. At the other end is the forensic anthropologist, who studies bodies that have already decomposed into skeletons or even into heaps of bones. In each of these extreme cases, these professionals usually work alone, without the need for the complementary intervention of the other. However, in all the other phases of the process (stages of decomposition), collaboration between them is essential.

There is, of course, no exact moment at which a multidisciplinary team becomes necessary, and this has to be decided on a case-by-case basis. However, it will be felt naturally, if each of the professionals involved has an open mind and recognizes self-limitations—one of the most important qualities of the true forensic expert. Somewhere in the middle of the spectrum, when the first signs of adipocere or mummification start to appear (this usually coincides with difficulties in identifying the body, determining sex, age, and so forth), the forensic pathologist will realize the advantages of working with a forensic anthropologist. At that point, objectives will more easily be achieved if tasks are shared. Assisting pathologists constituted the 5th of 11 main functions undertaken by anthropologists who participated in human rights investigations throughout the world (1990–1999), and the third if only fieldwork is considered *(10)*. This was particularly evident in the former Yugoslavia *(3,6,14,16)*, where many bodies were not yet skeletonized and therefore still had a great deal of soft tissue *(10)*.

If one continues moving right along the spectrum, the tasks gradually become increasingly anthropological in nature. Nonetheless, the pathologist should never resign or be dispensed because in a forensic case, the pathologist will always be necessary for determining the cause of death. Now, in almost all legal systems around the world, certifying cause of death is the exclusive responsibility of a medical doctor, in this case, a forensic pathologist.

In addition to justifying the relevance of such expertise and presenting the reasons why such teams are formed, the aim of this chapter is also to provide some practical guidelines for the investigation of cadavers at different stages of decomposition, ranging from the necessary materials to the main procedure to follow. These guidelines may be used by both pathologists and anthropologists, or indeed, other professionals involved in this kind of investigation. Whereas this procedure was developed mainly for routine forensic investigations and is oriented toward these guidelines, it is not limited to them and may, of course, be extended to cases of mass disasters or crimes against humanity.

2. MULTIDISCIPLINARY TEAM

2.1. Presuppositions

The existence of this multidisciplinary team therefore seems to be completely justified, even for isolated cases arising in forensic practice *(3,12–17)*. However, further evidence, so obvious as to seem anecdotal, is that four eyes always see better than two.

The complementary nature of teamwork avoids the risk (unfortunately not uncommon) of exaggerated self-sufficiency on the part of a particular specialist: *A pathologist with some skill in anthropology is not an anthropologist, just as an anthropologist is never a pathologist, even if he or she has assisted in many autopsies* (with the exception, of course, of those very rare cases of people who have training and proven experience in both branches).

Naming experts is not enough to compose a good team—this would be a serious error of human resource management. Such teams should be constituted not of those who want, but those who know. The best pathologists and/or anthropologists may perform very poorly in teams of this kind. In fact, a strong team spirit is necessary, manifest in the exact notion of the tasks and responsibilities of each. There must also be good communication between anthropologist and pathologist *(7)*. It is not sufficient simply to put two experts together. There must be some complicity between them, and above all, they need to know how to work on the frontier/interface of different kinds of knowledge, without intentionally invading the field of the other, as sometimes happens. This team spirit and complicity is even more justified if the conditions under which these teams work are considered, which are frequently difficult: bumpy terrains, unsafe places, irregular hours, and so forth. It is even more necessary in the case of transnational teams on missions to distant countries, where the hardships may be even more pronounced: language and cultural barriers (food in Muslim countries for a Westerner, for example, is not a small problem on long missions); extreme climate conditions (the cold of the Balkans or the heat of Africa) and bad accommodations; difficulties with social contact in regimes where there is a curfew and very little freedom; and severe security problems, sometimes involving risks to life (for in postwar environments, even when conflicts are over, there will still be areas and sites rife with unexploded mines). For this reason, some missions have had to be suspended (such as in Rwanda *[10]*), whereas others (such as current missions in Iraq, despite the urgency well justified by Stover *[8]*) still have not properly begun in an organized fashion.

2.2. Constitution

The basic structure of the multidisciplinary team presented here is the fruit of experience collected over various missions of the International Tribunal for the former Yugoslavia under the auspices of the United Nations, Human Rights Watch, Physicians for Human Rights, and other nongovernmental organizations, such as the various South American forensic anthropology teams, developed from the most important pioneer of them all, the Argentinean Team of Forensic Anthropology *(8,10)*. The team should consist of the forensic pathologist (who heads the team), and the forensic anthropologist, each of whom may bring one or two trainees (Table 1).

The team will also have autopsy technicians (one or two per table) and a scene of the crime officer (SOCO). This position, which does not exist in Mediterranean countries but is common in countries of Anglo-Saxon influence, the United States, and the United Kingdom *(18,19)*, operates half way between the autopsy technician and pathologist and has specific training in the gathering of nonbiological evidence, very helpful in this kind of autopsy. They will be present at both the site of exhumation and also during the autopsy itself *(7)*, accompanying the pathologist and anthropologist in the collection of all personal objects (keys, watches, rings, amulets, necklaces, military insignia, coins, banknotes, cigarette packets, etc.), clothing (of different types and footwear), documents and photographs, bandages, ribbons or blindfolds,

Table 1
Constitution of a Forensic Team

- Forensic pathologist: chief of the team
- Forensic anthropologist
- Interns/trainee students
- SOCO: scene of the crime officer
- Forensic odontologist
- Radiologist or radiology technician
- Forensic geneticist
- Forensic enthomologist
- Photographer
- Others

and ballistic evidence or instruments that could have produced traumas found on the body, all of which must be labeled with care. After washing and drying the clothes, they will study them (the type, color, size, labels, alterations, and defects) and will prepare files to record each of the objects collected to be included in the final report or form the basis of a particular report. They will also be responsible for transferring this information to the computer and including it in databases (7).

Other important specialists are the radiology or radioscopy technicians, particularly in cases involving firearms or where identification is carried out from bone lesions, and a photographer, who will free the other members of the team for their main tasks, as well as ensuring that the pictures are the best possible quality.

Specialists in other areas, such as forensic odontologists, geneticists, or entomologists are also welcome, though not always essential.

2.3. Equipment

As might be expected, the basic equipment required includes that used in both the autopsy of a fresh body (scalpel, pincers and saw, and so on) and for an anthropological study (osteometric table, compass, sliding caliper, and so on), listed in Table 2. However, it is also important to protect the experts and other participants against disease or accidents (with gloves, caps, aprons, antiradiation jacket, and so forth), particularly when the task at hand is situated toward the left-hand side of the spectrum. Pinheiro et al. (20), inspired by the Centers for Disease Control (US) publications, has already studied the risks of infection faced by workers in legal medicine, suggesting some recommendations. More recently, Galloway et al. (21) put forward safety mea-

Table 2
Equipment for a Multidisciplinary Expertise

- Brushes of different types
- Scalpels
- Scissors
- Pincers
- Sieve
- Tubs, vase
- Saw
- Reversible glue
- Sliding calipers
- Compass
- Metric bandage/osteometric table
- Stepladder
- Forms, charts, labels, packs
- Photographic cameras
- Protective equipment: gloves, masks, cups, aprons, and so on
- Water
- *Expert hands*

sures necessary for the protection of the workers adapted to the forensic anthropological context.

A model of an articulated skeleton is also extremely useful in the autopsy room to clarify certain anatomical details—even for those who claim to know everything about anatomy may find there is an area or structure that they have forgotten—and, particularly to have a notion of the relations between structures and the movements of body parts, very useful in the attempt to reproduce, three-dimensionally, the path of bullets from firearms.

Finally, and perhaps most importantly, are the two things that are essential for a good investigation: first, the *hands of the experts*, particularly the pathologist, which should not serve only to take notes but also to penetrate deep into the body mass and manipulate the cadaver, and second, water, which does not have to be running.

3. PROCEDURES

3.1. Examination of the Scene and Exhumation

It would be ideal if forensic pathologists—or at least practitioners trained in legal medicine—were always able to undertake their examination at the site where a body is found. This, however, is not usually possible, especially

Fig. 2. Scene investigation by criminal police in Portugal: a skull and some bones under a tree from whose branch a belt was suspended. An empty bottle of whiskey next to the cadaver, the autopsy, and posterior police investigation led to the conclusion of a suicide by hanging.

in Europe, where the anthropologist is even less available because these multidisciplinary teams are not yet implanted on the terrain locally. For this reason, remains are usually collected by the police in most cases (Fig. 2). When it is the criminal police, one hopes for some degree of rigor and detail in the description. However, if it is the normal police force, with little training in criminal procedures, then the results are likely to be less successful.

The need to train police in these matters and to incur the spirit of interdisciplinarity in them has been emphasized throughout Europe *(3)*.

Ideally, the pathologist and anthropologist, or at least one of them, should be present in all cases. With or without them, an excellent report about the exhumation or examination of the scene is desirable, given that this kind of contextual information is as valuable as the autopsy itself (indeed, sometimes even more so) for investigating the circumstances of death. This report (whoever is responsible for it) should be drawn up at the time and be available before the autopsy to avoid the loss of important evidence and signs. If it is not properly presented, it may lead to the pathologist's resignation in investigation into cause of death *(7)*. Indeed, there are some authors *(22)* who consider that, in situations of crimes against humanity, excavations carried out in a careless manner and that consequently do not lead to any charges may be perceived as a new violation of human rights.

3.2. Procedures Before the Autopsy

The first task is to check the labeling of the body. Then, there is the general photograph to be taken, with the label bearing the expert's number (for which a stepladder is very useful).

Following the photograph is the radioscopic or X-ray examination by the particular technician (Fig. 3). The aim of this is, of course, to investigate the existence of metal objects such as bullets, lead, shrapnel, and, in other situations, to identify traumatic lesions on the skeleton (such as fractures) or even in the soft tissue, either to determine the cause of death or to compare findings from the necropsy with antemortem data in order to achieve a positive identification. It also serves to identify pointed or sharp objects that could be hazardous for workers; these should be duly marked.

The advantage of radioscopy for this type of investigation is that it allows projectiles or shrapnel to be collected through direct vision, with the protection of antiradiation gloves, objects that may not be found during the necropsy and that might otherwise take a long time to be located.

When the examination is complete, any projectiles or other metallic or dense objects will be photographed and printed; the photograph is then affixed to the autopsy table, where it constitutes a precious aid for the identification and location of these during the autopsy itself.

3.3. During the Autopsy

Some preliminary recommendations should be made.

First, the entry into the mortuary or worksite of people not involved in the investigation should be controlled. Noise, confusion, and the constant

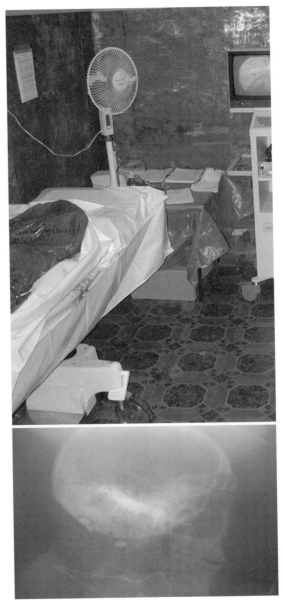

Fig. 3. A radioscopy room improvised in a theater of human rights abuse and an X-ray showing four bullets on the cervical region and head of a murder victim, which was extremely useful in the recovery of the bullets (*see* Fig. 13, Chapter 5 for case details).

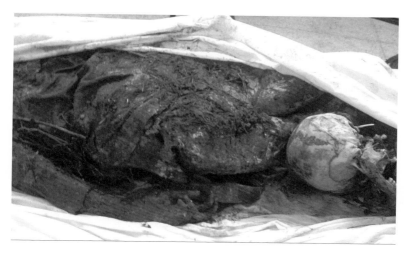

Fig. 4. The first thing to do after opening the body bag, before manipulating the body or undressing it, is to observe carefully the body or remains.

giving of opinions, that are not always informed, may be distracting and break the concentration needed for this type of examination: *a bad opinion is worse than no opinion at all.* Unfortunately, some think they know everything, and in these cases, few restrain themselves from expressing their opinions, sometimes prematurely, ungrounded, and often with little scientific value.

The duties of all the team members should also be checked, and no step should be taken—not even the general photograph—without the presence of the forensic pathologist.

At the beginning of the autopsy itself, the plastic bag should be opened and the cadaver or remains should be observed (Fig. 4). A careful look should be taken at what is there: a body in a greater or lesser state of conservation: a skeleton, complete or not, mixed with elements from the surrounding environment; or an indistinct body mass (that is, scarcely distinguishable as a body) containing bones or parts of bones, fragments of soft tissue or clothes, muddy and mixed with stones, sticks, leaves, iron, wire, glass, and personal objects (Fig. 5). The position of the body should be noted.

Then, if the body is clothed, it should of course be undressed. The clothes should not be torn or cut with scissors (a bad practice, unfortunately frequent even in autopsies of fresh bodies), but removed with care in order to preserve them as much as possible because they are extremely helpful in interpreting the orifices caused by bullets or other findings, also for identification by

Fig. 5. The body mass may contain bones, soft tissues mixed with sand or mud, stones, sticks, pieces of glass and iron, and leaves.

relatives, and sometimes in alerting to unsuspected organic pathologies (Fig. 6). In this task, the experience of autopsy technicians is essential, particularly as many saponified or mummified bodies or those that are not completely skeletonized may break up easily. If the clothes are mixed with the body mass, they should be removed, observed, described—with attention given to the labels (Fig. 7)—and handed over to the SOCO. Similarly, all personal items found in pockets, on the body (rings, collars, and so on; *see* Fig. 8), or in the bag itself should be handed over to the technician or to whomever exercises the same functions, who should assure the chain of custody.

When the bodies still have soft tissue (those situated farther to the left on the spectrum in Fig. 1), are putrefied, in adipocere, or are mummified, a complete autopsy, including an examination of the external surface and internal organs and the opening of the three cavities, is mandatory (Fig. 9). The details of a standard autopsy will not be present here because it is not the objective of this chapter. Let it only be stated that a standard autopsy requires a complete examination of the external habit, with meticulous investigation of traces of individualization; rigor in measuring traumatic lesions (scratches/abrasions, ecchymosis, bruises, cuts or gunshot wounds); recognition of signs or stigma of torture (bandages and ribbons, shaped lesions) or organized genocide (blindfolds); differential determination between soft tissue lesions that have been incurred ante-, peri-, and post-

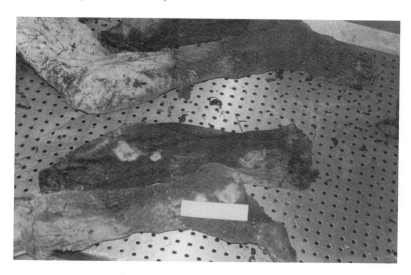

Fig. 6. To properly undress the cadaver is essential. If the socks of this woman had been cut with scissors, the ties she wore closer to the legs would not have been realized, which led to the discovery of an eventual pathology of the lower limbs (*see* Fig. 9, Chapter 14 for further details), later confirmed on autopsy and used as a factor for identification.

Fig. 7. Verifying the labels is always an important task that must not be forgotten.

Fig. 8. Looking for personal objects, essential for identification, such as this ring on the woman's hand (the same as Fig. 6), is sometimes a difficult task when the body is mud-covered and in adipocere.

mortem; and observation of genitals and collection of elements to determine the age at death.

On the level of the internal autopsy, the removal and study of all organs that are still conserved is obligatory (not forgetting the sexual orifices): seeking signs of preexisting disease or traumatic lesions important for identification and distinguishing them from those because of decomposition, determining the ante- or perimortem nature of the lesions, and establishing their correspondence with those observed externally, particularly in the case of gunshot wounds, i.e., the description of the trajectory of bullets (*see* Fig. 9).

When the bodies are more properly called human remains (i.e., when they are situated toward the right-hand side of the spectrum), the examination will have a markedly anthropological character, which will be described in some detail because it is the aim of this chapter.

3.3.1. *Preparation of the Remains*

Careful preparation of the bones is necessary to maximize the results of a forensic anthropology examination, identification and cause of death. Tasks that might appear to have little importance are indeed crucial to achieve the

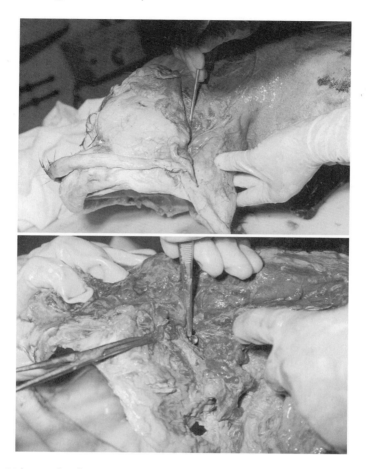

Fig. 9. When a body is saponified, a standard autopsy must be carried out. Here the first author is looking for the four bullets with which the victim was shot, on the skull and posterior neck. Note the white, waxy color of the saponified tissues, the hole on the occipital from a bullet already recovered, and the detail of another projectile being removed from a difficult place, between the occipital and the atlas (same case as in Fig. 13, Chapter 5).

two great objectives of the examination. For example, failure to properly remove the dried tissue that covers the pelvis may hide a sign that might be essential for identification, or a relevant perimortal lesion.

For this reason, the bones need to be prepared very carefully. The description given next is therefore a very important step in the forensic anthropology exam.

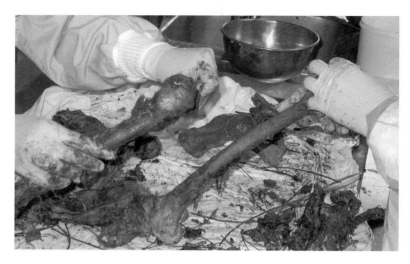

Fig. 10. Isolating body elements (bones, teeth, fingers) from the body mass is a painstaking task for the whole team.

The preparation is done in four broad stages, which may be subdivided. In the first, a rough dissection of the soft tissues is carried out. Then the bones are disarticulated, if useful. This is followed by the more detailed removal of the soft tissues. Finally, the bones are stabilized to be easily observed and manipulated *(23)*.

3.3.2. *IDENTIFICATION AND SEPARATION OF BODY PARTS*

In the case of bodies that have already undergone considerable decomposition, this step begins with the separation of body parts (bones, mummified and/or saponified soft tissue, teeth, and so forth; *see* Fig. 10) from stones, leaves, and so on (Fig. 11). This long-drawn-out and fastidious work is very detailed and should be done by the whole team—pathologists, anthropologists, trainees, and so forth, and not only by the technicians. Often the state of conservation of the remains can only be assessed after this process has been concluded.

On this point, it is of course important to exclude from the future analysis any animal bones that sometimes are mixed in with the body mass or bones. In most cases, this differential determination is not difficult, but if the bones are incomplete or reduced to fragments, the situation may become considerably more complex.

In this phase, with the aim of identification, particular attention should be given to the collection of the two fundamental elements, teeth (which

Fig. 11. Stones, soil, and mud to one side, body elements to the other, and the body bag almost empty.

are often lost postmortem and immersed in the body mass; *see* Fig. 12) and fragments of skin from the fingers (which should be identified) for the study of fingerprints, taken directly from the fingers (Fig. 13) or from the skin detached like a glove during decomposition. Fortunately, it is possible to reconstitute fingerprints even in the absence of skin from the pads of the fingers *(24)*, but when they cannot be collected, the reason should be given (e.g., taphonomic alterations, severe destruction of hands, and so on *[7]*).

At this time, the possible risks to professionals in the form of sharp or pointed objects that might cause injury should not be overlooked; these may be observed and marked in the radioscopy.

Any tattoos that there may be, when very faint, are better observed under infrared or ultraviolet radiation. Rings should be sought carefully because they may go unnoticed in the mud (*see* Fig. 8) or in carbonized remains.

At this time, the possible risks to professionals in the form of sharp or pointed objects that might cause injury should not be overlooked; these may be observed and marked in the radioscopy.

3.3.3. Disarticulation

The general removal of the soft tissue from the skull and other parts precedes disarticulation and requires great care and attention because it can supply crucial information.

Fig. 12. Recovery of teeth lost postmortem from the body mass. It is a fundamental task, not only for dental record, but also for future DNA analysis. Here a tooth immersed in soil that surrounded the skull to which it belonged, showing a plant root, can be studied by botanical specialists to get an idea of the time the skull was deposited.

Fig. 13. Two fingers recovered from the body mass of an old woman (the same as in Fig. 1, Chapter 5) disappeared after 2.5 mo: in this case, it was not necessary to take fingerprints.

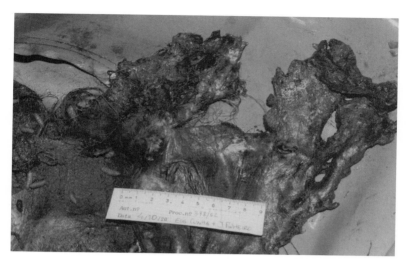

Fig. 14. The scalp of a murder victim recovered out of place, stained red, suggesting a bloody infiltration of an antemortem origin (*see* the bone traumatic pathology of this case in Fig. 15).

In one autopsy performed by the author, the importance of a mortal cranial fracture in a skeletonized body was reinforced by extensive infiltration of blood of the scalp recovered from another part of the body mass and from the vault (Figs. 14 and 15), thus providing further support for a determination of murder by blunt instrument *(12)*. Dried tissue stuck to the bone, which can hide important signs for identification, such as discrete traits and pathological alterations, should not be removed until a later stage of the process of bone preparation. The skull and pelvis bones should be cleaned particularly carefully because they provide precious information about the demographic profile of the individual.

In many situations of skeletonization, it may be important to separate the skull from the vertebral column, the upper limbs from the thorax, the pelvis from the backbone, and the lower limbs from the pelvis. This disarticulation may be more or less complex, depending on the quantity of tissues still existing, and should be assessed on a case-by-case basis.

Decapitation should be done between the second and third cervical vertebrae or lower down to avoid damaging the area of the atlanto-occipital joint *(23)*. The disarticulation of the jaw, usually facilitated by the disappearance of the ligaments and capsule of the temporomandibular joint, allows dental

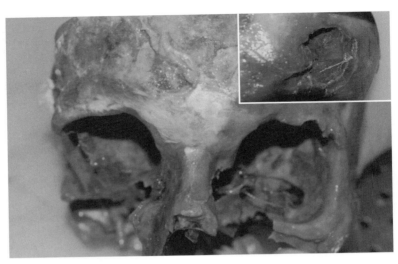

Fig. 15. Depressed fracture of the parietal bone (on the top right corner), stained because of blood leakage. This finding came from the front along the right part of the vault, together with the same staining of the scalp (Fig. 14) led to the establishment of the cause of death: a blunt trauma of the head.

formula to be collected and permits X-rays to be performed (Fig. 16). These may then be compared with antemortem records in periapical and bitewing incidences *(24)*.

Next, the pelvis should be separated from the fifth lumbar vertebrae. It may be particularly difficult to remove the head of the femur from the hip socket because of the amount of tissue and strong ligaments.

If incisions are accidentally made in the bones during this process, these should be recorded or the pathologist or anthropologist informed to avoid artifacts that could lead to the wrong conclusions.

3.3.4. WASHING AND REMOVAL OF REMAINING SOFT TISSUE

Once the bones have been disarticulated, they should be washed with care in order to allow possible lesions to be clearly seen and to avoid the addition of any artifacts (Fig. 17). This task should be carried out by everyone, using sieves, nail brushes, toothbrushes, and any other kind of cleaning equipment that might prove useful. To facilitate washing, the bones should be sorted into tubs, one for the backbone, another for each of the hands, and so forth (Fig. 18). This procedure avoids possible confusion as to which side of the body the bones come from, for example, and saves time.

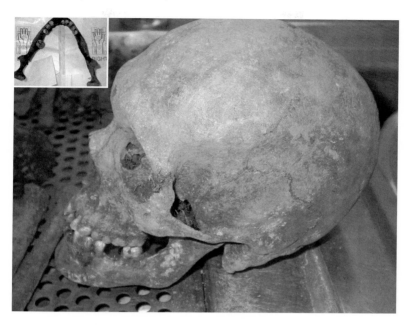

Fig. 16. The temporomandibular joint in skeletonized bodies is normally free of tissues and ligaments, turning the collection of the dental formula an easy task. On this mandible (on the top left corner), one can see that right molars and the left ones were lost antemortem, and left incisors were lost postmortem.

At this stage, there may be still some dried soft tissue clinging to the bones. To remove it, the most common procedure is to soften it in water. Care should be taken that the bones are not left too long in water (i.e., the task should be properly controlled). Afterward, any remaining soft tissue is removed with a hard brush and the fragments dried, preferably in open air, avoiding exposure to direct sunlight. An ordinary hairdryer may also be used.

When the bone fragments are very small, as happens with the skull when it has been hit with a blunt object and/or firearm, it is very important to ensure that all the pieces are recovered (Fig. 19). Conversely, if the skull is closed, then after it has been inspected and the external superficial lesions described, it should be opened with a saw in order to examine the interior (vault and basis of the skull). There may be bone splinters, teeth, metal fragments, colorings of the surface of the endocranium, and maybe even fissures on the inner table that are not reflected on the outside, as Galloway has pointed out recently *(25)*.

The body mass should also be reviewed to search for phalanges, teeth (especially single root) or small bones from the hands and feet.

Fig. 17. Washing bones is important to permit the visualization of eventual fractures, cuts, or other lesions. When under current water, it is important to not lose any element or sign, so a sieve must be used. Brushes of all types should be used, and for small bones, it is better to employ a receptacle with water.

3.3.5. Reconstruction

When the bones are dry, the next step is reconstruction, whenever this is required for the interpretation of lesions. Such a reconstruction is essential in many cases of crimes against humanity or gunshot wounds.

Fig. 18. When cleaned and washed, bones should be placed in receptacles according to their type or laterality: vertebral column, ribs, or limbs.

Special attention should be given to the skull because there are often traumatic lesions to be found in this part of the body *(18,19)*. Indeed, one can frequently learn the cause of death through the faithful reconstruction of the skull. In other words, it is often only possible to distinguish between different kinds of cranial lesions and determine their causes following reconstruction of the skull (Fig. 20).

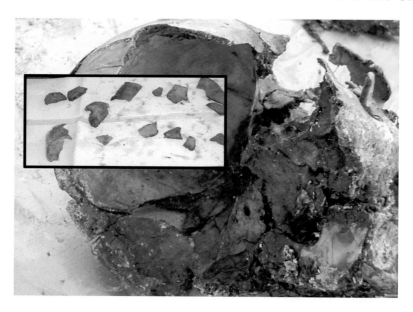

Fig. 19. Fragmented skulls must be studied very carefully as most of traumatic injuries are in the skull. It is important to recover each bone fragment in order to perform the reconstruction (*see* Fig. 21).

Some useful advice may be given at this stage: fragments should only be stuck together when it is certain they fit (whenever there is doubt, they should not be stuck). Do not stick fragments that are not properly dry; a bad reconstruction necessarily falsifies the reconstitution of the events. It also helps considerably to place the bones in sand (using a sandbox) while sticking them together (Fig. 21).

3.3.6. INDIVIDUALIZATION OF THE REMAINING BONES

When the bones have been reconstructed, an attempt should be made to attribute them to one or more individuals. Even in cases supposedly dealing with a single individual, it is not uncommon to detect an extra bone that is incompatible, indicating the presence of a second body.

This task is obviously more complicated in the case of heaps of bones, i.e., clusters of disarticulated mixed bones. This is relatively frequent in modern cemeteries when family members require the individualization of bone heaps, but it is usually possible to determine who is who in these situations (Fig. 22). However, in mass disasters, such as an airplane crash, it may become virtually impossible.

Fig. 20. The striking importance of a reconstructed skull: the hole visible on the lambda was, by the aspect of the fragments and the context, suspected to be an entrance bullet hole. Yet when glued, it was a wormian bone that was missing.

The individualization process should follow a particular order. First, adult and nonadult bones should be separated. Then, within each of these groups, the bones should be separated according to type, followed by division by laterality. The pairing of symmetrical bones should be attempted, with attention to size, hardness, and taphonomic, morphological, and pathological alterations.

3.3.7. Assembling the Skeleton

As the bones are attributed to a particular individual, the skeleton should be gradually assembled in the anatomical position (Fig. 23).

It is important to remember that duplication, even when it is only of a bone fragment, indicates the presence of another individual, which might mean that the material will need to be reanalyzed.

Particular attention should be given to the compatibility of various bone parts. There are particularly difficult situations: a typically female pelvis does not have to be associated with an absolutely feminine skull because many women have robust skulls.

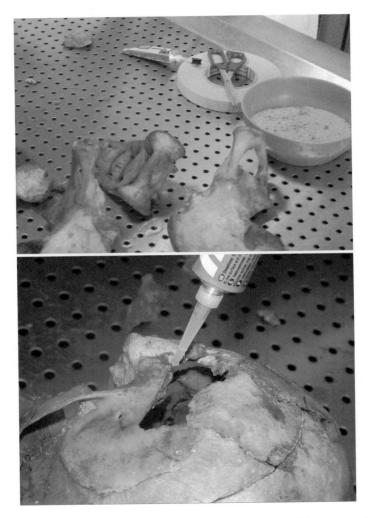

Fig. 21. Skull reconstruction: a laborious task essential for many diagnoses on human rights violation contexts. Experience, patience, and skills for solving puzzles are needed in this typical anthropological job.

As to confirming the joints, this is mostly done through a process of elimination. A femur that does not fit into a hip socket means that these bones definitely cannot be associated. However, if the femur is a little loose in a hip socket, this does not necessarily mean that the two bone pieces do not belong to the same individual. There are, however, joints that are easier to confirm,

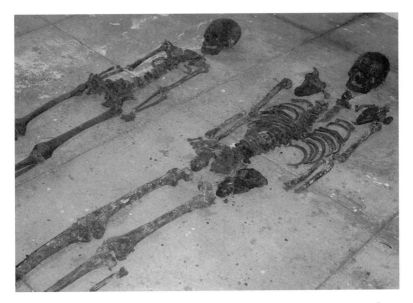

Fig. 22. Two adult skeletons have been individualized from a box containing commingling bones in a cemetery, an expertise increasingly asked of medicolegal services.

such as the temporomandibular joint. The mandibular condyles should fit relatively easily into the mandibular fosse. The atlanto-occipital joint should also not be overlooked. One should try, whenever possible, to join up the whole vertebrae, as well as the sacroiliac joints. The costovertebral joints may be impossible to reconstruct, however, or at least, it may not be worth spending too much effort for a result that yields so little information.

It is often difficult to assemble the ribs because these fragile bones decay easily; however, it should be tried as much as possible. Indeed, given the importance of the organs contained in the thoracic cavity, in the absence of any firearm wounds to the head, discrete orifices on one of the edges may indicate the entry of a bullet, thus allowing the case to be resolved (as has, in fact, happened in autopsies performed by J. Pinheiro on missions in the Balkans and Colombia [26]).

The parts of the appendicular skeleton should also be checked for consistency. Ideally, all physiological joints should be present. For example, the distal end of the fibula is always placed lower down than the corresponding distal end of the tibia.

Fig. 23. Assembling the skeleton: an anthropological task of the multi-disciplinary team.

3.3.8. INVENTORY

After the skeletons are assembled in the anatomical position, the inventory should be drawn up. This process is easier when diagrams or checklists of all bone elements are provided, which can simply be ticked off the list. It is useful to check at this stage that no mistakes have been made as to the laterality of the bones (if necessary bones can be marked). This inventory is one of the first and most important stages in the commingling analysis, where the mixing of various individuals (*see* Fig. 22) may be detected through the duplication of bones *(27)*.

All stages should be properly recorded and photographed. It is essential that the reconstruction of skeletons in the anatomical position is well documented photographically. All morphological and/or pathological peculiarities should also be recorded.

All the procedures described can be executed relatively well when the bones are well preserved. However, when they are in fragments, incomplete, or brittle, the results may be seriously compromised.

3.3.9. ANTHROPOLOGICAL EXAMINATION

This examination begins by determining the biological identity of the individual (the methodologies to achieve biological identity will not be detailed here as they will be deeply studied in other chapters of this book; *see* Chapters 9–11). The two large issues involved are determination of sex and estimation of age at death.

The identification of population affinities comes next, in which the attempt is made to distinguish at least between the three large geographic groups: Caucasian, Negroid, and Mongoloid, more recently renamed European, African, and Asiatic (*see* Chapter 12). Then comes the morphological assessment; the skeleton is scrutinized in order to estimate stature (*see* Chapter 13), strength, and laterality, based essentially on a series of anthropometric measurements.

Once the biological identity has been established, other individualization factors (morphological, pathological, and so on) are sought, which will make the skeleton into a unique observation in relation to the others.

There are cases in which a new radiological examination will have to be performed in order to (among other objectives): check the age (of nonadults), obtain a record of the frontal and maxillary sinuses, assess a fracture, and record dental formation from the jaws.

In order to safeguard a possible future facial reconstruction (among other reasons), craniometrical measurements should also be taken, or at least those that generally permit the assessment of the skull and nasal area.

Dental examination and odontogram must be done whenever possible by a forensic odontologist. However, because of the lack of these experts in many countries, both forensic anthropologists and even the pathologists must be technically prepared to do it (*see* Chapter 15).

All data should be rigorously recorded on a proper anthropological file. *If an error is made in determination of any these parameters, the unidentified body may remain unidentified forever (24).*

This is followed by the study and recording of lesions, and the respective ante-, peri-, and postmortem assessment, absolutely crucial for diagnosing cause of death (*see* Chapter 8 for more detail).

3.3.10. MULTIDISCIPLINARY INVESTIGATION:
FORENSIC AND ANTHROPOLOGICAL FINAL REPORT

After the anthropological study and the first draft of the forensic pathologist's report are completed, both specialists should get together at the table where the skeleton is laid and compare their respective finds, taking the opportunity to discuss particular fractures, bullet paths, lesions, and so forth. This is the most interesting phase for experts and is extremely stimulating. When conclusions have been reached and notes taken, each one will go ahead with the preparation of his or her respective report (normally at a later phase and in retirement). The use of body diagrams is advised, of which there are numerous versions, in addition to the photographic documentation already mentioned.

The models to be used for this report are obviously different from ordinary autopsy reports used for a fresh body. These should, however, be monitored in relation to internationally known models, such as the United Nations Minnesota Protocol *(28)* and Interpol's Disaster Victim Identification (DVI) *(29)* autopsy protocol, to ensure that they are compatible with international databases *(7)*.

The final report may take two forms. There may be two separate documents (the anthropological report and pathologist's report) or the two may be merged into one, with the conclusions concerning the essential objectives of the autopsy (signs relating to identification and cause of death) translating into a single version.

3.4. Procedures Following the Autopsy and Complementary Examinations

While the anthropologist and pathologist are undertaking their analysis and discussing results, samples should be collected for any complementary examinations that are to be carried out in addition to the radiological examinations already mentioned.

In the cases under consideration, the most important of these tests is the study of DNA polymorphisms for identification purposes. Various types of samples may be used for this, the most common being long bone fragments, molar teeth, or resistant organs such as the prostate or uterus, if these are still present. The custody chain should be respected and contamination avoided. Consider that at this moment, DNA is very overvalued, particularly by the media, as a panacea for all identifications; however, it does not dispense with the care and rigor of the classical forensic anthropological examination. This is as important as ever because there are families that do not accept positive identification without other discrimination factors, such as clothes, being consistent with DNA *(7)*. In addition, in situations where there are technical difficulties in extracting DNA from soft tissues or extremely burned bones *(30)* or commingling remains *(31)*, anthropology has a very important role to play. In the attack on the World Trade Center, DNA tests on soft tissues, if performed in isolation, would have brought problems: Budimlija et al. *(5)* describe two pelvis fragments of the same side with the same profile. Only DNA from the bone made it possible to conclude that there was contamination of the soft tissue of one pelvis with the other. This was because of the type of catastrophe and the extreme fragmentation of the remains. Unlike other disasters where each victim is identified, in this one, each human *fragment* had to be identified. Indeed, it was necessary to determine the minimum number of individuals present in each body bag. Forensic anthropologists thus had a new role: assessing the consistency of connected body parts. They reexamined 19,000 samples and found 69 to be inconsistent, which resulted in at least three new individuals *(5)*. Other authors *(32)* describe the same situation, urging the need for collaboration between geneticists and anthropologists. Similar situations, though of course on a much smaller scale, may occur after high-speed road accidents, fires in demolished buildings, or work accidents, common in daily forensic practice.

It may also be necessary to gather samples for toxicological studies, and for these, fragments of soft tissues are preferred, the less fatty the better. Hair and skin are also excellent for the search for various substances, particularly drugs and heavy metals, samples with which forensic experts today have a lot of experience *(33)*. The value of these samples is testified by their long durability, as has been proven by the vestiges of cocaine detected in the hair of 4000-yr-old mummies found in Peru *(34)*.

Samples may also be taken for use by forensic entomology, although this does not make part of the aims of this chapter. Whereas the analysis of insect and arthropod activity has little relevance on the right-hand side of our spectrum, it may be important for the establishment of the postmortem interval, to detect if the body has been moved postmortem, or determine the position of the body at the moment of death and the presence of wounds *(3)*.

With regard to clothing gathered by the SOCO (as described) they are usually covered in mud and very dirty, which means they need to be washed in order to facilitate study, description, and cataloging. This may be done immediately or at another time, usually by assistant technicians. A pressure machine, though not essential, a yard, and normal washing powder are required (Fig. 24). After a general washing, the clothes should be washed again in a household washing machine and dried for future study and recognition by the

Fig. 24. Washing clothing in a human rights abuse context: often indispensable to identification or for further analyses concerning bullet holes, tears by sharp instruments, and so on, when they are muddy, bloody, or dirty. A pressure machine can be useful for the first bulk washing.

victim's relatives (Fig. 25). If this equipment is not available, the articles should be summarily washed and dried in the autopsy room (Fig. 25).

3.5. Final Procedures

When the final reports have been completed by the forensic pathologist, they are handed over to hierarchical superiors, who will send them on to the competent authorities that have requested them: departments of justice, police, prosecutors, courts, international tribunals, and so on.

Throughout all stages of this investigation, care should be taken with ethics, to preserve the dignity and privacy of the body remains, as well as respect for human rights *(3,7)*. This should avoid the unnecessary and inadmissible problems raised by works whose aim is, precisely, to incriminate anyone who participated in or was responsible for the violation of those rights.

Data collected during the examination that relates to identification (those concerned with personal clothing and objects are the responsibility of the SOCO and may be part of an additional report) will constitute the postmortem data on that individual, destined to be compared with the antemortem records collected by police or other entities from the family, clinical records, previous X-ray examinations, hospitalizations, and so on. In some cases, these antemortem records

Fig. 25. When it is not possible to dry the clothing on the proper way, as with the picture above of a theater of crimes against humanity, one can improvise on the autopsy table (*see* clothing of the woman of Fig. 6).

may not exist at all or be very incomplete because in many regions, citizens do not have easy access to health services, and the signs described by relatives may be very imprecise. Indeed, there are cases described in the literature *(6)* of this kind of problem, with most failures occurring in the assessment of stature.

On large-scale international missions, this comparison obviously takes on another dimension, and databases have to be created with antemortem and postmortem records. These are regulated by international recommendations, such as the Minnesota Protocol and Interpol's DVI autopsy protocol *(28,29)*.

This work all takes place upstream of what has been described here, undertaken by other specialists, but that sometimes involves the participation of members of the forensic anthropology team *(9,10)*, essential for arriving at a positive identification. This strategy has been gradually perfected in mass disasters and natural catastrophes, such as the tsunami in Southeast Asia in December 2004, with the help of predefined forms well known to Interpol (DVI). As these are international and have been translated into various languages and used successfully in various events, they have enormous relevance, constituting a working tool whose great use has been recognized by all experts.

The arduous task of comparing ante- and postmortem data also has to be connected in many cases with the results of DNA tests, which may also require the collection of samples from relatives of the victims in their countries of origin.

4. CONCLUSIONS

The ideas, reflections, and procedures described here take into account the increasing need for this kind of investigation, not only on large-scale missions, as has been seen, but also in day-to-day forensic work. In this sense, it was our aim to make some practical recommendations, which could be used by any professional, irrespective of specialty, from either side of the spectrum (*see* Fig. 1).

There is, however, an urgent need to train experts to carry out these procedures and who are able to work harmoniously, with sound scientific grounding, in the complementary areas of forensic pathology and anthropology in accordance with the most modern trends verified throughout the world for these cases *(2,7,10,35)* (*see* Chapter 37). However, postgraduate training courses in the exhumation of mass graves are still in their infancy *(7)* and in 2001, none of four universities in Belgium provided training in physical anthropology, despite their established competence in mass disasters *(3)*. However, in some other countries, progress is gradually being made. In Portugal, for the last 4 yr, masters and other postgraduate courses in legal medicine open to doctors, anthropologists, police, jurists, biologists, technicians, and so on, have included a 30-h module on forensic anthropology, which follows the classic 90-h module in thanatology. In this module, the contents not only of this chapter, but also of most of this book, are taught by two coeditors of this book (and the authors of this chapter). At the University of Granada (Spain), a masters course in forensic anthropology is running for the third time, now also in a virtual, on-line format.

According to Steadman *(10)*, the efforts on the global scale will eventually endow experienced South American anthropologists with American superior academic qualifications, to which they do not have access. Inversely it would be necessary to generate opportunities for practical training and fieldwork for the academic-qualified students and staff from the United States or other parts of the world with a similar system. On the European level, there is still farther to go; however, legal medicine institutes are now functioning in various countries, as are transnational structures such as the Forensic Anthropologic Society of Europe (FASE *[35]*). Given the great appetite for the subject felt by everyone who works in the area, the future will certainly be auspicious. Indeed, as Steadman *(10)* has forecast, the present boom in such courses and the number of candidates attending them may even lead to an eventual job crisis. In the meantime, however, there is a growing need for forensics in Africa, Asia, and other parts of the world, with some urgent cases already catalogued in Iraq, where some 290,000 people are estimated to have disappeared *(8)*, providing justification for all these efforts in the area of training.

REFERENCES

1. Owslley, D. W., Ubelaker, D. H., Houck, M. M., et al. The role of forensic anthropology in the recovery and analysis of Branch Davidian Compound victims: techniques of analysis. J. Forensic Sci. 40:341–348, 1995.
2. Blewitt, G. T. The role of forensic investigations in genocide prosecutions before an international criminal tribunal. Med. Sci. Law 37:284–288, 1997.
3. Hunter, J. R., Brickley, M. B., Bourgeois, J., et al. Forensic archaeology, forensic anthropology and human rights in Europe. Sci. Justice 41:173–178, 2001.
4. Haglund, W. D. Recent mass graves, an introduction. In: Haglund, W. D., Sorg, M. H., eds., Advances in Forensic Taphonomy: Method, Theory and Archaeological Perspectives. CRC Press, Boca Raton, FL, pp. 244–259, 2002.
5. Budimlija, Z. M., Prinz, M. K., Zelson-Mundorff, A., et al. World Trade Center Human Identification Project: experiences with individual body identification cases. Croat. Med. J. 44:259–263, 2003.
6. Komar, D. Lessons from Srebrenica: the contributions and limitations of physical anthropology in identifying victims of war crimes. J. Forensic Sci. 48:713–716, 2003.
7. Skinner, M., Alempijevic, D., Djuric-Srejic, M. Guidelines for international forensic bio-archaeology monitors of mass grave exhumations. Forensic Sci. Int. 134: 81–92, 2003.
8. Stover, E., Haglund, W. D., Samuels, M. Exhumation of mass graves in Iraq: considerations for forensic investigations, humanitarian needs, and the demands of justice. JAMA 290:663–666, 2003.
9. Djuric, M. Anthropological data in individualization of skeletal remains from a forensic context in Kosovo—a case history. J. Forensic Sci. 49:1–5, 2004.
10. Steadman, D. W., Haglund, W. D. The scope of anthropological contributions to human rights investigations. J. Forensic Sci. 50:1–8, 2005.
11. Pinheiro, J., Cunha, E., Cordeiro, C., Vieira, D. N. Bridging the gap between forensic anthropology and osteoarchaeology—a case of vascular pathology. Int. J. Osteoarchaeol. 14:137–144, 2004.
12. Cunha, E., Pinheiro, J., Corte Real, F. Two Portuguese homicide cases: the importance of interdisciplinarity in forensic anthropology. ERES (Arqueología y Bioantropología) 13:66–72, 2005.

13. Cunha, E., Pinheiro, J., Ribeiro, I. P., Soares, J., Vieira, D. N. Severe traumatic injuries: report of a complex multiple homicide case. Forensic Sci. Int. 136:S164–S165, 2003.
14. Symes, S. A., Woytash, J. J., Kroman, A. M., Wilson, A. C. Perimortem bone fracture distinguished from postmortem fire trauma: a case study with mixed signals. Proceedings of the 54th American Academy of Forensic Sciences, Vol. 11. New Orleans, LA, pp. 288–289, 2005.
15. Pinheiro, J., Cunha, E., Cattaneo, C., Corte Real, F. Forensic anthropologist and forensic pathologist: why work together? Some illustrative cases of homicide. Proceedings of the 54th American Academy of Forensic Sciences, Vol. 11. New Orleans, LA, pp. 301, 2005.
16. Saul, F. P., Saul, J. M., Symes, S. A. The lady in the box. Proceedings of the 54th American Academy of Forensic Sciences, Vol. 11. New Orleans, LA, pp. 300, 2005.
17. Verano, J. Serial murder with dismemberment of victims in an attempt to hinder identification: a case resolved trough multidisciplinary collaboration. Proceedings of the 54th American Academy of Forensic Sciences, Vol. 11. New Orleans, LA, pp. 329, 2005.
18. Knight, B. Forensic Pathology, 2nd Ed. Arnold, London, pp. 1–47; 171–213, 1996.
19. Saukko, P., Knight, B. Knight's Forensic Pathology, 3rd Ed. Arnold, London, pp. 1–52; 174–222, 2004.
20. Pinheiro, J., Vieira, D., Silva, B. S., Antunes, I. Prevenção da transmissão da SIDA e da Hepatite B na investigação médico-legal [in Portuguese]. Arq. Med. 6:79–84, 1992.
21. Galloway, A., Snodgrass, J. J. Biological and chemical hazards of forensic skeletal analysis. J. Forensic Sci. 43:940–948, 1998.
22. Dirkmaat, D. C., Cabo, L. M., Adovasio, J. M. Mass graves, human rights and commingled remains: considering the benefits of forensic archaeology. Proceedings of the 54th American Academy of Forensic Sciences, Vol. 11. New Orleans, LA, pp. 316, 2005.
23. Byers, S. Introduction to Forensic Anthropology. Allyn & Bacon, Boston, MA, pp. 122–149, 2002.
24. Di Maio, V., Dana, S. E. Handbook of Forensic Pathology. Landes Bioscience, Austin, TX, pp. 27–34, 1998.
25. Galloway, A., Zephro, L. Internal cranial fractures. Proceedings of the 54th American Academy of Forensic Sciences, Vol. 11. New Orleans, LA, pp. 288, 2005.
26. Equipo Argentino de Antropologia Forense, Annual Report, 2001. Available at www.eaaf.org/reports/AR2001/07COLOMBIA.PDF. Last accessed on December 19, 2005.
27. Ubelaker, D. H. Advances in the assessment of commingling within samples of human remains. Proceedings of the 54th American Academy of Forensic Sciences, Vol. 11. New Orleans, LA, pp. 317, 2005.
28. UN manual on the effective prevention and investigation of extra-legal arbitrary and summary executions (Minnesota Protocol), United Nations, UN pub. sales no. E.91.IV.1 (doc.ST/CSDHA/12), 1991.

29. Interpol Disaster Victim Identification (DVI) autopsy protocol. Forensic page, Interpol. Available via www.INTERPOL.int/Public/Forensic. Last accessed on December 19, 2005.
30. Kaye, M., Pope, E. J., Cipriano, F., Smith, O'B. C. An experimental test of the accuracy of human forensic identification techniques for analysis of burn-damaged bone and tissue. Proceedings of the 54th American Academy of Forensic Sciences, Vol. 11. New Orleans, LA, pp. 308–309, 2005.
31. Yazedjian, L. N., Kesetovic, R., Boza-Arlotti, A., Karan Z. The importance of using traditional anthropological methods in a DNA-led identification system. Proceedings of the 54th American Academy of Forensic Sciences, Vol. 11. New Orleans, LA, pp. 312–313, 2005.
32. Mundorf, A. Z., Shaler, R., Bieschke, E. T., Mar, E. Marrying of anthropology and DNA: essential for solving complex commingling problems in cases of extreme fragmentation. Proceedings of the 54th American Academy of Forensic Sciences, Vol. 11. New Orleans, LA, pp. 315–316, 2005.
33. Pinheiro, J. O consumo, detecção e vigilância de drogas ilícitas em meio laboral: estudo analítico em amostras de cabelo [in Portuguese]. Dissertação de Mestrado, Coimbra, pp. 114–134, 1996.
34. Welch, M. J., Sniegoski, L. T., Allgood, C. C., Habram, M. Hair analysis for drugs of abuse: evaluation of analytical methods, environmental issues and development of reference materials. J. Anal. Toxicol. 17:389–398, 1993.
35. Cattaneo, C., Baccino, E. A call for forensic anthropology in Europe. Int. J. Legal Med. 116:N1–N2, 2002.

Chapter 8

Identification and Differential Diagnosis of Traumatic Lesions of the Skeleton

Conrado Rodríguez-Martín

Summary

The relationship between forensic anthropology and dry skeletal pathology has been a very useful tool in the investigation of violence, especially in a political context, and human rights violations. The interdisciplinary work between forensic anthropologists and osteopathologists is vital because the autopsy of an individual who died under arrest or other "unclear" circumstances is one of the most problematic tasks in legal medicine. To perform this type of research, it is necessary to adapt, in some way, to the *Manual on Effective Investigation and Documentation of Torture and Other Cruel, Inhuman or Degrading Treatment and Punishment*—the Istanbul Protocol (1999) and in some cases, to the *UN Manual of the Effective Prevention and Investigation of Extra-Legal, Arbitrary and Summary Executions* (1991).

There are different methods employed to kill an individual or to produce suffering: beatings of every possible type, crushing trauma, mechanical asphyxia, stretching suspension, and positional torture, gunshot wounds, sharp wounds, and electric shock. These methods produce different types of lesions, but the problem is that they are not specific. Different lesions may be caused by the same method, and several methods may produce the same lesion. This chapter deals with the identification and differential diagnosis of all these lesions (fractures, traumatic bone avulsion, dislocations, myositis ossificans traumatica, localized subperiosteal thickenings, lesions produced by sharp instruments including amputation, and gunshots), insisting on the "timing" of the lesions.

Key Words: Skeleton; trauma; identification; pathology; violence; torture; human rights violation; murder; punishment; investigation protocols.

From *Forensic Anthropology and Medicine:*
Complementary Sciences From Recovery to Cause of Death
Edited by: A. Schmitt, E. Cunha, and J. Pinheiro © Humana Press Inc., Totowa, NJ

1. Introduction

Skeletal pathology analysis in a forensic anthropological context, especially in those cases in which human rights violation is suspected, is a new, promising, and fundamental field for the elucidation, when possible, of the cause and manner of death, the traumatic events before death, and in some cases—when compared with antemortem medical and radiological records—for helping in the positive identification of the victim.

Dry skeletal pathology has experienced a great development in the last three decades because of the true "boom" of paleopathology (the study of disease in individuals and populations of the past, of every age) that has produced a huge number of papers dealing with most of the skeletal conditions observable on dry bone and several general works covering the whole subject (i.e., refs. *1–5*).

The relationship between forensic anthropology and dry skeletal pathology has been a very useful tool in the investigations of human rights violations that occurred in Latin America from the 1970s until the 1980s to 1990s, which coincide with insurgent or revolutionary movements and the arrival of military dictatorships in most of those countries. This leads to the tragic situation of the "missings," most of them buried in clandestine cemeteries after they were tortured during the period of arrest and killed in extralegal, arbitrary, and summary executions. This has occurred in different regions of Europe, the Balkans, or the countries of the former Soviet Union, and, of course, in other regions of the world as well.

These comments are enough to demonstrate that the interdisciplinary work between forensic anthropologists and osteopathologists (*see* Chapters 3, 5, and 7) is vital because it is clear that the autopsy of an individual who died under arrest, especially if illegal, is one of the most problematic and complicated tasks that can happen in legal medicine *(6)*.

2. Standards for the Investigation of Trauma in Dry Skeletal Tissue

The analysis of trauma on dry skeletal tissue has been performed in the past years according to the experience and routine of the experts dealing with different cases. However, in the author's experience and especially in those cases related to human rights violations, it is much better to adapt the study of traumatic lesions in the skeleton to the recommendations given by The *Manual on Effective Investigation and Documentation of Torture and Other Cruel, Inhuman or Degrading Treatment and Punishment*—the Istanbul Protocol *(7)* and, in some instances, to the *UN Manual on the Effective Prevention and Investigation Of Extra-Legal, Arbitrary and Summary Executions, (8)* mainly to the sections III ("Model Protocol for a Legal Investigation of Extra-Legal Arbitrary And Summary Executions" [the Minnesota Protocol]), IV ("Model Autopsy Protocol"), and V ("Model Protocol for Disinterment and Analysis of Skeletal Remains").* The Istanbul Protocol (1999) was not created specifically for skeletal tissue or even for dealing with corpses. It was written for other kinds of evidence and offers different recommendations for the investigation of possible cases of human rights violation, mostly for living persons. However, it is very useful for the study of suspected human rights violations and other types of violence showing stigmata on dry bone, and even for routine cases of forensic anthropology in which a violent, traumatic death is suspected. In summary, the most important of these recommendations regarding skeletal trauma include the following:

1. The experts must avoid speculation.
2. It is necessary to take into account the variability of the lesions, depending on age, sex, previous health, and nutritional status, and the severity of the lesion itself.
3. All lesions must be recorded and described according to their topography, detailing their size, shape, severity, and degree of healing and recovery (if they exist). For sure, all the lesions observed on the skeletal tissue, as occurs in all autopsies, have to be numbered.
4. The whole body has to be observed in detail.
5. It is essential to bear in mind the different methods of maltreatment, punishment, torture, and, finally, homicide used in the region in which the events took place (Table 1).

These recommendations can be complemented with those of Saul *(9)* for cases of suspected violent deaths that include the following:

1. Damage to the bone tissue has to be avoided during the cleaning process.
2. The whole skeleton has to be carefully examined because every bone can show lesions (this point agrees with the point 3 above).
3. Magnified observation of the lesions (with lenses of ×4 or ×10) is very useful for elucidating the degree of healing that is important for the timing of events before death.
4. The skeleton has to be placed in the correct anatomical position when examined because this helps to determine the type of lesion, its chronology, and the weapon or tool used to produce trauma.

---

* The goal of this paper does not focus on explaining all these procedures, and for those interested, additional information can be found through the "References" list and in Chapter 17.

Table 1
Lesions Related to Several Methods of Punishment or Torture

Method	Lesions
Beatings	Fracture, myositis ossificans traumatica, subperiosteal thickening, dislocation
Crushing trauma	Fracture
Mechanical asphyxia	Bone avulsion, hyoid, and calcified cartilages fracture
Stretching, suspension, and positional torture	Dislocation, traumatic bone avulsion
Gunshot wounds	Fracture, penetrating wound
Sharp instruments	Sharp bone section, penetrating wound
Electric shock	Bone avulsion, dislocation

5. The hyoid bone and calcified cartilages of the neck region must be analyzed in order to check possible cases of mechanical asphyxia (homicidal, suicidal, or accidental).
6. Defense fractures in the forearm may be present.
7. Fragments of bullets or other metallic objects may be embedded in the bone.
8. Blood signs inside the lesion or in its surrounding tissues indicate that it was inflicted antemortem.

The same author *(9)* also provides other general considerations that are important to take in account when dealing with trauma on dry skeletal tissue: more than one weapon could produce death or suffering to the victim, more than one part of the weapon could be used, and an ordinary object may be used in an extraordinary manner.

In addition to the recommendations given in the previous list, there are other routine methods to perform this type of investigation *(10)* including the following:

1. Interviews with witnesses, perpetrators, collaborators, fellows, relatives, and/or friends.
2. All the existing information has to be examined.
3. Collection of all medical and dental records of the victim (when they exist) has to be performed in order to check if the observed pathology must be dated before or after death. In the last case, this may be helpful for the identification.
4. Skeletal and dental radiographs shall be taken for identification purposes, diagnosis of the lesions, and comparison with antemortem records. Microscopy may also be needed in a few cases.

3. METHODS PRODUCING TRAUMA IN THE SKELETAL TISSUE

Independent of the context in which one deals (human rights violation investigation, violations to the humanitarian international right, or common cases of homicide or suicide), the methods used by the perpetrators to kill the victim or to produce suffering can be divided into categories given here (of course, the author is only referring to trauma observed in dry skeletal tissue):

1. Beatings of every possible type, with every possible weapon or tool, and in every possible anatomical place.
2. Crushing trauma in the head, fingers, or toes, produced with blows (masses, hammers, stones, bars).
3. Mechanical asphyxia: hanging, strangulation, "wet submarine" (head under water), or "dry submarine" (head inside a sack, a bag, or a tight mask).
4. Stretching, suspension, and positional torture.
5. Gunshot wounds.
6. Sharp wounds, including amputation, mutilation, or disfiguration.
7. Electric shock.

All these methods produce different types of lesions. However, it is important to emphasize that the specificity of these lesions is not ideal, meaning that different lesions may be produced by the same method, and several methods may produce the same lesion. This overlap of manifestations at the level of the dry skeletal tissue is clearly shown in Table 1.

4. PATHOLOGY OF SKELETAL TRAUMA

Besides the intrinsic importance of a correct diagnosis of the lesions, another important point is to know the chronology of the traumatic event, because the steps of the healing process provide key data to elucidate the length of survival of the victim after being injured. The time of recovery of a lesion can be determined in dry skeletal tissue; however, there may be problems that must be borne in mind:

1. There may be lesions that do not show recovery—the individual died because of the trauma or he or she survived a short time. This last case may also be complicated by the fact that the victim could have died as a result of other types of injury produced about the same time. This is the case of the so-called perimortem lesions.
2. The old Greek medical principle of "there are no diseases but sick persons" may be applied here, meaning that the time of recovery of a lesion varies depending of several factors: age (even sex), general health status, nutritional status, possibility of medical treatment at the time of the trauma, and so on.

4.1. Fractures

From a clinical and pathological point of view, a fracture is the interruption of the structural continuity of the bone and may be only a fissure, a cortical break, or a complete fracture. In normal conditions, bone is rather elastic and resistant to external forces. Therefore, to produce a bone fracture, it is necessary that one of the following three conditions has to be present *(11)*:

1. A single traumatic event. Traumatic fractures because of different types of sudden and excessive force that can work according to several mechanisms.
2. Repeated stress. Stress fractures because of minor trauma repeated on a bone or group of bones.
3. Abnormal weakening of the bone. Pathological fractures because of diseases like osteoporosis, some type of bone tumors, rickets, and so on.

However, when dealing with cadavers, it is essential that these fractures can be related to the moment of death in order to evaluate the role they played in the case's story. From this forensic point of view, fractures can be classified in three different types:

1. Antemortem fractures occurring before death showing bone reaction to form the callus.
2. Perimortem fractures or fractures occurring near the time of death.
3. Postmortem breakage because of the circumstances of the burial or bad archaeological or conservational techniques.

The last two types are difficult to distinguish because of lack of bone reaction, but there are several criteria that may help:

1. The topography of the lesion has to be taken into account (i.e., there are fractures that can determine the death of the victim because of their locations, whereas there are others, even more severe, that are not fatal because they do not involve vital structures). There are femoral fractures tearing the femoral artery that may lead the individual to die because of fatal hemorrhage, whereas even more severe fractures, from an orthopedic point of view, of the same bone may only produce long-term or permanent physical disablement (when they involve the condyle, for example). The author had a case where the unique lesion found was a traumatic injury of the shoulder with a clavicle fracture. It could be said that such a fracture can never be considered a cause of death. But in this case, because it had torn the subclavian artery, the fracture became lethal.
2. The margins of the lesion have to be carefully analyzed because the first evidence of healing should appear there, showing a smooth and rounded reaction observable under dissecting microscope. However, it has to be noted that this does not occur until after 1 wk.

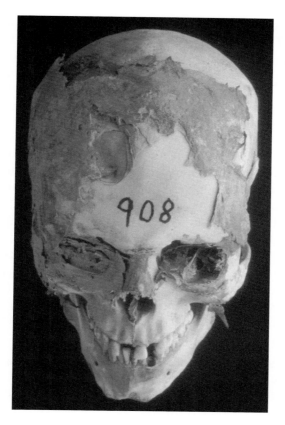

Fig. 1. Perimortem cranial fracture on the right part of the frontal bone. The fragments are in the anatomical position.

3. Color differences in the bones of the skeleton are useful as well. Bone fragments in perimortem fractures usually show the same patina between the margins of the lesion and the rest of the bone. Meanwhile, there are changes in color in cases of postmortem fractures, especially when the break occurs a long time after burial.
4. Small fragments of bone attached to the fracture margins indicate that it was produced when the periosteum and other soft tissues were still present, and this points to perimortem trauma *(2)*.
5. Perimortem cranial fractures (Fig. 1) usually show the fragments in the anatomical position because of the presence of cephalic tissue and soft tissue of the skull, whereas the same energy could cause complete crushing of a dry skull. However, bone elasticity can last for several weeks after death, and this may produce mistakes in the diagnosis.

Every type of fracture (transverse, oblique, spiroidal, comminute, crushing injuries, and the like), in every possible topographical location, may be found during the examination of the skeleton in a forensic context. However, there are fractures that show more interest in the forensic analysis of traumatic lesions, especially in suspected cases of human rights violation. Briefly, and in a topographical order, these fractures are presented here.

4.1.1. HEAD AND FACE

Two regions of the head may be involved, vault and base. The cranial vault may show depressed fractures, linear fractures, and sharp or penetrating wounds. It is important to emphasize that there is no strict relationship between the size of the fracture and the degree of encephalic damage. Also, as there is no relationship between fractures and the energy producing them (the fact that the scalp and hair absorb some of the energy that potentially can produce a cranial fracture has been taken into account). Stewart (12) points out that, in general, low-speed injuries involve a wide area, producing linear fractures, whereas high-speed trauma is responsible for smaller, depressed fractures.

In the author's experience, the radiographic patterns given by Lacroix (13) are useful for elucidating the length of survival in cases of traumatic cranial substance's loss:

1. A radiographic shadow, few millimeters wide, implies a short survival (few weeks).
2. Radiographic densities of around 10 mm indicate few months' survival.
3. Bone rarefaction around the margins of the lesion suggests survival of more than 1 yr.

Regarding fractures of the newborn skull, it is necessary to emphasize that in cases of suspected infanticide, it is necessary to make a differential diagnosis of birth injury or accidental trauma (14). This is always a difficult task, especially in a forensic anthropological context in which one deals with dry bones lacking scalp, brain, and hemorrhage signs that are vital for a research of this type.

Facial fractures are divided depending on the region in which they appear:

1. Upper facial third. These fractures are very similar to those of the vault and, in many cases, the eyes are involved as well.
2. Mid-facial third. Fractures here are the result of direct blows to the face and may involve nasal bones (the most common fractures in this area), malar bone (uncommon), zygoma, and maxilla. Maxillary fractures have been subdivided in the three types by Le Fort (Fig. 2).
   a. Type I. Fracture line separates the upper dental arch from the rest of the face, crossing the pterigoides.

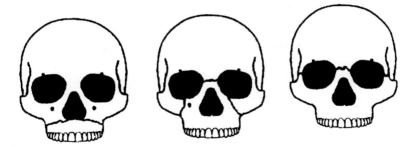

Fig. 2. (From left to right) Type I fracture line separates the upper dental arch from the rest of the face. Type II fracture line involves the maxilla and extends to the nasal bones. Type III transverse fracture line separating face and vault.

    b. Type II. Involves the maxilla and extends through the nasal bones, crossing the orbit and the orbit's margin.

    c. Type III. The line is transverse and high, producing a separation between vault and face. These lesions are often not isolated but associated with each other. Damage to the maxillary sinus, the orbital roof, or the dental arch is a common finding.

3. Mandible. Direct trauma produces fractures involving mostly the neck, body, and angle, which in 64% of the cases are bilateral *(15)*.

4.1.2. NECK

One has to focus on the fractures of the hyoid bone and the calcified cartilages (thyroid and cricoid) that usually result from mechanical methods of asphyxia, hanging and strangulation. In the latter method, the hyoid bone is sometimes broken *(12)*. Attention must be paid to the cervical vertebrae that may be affected too (the odontoid process of the axis may be broken in cases of hanging).

4.1.3. TRUNK

Ribs are the most commonly involved structures and, less commonly, the sternum and vertebrae.

Rib fractures may be single or multiple, and they are located between the 2nd and the 10th ribs at the level of the angle *(16)*. Single fractures are usually caused by direct blows, whereas multiple fractures appear because of violent trauma produced by a large object or by compression on the rib cage (i.e., the "turtle method of torture"). Two complications may appear in multiple fractures, visceral lesions (liver, spleen, kidney, digestive system) and the so-called flail chest that is responsible for "paradoxical breath," causing severe respiratory distress *(17)*.

Sternal fractures are caused by direct blows or forced, violent, flexion of the spine (as occurs in traffic accidents) and usually are accompanied by rib fractures. Not infrequently, damage to the viscera is observed *(18)*.

In general, spinal fractures are produced by hyperflexion, hyperextension, and compression, showing involvement of the vertebral bodies, and they may involve or not the spinal cord and the spinal nerves. However, in the context of human rights violation and violations of the humanitarian international right, vertebral fractures of interest are those produced by direct violence (like beatings) or indirect violence (like electric shock), showing partial fractures involving apophyses (the most common fractures at this level), posterior vertebral elements (spinous and lateral apophyses and vertebral arches) (uncommon), and the axial odontoid (in cases of hanging and even electric shock) *(10)*.

4.1.4. Appendicular Skeleton

Although all types of fractures (90% resulting from direct blows) can be observed during the forensic examination of the dry skeleton, the most interesting—especially in the context of human rights violations—are those involving hands and feet, because of the very extended practice of the "falaka" or "falanga" (repeated beatings on the sole or the palm). Metatarsals are the most commonly involved bones, although the phalanges and the tarsal bones may be injured too. Open fractures are common in the feet, and especially those involving the fingers. At the level of the hand, carpal bones are uncommonly affected.

Regarding fractures of other bones of the appendicular skeleton, it is interesting to note here that pelvic and long bone fractures are rather usual in cases of human rights violations in the Balkans, mostly by firearms injuries (J. Pinheiro, personal communication). With the exception of gunshot wounds in the limbs, the real nature of these fractures are not well known, although blows or even forced falls (as it occurs in some other parts of the world) have been speculated.

One of the most typical fractures observed in the upper limbs is the so-called defense fracture in the forearm bones that is often a parry fracture occurring when the victim tends to fend off an attack by another person *(5)*, and it usually involves the ulna, suggesting interpersonal violence. Fractures of the clavicle, humerus, and especially of the lower third of the radius (Colles fracture) are produced most commonly by accidents. Fractures of the lower limbs are less commonly observed in interpersonal violence, although direct blows on the limbs may fracture the bones of the leg (tibia and fibula; femoral fractures are uncommon in this context).

Pelvic fractures can be divided in different types depending of the site and degree of damage *(19)*:

1. Fractures that do not disrupt the pelvic ring (type I, including pubis or ischium, iliac wing, sacrum and coccyx, and accounting for almost one-third of all pelvic fractures).
2. Fractures with single breaks of the pelvic ring (type 2: fractures of two ipsilateral rami, symphysis pubis, and sacroiliac joint).
3. Fractures with double breaks of the pelvic ring (type 3: straddle fractures, Malpaigne fractures, and multiple fractures).
4. Acetabular fractures with or without displacement (type 4).

The most common causes of pelvic fractures according to clinical statistics are traffic and work accidents (falls) *(20)*. The importance of pelvic fractures is linked to the fact that this structure is closely related to vital internal organs, and the lesions itself may lead to important secondary complications like lesions of the urinary system and nerves or hemorrhages that sometimes can lead, solely, to the victim's death.

4.1.5. FRACTURE REPAIR

In order to get an idea of the chronology of the traumatic event, it is convenient to summarize here the stages of fracture repair:

1. Inflammatory stage. It is divided in two subphases, the hematoma phase occurring immediately after the fracture and the cellular phase, when the hematoma becomes organized (granulation tissue is noted during the interval between a few hours after the fracture and about the third day, or even before). No signs are observable in dry skeletal tissue.
2. Reparative stage. A fibrous callus (Fig. 3) is completed by the third week and fibroblasts, chondroblasts, and osteoblasts, along with vasculogenesis, take part in its formation. Fracture margins that show some osteogenic reaction with some spiculae and small pieces of bone attached to the fracture's margins are observed in the dry bone, and this is important from a forensic point of view because it means that the individual survived for a short time after trauma. Callus calcification (calcium comes from the fracture's margins) begins after the third week. This process takes months, and its length depends of the type of bone, health, and nutritional status, and other factors that will not be mentioned here.
3. Remodeling of the bone is the slowest stage and may last for many months and even years. When remodeling is completed, it is impossible to assess when the fracture happened.

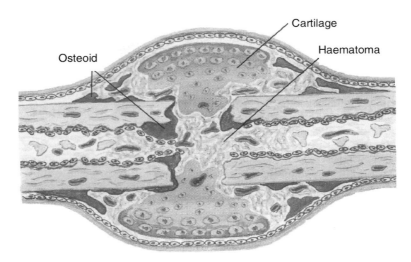

Fig. 3. Fibrous callus is completed by the third week and fibroblasts, chondroblasts, and osteoblasts (plus vasculoneogenesis) take part in its formation. Callus calcification begins after the third week.

4.1.6. Fracture Complications

It is important to emphasize that in a forensic osteological context, especially when dealing with possible cases of human rights violation, several possible fracture complications may be observed, usually because of lack of treatment and the poor living conditions of the victim.

Pseudoarthrosis is a lack of fusion of the fracture fragments. This is usually because of a lack of immobility, indicating bad or absent treatment, which is important in the context of human rights violation. Differential diagnosis with amputations may be needed. Amputation involves absence of the distal fragment of the limb (*see* Subheading 4.5.), and pseudoarthrosis reveals rounded ends with some cupping and marked radiographic sclerosis, whereas amputation does not demonstrate these changes (Fig. 4).

Poor alignment of the fragments produced by lack of reduction and immobility is also important in the osteopathological analysis of human rights violation.

Osteomyelitis in open or compound fractures is caused by lack of surgical treatment or antibiotic therapy. Differential diagnosis with severe degenerative joint disease has to be considered, and Morse *(21)* suggests that the presence of a fracture line in the involved bone and lack of bilateral asymmetry may be helpful.

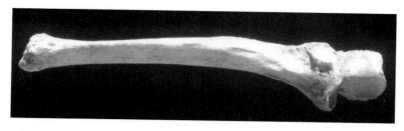

Fig. 4. Pseudoarthrosis (lack of fusion of the fracture fragments) of the ulna. Differential diagnosis with amputation is needed when one of the fragments is absent.

Secondary degenerative joint disease (osteoarthritis) is the result of incongruence of the joint surfaces or direct injury to the joint surfaces, leading, in some cases, to bony ankylosis *(3)*.

Bone necrosis because of insufficient blood supply may occur near bone ends, and it frequently leads to degenerative joint disease or pseudoarthrosis.

Posttraumatic osteodystrophy (Sudeck's atrophy) occurs in the limb bones (mostly in the hand) as a mottled osteoporosis, visible in the radiographs. It usually appears 2 mo after the injury and may persist for life. The usual cause is lack of treatment.

Posttraumatic osteoporosis. Differential diagnosis with Sudeck's atrophy may be needed, although posttraumatic osteoporosis involves the entire limb, not only a bone as is noted in Sudeck's atrophy.

4.2. Traumatic Avulsion

This lesion is also known in orthopedics as a traction or tension fracture and, indeed, it is a type of fracture produced by a violent and sudden muscular contraction detaching or tearing a fragment of bone in the area of tendon attachment *(3)*. However, in the context of forensic osteopathology, the author prefers to separate the condition from the rest of the fractures because its mechanism of production responds to specific methods of maltreatment or torture. In the author's experience, traumatic bone avulsion may be produced by suspensions, extremely forced positions, but especially by electric shock.

The lesion is observed as a small defect, several millimeters deep, rounded or oval in shape, and showing some trabeculae at the bottom of the lesion in the areas of muscle attachment to the bone. Obviously, recent lesions (weeks or months) are more clearly noted than the older ones, although there will always be signs of their presence. The most common location in the context of human rights violation is that of the upper humerus and it is usually produced

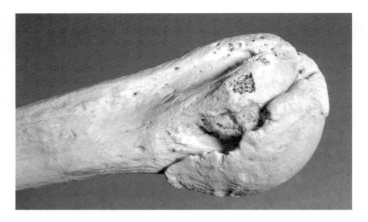

Fig. 5. Shoulder's dislocation showing important new bone formation, indicating lack of treatment (reduction and immobilization) and improper matching of joint surfaces.

by electric shock because of violent and sudden muscular contraction or by suspension *(10).*

Differential diagnosis with osteochondritis dissecans is sometimes required. However, the latter condition always involves the joint surface, whereas traumatic bone avulsion is restricted to areas of muscular attachment.

4.3. Dislocations

Dislocations are important injuries in the context of human rights violation more than in other types of crimes. They are of interest because they are caused by torture methods like electric shock (especially when repeated because this impairs the strength of the joint capsule) and, less commonly, direct blows, rotation mechanisms, or mechanical asphyxia (dry submarine).

The only way to detect dislocations in dry skeletal tissue is when orthopedic treatment (reduction) is absent—a very common fact in the context of human rights violation. This lack of treatment causes the joint surfaces to match improperly, leading to several skeletal changes after a period of approx 6 mo. These changes include degenerative joint disease, new bone formation in the joint surface, and production of false or secondary joints because of the compression of the articular surfaces of the bone on other bone (Fig. 5). All these changes may be accompanied by complications like avascular or aseptic necrosis, bone atrophy secondary to immobility, and infection in cases of open dislocation *(3,5).*

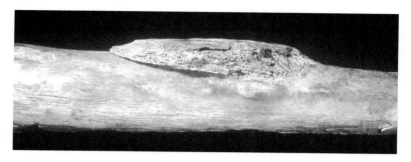

Fig. 6. Myositis ossificans traumatica. Woven bone is observed under the older layers of bone (centripetal ossification). (Photograph courtesy of Dr. Miguel Botella.)

Differential diagnosis needs to include severe degenerative joint disease, but in the latter condition, false joints are never present.

4.4. Myositis Ossificans Traumatica and Localized Subperiosteal Thickenings

This is a reactive lesion located in the soft tissues, especially muscles (localized myositis ossificans), or adjacent to the periosteum (periosteal myositis ossificans), resulting from direct blows or tendinous or muscular avulsion, leading to hematoma formation that becomes first calcified and then ossified in a centripetal manner, with the older layers of bone in the periphery and the soft, new bone in the central part of the lesion. Although ossification may begin as early as 7–10 d, the normal pattern is around 3–4 wk after trauma *(22)*, being visible around the 6th to 8th week, although the whole mass will not be mature for 3–6 mo (Fig. 6).

Differentiation must be performed between this condition and those like myositis ossificans progressiva, osteochondroma, and osteosarcoma. Myositis ossificans progressiva affects children, showing ossification of tendons, muscles, ligaments, and aponeuroses. It is a generalized disease that usually is accompanied by congenital malformations (microdactyly, carpal blocks, spina bifida, and so on), and death occurs by the second decade of life *(3)*. Osteochondroma is usually smaller and perpendicular to the diaphyseal plane, contains a rounded cap, and shows a common medullary cavity with the rest of the bone. Osteosarcoma usually shows the typical "sunburst" pattern. The context is always useful for the differential diagnosis.

Localized subperiosteal thickenings or calcified subperiosteal hematoma (also known as "localized traumatic periostitis," a confusing term) appear as a mass of new bone on the external surface of the bone diaphysis. These lesions have a similar morphological pattern and almost a common origin with myositis ossificans traumatica. Some authors have stated that both conditions are actually the same. However, the period of calcification is shorter in this case, around 2 mo (23).

Differential diagnosis with infectious periostitis has to be performed, although this last condition shows involvement of the entire bone. Another condition showing subperiosteal hematoma is chronic scurvy, but this feature is mainly observed in children as a generalized condition.

4.5. Lesions Produced by Sharp Instruments or Amputations

According to DiMaio and DiMaio (24), most deaths caused by these instruments are homicides, although suicides and, much less commonly, accidents are also observed. In their opinion, suicidal wounds vary in size and depth with usually only one or two final wounds, whereas in homicides, multiple, scattered, and deep lesions are found, mostly in the chest and abdomen and more infrequently in the head, neck, and spine.

These authors state that there are some requirements for inflicting fatal wounds: the condition of the knife, the resistance to penetration of the different tissues, the length and depth of the wound, and the amount of clothes and their composition. Most authors agree that these lesions are divided into the following types:

1. Penetrating wounds (stab wounds). These are produced by pointed weapons and may be sharp or blunt (14). They are characterized by a perforating, often conical, puncture showing a circular or ellipsoidal section (although sometimes may be linear or irregular) whose smooth, sharply defined edge is useful for differential diagnosis with postmortem erosions. The lesion is deeper than longer. The involvement of the skeletal tissue is possible, especially in areas like the head, chest, or back.
2. Wounds by sharp weapons or instruments (incised wounds). The lesion is linear or spindle-shaped and shows a triangular, V-shaped section or groove. Attention must be paid because there is a tendency of bone elasticity to partially close the wound after the weapon is withdrawn (25). It is longer than deeper. It is important to emphasize that most of these wounds do not produce marks on the skeletal tissue, and it is necessary to apply a large amount of force to create such marks; however, in some cases (wounds on the neck, head, chest, or back) the bones may be involved in some degree.
3. Wounds by heavy instruments with a cutting edge (chop wounds). Axes, jungle knives, and machetes produce incised wounds with underlying fractures or grooves in the bones. The shape of the lesion is usually irregular. Almost all of these lesions produce skeletal changes.
4. Mixed wounds because of blunt, sharp tools.

All of these lesions may be located on any part of the body. However, with regard to the context of human rights violation and violations to the humanitarian international right, the typical areas are the bones of the upper limbs (humerus, ulna, and radius) and those of the face and trunk. It is important to emphasize that the pattern of the lesion will always depend of the angle of attack *(24,26)*.

When dealing with these wounds, it is useful to follow the Sauer's protocol *(27)* as follows in order to asses their origin and to check if the individual survived to the traumatic event, even shortly:

1. Checking if bone tissue formation is present; a magnifying lens is useful for this task.
2. Radiographs of the injured bones are important to check if any bone reaction and metallic particles exist in the injured area.
3. Differential diagnosis between these lesions and those caused by compression have to be considered.
4. Examination of the color of the whole bone surface is crucial to exclude or implicate the effects of water and environment of the burial.
5. Analysis of the whole skeleton to exclude signs of animal activity mimicking skeletal lesions is very important too.

Regarding intentional amputation, it is well known that it has been practiced in some regions of the planet as a method of torture or punishment for a long time. The problem in analyzing amputated bones, both in the osteoarchaeological and forensic osteopathological contexts, lies in the differential diagnosis between intentional and accidental amputations, where the context is always very useful. Differentiation between amputation produced about the time of death and postmortem broken bones may be a difficult task. The edges of the amputated bone are always more clearly defined. Differential diagnoses between amputated bones and pseudoarthrosis when bone fragments are missing have to be made too (*see* discussion on pseudoarthrosis under Subheading 4.1.6.).

According to Steinbock *(1)*, bone reaction is observed after 1 wk; therefore, before that period, it would be impossible to make an accurate diagnosis. In this case, examination under a dissecting microscope of the sectioned surface may be of value *(28)*.

Aufderheide and Rodríguez-Martín *(3)* point out the following criteria for a chronological diagnosis of amputation:

1. Less than 1 wk after trauma: no vital signs appear.
2. Between 1 and 2 wk: vascular erosion is noted in the injured area.
3. Around 14 d: an endosteal callus begins to appear in the margins of the bone.
4. Several weeks–several months: narrowing and final obliteration of the medullary cavity leaves a soft and rounded end of the amputated bone that is easily observed.

5. Several years after trauma: osteoporosis and bone atrophy along with a lesser size in the amputated limb (because of disuse) are the most common findings.

4.6. Firearm Lesions (Gunshot Wounds)

There are two classical types of firearm lesions, those caused by bullets and those caused by pellets. However, it is interesting to include here certain lesions produced by explosions.

4.6.1. LESIONS PRODUCED BY BULLETS

Wounds produced by bullets show, theoretically, an entrance wound, a trajectory ("bullet track"), and an exit hole or wound, but when dealing with dry bone, this statement is in most cases only valid for the skull and, in some instances, the trunk, and the bullet track has to be supposed because of lack of soft tissue. The lesions in the limbs usually lack both holes (although this fact is always dependent of the caliber of the bullet), and the pattern corresponds to a compound, comminuted fracture.

In general, both holes differ in size and shape, and their classic patterns as in the cranium are as follows:

1. The entrance wound is usually smaller and related to the caliber of the ammunition, ragged or, most commonly, circular in shape, and the inner table shows beveled edges (Fig. 7). As Gordon et al. *(14)* point out, under certain circumstances, an entrance wound may be irregular in shape. However, in most of the cases, the direction of fire may be established taking in account the margins of the lesion (circular if the bullet was shot at right angle or oval if was shot in an oblique angle).
2. The exit hole or wound is almost always larger and irregular in shape because of the fact that there is a mass of cephalic and skin tissue and fragments of bone accompanying the bullet, which, along with bullet's energy, increases the intracranial pressure, so the damage produced at that level is bigger than that of the entrance wound. The margins of the hole are usually everted and, not infrequently, radiating fracture lines, comminution, and loss of bone fragments, as well as outer table beveling, are present (*[3]*; Fig. 8). An important exception is the contact shots that may show a smaller exit hole than the entrance wound *(14)*.

Regarding the trajectory or bullet track of the shot, it is important to note that it is not always straight because the bullet may be deflected when crashing against intracranial structures, especially bones.

According to Morse *(21)*, the destructive capacity of the bullet depends on the following factors: weight and mass, shape, content, and area of impact in the body.

There are two types of lesion, depending on the caliber of the bullet. The first is small caliber, when the bullet may stay embedded in the bone ("embed-

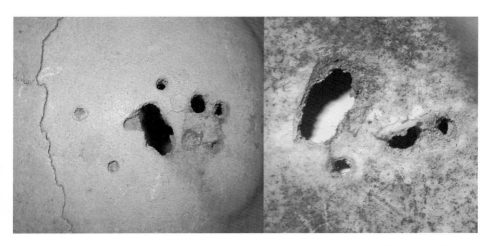

Fig. 7. Four typical entry holes on the frontal bone, probably of different ammunitions, the outer table diameter being inferior to the one of the inner table. Note on the latter, the inner beveling, which permits to qualify these as entrance wounds. (Photograph courtesy of João Pinheiro and Eugénia Cunha.)

Fig. 8. A typical exit hole of a gunshot wound: beveled on the outer table, with a superior diameter on this table when compared with the inner table. (Photograph courtesy of João Pinheiro and Eugénia Cunha.)

ding shot"). The second is large caliber, when the bullet may perforate the whole bone ("perforating shot"). However, it is convenient to repeat here that the usual pattern of a gunshot at the level of the bones of the limbs is that of a comminuted, compound fracture.

The estimation of the shooting distance is always a request in a forensic autopsy, but often a very difficult task. Following Gordon et al. *(14)* and Font Riera *(29)*, the lesions produced by firearm weapons may be divided, depending on the distance between the weapon and the target:

1. Close-range and contact wounds, which may be divided into two types of lesions:
   a. Weapon touching the target ("shot with touching barrel"). The entrance wound has a ragged appearance. Blackening (tattooing) of the bone may be observed in these lesions.
   b. "Burning shots," when the flame of the shot reaches the target (shots of around 15 cm). The entrance wound is circular in shape. As in the previous case, some tattooing of the bone surface may be observable.
2. Short-distance shots at 60–70 cm. The entrance wound is usually circular in shape too. Tattooing is not present most of the times.
3. Long-distance shots.

When involving the skull, the first two types are of great interest in the context of human rights violation (because they are the common method of extralegal arbitrary and summary executions), violations of the humanitarian international right, terrorist selective killing, and, in those cases of close range and contact wounds, suicide.

4.6.2. LESIONS PRODUCED BY PELLETS

The damage depends on the distance between the weapon and the target because the effect is very different between short- and long-distance shots:

1. Short-distance shots (less than 1 m): the pellets behave as a large-caliber bullet because they will be very close, like a single mass, and the lesions are even much more severe and destructive than those of a bullet (i.e., the skull may literally explode). Burning and blackening are seen even in the bone surface (*[14]*; Fig. 9).
2. Long-distance shots (Fig. 10): as the pellets separate as distance increases, the lesions will be separated as well, and the effect on the target will be less than in the previous case. Most of the cases do not show an exit hole, and the pellets will be embedded in the bone.

The direction of fire may be only elucidated in cases of close-range wounds *(14)*.

4.6.3. EXPLOSIONS

Aside from the typical "blast syndromes" (pulmonary, ocular, encephalic, gastric) that different authors include as firearm lesions, other injuries of interest are those produced by fragments of bombs or other kinds of explosive artifacts.

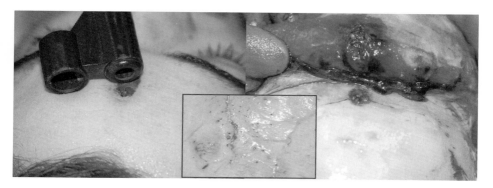

Fig. 9. The black tattoo on the bone produced by a close-range shot, as the one illustrated. Observe the sequence of the events: The tattoo overlaps the skin, reaches the periosteum and the bone, where it can stay for years until this forensic case could be an anthropological one. Typical fracture lines irradiate from the hole to the sides of the vault. Little pieces of shrapnel were found on the interparietal region, and the bullet was found nearby. (Photograph and case study courtesy of João Pinheiro.)

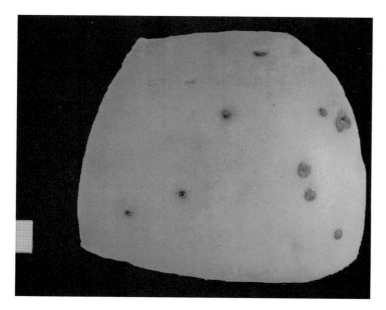

Fig. 10. The effect of long-distance shots with pellets is less than that of a bullet; most of the cases do not show an exit hole. The pellets are embedded in the bone. (Photograph courtesy of Dr. Francisco Etxeberria.)

Marino *(30)* states that these lesions are divided into those resulting from small fragments of the artifacts acting like true bullets (mitraille) and those lesions produced by large fragments that, because of their mass and speed, are much more destructive. Along with the fragments, one has to consider here the effects of other objects "flying" in the air because of the tremendous energy of the explosion and the "flying victim" crashing against different obstacles because of the expansive wave. All these things produce a varied spectrum of fractures, contusions, cuts, amputations, and so forth that have to be considered when analyzing human remains destroyed by explosive devices, as occur in terrorist attacks or, even accidental explosions.

In all the cases of firearm lesions, including explosions, it is very important to perform a radiographic study in order to help the recovery of bullet fragments, because their later analysis will permit the comparative study with other possible fragments found in the neighborhood of the crime *(31)* and the identification of the gunshot involved. However, when these fragments are absent, this does not exclude a gunshot, especially in cases of high-speed bullets *(25)*.

Examination of the radiographs with a magnifying lens will help in this task *(3,25)*.

5. CONCLUSIONS

The pathological analysis of dry bones in a forensic context is always a difficult matter, even for the most experienced specialist. Lack of soft tissues is an obstacle for the research because soft tissues provide information that is normally not shown in the dry skeleton. Therefore, it presents limitations that may preclude final and definite conclusions.

There are other circumstances to take into account: the environment of the burial and the context in which the research is carried out. The first is paramount for the preservation of the skeletal tissue, the second is fundamental for knowing what could have happened to the victim, and both are crucial for the possibilities of success of the research. The study of the data before, around, and after death, along with a correct archaeological work, is a priority before performing the analysis in the laboratory or morgue because they provide important additional information.

The above-stated is even more complicated when dealing with cases of mass violence (human rights violation, violations to humanitarian international right, or other type of ethnic, social, religious, or political violence) because many times the work is performed in mass burials or ossuaries, where relevant information can be lost.

Interdisciplinary work is essential in this type of research. Osteopathologists, archeologists, anthropologists, forensic pathologists, and radiologists must work together because they look not only for the identification of the victim and the manner of death, but also to know if there are pathological signs related to violence or other cruel, inhuman or degrading treatment, like torture.

Although osteopathology has been neglected many times as an useful tool in the forensic anthropological context, it is obvious that its correct use can produce information that forensic anthropology itself cannot provide: additional data for the positive identification of the individual based on the comparison with the antemortem medical records, data for the determination of the manner of death, data for the events during the period of arrest (i.e., cases of political or ethnic violence, or kidnapping), and keys for the differential diagnosis between antemortem pathology and postmortem artifacts.

Dry bone pathological analysis in the forensic context still needs more research on laboratory collections to standardize the investigation because this will permit to know the true limits and the actual value of the discipline. Identification of a lesion, determination of its antemortem or perimortem nature, and its interpretation in terms of its responsibility to the victim's death are the basic questions that either a forensic anthropologist or pathologist must be prepared to answer wherever he or she works. The matters dealt with in this chapter are essential for these purposes. Therefore, it seems of absolute relevance that the forensic anthropologist is trained in basic skeletal pathology, which will help with the specialized work in the morgue and, certainly pathologists must also be familiar with the basics of forensic anthropology.

With a correct preliminary research (archives, interviews, antemortem records, and the like) and the statements made here, the use of osteopathology in the forensic context will show, very soon, its real possibilities.

REFERENCES

1. Steinbock, R. T. Paleopathological diagnosis and interpretation. Charles C. Thomas, Springfield, IL, 1976.
2. Ortner, D. G., Putschar, W. G. J. Identification of pathological conditions in human skeletal remains. Smithsonian Institution Press, Washington, D.C., 1985.
3. Aufderheide, A. C., Rodríguez-Martín, C. The Cambridge Encyclopedia of Human Paleopathology. Cambridge University Press, Cambridge, 1998.
4. Campillo, D. Introducción a la Paleopatología [in Spanish]. Bellaterra, Barcelona, 2001.
5. Ortner, D. J. Identification of pathological conditions in human skeletal remains, 2nd Ed. Academic, San Diego, CA, 2003.

6. Palomo Rando, J. L., Ramos Medina, V., Santos Amaya, I. M. Muerte en privación de libertad (MPL) [in Spanish]. Cuad. Med. Forense 35:37–50, 2004.
7. Iacopino V, Ozcalipci O, Schlar C. The Istanbul Protocol. The manual in effective investigation and documentation of torture and other cruel, inhuman or degrading treatment or punishment. United Nations, 1999.
8. UN Manual on the Effective Prevention and Investigation of Extra-Legal, Arbitrary and Summary Executions. United Nations, 1991.
9. Saul, J. M. Trauma analysis. IXth Annual Forensic Anthropology Course. National Museum of Health and Medicine, Bethesda, MD. AFIP. USUHS, 1996.
10. Rodríguez-Martín, C., Martín Oval, M., Patiño Umaña, A. Patología ósea del abuso y maltrato físicos [in Spanish]. ERES-Serie Arqueol./Bioantropol. (Santa Cruz de Tenerife) 13:37–53, 2005.
11. Apley, A. G., Solomon, L. Manual de Ortopedia y Fracturas, 1a Ed. [In Spanish.] Masson-Salvat, Barcelona, 1995.
12. Stewart, T. D. Essentials of Forensic Anthropology. Charles C. Thomas, Springfield, IL, 1979.
13. Lacroix, M. Etude Médico-Legale des Pertes de Substance de la Voute du Cráne [in French]. Masson, Paris, 1972.
14. Gordon, I., Shapiro, H. A., Berson, S. D. Forensic Medicine: a Guide to Principles, 3rd Ed. Churchill Livingstone, New York, NY, 1988.
15. Cramer, L. M., Brobyn, T. Plastic and reconstructive surgery. In: Schwartz, S. I., Shires, G. T., Spencer, F. C., Storer, E. H., eds., Principles of Surgery, 3rd Ed. McGraw-Hill, New York, NY, pp. 2055–2106, 1979.
16. Adams, J. C. Manual de Ortopedia, 4th Ed. Toray, Barcelona, 1986.
17. Birnstingl, M. A. Traumatismos de tórax y abdomen. In: Wilson, J. N., Watson-Jones, R., eds., Fracturas y Heridas Articulares, Vol I, 3rd Ed. [In Spanish.] Salvat, Barcelona, pp. 155–177, 1980.
18. Spatola, J. Traumatismos torácicos. In: Michans, J. R, ed., Patología Quirúrgica, Vol. III, 2nd Ed. [In Spanish.] El Ateneo, Buenos Aires, pp. 99–118, 1971.
19. Resnick, D., Goergen, T. G., Niwayama, G. Physical trauma. In: Resnick, D., ed., Bone and Joint Imaging. Saunders, Philadelphia, PA, pp. 801–898, 1989.
20. Lòpez-Duràn, L. Traumatología y Ortopedia, 2nd Ed. [In Spanish.] Luzán, Madrid, p. 5, 1995.
21. Morse, D. The skeletal pathology of trauma. In: Morse, D., Duncan, J., Stoutamire, J., eds., Handbook of Forensic Archaeology and Anthropology. Rose, Tallahassee, FL, pp. 145–185, 1983.
22. Resnick, D. Tejidos blandos. In: Resnick, D., ed., Huesos y Articulaciones en Imagen [in Spanish]. Marban, Madrid, 1240–1272, 1998.
23. Casagrande, P. A., Frost, H. M. Fundamentos de Ortopedia Clínica [in Spanish]. Salvat, Barcelona, 1955.
24. Dimaio, D. J., Dimaio, J. M. Forensic Pathology. Elsevier, New York, NY, 1989.
25. Maples, W. R. Trauma analysis by the forensic anthropologist. In: Reichs, K. J., ed., Forensic Osteology: Advances in the Identification of Human Remains. Charles C. Thomas, Springfield, IL, pp. 218–228, 1986.

26. Ubelaker, D. H., Scammel, H. Bones: a Forensic Detective's Casebook. Harper Collins, New York, NY, 1992.
27. Sauer, N. J. Manner of death: skeletal evidence of blunt and sharp trauma. In: Rathbun, T. A., Buikstra, J. E., eds., Human Identification: Case Studies in Forensic Anthropology. Charles C. Thomas, Springfield, IL, pp. 176–184, 1984.
28. Roberts, C., Manchester, K. The Archaeology of Disease, 2nd Ed. Cornell University Press, Ithaca, NY, 1995.
29. Font Riera, G. Atlas de Medicina Legal y Forense [in Spanish]. J.M. Bosch Editor, Barcelona, 1996.
30. Marino, H. Traumatismos. In: Michans, J. R., ed., Patología Quirúrgica, Vol. I., 2nd Ed. [in Spanish.] El Ateneo, Buenos Aires, pp. 90–134, 1971.
31. Spitz, W. U. Gunshot wounds. In: Spitz, W. U., Fischer, R. S., eds., Medicolegal Investigation of Death. Guidelines for the Application of Pathology to Crime Investigation, 2nd Ed. Charles C. Thomas, Springfield, IL, pp. 216–274, 1980.

PART IV

Biological Identity

Chapter 9

Methodology and Reliability of Sex Determination From the Skeleton

Jaroslav Bruzek and Pascal Murail

Summary

Once a body is completely decomposed, it is necessary to determine sex from the skeleton. The hip bone is the most reliable indicator for sex determination because the pattern of sexual dimorphism is common to the whole human race. Two reliable visual methods are suggested to assess sex from the hip bone. However, the authors recommend the use of a method based on discriminant function analysis including a probabilistic approach that the authors recently developed with a large sample of known-sex individuals. The population specificity of sexual dimorphism of the other parts of the skeleton is also discussed. The authors particularly insist on the inherent limits of discriminant functions on extrapelvic measurements.

Key Words: Sex determination; adult; hip bones; pelvic measurements; probability; discriminant function.

1. INTRODUCTION

For forensic anthropologists and bioanthropologists, studying skeletal remains from past populations, estimating age, and sex is a fundamental step for establishing the biological profile of an individual *(1–4)*. In the forensic context, it is necessary to use bone and dental indicators on decomposed bodies

From *Forensic Anthropology and Medicine:*
Complementary Sciences From Recovery to Cause of Death
Edited by: A. Schmitt, E. Cunha, and J. Pinheiro © Humana Press Inc., Totowa, NJ

for age-at-death assessment, but sex determination is more problematic when the body is skeletonized than at other times. If the aims of sex determination differ in paleoanthropological studies and police investigations, both fields are confronted with the same biological and methodological limits and require a high level of reliability. However, the reliability and accuracy of sex assessment from skeletal remains depends on the anatomical region available.

After presenting the fundamental theoretical backgrounds of performing sex assessment methods, this chapter suggests the reliable methods to assess sex from the hip bone and the skull, and comments on the application of the methods based on the other bones of the skeleton.

2. WHAT IS A RELIABLE METHOD TO ASSESS SEX FROM THE SKELETON?

The identification process from skeletal remains requires the use of methodological approaches and methods whose performance is demonstrated. One should not confuse the accuracy and the reliability of a method. The *accuracy* is the percentage of skeletons whose sex is correctly assigned in the sample on which the method is elaborated. The *reliability* is evaluated by testing the method on an independent population. As the legal consequences of the identification of individuals are significant, the level of reliability needs to be higher in the legal context than those presented in current sexing methods (around 85%). A minimum threshold of 95% is required *(5)*.

When a biological character and/or the preservation of skeletal remains prevent such reliability, the result of sex assessment must be expressed by the probability of a skeleton being male or female. Moreover, the risk of error must be specified by the expert in charge of the identification. The risk of sex misclassification should be underlined in any expert opinion.

Over the last two decades, gradual loss of empirical and typological approaches to elaborate methods of sex determination from the skeleton was observed. Recent methods are instead based on biological and statistical backgrounds.

Describing morphological sexual differences on the skeleton is not enough to elaborate a method of sexing. No single trait of the human skeleton enables a reliable sex determination *(6)*. For example, the "mandibular ramus flexure," which is supposed to be present in males mandibles and missing in females mandibles, is asserted to be a reliable indicator of sex by Loth and Henneberg *(7,8)* because the reliability level reaches 94% of cases. However, when tested by others authors, the results fail to give such reliability (80% and less *[5,9,10]*).

It is not appropriate either to use extreme values of a single measurement, such as the femur head diameter, when applied to a population different from the reference sample. Neither the technique of demarking points *(11)* nor indices that are also population-specific *(12)* are appropriate for sexual assessment.

When testing sex determination methods, trained scientists with long-term practice obtain a higher accuracy level; their experience is sufficient to supply the putative lack of precise and reliable methods. It is rather difficult to quantify the part of observer experience when assessing accuracy and reliability of a method *(13)*. Both new and experienced observers should achieve the same level of reliability in determining the sex of an individual.

Only a combination of an optimum number of traits (or measurements), which are evaluated (or measured) according to precise definitions, provides a reduction of the subjectivity and enables the reproducibility of observations and, therefore, a correct sex determination. Only such approaches, including well-documented instructions, can be considered as correct methods. In addition, each method must be elaborated on osteological collection of known sex and its practical and effective reliability tested on independent samples.

3. SEX DETERMINATION FROM THE HIP BONE: THE MOST RELIABLE SEX DETERMINATION

3.1. The General Pattern of Sexual Dimorphism of the Hip Bone

It is widely accepted that the hip bone is the part of the skeleton that provides the most accurate and reliable results for sex determination. The hip bones exhibit the most sexually dimorphic elements of the skeleton. The discrete sex-specific differences in size and shape are based on the differing reproductive roles of males and females. Sexual dimorphism of the hip bone is the result of functional modification and evolutionary adaptation. The male pelvis is adapted to bipedal striding. In females, the pelvis reflects a compromise between locomotion and parturition that requires a voluminous pelvis in female for the safe passage of a large fetal head through the birth canal. This specificity absent in males leads to a biomechanical advantage for more efficient locomotion. Therefore, male pelvises are generally narrower than the female's.

The hip bone can be divided into three morphofunctional parts or segments. The first part is the sacroiliac segment; it concerns the auricular surface of the sacroiliac joint and its surroundings structures. The most important sexual difference that increases with age is the shape of the sciatic notch. The second part is the ischiopubic segment, whose sexual dimorphism occurs in puberty because of the hormonally controlled transformation of the pelvis in females (open subpubic angle and relatively greater length of pubis than ischium). The third morphofunctional part of the pelvis is the acetabular segment; it reflects the spatial organization of the three bones that form the pelvis and contributes to its general architecture.

This pattern of sexual dimorphism of the pelvis is common in the human race and has existed for at least 100,000 yr *(14)*. Sexual dimorphism of the pelvis as the whole is also presented in isolated hip bones. Because the relationship between locomotion and reproduction is not population-specific, morphometric methods of sex determination by discriminant function analysis (DFA) are not population-specific. However, it is necessary to use these DFAs in an appropriate manner.

Observing traits or taking measurements of a single morphofunctional segment of the hip bone is not appropriate. The sexual dimorphism observed on a single segment is often influenced by size and thus, population-specific. This is the case with Phenice's method *(15)*, which is based on the pubic bone. A test of this method showed a reliability ranging from 60 to 90%, depending on the population studied *(16)*. Similar conclusions are valid for sex determination from the posterior pelvis and the sacroiliac joint surface *(17–19)*. In fact, the variation in sexual dimorphism of one segment of the hip bone influences the variation in the other segments of the hip bone. This equifinality principle of sexual dimorphism is observed on the hip bone considered as a whole *(13,16,20)*.

Sexing immature skeletons is a point largely debated among both forensic and osteoarchaeological communities. Nevertheless, until the fusion of the three different segments of the hip bone, sex dimorphism is not sufficiently expressed to elaborate a reliable method for sexing immature individuals.

3.2. Reliable Methods of Sex Determination

Reliable sex assessment from the hip bone is obtained either by visual techniques based on the evaluation of morphological traits or by statistical tools with hip bone measurements.

Two visual methods that take into account the total sexual dimorphism of the hip bone provide a reliable sex determination and are highly recommended for sex determination *(20,21)*. Those methods are described in details in the cited literature. From a practical point of view, it is necessary that the methods employ a limited number of traits. Increasing the number of variables does not provide a higher accuracy; it is time-consuming and gives redundant results.

Table 1
Four Reliable Discriminant Functions Using Hip Bone Measurements

Reference	Discriminant function	Discriminant value
Novotny, 1975 *(22)*	SD = (7.178 ISM) – (4.789 PUM) – (4.262 AC) – (0.788 IIMT)	$F < 292.53 < M$
Bruzek, 1991 *(16)*	SD = (0.4666 HOAC) – (0.2126 PUBM) + (0.2959 ISM) – (0.2849 AC) – 37.307	$F < 0.093 < M$
Bruzek, 1985 *(23)*	SD = (0.1942 HOAC) – (0.15688 PUM) + (0.10323 ISM) – (0.0273 IIMT) – (0.05105 AC) – 7. 44678	$F < 0.402 < M$
Schulter-Ellis et al., 1985 *(24,25)*	SD = 25.1462 (HOAC ÷ PUM) + (0.1318 ISMM) – 31.8388	$F < 0 < M$

The dimensions used and their definitions are as follows, where "M" corresponds to the marking according to Martin *(61)*: HOAC (M.22), PUM (M.14), IIMT (M.15.1), ISM *(62)*, ISMM, PUBM (24-25), AC *(22)*.
F, female value; M, male value.

However, visual methods, if reliable, are quite difficult to apply for new applicants. Therefore, it is much easier to use metrical methods. Four discriminant functions *(22–25)* previously published have been shown to be reliable after tested on several independent samples (*[26]* Table 1). However, the sex determination of an individual depends on the discriminant score obtained compared with the discriminant value (this particular point is developed under Subheading 4.2.2). To avoid this problem, the authors recently developed a method based on discriminant function analysis including also a probabilistic approach for sex assessment *(27,28)*. Current developments in software enable extension of the classic computation of DFAs to the calculation of posterior probabilities of a skeleton being male or female, without discussing the discriminant value (Fig. 1). The method the authors proposed was elaborated on a large sample of hip bones ($n = 2040$) of known-sex individuals. This sample was composed of several populations from preindustrial and contemporary periods and diverse geographical areas (Europe, Africa, Asia, North America) (Table 2). The aim was to take into account a large variability of human hip bone sexual dimorphism. The measurements used for this approach were selected from published osteometric studies of sex determination according to their relevance in discriminating sex. The level of reliability of the authors' method (for a posterior probability ≥0.95) is impressive. Using a combination of eight or four measurements, it varies from 98.7

A

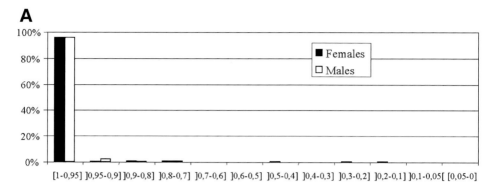

B

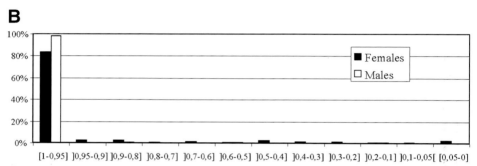

Fig. 1. Principles of probabilistic sex determination. Classification of the posterior probabilities (probability for a specimen to be classified in the good category) in the European sample **(A)**. At a 0.95 threshold, sex is assessed for 95.9% of the sample. The level of reliability is 100%. It demonstrates that these three different samples (from England, France, and Portugal) share the same sexual dimorphism of the hip bone. This model is tested on an African-American sample (Terry and Hamann-Todd Collection); probabilities are calculated from the European sample **(B)**. At a 0.95 threshold, sex is assessed for 92% of the sample, and the reliability is 98.6% (error rate is 1.4%). Pelvic measurements describe a common sexual dimorphism among different populations (*see also* Table 1 for other tests). The final version of the probabilistic tool includes all the samples of different origins as a reference sample.

to 100%, depending of the target samples (Table 3). In addition, it is possible to select various combinations of measurements, depending on the state of preservation of the hip bone. For each case, posterior probability is calculated from the whole reference sample. It allows assessment the sex of an individual, knowing the exact probability of being male or female, which is of

Table 2
Material Used in the Probabilistic Sex Determination

Country	City	Collection	Group	Date (century)	Females	Males	Total
Europe							
France	Paris	Olivier	—	Early 20th	62	98	160
England	London	Spitalfields	—	18th, 19th	31	31	62
Portugal	Coimbra	Tamagnini	—	19th, 20th	130	102	232
Lituania	Vilnius	Garmus	—	20th	112	108	220
Africa							
South Africa	Johannesburg	Dart	Zulu	Early 20th	153	153	306
			Soto	Early 20th	58	52	110
			Afrikaner	Early 20th	56	56	112
North America							
United States	Cleveland	Hammann-Todd	Black	Early 20th	57	56	113
			White	Early 20th	56	56	112
	Washington D.C.	Terry	Black	Early 20th	110	106	216
			White	Early 20th	102	97	199
Asia							
Thailand	Chiang-Mai	Forensic	—	Late 20th	96	102	198
Total					1023	1017	2040

Adapted from ref. 28.

Table 3
Reliability of the Pooled European and American Model of Probabilistic Sex Determination From Hip Bone Measurements and Its Testing in Other Populations

Population	Combination of eight variables			Best combination of four variables		
	Wilks' λ statistic	Sexing (%)	Reliability (%)	Wilks' λ statistic	Sexing (%)	Reliability (%)
Reference sample of European and American samples	0.179	99.7	99.3	0.196	86.9	99.7
Thai		94.1	100		90.5	100
Zulu (Dart Collection)		88.7	98.8		84.6	98.8
Soto (Dart Collection)		86	100		84.4	100
Afrikaner (Dart Collection)		95.1	100		88.8	100
Lithuanian		94.4	100		91.7	100

Wilks' λ is the discriminatory power of the discriminant function analysis. Sex is assessed for individuals whose posterior probability is ≥0.95 (cf. percentage of sexing).

232

great interest in forensic context. This method under publication *(28)* is easy to run via software, which is available on request to the authors (jbruzek@ u-bordeaux1.fr).

4. HOW TO DETERMINE SEX WHEN THE HIP BONES ARE NOT PRESERVED

4.1. Sex Assessment From the Skull

The skull is the second element of the skeleton that expresses a relevant sexual dimorphism. Therefore, it is possible to use a classic visual technique by skull dimorphism *(29)*. However, one should keep in mind that sexual dimorphism of the skull depends on the population observed. Sex determination from cranial morphological features is less reliable than sex assessment from the hip bone. Therefore, it is more appropriate to use cranial measurements of a specimen and to compare them to a large reference database, such as the one published by Howells. This database includes a worldwide variation of human skull measurements *(30)*. The software FORDISC 2.0 enables application of such a principle *(31)*. However, this system determines sex by the greater probability. For example, if a specimen has a probability of 0.48 of being male and 0.52 of being female, the specimen is determined to be female. Taking into account the discriminant value reduces the reliability of the determination, the authors therefore recommend using FORDISC 2.0 by limiting sex assessment to the specimens whose the probability of being male or female is greater than 0.95. Another possibility is to compute the probabilities from the Howells database *(30)*. Depending of the case studied, one may choose one or several reference populations to calculate specific DFAs according to the available measurements in the specimen. In this case, measurements are also selected according to previous works that already showed satisfactory results *(32–34)*. Most of statistical software enables computation of probabilities and estimation of the reliability of such analysis. Again, the sex of a specimen should be assessed according to a probability higher than 0.95. Because sexual dimorphism of the skull is more population-specific than the hip bone, it is not surprising that the sex of some individuals will not be determined.

4.2. Sex Determination When Hipbones and Skull Are Absent: A Fundamental Problem

When hip bones and skull are missing, it is commonly accepted to apply DFAs elaborated on measurements of other elements of the skeleton, such as long bones. However, this solution is not appropriate because the sexual dimorphism is population-specific.

4.2.1. Population Specificity of Extrapelvic Osteometric Methods for Sex Determination

In general, males have larger body size, more massive joints, and stronger musculature compared with females. However, the degree of this sexual dimorphism varies between populations. Therefore, methods of sex determination that use measurements are population-specific. Many authors have demonstrated the population specificity of the DFAs (29,35–37). To remove the variations affecting discriminant values when applied to a sample different from the sample on which the DFA was computed, it was proposed modifying the discriminant value by a new target sample of bones. Because of the lack of suitable data, this proposal is not applicable (16).

Işcan (38) proposed elaboration of specific DFAs for each population. The calculation of new discriminant functions is nowadays an easy task with common software. Therefore, the number of publications proposing DFAs from most of the bones of the skeleton to determine sex increased in the last decade (reviewed in ref. 5) and are still being developed (39–42). However, one might ask the legitimate question of whether these publications actually serve any purpose. The assessment of ethnic origin remains one of the most difficult tasks in forensic osteology, as culturally and politically defined groups do not necessarily coincide with biological parameters (31–43). In the context of the current globalization, a phenomenon characterized by the flow of individuals (and populations) over great distances, there is no guarantee that any discovered skeletonized body in one country belongs to the local population group living in this geographic area. Therefore, there is no reason to use a specific national or regional population standard. In past populations, migration and population movements may have led to modifications of the biological characteristics by the influence of rapid changing conditions.

Therefore, any population standard is only valid for individuals who belong to this population. The authors assert that population-specific discriminant function analyses do not enable reliable sex determination in archaeological and legal contexts. Their application may actually be erroneous and misleading. For example, specific discriminant functions derived from the dimensions of the long bones in the limbs of a recent American population sample (44) were applied on a Neolithic population sample from Denmark. Parallel to the establishment of the biological profile, DNA analysis was conducted. This study showed that the sex determination by DFAs failed to give the same results than those obtained by DNA analysis ([45] see also Fig. 2).

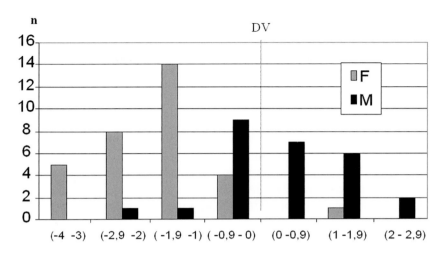

Fig. 2. Population specificity of extrapelvic discriminant function analysis (DFA). The DFA proposed by Iscan and Miller-Shaivitz *(33)* takes into account two variables of the femur (M21 and M18). Elaborated in a North American sample of known-sex skeletons (Hamann-Todd: 56 males and 55 females), its accuracy level is 91%. Nevertheless, its application in another sample of known sex (Spitalfields, London: 32 females and 26 males) shows that the reliability level is reduced to 42%. This DFA is specific to the original population: 11 males are misclassified (reliability is only 58% for the male group). Wrong sexual determination may be explained by a specific size pattern of sexual dimorphism that introduces the shift of the discriminant value. This DFA should not be applied to individuals from a different origin. F, female; M, male; DV, discriminant value.

Inferring ethnic origin from bones in order to choose the appropriate DFA is not recommended for two reasons. First, sex dimorphism varies among individuals from the same origin. Second, inferring ancestry from bones is not a reliable process. Goodman *(46)* related a famous example: "A left leg was found in the debris of the Oklahoma City bombing. By measuring the lower leg and plugging the numbers into computer programs that categorize bones by race and sex, Snow confirmed the hunch: the leg probably came from a white male." It was asserted later that "the leg belonged to Lakesha R. Levy," who was female, and "'obviously black'."

Even the sexual dimorphism in a single population modifies through time. The secular trend causes not only changes in size and height between generations *(47,48)*, but also modifies the size of individual bones *(49–53)*. A population-specific standard elaborated in a well-documented osteological collection from the past should not be applied to recent individuals from the same origin. The sexual dimorphism observed on the osteological sample would not reflect the sexual dimorphism of the current population.

4.2.2. PITFALL FOR USERS: THE INTERVAL OF OVERLAPPING VALUES IN DFAS

The other limit of DFAs is the overlapping value, which can reach 85% *(54)*. A DFA computed by combined measurements reduces the range of the overlapping area, but it is not completely removed (Fig. 3A). Success of a DFA is generally evaluated by its statistical power, expressed by a Wilks' lambda statistic (varying from 0 to 1). The lower the value is, the greater the power of DFA. However, results of a DFA emphasize the classification accuracy, depending on the discriminant value. Level of accuracy is highly variable and covers a wide range: 66% for skull fragments *(55)*, between 75 and 85% for long bones *(56,57)*, the highest values being for the hip bone (*see* Subheading 2.2).

When determining sex, the overlapping values area is not taken into account because it may change the success of a DFA into a completely useless tool. Use as an example a DFA with a discriminant value equal to 0, where "female" corresponds to negative values and "male" to positive values. If the determination of the sex of an unknown forensic specimen or from a cemetery is by the same DFA (*see* Fig. 3B) in the overlapping area, there is no rule to decide whether the individual's sex has been correctly determined. Moreover, the variation of the discriminant value between populations increases the influence of the overlapping area and may lead to important misclassification (*see* Fig. 2). In the forensic context, a DFA that fails to provide a maximum error rate of 5% is useless. Yet, this is the case of the majority of published DFAs, regardless of the population on which they were elaborated. This failure comes from the use of the discriminant value as a classification criterion. A discriminant value corresponds to a probability of 0.5, whereas the classification reliability of a DFA should reach an optimum value of 95%.

Sex assessment when the hip bone and the skull are absent is problematic. Metric analyses are population-specific and are not reliable enough when applied to individuals of unknown origin. As the origin of a skeletonized body is unknown, it is not recommended to assess sex based on isolated bones.

In archaeological context, there is a solution for sexing skeleton missing hip bones. The authors call it "secondary sex diagnosis" *(58)*. The first step is to perform sex determination for skeletons with hip bones, using one of the

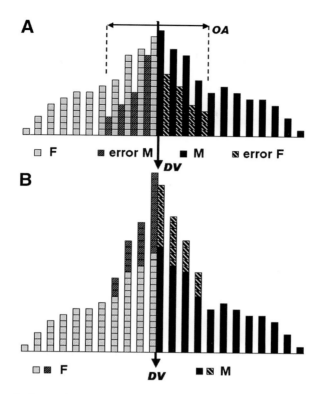

Fig. 3. Discriminant function analysis (DFA) in a sample of known-sex specimens **(A)** vs its application to an unidentified skeleton **(B)**: pitfall of discriminant value (sectioning point). In a series of bones belonging to subjects of known sex (A), the DFA separates males and females with an error rate (misclassification) that corresponds to the percentage of the subjects misclassified. This DFA applied in a sample of unknown sex ([B] forensic or archaeological samples) separates subjects in an exhaustive way. Distinguishing true and false allocations of sex in the overlapping area is impossible. Furthermore, the zone of overlapping is unknown. Thus, the use of discriminant value is not recommended for most DFAs. Probabilistic assessment is highly recommended. F, female; M, male; DV, discriminant value; OA, overlapping area.

methods listed previously. The second step consists of elaborating specific DFAs from this subsample. After verifying their reliability, it is possible to apply the DFAs to the others skeletons. Stojanowski *(59)* has recently used nearly the same principle.

5. CONCLUSION

Sex determination from the skeleton can be assessed with reliability when the methods take into account a common sexual dimorphism between populations. The best indicator is the hip bone. At least three reliable methods based on this element can be applied (visual, pelvic DFA, and probabilistic approaches). When the hip bone is missing, it is recommended examining cranial sexual dimorphism by visual methods or by computing the sex affinity of the specimen from wide reference morphometric data. However, for cranial methods, when a specimen exhibits no marked sex dimorphism or when cranial measurements provide a lower probability than the required threshold, one should not determinate sex. One has to accept that the quest for reliability leads to unidentified individuals. For isolated bones, sex determination is rather problematic. Sexual dimorphism is population-specific, and furthermore, ethnic origin determination is limited on skeletonized remains. Consequently, population specific standards are useless.

For nonadult skeletons, no reliable methods have been proposed yet. One solution is to perform molecular diagnostics by genetic markers on X/Y chromosomes *(60)*. This technique may also solve the problem of sex determination with isolated bones.

ACKNOWLEDGMENTS

The work on probabilistic sex determination on the hip bone required the study of many osteological samples. We are particularly grateful to the persons in charge with the reference collections: F. Demoulin (Paris, France), T. Molleson and L. Humphrey (London, England), E. Cunha and M. Laranjeira Rodrigues de Areia (Coimbra, Portugal), R. Jankauskas and A. Garmus (Vilnius, Lituania), B. Latimer and L. Jellema (Cleveland, OH), D. Ubelaker and D. Hunt (Washington, D.C.), K. L. Kuykendall (Johannesburg, South Africa), and P. Mahhakanukrauh (Chiang-Mai, Thailand).

REFERENCES

1. Bass, W. M. Human Osteology: a Laboratory and Field Manual, Third Ed., Special Publication No. 2. Missouri Archaeological Society, Colombia, p. 987, 1987.
2. Krogman, W. M., Işcan, M. Y. The Human Skeleton in Forensic Medicine. Charles C. Thomas, Springfield, IL, 1986.
3. Buikstra, J. E., Ubelaker, D. H. Standards for Data Collection from Human Skeletal Remains: Proceedings of a Seminar at the Field Museum of Natural History. Arkansas Archeological Survey Research Series, Fayetteville, AR, p. 44, 1994.

4. Burns, K. R. Forensic Anthropology Training Manual. Prentice Hall, Saddle River, NJ, 1999.
5. Scheuer, L. Application of osteology to forensic medicine. Clin. Anat. 15:297–312, 2002.
6. Sjøvold, T. Geschlechtsdiagnose am Skelett. In: Knußmann, R., ed., Anthropologie. Handbuch der Vergleichenden Biologie des Menschen [in German]. Gustav Fischer, Stuttgart, pp. 444–480, 1988.
7. Loth, S. R., Henneberg, M. Mandibular ramus flexure: a new morphologic indicator of sexual dimorphism in the human skeleton. Am. J. Phys. Anthropol. 99:473–485, 1996.
8. Loth, S. R., Henneberg, M. Mandibular ramus flexure is a good indicator of sexual dimorphism. Am. J. Phys. Anthropol. 5:91–92, 1998.
9. Hill, C. A. Technical note: evaluating mandibular ramus flexur as a morphological indicator of sex. Am. J. Phys. Anthropol. 111:573–577, 2000.
10. Kemkes-Grottenthaler, A., Löbig, K., Stock, F. Mandibular ramus flexure and gonial eversion as morphologic indicator of sex. Homo. 53:97–111, 2002.
11. Asala, S. A. Sex determination from the head of the femur of South African whites and blacks. Forensic Sci. Int. 117:15–22, 2001.
12. Sullivan, N. C., Hall, R. A critique of index methods of determining the sex of the innominate. Can. Rev. Phys. Anthropol. 3:68–72, 1981.
13. Novotný, V. Pohlavní rozdíly a identifikace pohlaví podle panevní kosti (Sex differences and identification of sex in pelvic bone [in Czech]). Ph.D. Thesis, Brno, Purkyne University, Brno, Czech Republic, 1981.
14. Rosenberg, K., Trevathan, W. Birth, obstetrics and human evolution. Br. J. Obstet. Gyneacol. 109:1199–1206, 2002.
15. Phenice, T. W. A newly developed visual method sexing the pubis. Am. J. Phys. Anthropol. 30:297–302, 1969.
16. Bruzek, J. Fiabilité des procédés de détermination du sexe à partir de l'os coxal. Implications à l'étude du dimorphisme sexuel de l'Homme fossile [in French]. Ph.D. Thesis, Institut de Paléontologie Humaine, Paris, 1991.
17. Işcan, M. Y., Derrick, K. Determination of sex from the sacroiliac joint: a visual assessment technique. Fla. Sci. 47:94–98, 1984.
18. Ali, R. S., McLaughlin, S. M. Sex identification from the auricular surface of the adult human ilium. Int. J. Osteoarchaeol. 1:57–61, 1991.
19. Bruzek, J., Castex, D., Majo, T. Evaluation des caractères morphologiques de la face sacro-pelvienne de l'os coxal. Proposition d'une nouvelle méthode de diagnose sexuelle [in French]. Bull. Mém. Soc. Anthropol. Paris 8:491–502, 1996.
20. Bruzek, J. A method for visual determination of sex, using the human hip bone. Am. J. Phys. Anthropol. 117:157–168, 2002.
21. Ferembach, D., Schwidetzky, I., Stloukal, M. Recommendations for age and sex diagnoses of skeleton. J. Hum. Evol. 9:517–549, 1980.
22. Novotný, V. Diskriminantanalyse der Geschlechtsmerkmale auf dem Os coxae beim Menschen. Papers of the 13th Congress of Anthropologist Czechoslovak [in Czech]. Czech Anthropological Society, Brno, pp. 1–23, 1975.

23. Bruzek, J. Dimorphisme sexuel de l'os coxal de l'Homme du point de vue ontogénique et phylogénique [in French]. Ph.D. Thesis, Université Charles, Prague, 1985.

24. Schulter-Ellis, F. P., Schmidt, D. J., Hayek, L. C., Craig, J. Determination of sex with a discriminant analysis of new pelvic bone measurements: part I. J. Forensic Sci. 28:169–180, 1983.

25. Schulter-Ellis, F. P., Hayek, L. C., Schmidt, D. J. Determination of sex with a discriminant analysis of new pelvic bone measurements: part II. J. Forensic Sci. 30:178–185, 1985.

26. Bruzek, J. Fiabilité des fonctions discriminantes dans la détermination sexuelle de l'os coxal. Critiques et propositions [in French]. Bull. Mém. Soc. Anthropol. Paris 4:67–104, 1992.

27. Bruzek, J., Murail, P., Houët, F. Stability of the human pelvic sexual dimorphism pattern allows probabilistic sex diagnosis among *Homo sapiens sapiens*. Pre-acts 12th Congress of the European Anthropological Association, Cambridge, 8–11 September 2000 (Abstr.):55–56.

28. Murail, P., Bruzek, J., Houët, F., Cunha, E. A probabilistic sex diagnosis tool using world wide variation of pelvic measurements. Bull. Mém. Soc. Anthropol. Paris, in press. http://www.pacea.u-bordeaux1.publication/dspv1.html.

29. Walrath, D. E., Turner, P., Bruzek, J. Reliability test of the visual assessment of cranial traits for sex determination. Am. J. Phys. Anthropol. 125:132–137, 2004.

30. Howells, W. W. Howells' craniometric data on the Internet. Am. J. Phys. Anthropol. 101:441–442, 1996.

31. Ousley, S. D., Jantz, R. L. FORDISC 2.0. Personal computer forensic discriminant functions. University of Tennessee, Knoxville, TN, 1996.

32. Hanihara, K. Sexing of Japanese skeleton and teeth by discriminant function method. J. Anthropol. Soc. Nippon 89:401–418, 1980.

33. Giles, E., Elliot, O. Sex determination by discriminant function analysis. Am. J. Phys. Anthropol. 21:53–68, 1963.

34. Šefčáková, A., Mizera, I., Thurzo, M. New human fossil remains from Slovakia. The skull from Moča (Late Upper Paleolithic, South Slovakia). Bull. Slov. Antropol. Spol. 2:55–63, 1999.

35. Henke W. On the method of discriminant function analysis for sex determination of the skull. J. Hum. Evol. 6:95–100, 1977.

36. Kieser, J. A., Groeneveld, H. T. The unreliability of sex allocation based on human odontometric data. J. Forensic Odontostomatol. 7:1–12, 1989.

37. Bidmos, M. A., Dayal, M. R. Further evidence to show population specificity of discriminant function equations for sex determination using the talus of South African blacks. J. Forensic Sci. 6:1165–1170, 2004.

38. Işcan, M. Y. Rise of forensic anthropology. Yearb. Phys. Anthropol. 31:223–230, 1988.

39. Šlaus, M., Strinović, D., Škavić, J., Petrovečki, V. Discriminant function sexing of fragmentary and complete femora: standards for contemporary Croatia. J. Forensic Sci. 48:509–512, 2003.

40. Purkait, R., Chandra, H. A study of sexual variation in Indian femur. Forensic Sci. Int. 146:25–33, 2004.
41. Zanella, V. P., Brown, T. M. Testing the validity of metacarpal use in sex assessment of human skeletal remains. J. Forensic Sci. 48:17–20, 2003.
42. Kemkes-Grottenthaler, A. Sex determination by discriminant analysis: an evaluation of the reliability of patella measurements. Forensic Sci. Int. 147:129–133, 2005.
43. Ubelaker, D. H., Ross, A. H., Graver, S. M. Application of forensic discriminant functions to a Spanish cranial sample. Forensic Sci. Comm. 4:1–5, 2002.
44. Işcan, M. Y., Miller-Shaivitz, P. Determination of sex from the femur in Blacks and Whites. Coll. Antropol. 8:169–177, 1985.
45. Götherström, A., Lidén, K., Ahlström, T., Källersjö, M., Brown, T. A. Osteology, DNA and sex identification. Int. J. Osteoarchaeol. 7:71–81, 1997.
46. Goodman, A. H. Bred in the bone? Sciences 37:20–25, 1997.
47. Meadows, L., Jantz, M. L. Allometric secular change in the long bones from the 1800s to the present. J. Forensic Sci. 40:762–767, 1995.
48. Klepinger, L. L. Stature, maturation variation and secular trends in forensic anthropology. J. Forensic Sci. 46:788–790, 1999.
49. Introna, Jr., F., DiVella, G., Campobasso, C. P., Dragone, M. Sex determination by discriminant analysis of calcanei measurements. J. Forensic Sci. 42:725–728, 1997.
50. Riepert, T., Drechsler, T., Schild, H., Mattern, R. Zur säkularen Akceleration des Calcaneus-Analyse auf der Grundlage von Röntgenaufnahmen der Ferse (Study of the secular acceleration of the calcaneus based on radiogram of the ankle [in German]). Homo. 49:13–20, 1998.
51. Jantz, L. M., Jantz, R. L. Secular change in long bone length and proportion in the United States, 1800–1970. Am. J. Phys. Anthropol. 110:57–67, 1999.
52. Jantz, R. L. Cranial change in Americans: 1850–1975. J. Forensic Sci. 46:784–787, 2001.
53. Alunni-Perret, V., Staccini, P., Quatrehomme, G. Reexamination of a measurement for sexual determination using the supero-inferior femoral neck diameter in a modern European population. J. Forensic Sci. 48:517–520, 2003.
54. Loth, S. R., Işcan, M. Y. Sex determination. In: Siegel, J. A., Saukko, P. J., Knupfer, G. C., eds., Encyclopedia of Forensic Sciences. Academic, London, pp. 252–260, 2000.
55. Graw, M. J., Wahlb, J., Ahlbrecht, M. Course of the meatus acusticus internus as criterion for sex differentiation. Forensic Sci. Int. 147:113–117, 2005.
56. Stojanowski, C. M. Sexing potential of fragmentary and pathological metacarpals. Am. J. Phys. Anthropol. 109:245–252, 1999.
57. Bidmos, M. A., Asala, S. A. Sexual dimorphism of the calcaneus of South African blacks. J. Forensic Sci. 49:446–450, 2004.
58. Murail, P., Bruzek, J., Braga, J. A new approach to sexual diagnosis in past populations. Practical adjustments from van Vark's procedure. Int. J. Osteoarchol. 9:39–53, 1999.
59. Stojanowski, C. M. Matrix decomposition model for investigating prehistoric intracemetery biological variation. Am. J. Phys. Anthropol. 122:216–231, 2003.

60. Mannucci, A., Sullivan, K. M., Ivanov, P. L, Gill, P. Forensic application of a rapid and quantitative DNA sex test amplification of the X-Y homologous gene amelogenin. Int. J. Legal Med. 106:190–193, 1994.

61. Bräuer, G. Osteometrie. In: Knußmann, R., et al., ed., Anthropologie. Handbuch der vergleichenden Biologie des Menschen. Zugleich 4. Band I. Wesen und Methoden der Anthropologie [in German]. Gustav Fischer, Stuttgart, pp. 160–232, 1988.

62. Thieme, F. P., Schull, W. J. Sex determination from the skeleton. Hum. Biol. 29:242–273, 1957.

Chapter 10

Age Assessment of Child Skeletal Remains in Forensic Contexts

Mary E. Lewis and Ambika Flavel

Summary

Of all the techniques used to identify children's skeletal remains, age assessment is the most reliable a forensic anthropologist can provide. In forensic contexts, assigning an age to a living child of unknown identity may be necessary when the child is the victim of a crime, suspected of a crime, when penal codes differentiate law and punishment for children of different ages, or if the child is a refugee of uncertain age. This chapter outlines the methods and caveats of skeletal and dental age estimations in non-adult skeletal remains, with published case studies and experiences from investigations after the Guatemalan armed conflict.

Key Words: Forensic anthropology; dental age; skeletal age; Guatemala.

1. INTRODUCTION

Of all the techniques used to identify children's skeletal remains, age assessment is the most reliable. In biological anthropology, the age at death of a child is used to make inferences about infant and child mortality rates, growth and development, morbidity, weaning ages, congenital and environmental conditions, palaeodemography, and infanticide. In forensic contexts, assigning an age to a living child of unknown identity may be necessary when the child is suspected of a crime, when penal codes differentiate law and punishment for children of different ages (1,2), or if the child is a refugee of

From *Forensic Anthropology and Medicine:*
Complementary Sciences From Recovery to Cause of Death
Edited by: A. Schmitt, E. Cunha, and J. Pinheiro © Humana Press Inc., Totowa, NJ

uncertain age. For the deceased child, age estimation is the most accurate biological identifier that a forensic anthropologist can provide.

Age estimation of non-adult individuals is based on a physiological assessment of dental or skeletal maturation and relies on the accurate conversion of biological into chronological age. Error in the accuracy of this conversion can be introduced by random individual variation, the effects of the environment, disease, secular changes, and genetics *(3,4)*. Most importantly, the age of development of the dentition and skeleton are known to differ between the sexes, a biological assessment that has yet to be carried out successfully in forensic anthropology *(5)*. As with adult skeletal remains, studies on the development rates of children from various countries is hindered by the lack of modern skeletal collections. Parents rarely choose to donate the bodies of their deceased children to medical science and therefore, large collections of known infant and child skeletons are limited. In addition, the recent changes to the laws governing access to medical radiographs of living children have hindered research into growth and stature *(6)*.

2. DENTAL DEVELOPMENT

Dental development is less affected by environmental influences than skeletal growth and maturation *(7)*, and mineralization of the dentition is the preferred method for producing an age estimate for non-adults. The development of the permanent dentition covers a period from birth to around 12 yr of age. Here, differences between the sexes are evident, with females being, on average, 1–6 mo ahead in their development than males. This variability is also evident in individual teeth, with the canines considered the most sexually dimorphic, and females being as much as 11 mo ahead of males in their development *(8)*. However, caries, severe malnutrition, or premature shedding of the deciduous teeth may delay the eruption of the succeeding dentition *(3,9)*.

There is a wealth of literature on the development and eruption of the deciduous and permanent dentition in children, and standards exist for various populations (Table 1), which employ both radiographic and macroscopic techniques. Although such estimates are usually best left to the forensic odontologist, it is often necessary for the anthropologist to provide an age estimate in cases where odontologists or dental records are not available. Dental development follows a typical pattern and can be divided into convenient stages, beginning with cusp mineralization of the deciduous maxillary incisors, and normally ending in root apex closure of the third molar. However, the timing of this development varies between populations *(10–14)*, and the

Table 1
Studies Available for the Dental Age Assessment of Children From Different Geographical Areas

Source	Population	Sample size	Notes
Moorrees, Fanning, and Hunt (29,69)	White American	246	Formation stages for deciduous and permanent mandibular teeth.
Gustafson and Koch (70)	Northern European	ns	Combined published data for deciduous and permanent teeth.
Demirjian et al. (71)	French-Canadian	2928	Mandibular permanent dentition.
Demirjian and Goldstein (72)	French-Canadian	2407 males 2349 females	Updated and simplified method following Demirjian et al. (1973).
Holman and Jones (11)	Bangladeshi Guatemalan Japanese Javanese	397 1271 114 468	Deciduous tooth emergence times.
Willems et al. (14)	White Belgians	2116	Corrected Demirjian et al.'s (1973) permanent tooth development technique.
Gunst et al. (73)	White Belgians	2513	Third molar development.
Bolaños et al. (17)	Spanish	786	Third molar development. Tested Nolla's (1960) data.
Gillett (23)	Zambian	721	Permanent tooth emergence.
Nichols et al. (74)	Mexican Americans	500	Compared with Demirjian et al.'s (1973) French-Canadian data.
Harris and McKee (10)	American blacks American whites	335 655	Mineralization of permanent teeth in males and females.
Loevy (12)	American black, white, and Latino	1085	Mineralization of permanent dentition.
Dahlberg and Menegaz-Bock (20)	Pima Indian	957	Compared eruption times of permanent dentition.
Chagula (75)	East African	990 males	Eruption of third molars.
Davis and Hägg (76)	Chinese	204	Tested Demirjian et al.'s (1973) permanent tooth development technique.
Garn et al. (21)	American blacks	3868	Permanent tooth emergence in low-income population.
Fanning and Moorrees (15)	Australian Aborigine, Australian, New Zealand whites	210	Mineralization of the permanent molars.

third molar in particular has been shown to be highly variable *(15–17)*. By contrast, dental eruption is a continuous process with few biological markers and is thought to begin with the mineralization of the cleft *(18)*. Evidence of clinical eruption, or the emergence of the tooth through the gingiva, is distinct from the eruption though the alveolar bone, seen in the hard tissues, which occurs slightly earlier *(19)*. Again, the timing and sequence of tooth emergence has been shown to vary among populations and with certain diseases *(20–23)*.

In order to simplify recording stages of development, Liversidge and Molleson *(24)* produced a method for measuring tooth length macroscopically and from radiographs based on archaeological remains. When this and two other dental estimates were tested for accuracy on a modern sample, ages were underestimated, and accuracy decreased with age *(25)*. Caution is therefore advised when choosing a method for dental aging for skeletonized remains when developmental and eruption timings were derived from archaeological samples and vice versa. Muller-Bolla and colleagues *(26)* have recently introduced a simplified method of dental age, using counts of erupted permanent teeth, based on 5848 modern (2000–2001 AD) white children from France. However, there have been few studies that test established methods on modern forensic cases from Europe and North America. In 1996, Lampl and Johnson provided a cautionary tale when they tested a popular dental aging standard (Demirjian 1978, 1979) on similarly modern healthy children, and estimated they were underaged by as much as 3.5 yr! More recently, Bolaños and colleagues *(27)* stated that age estimations based on dental development in modern children are most precise for those under 10 yr of age, perhaps because of the greater number of stages to be scored and teeth that can be observed. In addition, they suggest the most accurate ages can be gained from the central maxillary incisors, the first mandibular molar, and the canine in boys, and the central maxillary incisors and the first and second mandibular molars in girls.

For fetal remains, dental development standards have been published by Schour and Massler *(28)*, Moorrees et al. *(29)*, Kraus and Jordan *(30)*, Lunt and Law *(31)*, Deutsch et al. *(32)*, and more recently, Nyström et al. *(33,34)*. The deciduous dentition is considered less environmentally influenced than the permanent teeth, but ancestral and sex differences still exist *(25)*. For example, Demirijian *(3)* found that all the teeth, with the exception of the first deciduous molar, emerged 1 mo earlier in boys than in girls. However, few standards exist for the formation of deciduous crowns based individuals of known gestational age *(4)*, and in fetal skeletal remains, the developing crowns sit in large open crypts, which often results in the loss of tooth germs during excavation and storage.

In some situations, it may be necessary to use macroscopic methods to assign an age using radiographic data. This may produce errors, as a higher stage of development is often scored when viewing the tooth itself rather than its image on X-ray. Radiographs will show a slightly later time for the formation of crowns and roots than those based on dissected material because the dental tissue needs a greater degree of calcification before being visible on a radiograph *(19)*. For example, the first permanent molar does not show up on a clinical radiograph until 6 mo, despite being calcified prenatally *(35)*. On a radiograph of dry bone, teeth may rotate in the jaw and obscure the true developmental stage of the tooth. Similarly, fragile mineralized material (for instance, the cleft at the start of root development) may be lost postmortem, resulting in a lower score for the macroscopic assessment.

One way to combat the errors in interpreting chronological from biological age, and underestimates that may be introduced by damaged teeth, is to examine microscopic features to assign an individual age. Microscopic aging techniques are based on the incremental markings within the dental microstructure. Unlike macroscopic or radiographic aging methods, chronological age does not need to be extrapolated from a set of standards, therefore introducing error as a result of interpopulation variability, but can be assessed directly *(35)*. Dental growth layers reflect a physiological rhythm and are represented by incremental markers, such as cross-striations, striae of Retzius, and perikymata. Cross-striations along the length of the enamel prisms are thought to result from a 24-h variation in the enamel matrix secretion *(36)*, whereas the coarser striae of Retzius (seen on the surface as perikymata) appear to represent near weekly (4–11 d) variation *(35)*. The first study on microscopic dental aging was carried out by Asper in 1916 *(37)* on human permanent canines. This was followed by Massler and Schour in 1946 *(38)*, who provided a technique for estimating age in days. A method by Boyde *(36)* originally conducted on two forensic and one archaeological case was employed by Huda and Bowman *(35)* to distinguish more precisely between commingled non-adult remains when macroscopic dental assessment and skeletal development proved inadequate. However, they warned that observer experience, decomposition of partially mineralized enamel, and variations in the plane of the thin section can all effect the accuracy of the technique.

3. SKELETAL DEVELOPMENT AND MATURATION

When dentition is unavailable, estimates of age on non-adult remains relies on the development, growth, and maturation of the skeleton. Establishing the age of fetal remains is mainly carried out with diaphyseal lengths and is critical in many forensic cases as a means to assess the viability of the fetus, or to assist in cases of abortion legislation and infanticide. Errors in the relationship between long bone diaphyseal lengths and gestational age are well known but difficult to control for in forensic contexts. The nutritional status of the mother during pregnancy, her weight, and her height all affect the size and weight of the child at birth and hence, the length of the diaphyses *(39,40)*. Additional stress factors, such as noise pollution and smoking, will decrease size for age *(41,42)*. It has also been proposed that female fetuses mature earlier than males in both leg length and weight *(43)*, potentially resulting in longer diaphyseal lengths and older age estimates in a female-dominated sample. Some researchers have explored the issue of shrinkage of the diaphyses in fetal remains, first raised by Rollell in the 1800s *(44)*. Studies of wet-to-dry bone have shown up to 10% shrinkage, and from wet-to-burned bone up to 32% shrinkage in fetuses of 4 lunar mo, decreasing to 1 and 2%, respectively, in newborns *(45,46)*. However, Warren *(47)* reported no significant differences in ages derived from radiographic (wet) diaphyseal lengths compared with dry-bone measurements.

A variety of data for aging fetal remains from diaphyseal lengths have recently been published by Scheuer and Black *(48)*, and attempts are being made to provide updated radiographic data of fetal remains with methods that can be applied to dry bone *(47,49,50)*. However, caution is advised when attempting to age fetuses with known or suspected congenital pathology *(51)*. Huxley and colleagues *(52)* provide a conversion chart for the transfer of ages reported in lunar months (anthropological sources) or gestational weeks (clinical sources) to allow viability of the fetus to be accurately assessed. More general assessment of age for perinates (whether ante- or postnatal) have been devised based on the appearance and fusion of growth centers and bone size; these include the temporal ring and plate *(48)* and the suture mendosa and pars basilaris of the occipital *(53)*. In addition, new data based on the dimensions of the fetal atlas and axis *(54)* and mandibular ramus *(55)* have been suggested. Most recently, Piercecchi-Marti and colleagues *(56)* have reported that a combination of the maturational assessment of surviving fetal viscera and femoral diaphyseal lengths can increase the accuracy of age at death in forensic cases.

In older children and adolescents, age estimates in the absence of the dentition are based on the appearance and fusion of the secondary growth centers, or epiphyses, to the diaphyses. The usual clinical method of assessing hand and foot maturation based on the appearance of secondary ossification centers (e.g., Greulich-Pyle Atlas, Tanner Whitehouse System) are not reliable for skeletal remains recovered from clandestine graves, as these tiny epiphyses are susceptible to taphonomic processes and are rarely recovered, although the method may be of use in partially skeletonized individuals or cadavers. Adolescents may enter the forensic record as teenage suicides, child soldiers, or they may have been vulnerable because of living on the streets. In the latter case, they are likely to be malnourished or neglected, resulting in a delay in their maturation.

In general, the maturation of girls is recognized to be 2 yr in advance of boys, with differences between populations being evident. For example, Pakistani and American black children tend to mature earlier than white Americans (57,58). However, there are few studies available that examine epiphyseal fusion rates in large samples of children of different ancestry from good economic backgrounds that would allow the assessment of true ancestry differences to be carried out. In India, Sahni and Jit (59) aged girls under 16 yr by nonfusion of the medial epicondyle of the humerus and head of the radius in criminal cases when sex with a minor was suspected. Other potentially useful biological markers in adolescence are the fusion of the hook of the hamate, and capping of the epiphysis of the third metacarpal and, in white children, the completion of the root (but not apical closure) of the canine, all of which are thought to signify the beginning of the growth spurt and puberty (60).

In general, the sequence of epiphyseal fusion begins at the elbow and through to the hip, ankle, knee, wrist, and finally, the shoulder. Data for age based on skeletal maturation appear in many texts, and most standards require the observer to score whether the growth plate is open, partially fused, or completely fused (61). Assessments will differ depending on whether the specimen is viewed as dry bone or on a radiograph, where the fusion line will persist when all external traces of fusion have gone (62). For example, Cope (63) reported the radiographic persistence of the fusion line on the distal femur and proximal tibia in an individual over 70 yr of age!

Once fusion of the long bones is complete, late fusing epiphyses, such as the basilar occipital synchondrosis, are used for adolescent aging, but recent research on modern cadavers has indicated it is only reliable for females (64), making this a difficult feature to use in individuals of unknown sex. Other methods, such as the fusion of the thoracic and lumbar vertebral rings in males and females, have helped to refine aging methods in adolescents (65–67).

4. PRACTICAL APPLICATIONS: THE GUATEMALAN ARMED CONFLICT

The Guatemalan armed conflict is an example that embodies many of the challenges involved in estimating age of non-adult individuals, resulting from poor preservation, conditions before and surrounding death, and the often immense scale of the task.

The Comisión para el Esclarecimiento Histórico (CEH) estimates that 200,000 Guatemalans died in the armed conflict between the years 1962 and 1996 *(68)*, with the peak of deaths (48%) occurring in 1982. Of those individuals whose age could be determined, 18% were children. The deceased were either buried in single or multiple graves or thrown down wells or caves. Such depositions result in challenges for the excavation of complete remains, and comingling is common. In addition, the period for which remains are interred cannot be relied on to predict the extent of preservation of the remains. Figure 1 shows the remains of two Guatemalan children recovered by the Fundación de Antropología Forense de Guatemala in 2003. In the first case (Fig. 1A), the lack of physical evidence limited age estimation, although sex could be presumptively assigned from the clothing, whereas in the second case (Fig. 1B), complete survival of the remains allowed a full age estimate to be carried out; both bodies were interred at the same time.

It is not always possible to control the environment in which remains are recovered. Scattered skeletal elements on the surface, scavenged by local wildlife, may result in the collection on fragmentary and commingled remains. Similarly, fragmentary remains can be recovered from robbed or incompletely excavated graves. Extremities (hands and feet), individual teeth, and unfused epiphyses are commonly left behind, either within the original grave cut or in the immediate vicinity. This was exemplified recently in Iraq, when local community groups and relatives removing loved ones from clandestine mass graves left a scattering of small bones, teeth, and epiphyses in the general area, observed during field walking. The presence of unfused epiphyses in this context has potential forensic implications, ranging from the killing of innocent children to the recruitment of child soldiers.

The manner and circumstances surrounding death may also obscure attempts to age non-adult remains. The CEH reports that 20% of all "arbitrary executions" in Guatemala were children. Witnesses report that many pregnant women and children were killed with gunfire, invariably resulting in polyfragmentation of the skeleton. Others were subjected to sharp or blunt force trauma, strangulation, or burning:

> " . . . *pero los soldados entraron a las casas disparando a toda la gente, hasta los niños y las mujeres embarazadas* . . . " *(CEH, 1999)* [" . . . *but the soldiers entered the houses shooting at everyone, even the children and pregnant women* . . . "]

> " . . . *la militar vino a quemar a varias familias enteras, vino a quemar sus viviendas y no solamente las viviendas sino las personas mismas, murieron hombres, mujeres y niños quemados, incinerados* . . . " *(ibid.)* [" . . . *the*

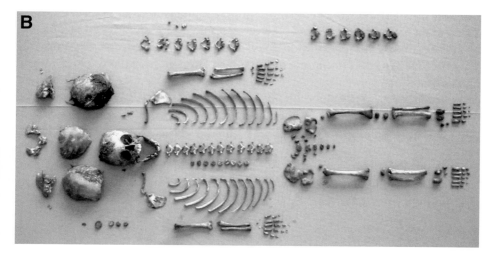

Fig. 1. Range of preservation of non-adult remains recovered from a buried environment by the Fundación de Antropología Forense de Guatemala, in Guatemala, 2003. The remains on the top **(A)** could not be assigned an age because of their incomplete and fragmentary condition. The remains on the bottom **(B)** were recovered in an almost complete state; therefore, both dental and skeletal aging methods could be utilized. Both individuals were buried for a similar period.

military came to burn several entire families, they came to burn their homes, not only their homes, also the people themselves, men, women and children died, burned, incinerated . . . "]

Investigations in Guatemala revealed the charred remains of several individuals in woodlands, represented mostly by deciduous teeth and os petrosa. Although anthropologists were unable to identify the individuals, it was possible to exclude the fact that adults were present in the grave as all the remains were from non-adults.

In Guatemala, as in other countries affected by mass killings and genocide, there is a tendency for people to bury women and children in graves separate from the adult men, with discrete families often buried together. Such knowledge can be of assistance when birth certificates are not issued. For example, three sisters were executed and buried together in a known location. Their exact age was unknown, but they were believed to be less than 8 yr old, with little more than 1 yr between them. The anthropologist was able to determine an age at death for the remains of each child, and although the age of the sisters may have been underestimated, the difference between all three was sufficient to allocate presumptive identifications to the remains.

In many cases of genocide, the majority of victims are minority groups often at lower socioeconomic status; for example, 83.33% of the victims in Guatemala were Mayan. Hence, the development and maturity of the youngest members of this population may be retarded because of malnutrition, especially when the communities have been impoverished by displacement and/or years of subjugation. Although it is abhorrent that such large numbers of children are involved in genocide or mass fatality investigations, this situation may assist in the development of population specific standards, not possible when estimating age of single individuals. It is therefore imperative that the forensic anthropologists charged with assessing the biological age in genocide cases with large numbers of individuals from distinct cultural or geographic environments employ aging methods that are accurate for that group, if not population-specific.

5. CONCLUSIONS

The personal identification of non-adult remains in forensic anthropology remains a problematic area, with many techniques applied to adult remains considered too imprecise for use in forensic circumstances involving children. One exception is the estimation of age at death, where the observation of dental development to assign age is considered one of the most accurate identifiers a forensic anthropologist can provide. Assessments of age based on the dentition and skeletal markers are hindered in remains recovered from clandestine and mass graves, as diagenesis and recovery techniques may result in the loss of the fragile developing dental crowns and primary and secondary ossification centers. In addition, the lack of large modern samples of non-adult skeletons of all ages and from different geographical areas limits the accuracy of the data that can be currently employed. In a situation like that of Guatemala, when large numbers of a distinct group of people were displaced and murdered, established aging methods should be tested on known samples for accuracy. Long-term projects should involve the development of population-specific standards to ensure accurate, uniform, and consistent analyses.

REFERENCES

1. Schmeling, A., Olze, A., Reisinger, W., Geserick, G. Age estimation of living people undergoing criminal proceedings. Lancet 358:8990, 2001.
2. Foti, B., Lalys, L., Adalian, P., et al. New forensic approach to age determination in children based on tooth eruption. Forensic Sci. Int. 3521:18, 2003.
3. Demirjian, A. Dentition. In: Falkner, F., Tanner, J. M., eds., Human Growth: a Comprehensive Treatise, Vol. 2. Plenum, New York, NY, pp. 269–297, 1990.
4. Saunders, S. R. Subadult skeletons and growth-related studies. In: Katzenberg, A., Saunders, S. R., eds., Biological Anthropology of the Human Skeleton. Wiley-Liss, New York, NY, pp. 135–161, 2000.
5. Lewis, M., Rutty, G. The endangered child: the personal identification of children in forensic anthropology. Sci. Justice 43:201–209, 2003.
6. Burton, J., Wells, M. The Alder Hey affair. J. Clin. Pathol. 54:820–823, 2001.
7. Acheson, R. M. Effects of starvation, septicaemia and chronic illness on the growth cartilage plate and metaphysis of the immature rat. J. Anat. 93:123–134, 1959.
8. Demirjian, A., Levesque, G. Y. Sexual differences in dental development and prediction of emergence. J. Dent. Res. 59:1110–1122, 1980.
9. Larsen, C. S. Bioarcheology: Interpreting Behavior from the Human Skeleton. Cambridge Studies in Biological Anthropology 21. Cambridge University Press, Cambridge, 1997.
10. Harris, E., McKee, J. Tooth mineralization standards for blacks and whites from the middle southern United States. J. Forensic Sci. 35:859–872, 1990.
11. Holman, D. J., Jones, R. E. Longitudinal analysis of deciduous tooth emergence II: parametric survival analysis in Banladeshi, Guatemalan, Japanese, and Javanese children. Am. J. Phys. Anthropol. 105:209–230, 1998.
12. Lovey, H. Maturation of permanent teeth in Black and Latino children. Acta Odontol. Pediatr. 4:59–62, 1983.
13. Tomkins, R. L. Human population variability in relative dental development. Am. J. Phys. Anthropol. 99:79–102, 1996.
14. Willems, G., Van Olmen, A., Spiessens, B., Carels, C. Dental age estimation in Belgian children: Demirjian's technique revisited. J. Forensic Sci. 46:893–895, 2001.

15. Fanning, E., Moorrees, C. A comparison of permanent mandibular molar formation in Australian Aborigines and Caucasoids. Arch. Oral Biol. 14:999–1006, 1969.

16. Kullman, L. Accuracy of two dental and one skeletal age estimation method in Swedish adolescents. Forensic Sci. Int. 75:225–236, 1995.

17. Bolaños, M., Moussa, H., Manrique, M., Bolaños. M. Radiographic evaluation of third molar development in Spanish children and young people. Forensic Sci. Int. 133:212–217, 2003.

18. Gleiser, I., Hunt, E. The permanent mandibular first molar: its calcification, eruption and decay. Am. J. Phys. Anthropol. 13:253–281, 1955.

19. Hillson, S. W. Studies of growth in dental tissues. In: Lukacs, J. R., ed., Culture, Ecology and Dental Anthropology. J. Hum. Ecol. Special Issue, 7:7–23, 1992.

20. Dahlberg, A., Menegaz-Bock, R. Emergence of the permanent teeth in Pima Indian children. J. Dent. Res. 37:1123–1140, 1958.

21. Garn, S., Sandusky, S., Nagy, J., Trowbridge F. Negro-Caucasoid differences in permanent tooth emergence at a constant income level. Arch. Oral Biol. 18:609–615, 1973.

22. Niswander. J. D. Permanent tooth eruption in children with major physical defects and disease. J. Dent. Child. 32:266–268, 1965.

23. Gillett, R. M. Dental emergence among urban Zambian school children: an assessment of the accuracy of three methods in assigning ages. Am. J. Phys. Anthropol. 102:447–454, 1997.

24. Liversidge, H. M., Molleson, T. Developing permanent tooth length as an estimate of age. J. Forensic Sci. 44:917–920, 1999.

25. Liversidge, H., Lyons, F., Hector, M. The accuracy of three methods of age estimation using radiographic measurements of developing teeth. Forensic Sci. Int. 131:22–29, 2003.

26. Muller-Bolla, M., Lupi-Pegurier, L., Quatrehomme, G., Velly, A., Bolla, M. Age estimation from teeth in children and adolescents. J. Forensic Sci. 48:140–148, 2003.

27. Bolaños, M., Manrique, M., Bolaños, M., Briones, M. Approaches to chronological age assessment based on dental calcification. Forensic Sci. Int. 110:97–106, 2000.

28. Schour, I., Massler, M. The development of the human dentition. J. Am. Dent. Assoc. 28:1153–1160, 1941.

29. Moorrees, C. F. A., Fanning, E. A., Hunt EE. Formation and resorption of three deciduous teeth in children. Am. J. Phys. Anthropol. 21:205–213, 1963.

30. Kraus, B. S., Jordan, R. E. The Human Dentition Before Birth. Henry Kimpton, London, 1965.

31. Lunt, R. C., Law, D. B. A review of the chronology of calcification of deciduous teeth. J. Am. Dent. Assoc. 89:599–606, 1974.

32. Deutsch, D., Tam, O., Stack, M. Postnatal changes in size, morphology and weight of developing postnatal deciduous anterior teeth. Growth 49:202–217, 1985.

33. Nyström, M., Peck, L., Kleemola-Kujala, E., Evälahti, M., Kataja, M. Age estimation in small children: reference values based on counts of deciduous teeth in Finns. Forensic Sci. Int. 110:179–188, 2000.

34. Nyström, M., Ranta, H. Tooth formation and the mandibular symphysis during the first five postnatal months. J. Forensic Sci. 48:1–5, 2003.

35. Huda, T. F. J., Bowman, J. E. Age determination from dental microstructure in juveniles. Am. J. Phys. Anthropol. 97:135–150, 1995.
36. Boyde, A. Estimating age at death of young human remains from incremental lines in dental enamel. Third International Meeting of Forensic Immunology, Medicine, Pathology and Toxicology, Plenary Session, London, 1963.
37. Asper H. Ueber die "Braune Retzius' sche parallelstreifung" im schmelz der menschlichen zähne [in German]. Schweiz. Vierteljahrschr. Zahneilkd. 26: 275, 1916.
38. Massler, M., Schour, I. The appositional life span of the enamel and dentine forming cells. I. Human deciduous teeth and first permanent molars. J. Dent. Res. 25:145–150, 1946.
39. Hauspie, R., Chrzastek-Spruch, H., Verleyen, G., Kozlowska, M., Suzsanne. C. Determinates of growth in body length from birth to 6 years of age: a longitudinal study of Dublin children. Int. J. Anthropol. 9:202, 1994.
40. Adair, L. Fetal adaptations to maternal nutritional status during pregnancy. Am. J. Phys. Anthropol. 38:50, 2004.
41. Schell, L. M. Environmental noise and human prenatal growth. Am. J. Phys. Anthropol. 56:63–70, 1981.
42. Sobrian, S. K., Vaughn, V. T., Ashe, W. K., Markovic, B., Djuric, V., Jankovic, B. D. Gestational exposure to loud noise alters the development and postnatal responsiveness of humoral and cellular components of the immune system in offspring. Environ. Res. 73:227–241, 1997.
43. Lampl, M., Jeanty, P. Timing is everything: a reconsideration of fetal growth velocity patterns identifies the importance of individual and sex differences. Am. J. Hum. Biol. 15:667–680, 2003.
44. Ingalls, N. Studies on femur III: effects of maceration and drying in the White and the Negro. Am. J. Phys. Anthropol. 10:297–321, 1927.
45. Huxley, A. Analysis of shrinkage in human fetal diaphyseal lengths from fresh to dry bone using Petersohn and Köhler's data. J. Forensic Sci. 43:423–426, 1998.
46. Huxley, A., Kósa, F. Calculation of percentage shrinkage in human fetal diphyseal lengths from fresh bone to carbonised and calcined bone using Petersohn and Köhler's data. J. Forensic Sci. 44:577–583, 1999.
47. Warren, M. W. Radiographic determination of developmental age in fetuses and stillborns. J. Forensic Sci. 44:708–712, 1999.
48. Scheuer, L., Black, S. Developmental Juvenile Osteology. Academic, London, 2000.
49. Adaline, P., Piercecchi-Marti, M. D., Bourliere-Najean, B., et al. Postmortem assessment of fetal diaphyseal femoral length: validation of a radiographic methodology. J. Forensic Sci. 46:215–219, 2001.
50. Piercecchi-Marti, M.-D., Adalian, P., Bourliere-Najean, B., et al. Validation of a radiographic method to establish new fetal growth standards: radio-anatomical correlation. J. Forensic Sci. 47:328–331, 2002.
51. Sherwood, R., Meindl, R., Robinson, H., May, R. Fetal age: methods of estimation and effects of pathology. Am. J. Phys. Anthropol. 113:305–315, 2000.
52. Huxley, A. K., Angevine, J. B. Determination of gestational age from lunar age assessments in human fetal remains. J. Forensic Sci. 43:1254–1256, 1998.

53. Scheuer, L., Maclaughlin-Black, S. Age estimation from the pars basilaris of the fetal and juvenile occipital bone. Int. J. Osteoarchaeol. 4:377–380, 1994.
54. Castellana, C., Kósa. F. Estimation of fetal age from dimensions of atlas and axis ossification centers. Forensic Sci. Int. 117:31–43, 2001.
55. Norris, S. Mandibular ramus height as an indicator of human infant age. J. Forensic Sci. 47:8–11, 2002.
56. Piercecchi-Marti, M.-D., Adalian, P., Liprandi, A., Figarella-Branger, D., Dutour, O., Leonetti. G. Fetal visceral maturation: a useful contribution to gestational age estimates in human fetuses. J. Forensic Sci. 49:912–917, 2004.
57. Rikhasor, R., Qureshi, A., Rathi, S., Channa, N. Skeletal maturity in Pakistani children. J. Anat. 195:305–308, 1999.
58. Garn, S. M., Clark, D. C. Problems in the nutritional assessment of black individuals. Am. J. Public Health 66:262–267, 1976.
59. Sahni, D., Jit, I. Time of fusion of epiphyses at the elbow and wrist joints in girls in Northwest India. Forensic Sci. Int. 74:47–55, 1995.
60. Chertkow, S. Tooth mineralization as an indicator of the pubertal growth spurt. Am. J. Orthod. 77:79–91, 1980.
61. Buikstra, J. E., Ubelaker, D. Standards for data collection from human skeletal remains. Arkansas Archaeological Survey Research Series 44. Arkansas Archeological Survey, Fayetteville, 1994.
62. Ubelaker, D. H. The estimation of age at death from immature human bone. In: Işcan, M. Y., ed., Age Markers in the Human Skeleton. Charles C Thomas, Springfield, IL, pp. 55–69, 1989.
63. Cope, Z. Fusion lines of bones. J. Anat. 25:280–281, 1946.
64. Kahana, T., Birkby, W., Goldin, L., Hiss, J. Estimation of age in adolescents—the basilaris synchondrosis. J. Forensic Sci. 48:1–5, 2003.
65. Albert, A., Maples, W. Stages of epiphyseal union for the thoracic and lumbar vertebral centra as a method of age determination for teenage and young adult skeletons. J. Forensic Sci. 40:623–633, 1995.
66. Albert, A. The use of vertebral ring epiphyseal union for age estimation in two cases of unknown identity. Forensic Sci. Int. 97:11–20, 1998.
67. Albert, A., McCallister, K. Estimating age at death from thoracic and lumbar vertebral ring epiphyseal union data. Am. J. Phys. Anthropol. 38:51, 2004.
68. Histórico/AAAS CpeE. Guatemala, memoria del silencio. Edición íntegra del informe de la Comisión para el Esclarecimiento Histórico de las Violaciones a los Derechos Humanos y los Hechos de Violencia que han Causado Sufrimientos a la Población Guatemalteca, 2000 [in Spanish].
69. Moorrees, C. F. A., Fanning, E. A., Hunt, E. E. Age variation of formation stages for ten permanent teeth. J. Dent. Res. 42:1490–1502, 1963.
70. Gustafson, G., Koch, G. Age estimation up to 16 years of age based on dental development. Odontol. Revy. 25:297–306, 1974.
71. Demirjian, A., Goldstein, H., Tanner. J. M. A new system of dental age assessment. Hum. Biol. 45:211–227, 1983.
72. Demirjian, A., Goldstein, H. New systems for dental maturity based on seven and four teeth. Ann. Hum. Biol. 3:411–421, 1976.

73. Gunst, K., Mesotten, K., Carbonez, A., Willems, G. Third molar root development in relation to chronological age: a large sample sized retrospective study. Forensic Sci. Int.136:52–57, 2003.
74. Nichols, R., Townsend, E., Malina, R. Development of permanent teeth in Mexican-American children. Am. J. Phys. Anthropol. 60:232, 1983.
75. Chagula, W. The age at eruption of third permanent molars in male East Africans. Am. J. Phys. Anthropol. 18:77–82, 1960.
76. Davis, P., Hägg, U. The accuracy and precision of the "Demirjian System" when used for age determination in Chinese children. Swed. Dent. J. 18:113–116, 1994.

Chapter 11

Determination of Adult Age at Death in the Forensic Context

Eric Baccino and Aurore Schmitt

Summary

   Age-at-death assessment faces biological and methodological problems. Age-related processes show great variation, both within and between populations. However, in forensic contexts, this parameter is crucial for identification, and both accuracy and reliability are required. Rather than proposing a list of various methods, the aim of this chapter is to suggest the most appropriate methods according to the indicators available for each case. The advantages and limits of the techniques presented are discussed. When most appropriate indicators are not available, the authors recommend avoiding age-at-death estimation.

   Key Words: Age at death; adult; pubis symphysis; sacropelvic surface; fourth rib; clavicle; periodontosis; root translucency.

1. INTRODUCTION AND PRELIMINARY REMARKS

1.1. Age-Assessment Objective in the Forensic Context

   Accurate estimation of age at death is a prerequisite for forensic identification *(1)* and paleoanthropological studies. However, the aims and constraints of paleoanthropology and forensic anthropology are different, although both fields apply the same methods. For past populations, estimation of age at death in skeletal material enables development of a demographic profile to discuss biology of past peoples and their burial practices. In forensic investigation, age

From *Forensic Anthropology and Medicine:*
Complementary Sciences From Recovery to Cause of Death
Edited by: A. Schmitt, E. Cunha, and J. Pinheiro © Humana Press Inc., Totowa, NJ

assessment is a part of establishing the biological profile of unidentified human remains. The value of this estimation is particular. Identification is essential for police or justice, as unidentified human remains arouse suspicion. Identification of a deceased person is also very important to the next of kin for economic and financial reasons (life insurance premium and salary payments of the deceased); for administrative reasons (funerals, inheritance, remarriage); and last, but not least, for psychological reasons. It is often more painful and difficult for the relatives to go through the mourning process when the body of their beloved person is not present.

1.2. Particularities of Forensic Cases

From a study made between 1997 and 2001 in the Montpellier area (population, approx 1.5 million), extrapolated to the whole country of France, it can be assumed that more than 1500 bodies admitted in the French medicolegal structures raise some kind of identification issue each year *(2)*.

Among these so-called John Does, 10% are well preserved, 33% are charred bodies, 33% are decomposed (to various degrees, but making a visual definite identification impossible), and only 20% are skeletonized.

This repartition has several practical implications for age estimation in a "daily" (not mass disaster) forensic activity. When a body is well preserved or moderately decomposed, it will have to be presented to the family for the wake; this implies that aging methods that are too destructive for the external appearance of the body (e.g., cranial suture closures and the sacroiliac joint) must be avoided. Therefore, in addition to being accurate and reliable, an aging method in forensic cases has to be elaborated on small parts of the body (i.e., easy to access and collect).

Moreover, because of the needs of police investigations, the age estimate must be given swiftly (within hours or days). Forensic anthropology has to deal with time factor. If the body is not skeletonized, it is necessary to clean the bones that are analyzed for age assessment. This bone cleaning takes 1–2 h with boiling water, bleach, and a metallic brush. It must be underlined that most of age-at-death assessment methods are elaborated on dry bones collections or samples *(3–6)* and do not take into account this parameter.

In most countries, working for justice means also keeping costs down. Therefore, in this chapter, the focus is on the "easy-to-run" methods, available to the majority of forensic teams.

This chapter excludes methods that are described as "reference" ones, such as aspartic acid racemization in dentine *(1)*, which the authors have been unable to carry out because of technical difficulties. These difficulties are shared by other teams. In addition, the reliability of this method has not been tested and compared with the more widely used ones described here.

1.3. Inherent Problems to Adult Age-At-Death Assessment From the Skeleton

Adult age-at-death assessment faces well-known problems developed in forensic and paleoanthropological papers *(6–9)*.

Adult age estimates are based on "wear-and-tear" indicators, such as skeletal degeneration, dental, and bone remodeling. It is nowadays largely accepted that methods of age assessment are flawed. The main source of the problem is the nature of human senescence. Senescence is characterized by an accumulation of metabolic disorders *(10)*. Age-related processes show great variation in the level and degree of change both within and between populations with increasing age *(11)*. Individual senescence is determined by a complex set of ongoing interactions (genes–culture–environment). Variation in the biological aging process has profound effects on age-at-death assessment. The relationship between chronological age and skeletal age indicators is neither constant nor linear. Skeletal changes have some relationship with age, but this relationship is governed by many factors *(12)*. The assumption that the underlying biological basis of the age/indicator relationship is constant across populations is erroneous. Therefore, the age of any unknown individual cannot be estimated by applying any methods. From a forensic point of view, it is necessary to take into account that age changes are not uniform across populations *(13)*. When applied to independent populations of known age at death, methods prove less reliable than the results obtained from the samples used to elaborate the methods *(14–17)*. Therefore, in forensic contexts, it is necessary to use specific population standards methods *(6)*. However, one must not forget the variability between individuals within the same population, a parameter that is often underestimated *(18)*. Further, ancestry of an individual whose body is skeletonized or decomposed is difficult to determine.

1.4. Theoretical Basis for the Choice of the Methods

As chronological changes of age indicators in the human body do not occur at the same pace during the life-span, the first step in age estimating is to preclassify the case in question within one of two age brackets, children up to 12 yr (when dental development will be crucial) and subadults up to 20 yr (based mainly on epiphyses study).

For adults, there are three additional subgroups: the young adults (up to 40 yr); the mature adults (over 40 yr); and the senior adults, or the elderly (over 65 yr), for which there is no reliable method allowing an age estimation more precise than "65 and over." Considering that they are a fast-growing percentage of the population in developed countries and that they often die isolated, i.e, found decomposed in their apartment or outside (dementia and run away), the identification problem of the elderly has to be solved.

One key factor for the choice of the appropriate method for aging adult remains is the quality of the preservation of these remains; dealing with a well-preserved entire body is a completely different problem than trying to age fragmented body parts (8). It is through this constraint imposed by the case that the authors have developed views about assessing age at death of adult human remains.

This chapter aims to provide practical information to professionals who are faced with aging in forensic cases; therefore, rather than proposing a list of various methods, the most appropriate methods, according to the indicators available on each case (fragments, skeleton, body, etc.) will be presented.

2. AGE DETERMINATION OF COMPLETE BODIES IN ADULTS (SKELETONIZED OR DECOMPOSED)

2.1. Two-Step Procedure

The authors have developed and used the two-step procedure (TSP) for 15 yr (19). The advantage of this method is its accuracy/simplicity ratio (19). TSP is an easy-to-run method that can be used by most forensic teams, with results rapid and accurate enough to cope with the investigation needs.

The principle of TSP (20) is to combine chronologically, not mathematically, the Suchey-Brooks System (SBS) for the pubic symphysis with the dental method of Lamendin. SBS (13,21,22) is an age-interval method that is accurate for aging individuals between 17 and 40 yr old. The pubic symphysis matures late in life. These modifications are distinct enough to enable assessment of age at death. Once the maturation process is over, morphological changes are degenerative and highly variable between individuals (4,19,23,24). The method of Lamendin is a formula method that gives better result for deceased individuals between 40 and 65 yr old (19,25). The first step consists of the examination of the pubic symphysis for a prechoice. It enables classification of the case as a young adult (phase I, II, or III of SBS) or an older one (phases IV, V, VI).

For SBS phases I, II, and III, the age estimate is given using the chronological interval corresponding to each phase. If the SBS phase is IV, V, or VI, the Lamendin method is applied.

TSP is based on the hypothesis that a single method is not relevant for the entire life-span. With TSP, the methods used are complementary and not combined. This approach is completely different from the multi-indicators methods recommended by many authors *(26–28)* and recently challenged. Combining methods that were elaborated on different reference samples leads to a fundamental error. Variability between populations does not allow such an approach. Moreover, it is not possible to associate mathematically a method giving an age estimate with a standard deviation with a method giving an age category *(6)*.

2.2. First Step: Pubic Symphysis Examination With SBS

2.2.1. CHARACTERISTICS OF SBS: ADVANTAGES AND WEAKNESSES

Among the pubic symphysis aging methods *(3,8,29)*, the authors prefer SBS for several reasons. First, its application is simple. Morphological modifications are divided into six phases. In addition, pubic casts are available for visual comparison, which is of great interest for the less experienced observers *(19,30)*. This method has been elaborated on a modern, multiregional, and forensic population (autopsy samples of Los Angeles Coroners Office), and the data processing takes into account the variability between individuals. For each phase, two age intervals are provided, 66 and 95% confidence intervals. Working with this technique since 1988, Baccino *(19)* has shown that it can be used with reliability on a European sample for individuals under 40 yr of age.

However, SBS presents some disadvantages. Gender and ancestry are prerequisites, and the symphyseal face is often damaged in ancient skeleton cases and in charred bodies.

2.2.2. COLLECTION AND PREPARATION OF THE PUBIC SYMPHYSIS

Soft tissue often abundant in forensic cases must be dissected on the autopsy table to gain access to the bone. An electric saw is necessary to cut the ischio- and iliopubic ramus (at least 2-cm long) in order to keep all the information. Preparation of the pubic symphysis is simple: after removing as much soft tissue as possible with a lance, forceps, and a metallic brush, the sample is put into boiling water. The process may last 10 min to 1 h, depending on the density of bone and how strongly cartilage is attached to the bone surface. It means that boiling must be watched regularly; the goal is to clean the symphyseal surface from soft tissues without losing information. A harsh preparation might destroy age criteria. Once prepared, if no chemical was used, the sample can be stored indefinitely at room temperature.

2.2.3. AGE-AT-DEATH ASSESSMENT WITH SBS

A detailed visual comparison with the casts allows, most of the time, any observer to a single phase choice.

The first feature observed is the aspect of the articular surface, which is billowy with clearly marked ridges and furrows in young individuals. The surface becomes flat in the 40s and eventually becomes excavated and irregular because of porosity, bone destruction, and construction.

The second criterion is the dorsal and ventral rims, which are absent in initial stages. The dorsal formation begins first, the upper part of the ventral margin being the last to be completed. Only in the fourth phase is an oval, articular surface achieved.

The evaluation of the completion of the upper and lower extremities enables differentiation of the three earlier phases. They are absent in phase I, incomplete in phase II, and complete in phase III.

A few practical recommendations can be made. It is necessary to compare both sides of the articulation as maturation may vary between the left and the right side. In order to accentuate the relief, the regular surface should be watched by using a dark background. The articular surface must be moved during examination in front, profile, and oblique view.

Figure 1 illustrates the six phases of SBS for males (Fig. 1A) and females (Fig. 1B), with mean age at death, standard deviation, and a 95% range as given by Brooks and Suchey *(22)*.

2.3. Second Step: A Single Rooted Tooth Examination With the Lamendin Method

2.3.1. CHARACTERISTICS OF THE LAMENDIN METHOD

As with most of dental methods for age-at-death assessment, the Lamendin method originates from the microscopic method of Gustafson *(31)*, which was based on the assessments of six dental features. In addition to the complexity of its realization (longitudinal thin sections of the tooth needed), the main flaw of this method was the use of the reference sample (from which the formula was established) to test the accuracy of the method. As a result, no further studies were able to show results as good as the initial publication *(32–34)*. In the 1980s, Lamendin *(35)* applied multivariate analysis to a large

Fig. 1. Suchey-Brook male **(A)** and female **(B)** pubic age determination with descriptive statistics. sd, standard deviation; 95% range, age interval for 95% of the sample.

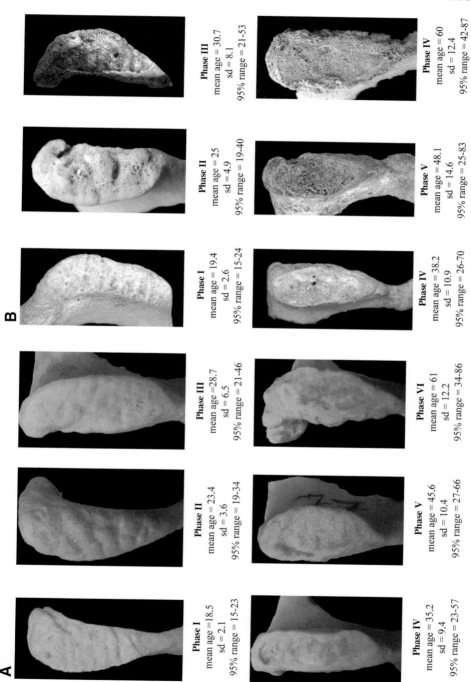

modern sample collected in dental offices (400 individuals) and showed that root translucency was the most important factor of the seven Gustafson criteria. It also demonstrated that, among all criteria, only periodontosis was statistically independent from root translucency. Translucency is because of the deposition of hydroxyapatite crystals in the dentin tubuli and appears usually after the age of 25. It is a natural phenomenon independent from acquired factors. This is not the case for periodontosis, which is highly dependent on diet and oral hygiene and which improves significantly (but slightly) the accuracy of the two-criteria age-determination formula of Lamendin. The use of root length as a denominator eliminates the influence of the tooth size on age evaluation.

2.3.2. AGE-AT-DEATH ASSESSMENT WITH THE LAMENDIN METHOD

A single rooted tooth (incisor or canine), a light source (such as a 16-W light box), a ruler, and a caliper square are needed. The measurements are made on the entire extracted tooth, without any preparation. During the development of this method, it was shown that the type and side of the tooth on which measurements are made, the mean of measurement values obtained from several teeth vs one tooth, have no significant influence on the performances of the method *(36)*. When a tooth has been extracted, the measurements of the translucency, periodontosis, and root height must be done on the same side of the tooth where the measurements seem the easiest to take. Root length is the distance between the apex of the root and at the crown (cementoenamel junction). Periodontosis is the distance between the crown and the soft tissue attachment line, visible as a brownish line and often detectable by touching. Translucency is easily visible by looking at the tooth exposed to a light box; the length of the transparent zone at the apex of the root is measured. Figure 2 shows these three distances.

Once measurements are made, age at death is obtained by the following formula:

$$Age = \left[\left(\frac{periodontosis}{root\ length} \times 0.18 \right) + \left(\frac{transculency}{root\ length} \times 0.42 \right) \right] \times 100 + 25.53$$

The mean error on the estimation, given for each decade, represents the average error between the actual and estimated age obtained from an evaluation of the method on real independent forensic cases *(19,36)*. For example, when the calculated age is 46 yr, there is a 66% chance that the actual age is between 35 and 55 yr (it corresponds to the estimated age ±9.9 yr). To obtain a 95% chance, it is necessary to double the average error. Experts should take into account this error interval when evaluating age at death by this method.

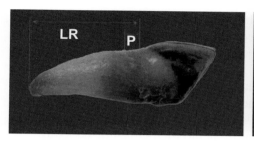 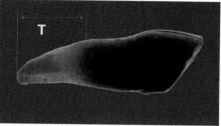

Fig. 2. Lamendin's method: measurements of the root length (LR), periodontosis (P), and translucency (T).

2.3.3. ADVANTAGES AND WEAKNESSES OF THE LAMENDIN METHOD

Because root translucency develops later in life, this method does not work with young individuals but provides acceptable confidence ranges from the age of 40 until 65. Below this limit, the confidence interval is more than 10 yr.

The application of the Lamendin method is simple, and differences between observers are low *(37)*. A recent study validated this method on a large-scale study done on a North American sample from the Terry Collection *(25)*. The results gave a smaller mean error (7.7 on the US sample vs 8.4 on the French one) than those from the original publication. In addition, Prince showed that by establishing gender- and population-specific formulae, the accuracy is only slightly improved (1 yr maximum). However, the same author *(38)* demonstrated that it is necessary to recalculate the formula from an appropriate reference sample to reduce the mean error of age-at-death assessment when applied to populations from the Balkans. It seems, therefore, that specific population standards have to be elaborated to obtain reliable results when applied to individuals from a different area than the reference sample.

A study *(39)* compared eight dental methods, both macroscopic and microscopic (sectioned teeth), and found that the Lamendin method had a "high" reliability, a low repeatability, a "high" usability, and a need for "standard" equipment. It is advisable to choose the method that has the best profile for the case in question, the Lamendin method being recommended for mass identification and "precious anthropological" cases. Unfortunately, this study is of limited interest as it is based on a small sample (20 cases) including individuals from the age of 14 (the exact number of individuals under 30 yr is not mentioned), an age period where the Lamendin method is not reliable (and should not be used).

As expected, the Lamendin method gives unreliable age-at-death assessment on individuals with major periodontal disease *(40)*.

The absence of single rooted teeth, frequent in the elderly, remains an obstacle to the method.

In case of a long postmortem delay (at least decades), translucency might be affected (unpublished study on the Coimbra Collection). As the range of these modifications and the factors involved are not established, caution is recommended when using the Lamendin method with ancient skeletons.

2.4. TSP: A Reliable Tool for Age Assessment

As expected, the efficiency of TSP is higher than the Lamendin method and SBS used alone *(41)* because of the two methods that make TSP perform better in a particular chronological interval. The first quality of TSP is to be elaborated from methods whose application is simple and fast, with low interobserver differences *(41)*. In addition, both methods were established from large and multiregional reference samples and have been (and are still being) evaluated on several independent samples, with satisfactory results.

TSP presents also significant limits, the first being the lack of one or two of the indicators. Second, some of the weaknesses of each of the constitutive methods remain. For instance, in a young individual where SBS will be chosen, it might be difficult to determine the ancestry on a decomposed or skeletonized cadaver. As the use of a population-specific standard is recommended, this methodological limit could be avoided by using a multiregional standard including the widest variability *(6,7)*. In the elderly, the Lamendin method does not perform for individuals over 65 yr of age. The application of Bayes' methodology *(7,42,43)* to TSP might fill, at least partly, this gap. Recently *(44)*, it was proposed adding a seventh phase to SBS to improve accuracy of aging the elderly female pubic symphysis, but considering the bad performances of phases IV, V, and VI, the authors' expectations are low.

2.5. Complementary Methods

There are two methods that can be useful in peculiar entire-body cases, even when the pubic symphysis and a single rooted tooth are available.

2.5.1. UNION OF CLAVICLE AND ILIAC CREST EPIPHYSES

From an anthropological point of view, adulthood can be defined as the time when epiphyses are fused, which indicates the end of bone growth.

Two epiphyses are of special interest for aging young individuals, the sternal end of the clavicle and the iliac crest of the ilium. Both epiphyses are easy to collect at autopsy. The medial end of the clavicle is cut with chisels;

the iliac crest needs an electrical saw. Caution must be taken in the earlier stage of union. The epiphyses are very thin, and fragile pieces of bone that may be damaged or even lost during boiling and cleaning.

As the fusion of these two epiphyses occurs between 17 and 30 yr of age, when an individual possesses a pubic symphysis in phase I or II, they provide relevant information to improve the accuracy of age-at-death assessment.

There are three stages: lack of union (the epiphyses are completely independent from the rest of the bone), partial union, and complete union.

The iliac crest of the ilium begins to fuse with the ilium between 14 and 23 yr of age, with complete union at 24 yr for both sexes *(45)*. However, as there are differences between populations *(46)*, it is recommended using the proper population standard. The fusion of the iliac crest has also been studied in clinical medicine as it is used as a biological age indicator for the end of the vertebral column growth *(47)* for scoliosis treatment in subadults.

The union of the medial clavicle begins at different age, depending on the population studied *(45)*. Table 1 summarizes the age interval of each of the three stages according to 11 studies from different geographical area. As for the iliac crest, it is recommended using a population-specific standard for higher accuracy.

2.5.2. AGE ASSESSMENT FROM THE STERNAL END OF THE FOURTH RIB

This method of using the sternal end of the fourth rib *(57–59)* is of interest when one hesitates between two phases of SBS, especially when the differentiation between phase III an IV is difficult.

The collection of a sternal part of a rib can be made by chisels. However, the chondrosternal joint is fragile. It may be damaged both by taphonomic conditions (fire, long postmortem delays, scavengers, and so forth), and preparation must therefore be more cautious than for the pubic symphysis. It is recommended collecting two ribs (the same on both sides) and cleaning completely the articulation surface on one side while keeping the cartilage on the other side in order to preserve all indicators. It has been demonstrated that this method can be applied from the third to the eighth rib, with equivalent performances *(60)*.

The method, initially based on the modification with age of the sternal end of fourth rib, consists of observing several features in order to classify the specimen in one of the nine phases proposed by the authors. Casts are available to make visual comparison of the following criteria:

1. The depth and the shape of the articulation ("the pit") that is flat in early stages, deepens slightly, with a V-shape and a billowy surface, becoming much deeper with a U-shape and an irregular surface in older stages.

Table 1
Age of Union of the Medial Clavicle in 11 Different Samples

Authors	Origin of sample	N	Technique	Nonunion (maximum age)	Partial union	Complete union (minimum age)	Complete union (100% of the sample)
Flecker (48)	Australia	437	X-ray	26	nd	22	26
Galstaun (49)	Bengal	654	X-ray	19	nd	19	25
Ji et al. (50)	Japan	54	Anatomical	<22		19	
Jit and Kulkarni (51)	North India	684	X-ray	19	18–24	22	25
Kreitner (52)	Europe	380	CT	22	16–26	22	27
Mc Kern and Stewart (29)	United States (of European origin)	374	Anatomical	nd	18–30	23	31
McLaughlin (53)	Portugal	32	Anatomical	<20	24–27		29
Owing Webb and Suchey (45)	United States (of European, African, and Mexican origin)	859	Anatomical	≤25	16–33	21	34
Stevenson (54)		110	Anatomical	>20	>22		28
Szilvassy (55)	Austria	140	Anatomical	>20	21–25	26	
Todd and D'Errico (56)	United States (of European and African origin)	166	Anatomical	nd	19–27	22	28

nd, no data; CT, computed tomography.

2. The edges of the rims, initially flat, become rounded and thick, then scalloped and thinner, and finally, irregular and sharp, with cartilage calcifications in the elderly (rounded in females, linear in males).

The authors suggest making visual observation from different angles, using a dark surface in the background to facilitate detailed examination.

The very small size of the initial Caucasian sample *(57,58)* used to elaborate the method, as well as the size of the black population sample assessed to evaluate racial variations *(59)*, make the statistics provided by the authors (mean and standard deviation) quite irrelevant; moreover, the choice of nine phases results in a very narrow age estimation. It is therefore not surprising that testing of the method by other teams failed to give as reliable result as expected. For instance, when using the nine phases, even experienced observers were wrong in 50% of cases *(61)*. Furthermore, many tests on independent samples confirmed that there were differences between populations *(15,62,63)*. Thus, this method must be used only as a complementary of TSP. Its use as a single method may lead to wrong age-at-death assessment, unless evaluation is given using two adjacent phases, diminishing precision but resulting in an acceptable reliability *(61,62)*.

3. AGE DETERMINATION WHEN TSP IS NOT POSSIBLE (FRAGMENTED, PARTIALLY RECOVERED BODY)

Rather that giving a long list of all available methods (there are more than 30 of them), the authors prefer to propose to the reader what they experienced as being the best strategy in each of the most common practical forensic situations. As expected, in those cases, methods available are less reliable or/and accurate.

3.1. Skull Alone

As decapitation and postmortem dismemberment cases are rare, aging an isolated skull occurs mainly when the remains are skeletonized. Usually, the skull stays at the death site, whereas other bones, which can be grabbed by small carnivores, are destroyed or moved. Sometimes, under the action of water (flood, river, sea), it is the skull that, because of its spherical shape, rolls away.

According to some textbooks *(8)*, the method of choice is cranial suture closure assessment, as proposed by Meindl and Lovejoy *(64)*. Ten sites of well-located ectocranial sutures are evaluated on a 1-cm length area for their stage of closure (open, minimal, advanced, closed, with corresponding numbers of 0, 1, 2, 3).

Two scores can then be obtained by adding the number attributed to each site, the vault system that groups seven sites and the lateral–anterior system that groups five sites (the two systems overlap for two sites in common).

The vault system provides 8 composite scores with a standard deviation from 7.8 to 12.6 yr, whereas the lateral–anterior system provides 9 with a standard deviation from 6.2 to 10.5 yr.

This method does not need any preparation (if skeletonized) and is easy to use even by beginners, but the authors agree with Masset's *(65)* conclusion that the relationship between chronological age and suture closure is only statistical. Moreover, unlike most of age indicators that change progressively with age, in some individuals, sutures never close. It may be because of the fact that suture closure is a maturation indicator rather than an aging one *(7)*. Thus, this indicator may lead to unreliable estimation.

The authors therefore recommend applying the Lamendin method when single rooted teeth are available (and if the skeleton is not too old). When there is no translucency, the Lamendin method is still useful. In this situation, it assures that the skull belongs to a young adult. When teeth other than single rooted ones are available, other dental age-estimation methods, such as Kvaal's or Solheim's intact methods *(39)*, cementum annulation *(66)*, pulp cavity index *(67)*, or even aspartic acid racemization *(1)*, should be preferred to cranial sutures if time and equipment are available. However, the age-at-death assessment must be provided with the proper standard error.

3.2. Body Without Teeth

When dentition is missing, the pubic symphysis is first observed for young adults under 40 yr, as in TSP. The fourth rib may help to age the elderly without really replacing the estimate from the tooth. Then, an alternative is to use the sacropelvic surface of the *ilium* (we prefer this term to *auricular surface*, as it includes the iliac tuberosity), but with a different methodology that the one proposed by Lovejoy et al. *(4)*. Several studies have proposed new scoring system and data processing *(68–70)*, but the method proposed by Schmitt and colleagues *(6,71)* is the most relevant at it avoids most of methodological biases common to current methods. It has been elaborated for studies of past populations *(72)*, but its contribution in forensic contexts may be valuable in badly preserved cadavers. Intra- and interobservers error was avoided by the elaboration of a simple scoring system. Four features were scored independently *(71)*. As age/indicator relationship varies among samples from different geographical regions, nine different samples from four continents (Europe, North America, Asia, and Africa) were studied in order to take into account the widest variability of aging patterns. The age-at-death estimation was made by the Bayesian approach. The probability of belonging to an age category conditional on knowledge of the indicator state is the most appropriate computation. As European samples follow the same trend of variation, a European model was created, without gender determination requisite *(73)*. For illustration, Table 2 shows the probability obtained from the different combination of the four features observed, computed from a sample whose age distribution is homogeneous. Chronological intervals are large but reliable.

3.3. Body Without Pubic Symphysis

The method based on the fourth rib *(57–59)* can be used as a substitute of SBS to do the screening of TSP. From phases I to V, the method can be used alone with the modifications mentioned already, giving an estimation with the interval of two phases rather than only one. However, Lamendin's method alone will be preferred to phases V to IX.

3.4. Body Without Teeth and Pubic Symphysis

When both indicators of TSP are missing, the alternative is to use the fourth rib or the sacropelvic surface of the ilium as described under Subheading 3.2. The estimation will, of course, lose accuracy.

3.5. Cases Represented by Long Bones and Various Fragments (Comingled Remains)

If no indicators described above are available, age-at-death assessment becomes a difficult task. In the large number of methods that have been developed for 50 yr, age-at-death assessment methods from long bones are based either on bone loss by X-ray *(5,74,75)* or histological analysis by microscopic observations of cortical bone structures *(76–80)*. However, the biological processes underlying bone loss and bone turnover are highly variables between sexes, within individuals from the same population, and between populations. The interaction of many parameters (heredity, environmental factors, physical activity, smoking, alcohol, medical treatment) are responsible for the metabolism of the bone tissue. Moreover, the techniques are time-consuming and destructive. The identification of cortical structure is difficult, and there are differences between observers *(41,81–83)*.

The little sample sizes constituted most of the time for the elderly are not appropriate. Age at death is predicted from regression, which overestimates the age of the youngest and underestimates the age of the oldest *(84)*. Thus, when the human remains are represented by fragments and/or long bones, age-at-death assessment is not possible. Consequently, process of identification is largely limited.

Table 2
Distribution of the Posterior Probabilities
From a Reference Population Whose Age Distribution is Uniform

Score				Probabilities					Estimation
SSPIA	SSPIB	SSPIC	SSPID	20–29	30–39	40–49	50–59	>60	
1	1	1	1	0.89	0.08	0.03	0.00	0.00	20–29
1	1	1	2	0.63	0.22	0.15	0.00	0.00	20–39
1	1	2	1	0.81	0.11	0.09	0.00	0.00	20–29
1	1	2	2	0.45	0.23	0.32	0.00	0.00	20–49
1	2	1	1	0.40	0.32	0.19	0.09	0.00	20–49
1	2	1	2	0.11	0.32	0.33	0.23	0.01	<60
1	2	2	1	0.23	0.25	0.31	0.19	0.02	<60
1	2	2	2	0.04	0.18	0.38	0.34	0.05	30–59
2	1	1	2	0.40	0.37	0.23	0.00	0.00	20–49
2	1	2	1	0.63	0.21	0.16	0.00	0.00	20–39
2	1	2	2	0.25	0.32	0.43	0.00	0.00	20–49
2	1	1	1	0.75	0.18	0.07	0.00	0.00	20–39
2	2	1	1	0.20	0.42	0.23	0.13	0.01	20–49
2	2	1	2	0.04	0.34	0.32	0.27	0.03	30–59
2	2	2	1	0.10	0.29	0.33	0.23	0.05	20–29
2	2	2	2	0.02	0.17	0.34	0.36	0.11	30–59
1	3	1	1	0.07	0.16	0.33	0.31	0.13	20–29
1	3	1	2	0.01	0.08	0.29	0.40	0.22	>40
1	3	2	1	0.02	0.06	0.27	0.31	0.34	>40
1	3	2	2	0.00	0.03	0.19	0.33	0.46	>40
2	3	1	1	0.03	0.15	0.28	0.30	0.25	>40
2	3	1	2	0.00	0.07	0.21	0.35	0.36	>40
2	3	2	1	0.01	0.05	0.18	0.25	0.52	>40
2	3	2	2	0.00	0.02	0.11	0.24	0.63	>50
1	4	1	1	0.00	0.26	0.14	0.38	0.23	>30
1	4	1	2	0.00	0.12	0.11	0.44	0.33	>40
1	4	2	1	0.00	0.09	0.09	0.32	0.50	>50
1	4	2	2	0.00	0.03	0.06	0.31	0.60	>50
2	4	1	1	0.00	0.21	0.10	0.32	0.37	>40
2	4	2	1	0.00	0.05	0.05	0.22	0.67	>50
2	4	1	2	0.00	0.09	0.07	0.34	0.50	>50
2	4	2	2	0.00	0.02	0.03	0.20	0.75	>50

SSPIA, transverse organization; SSPIB, surface modification; SSPIC, apical modification; SSPID, iliac tuberosity modification.

Age categories are added to reach a threshold of 0.8.

4. CONCLUSION

Rosing and Kvaal *(85)* stated that "methods with standard errors of regression of more than 5–7 yr were not suitable for routine forensic application." The authors think that it is a purely theoretical limit, without practical basis. Consider that adult age-at-death assessment is reliable and accurate enough from a legal point of view when the cadaver is well preserved. TSP yields satisfactory results. However, the Lamendin method requires more tests on populations from various areas in order to study and take into account the variability of the indicators involved with age.

When the teeth are missing, the Lamendin method can be replaced either by the observation of the sternal end of the fourth rib or by the sacropelvic surface of the ilium applying, respectively, the method of Işcan and Loth *(57–59)*, modified by Baccino and colleagues *(61,62)*, and the method elaborated by Schmitt *(6,71,73)*. However, one must keep in mind that the reliability of the former method and accuracy of the latter are lower than TSP. The study of the variability of aging modifications of the fourth rib, with appropriate statistical treatment, should be developed. By now, the evaluation of age by this indicator has to be considered with caution.

When both indicators of TSP (pubic symphysis and teeth), the fourth rib and the sacropelvic surface of the ilium are missing, age assessment is too unreliable and inaccurate, and its estimation is not recommended.

The biggest limit of age-at-death assessment, whatever the methods used, is the absence of identification of the elderly. After 65 yr of age, it is difficult to determine accurate age at death. Efforts in this direction are necessary.

REFERENCES

1. Ritz-Timme, S., Cattaneo, C., Collins, M. J., et al. Age estimation: the state of the art in relation to the specific demand of forensic practice. Int. J. Legal. Med. 113:129–136, 2000.
2. Boismenu, L., Bertolotti, C., Salerio, G., Baccino, E. L'identification Médico légale anthropologique, bilan d'activité autopsique du service de médecine légale de Montpellier au cours des années 1997–2001 [in French]. Presented at the 3rd Congress of Medico-Legal Anthropology, Nice, France, November 2001.
3. Todd, T. W. Age changes in the pubic bone. Am. J. Phys. Anthropol. 4:1–70, 1921.
4. Lovejoy, C. O., Meindl, R. S., Prysbeck, T. R., Mensforth, R. P. Chronological metamorphosis of the auricular surface of the ilium: a new method for the determination of adult skeletal age at death. Am. J. Phys. Anthropol. 68:15–28, 1985.
5. Walker, R. A., Lovejoy, C. O. Radiographic changes in the clavicule and proximal femur and their use in the determination of skeletal age at death. Am. J. Phys. Anthropol. 68:67–78, 1985.

6. Schmitt, A., Murail, P., Cunha, E., Rougé, D. Variability of the pattern of aging on the human skeleton: evidence from bone indicators and implications on age at death estimation. J. Forensic Sci. 47:1203–1209, 2002.
7. Schmitt, A. Estimation de l'âge au décès des adultes: des raisons d'espérer [in French]. Bull. Mem. Soc. Anthropol. Paris 14:51–73, 2002.
8. Ubelaker, D. K. Human Skeletal Remains: Excavation, Analysis, Interpretation, 3rd Ed. Taraxacum, Washington, D.C., 1999.
9. Bass, W. M. Human Osteology: a Laboratory and Field Manual of the Human Skeleton. Special publication. Missouri Archeological Society, Columbia, MO, 1971.
10. Rose, M. R. Evolutionary Biology of Aging. Oxford University Press, New York, NY, 1991.
11. Harper, G. J., Crews, D. E. Aging, senescence, and human variation. In: Stinson, S., Bogin, B., Huss-Ashmore, R., O'Rourke, D., eds., Human Biology: an Evolutionary and Biocultural Perspective. Wiley-Liss, New York, NY, pp. 465–505, 2000.
12. Jackes, M. Building the bases for paleodemographic analysis:adult age determination. In: Katzenberg, M. A., Saunders, S. R., eds., Biological Anthropology of the Human Skeleton. Wiley-Liss, New York, NY, pp. 417–466, 2000.
13. Katz, D., Suchey, J. M. Races differences in pubic symphyseal aging patterns in the male. Am. J. Phys. Anthropol. 80:167–172, 1989.
14. Murray, K. A., Murray, T. A test of the auricular surface aging technique. J. Forensic Sci. 36:1162–1169, 1991.
15. Saunders, S. R., Fitzgerald, C., Rogers. T., Dudar, C., McKillop, H. A test of several methods of skeletal age estimation using a documented archaelogical sample. Can. Soc. Forensic Sci. 25:97–118, 1992.
16. Schmitt, A. Age at death assessment using the os pubis and the auricular surface of the ilium: a test on an identified Asian sample. Int. J. Osteoarcheol. 14:1–6, 2004.
17. Schmitt, A., Murail, P. Is the first rib a reliable age indicator of age at death assessment? Test of the method elaborated by Kunos et al. (1999). Homo. 54:207–214, 2004.
18. Ubelaker, D. H. Methodological consideration in the forensic applications of human skeletal biology. In: Katzenberg, M. A., Saunders, S. R., eds., Biological Anthropology of the Human Skeleton. Wiley-Liss, New York, NY, pp. 41–67, 2000.
19. Baccino, E., Tavernier, J. C., Lamendin, H., Frammery, D., Nossintchouk, R, Humbert, J. F. Recherche d'une méthode multifactorielle simple pour la détermination de l'âge des cadavres adultes [in French]. J. Med. Leg. Droit Med. 34:27–33, 1991.
20. Baccino, E., Zerilli, A. The two-step strategy or the right way to combine a dental (Lamendin) and an anthropological (Suchey-Brooks System) method for age determination. Proc. Am. Acad. Forensic Sci. 3:150, 1997.
21. Suchey, J. M., Katz, D. Age determination of the male pubic bones. Am. J. Phys. Anthropol. 69:269, 1986.
22. Brooks, S., Suchey, J. M. Skeletal age determination based on the os pubis: a comparison of the Acsadi-Nemeskeri and Suchey-Brooks methods. Hum. Evol. 5:227–238, 1990.
23. Bocquet-Appel, J. P., Maia Neto, M. A., Tavares da Rocha, M. A., Xavier de Morais, M. H. Estimation de l'âge au décès des squelettes d'adultes par regressions multiples [in Portuguese]. Contrib. Estudo Antropol. Port. 10:107–167, 1978.

24. Meindl, R. S., Lovejoy, C. O., Mensforth, R. P., Walker, R. A. A revised method of age determination using the os pubis, with a review and tests of accuracy of other current methods of pubic symphyseal aging. Am. J. Phys. Anthropol. 68:29–45, 1985.
25. Prince, D. A., Ubelaker, D. H. Application of Lamendin's adult dental aging technique to a diverse skeletal sample. J. Forensic Sci. 47:107–116, 2002.
26. Işcan, M. Y., Loth, S. Osteological manifestation of age in the adult. In: Işcan, M. Y., Kennedy, K. A. R., eds., Reconstruction of Life from the Skeleton. Wiley-Liss, New York, NY, pp. 23–40, 1989.
27. Russel, K. F., Simpson, S. W., Genovese, J., Kinkel, M. D., Meindl, R. S., Lovejoy, C. O. Independent test of fourth rib aging technique. Am. J. Phys. Anthropol. 92: 53–62, 1993.
28. Meindl, R. S., Russel, K. F. Recent advances in method and theory in paleodemography. Annu. Rev. Anthropol. 27:375–399, 1997.
29. McKern, R. W., Stewart, T. D. Skeletal age changes in young American males. Technical report EP45, Environmental Protection Division, US Army Quartermaster Research and Development Center, Natick, MA, 1957.
30. Baccino, E., Coat, J. P., Masse, R., Develay-le Gueut, M. A. Problèmes d'identification posés par un cadavre momifié: intérêt de l'utilisation des kits osseux SUCHEY-BROOKS [in French]. J. Med. Leg. Droit Med. 32:267–271, 1989.
31. Gustafson, G. Age determination of teeth. J. Am. Dent. Assoc. 41:45–54, 1950.
32. Maples, W. R., Rices, P. M. Some difficulties in the Gustafson dental age estimations. J. Forensic Sci. 24:168–172, 1979.
33. Nkhumeleni, F. S., Raubenheimer, E., Monteith, B. D. Gustafson's method for age determination revised. J. Forensic Odontostomatol. 7:13–16, 1989.
34. Lucy, D., Pollard. A. M. Further comments on the estimation of error associated with the Gustafson dental age estimation Method. J. Forensic Sci. 40:222–227, 1995.
35. Lamendin, H. Determination de l'age avec la méthode de Guftason "simplifiée" [in French] Chir. Dent. Fr. 58:43–47, 1988.
36. Lamendin, H., Baccino, E., Humbert. J. F., Tavernier, J. C., Nossintchouk, R., Zerilli, A. A simple technique for age estimation in adult corpses: the two criteria dental method. J. Forensic Sci. 37:1373–1379, 1992.
37. Willems, G., Moulin-Romsee, C., Solheim, T. Non-destructive dental-age calculation methods in adults: intra- and inter-observer effects. Forensic Sci. Int. 126:221–226, 2002.
38. Prince, D. A., Konigsberg, L. W. New formulae for estimating age in the Balkans utilizing Lamendin's dental technique. Proceedings of the 56th Annual American Academy of Forensic Sciences, 16–21 February 2003, Dallas, TX. p. 279, 2004.
39. Soomer, H., Ranta, H., Lincoln, M. J., Pentilla, A., Leibur, E. Reliability and validity of eight dental age estimation methods for adults used in forensic odontology. J. Forensic Sci. 48:149–152, 2003.
40. Foti, B., Adalian, P., Signoli, M., Ardagna, O., Dutour, O., Leonetti. G. Limits of the Lamendin method in age determination. Forensic Sci. Int. 122:101–106, 2001.
41. Baccino, E., Ubelaker, D. H., Hayek, L., Zerilli, A. Evaluation of seven methods of estimating age at death from mature human skeletal remains. J. Forensic Sci. 44:39–44, 1999.

42. Konigsberg, L. W. Local standards vs. informative priors in applied forensic anthropology. Proceedings of the American Academy of Forensic Sciences, 16 February 2004, Dallas, TX, p. 276.
43. Chamberlain, A. Problems and prospects in paleodemography. In: Cox, M., May, S., eds., Human Osteology in Archeology and Forensic Science. Greenwich Medical Media, London, pp. 101–115, 2000.
44. Berg, G. E., Kimmerle, E. Aging the elderly: a new look at an old method. Proceedings of the American Academy of Forensic Sciences, 16 February 2004, Dallas, TX, p. 277.
45. Owing Webb, P. A., Suchey, J. M. Epiphyseal union of the anterior iliac crest and medial clavicule in a modern multiracial sample. Am. J. Phys. Anthropol. 68:457–466, 1985.
46. Scoles, P. V., Salvagno, R., Villalba, K., Riew, D. Relationship of iliac crest maturation to skeletal and chronologic age. J. Pediatr. Orthop. 8:639–644, 1988.
47. Risser, J. C. Important practical facts in the treatment of scoliosis. AAOS Instructional Course Lectures. V:248–2690, 1948.
48. Flecker, H. Roentgenographic observations of the times of appearance of epiphyses and their fusion with the diaphyses. J. Anat. 67:118–164, 1933.
49. Galstaun, G. A study of ossification as observed in Indian subjects. Indian J. Med. Res. 25:267–324, 1937.
50. Ji, L., Terazawa, K., Tsukamoto, T., Haga, K. Estimation of age from epiphyseal union degrees of the sternal end of the clavicle [in Japanese]. Hokkaido Igaku Zasshi 69:104–111, 1994.
51. Jit, I., Kulkarni, M. Times of appearance and fusion of epiphysis at the medial end of the clavicle. Indian J. Med. Res. 64:773–782, 1976.
52. Kreitner, K. F., Schweden, F. J., Riepert, T., Nafe, B., Thelen, M. Bone age determination based on the study of the medial extremity of the clavicle. Musculoskelet. Radiol. 8:1116–1122, 1988.
53. MacLaughlin, S. M. Epiphyseal fusion at the sternal end of the clavicle in a modern Portuguese skeletal sample. Antropol. Port. 8:59–68, 1990.
54. Stevenson, P. H. Age order of epiphyseal union in man. Am. J. Phys. Anthropol. 7:53–93, 1924.
55. Szilvassy, J. Age determination on the sternal articular faces of the clavicula. J. Hum. Evol. 9:609–610, 1980.
56. Todd, T. W., D'Errico, J. The clavicular epiphyses. Am. J. Anat. 41:25–50, 1928.
57. Işcan, M. Y., Loth, S. R., Wright, R- K. Age estimation from the rib phase analysis: white males. J. Forensic Sci. 29:1094–1104, 1984.
58. Işcan, M. Y., Loth, S. R., Wright, R. K. Age estimation from the rib phase analysis: white females. J. Forensic Sci. 30:853–863, 1985.
59. Işcan, M. Y., Loth, S. R., Wright, R. K. Racial variation in the sternal extremity of the rib an its effect on age determination. J. Forensic Sci. 32:452–466, 1987.
60. Yoder, C., Ubelaker, D. H., Powell, J. F. Examination of variation in sternal rib end morphology relevant to age assessment. J. Forensic Sci. 46:223–227, 2001.
61. Baccino, E., Souaiby, N., Vergnes, M. D. Evaluation of the Işcan method for age determination from the sternal end of the fourth rib on a French forensic male sample

(n = 131): results and propositions of modifications. Proceedings of the American Academy of Forensic Sciences, 52nd annual meeting, Reno, NV, 2000, p. 234.

62. Baccino, E., Cuesta Tormo, M. C., Souaiby, N., et al. Evaluation of the Işcan method for age determination from the sternal end of the fourth rib on a French forensic male sample (n = 131) and a Spanish forensic female sample (n = 168): results and propositions of modifications. Indopacific Association of Legal Medicine and Forensic Sciences, Melbourne, Australia, September 2001.

63. Dudar, J. C., Pfeiffer, S., Saunders, S. R. Evaluation of morphological and histological adult skeletal age-at-death estimation techniques using ribs. J. Forensic Sci. 38:677–685, 1993.

64. Meindl, R. S., Lovejoy, C. O. Ectocranial suture closure: a revised method for the determination of skeletal age at death based on the lateral-anterior sutures. Am. J. Phys. Anthropol. 68:57–66, 1985.

65. Masset, C. Où en est la paléodémographie [in French]? Bull Mem. Soc. Anthropol. Paris 2:109–122, 1990.

66. Wittwer-Backofen, U., Campe, J., Vaupel, J. W. Tooth cementum annulation for age estimation: results from a large known age validation study. Am. J. Phys. Anthropol. 123:119–129, 2004.

67. Drusini, A. G., Toso, O., Ranzato, C. The coronal pulp cavity index: a biomarker for age determination in human adults. Am. J. Phys. Anthropol. 103:353–363, 1997.

68. Usher, B. M., Boldsen, J. J., Holman, D. Age estimation at Tirup Cemetery: an application of the transition analysis method. Am. J. Phys. Anthropol. 30:S307, 2000.

69. Buckberry, J. L., Chamberlain, A. Age Estimation from the auricular surface of the ilium: a revised method. Am. J. Phys. Anthropol. 119:231–329, 2002.

70. Boldsen, J. L., Milner, G. R., Konisberg, L. W., Wood, J. W. Transition analysis: a new method for estimating age from skeletons. In: Hoppa, R. D., Vaupel, J. W., eds., Paleodemography: Age Distribution from Skeletal Samples. Cambridge University Press, Cambridge, pp. 73–106, 2002.

71. Schmitt, A., Broqua, C. Approche probabiliste pour estimer l'âge au décès a partir de la surface auriculaire de l'ilium [in French]. Bull. Mem. Soc. Anthropol. Paris 12:279–301, 2000.

72. Debono, L., Mafart, B., Guipert, G., Jeusel, E. Application pratique de la méthode d'estimation de l'âge au décès de Schmitt et Broqua (2000) [in French]. Bull. Mem. Soc. Anthropol. Paris 16:115–120, 2004.

73. Schmitt, A. Une nouvelle méthode pour estimer l'âge au décès des adultes à partir de la surface sacro-pelvienne iliaque [in French]. Bull. Mem. Soc. Anthropol. Paris 17:89–101, 2005.

74. Acsadi, G., Nemeskeri, J. The complex method. In: Acsádi, G., Nemeskeri, J., eds., Human Life Span and Mortality. Akadémiai Kiado, Budapest, pp. 122–135, 1970.

75. Thomas, C. D. L., Stein, M. S., Feik, S. A., Wark, J. D., Clement, J. G. Determination of age at death using combined morphology and histology of the femur. J. Anat. 196:463–471, 2000.

76. Kerley, E. R., Ubelaker, D. H. Revisions in the microscopic method of estimating age at death in human cortical bone. Am. J. Phys. Anthropol. 49:545–546, 1978.

77. Ericksen MF. Histological estimation of age at death using the anterior cortex of the femur. Am. J. Phys. Anthropol. 84:171–179, 1991.
78. Stout, S. D., Paine, R. R. Brief communication: histological age estimation using rib and clavicule. Am. J. Phys. Anthropol. 87:111–115, 1992.
79. Iwaniec, U. T., Crenshaw, T. D., Shoeninger, M. J., Stout, S. D., Ericksen, M. F. Methods for improving the efficiency of estimating total osteon density in the human anterior mid-diaphyseal femur. Am. J. Phys. Anthropol. 107:13–24, 1998.
80. Cho, H., Stout, S. D., Madsen, R. W., Streeter, M. A. Population-specific histological age-estimating method: a model for known African-American and European-American skeletal remains. J. Forensic Sci. 47:12–18, 2002.
81. Stout, S. D. Histomophometric analysis of human skeletal remains. In: Işcan, M. Y., Kenneth, A. R., eds., Reconstruction of Life from the Skeleton. Wiley-Liss, New York, NY, pp. 41–52, 1989.
82. Lynnerup, N., Thomsen, J. L., Frohlich, B. Intra- and inter-observer variation in histological criteria used in age at death determination based on femoral cortical bone. Forensic Sci. Int. 91:219–230, 1998.
83. Wallin, J. A., Tzock, I., Kristensen, G. Microscopic age determination of human skeletons including an unknown but calculable variable. Int. J. Osteoarchaeol. 4:353–362, 1994.
84. Aykroyd, R. G., Lucy, D., Pollard, A. M., Solheim, T. Technical note: regression analysis in adult age estimation. Am. J. Phys. Anthropol. 104:259–265, 1997.
85. Rösing, F. W., Kvall, S. I. Dental age in adults: a review of estimation methods. In: Rösing, F. W., Teschler-Nicola, M. eds., Dental Anthropology, Fundamentals, Limits, and Prospects. Springer, New York, NY, pp. 443–468, 1997.

Chapter 12

Is It Possible to Escape Racial Typology in Forensic Identification?

John Albanese and Shelley R. Saunders

Summary

This chapter provides a review of metric and morphological methods for determining ancestry from skeletal forensic cases, as well as a comparative look at emerging genetic "origins"-determination methods. The authors address two major issues with respect to these methods. Are the methods consistent with observable patterns of human biological variation and with the apportioning of variation in skeletal reference samples used to represent population groups? Do the methods have any utility for positive identification of unknowns? In addition, the authors provide examples of the patterns of variation in cranial measurements, infracranial measurements, and morphological characters as observed in skeletal reference samples to illustrate some of the limitations of the underlying assumptions of "race"-determination methods.

The reality of human variation is not consistent with how forensic anthropologists have used (and continue to use) human variation to identify unknown individuals, and the substitution of various terms without a critical reanalysis of the underlying assumptions has not remedied the situation. False or misleading information is far worse than a lack of information. The relatively high risk of false information may outweigh the value of determining "race" may possibly have for the positive identification of an unknown individual.

Key Words: Race; personal identification; population affinities; ethnicity; discriminant function; morphological characters; anthroposcopic traits; nonmetric traits.

From *Forensic Anthropology and Medicine:*
Complementary Sciences From Recovery to Cause of Death
Edited by: A. Schmitt, E. Cunha, and J. Pinheiro © Humana Press Inc., Totowa, NJ

1. INTRODUCTION

The determination of ancestry population affinities or ethnicity (in the past, referred to as "race") is the most controversial question that a forensic anthropologist must face when assisting in identifying unknown individuals. In some parts of the world (for example, the United States, South Africa, etc.), there is a history of the use of racial classification as part of personal identification, and forensic anthropologists continue to be called on to address this question when positively identifying an individual. The recent trend in the forensic literature has been to use the term "ancestry" instead of "race," with no change in the underlying concepts, so that determining continental origin has been substituted for color terminology. Regardless of the terminology used, the underlying assumption *in forensic applications* is the same: using morphological, metric, or a combination of data, it is possible to assign an unknown individual into one of a limited number of continental or racial groups (usually two to six groups).

In this chapter, the authors provide a review of some of the metric and morphological methods for determining ancestry, as well as a comparative look at emerging genetic "origins"-determination methods. Two major issues with respect to these methods are addressed: are the methods consistent with observable patterns of human biological variation and with the apportioning of variation in reference samples used to represent population groups? Do the methods have any utility for positive identification of unknowns? In addition, two examples are provided, one cranial and one infracranial, to illustrate some of the limitations of the underlying assumptions of "race"-determination methods.

2. THEORIES AND METHODS FOR ALLOCATING UNKNOWNS: AN HISTORICAL PERSPECTIVE

Some of the earliest applications of skeletal biological methods to forensic cases date back to the 1930s in the United States. However, the racial approach to research during earlier periods had an enormous influence on physical anthropology throughout the 20th century and into the 21st century *(1–5)*. Comparative morphological and metric investigations of human variation related to race or continental origin date back to the mid-19th century in North America, with work by Samuel Morton and in Europe with research by Paul Broca *(6)*. Many of those investigations focused on the identification of racial traits, usually in the cranium, which were erroneously used to assess mental ability, rank various groups, support nationalist views, and justify social and economic inequality *(6)*. Although those approaches were theoretically and methodologically flawed (*see* ref. *6* for a comprehensive review), they had an enormous influence on how physical anthropologists framed investigations of human variation throughout the 20th century.

These early approaches are more closely analogous to recent studies of population distance to *discriminate* between populations rather than *allocate* unknown individuals. Research directly related to allocating unknowns began when large documented "multiracial" collections became available in the United States (*7*). Anatomists T. Wingate Todd and Robert J. Terry began amassing respective collections at medical institutions in Cleveland, OH and St. Louis, MO in the first decades of the 20th century (*7,8*). These collections were formed at a time when race, as it was socially constructed in the first half of the 20th century, was considered as biologically meaningful as age or sex when investigating skeletal variation. The 19th century racial approach for investigating human variation is evident in how the collections were put together, what documentary data were collected and curated with the skeletal material, and in the research of the collectors (*see* refs. *9–12*). The racial designations in the Hamann-Todd Collection and the Terry Collection predate the adoption of modern evolutionary theory by physical anthropologists (*see* ref. *13*).*

By the latter half of the 20th century, at least three distinct race concepts emerged in the biological and social sciences: social race, bureaucratic race, and biological race (*see* refs. *14–17*) for different perspectives in a forensic context). Social and bureaucratic race are *socially constructed* concepts for grouping humans that are self-defined by individuals or groups, imposed by certain socioeconomic levels of society on others, or both. The biological race concept is theoretically based on phenotypic and genotypic variation. When asked to determine race or ancestry, forensic anthropologists are asked to determine social race or bureaucratic race based on morphological and/or metric variation. Whereas social race and bureaucratic race are real concepts that have social and economic effects on peoples' lives (an extreme example is Apartheid), the overwhelming evidence from many different studies—but particularly in the last 35 yr with the advent of protein and DNA analysis—clearly show that the race concept is not a valid biological concept, and that racial groups are not coarse but useful categories for investigating human variation (*4,18–26*). The conclusions are consistent and clear (*21,22,25,27–29*):

---

* Racial terms are presented here in quotation marks to highlight that these designations in reference collections are not based on phenotype and genotype.

1. Intrarace variation is *much* greater than interrace variation.
2. Only 6–13% of genetic and morphometric variation is attributable to race.
3. There is *no concordance* of human genetic and morphometric variation with racial categories, continental origin, or skin pigmentation.

Another trend in forensic literature in the last decade of the 20th century was to use the term "ancestry" instead of race. The terms "European," "African," and "(East) Asian" have replaced "Caucasoid/White," "Negroid/Black," and "Mongoloid/Yellow/Red." An example of this trend can be found in *A Lab Manual and Workbook for Physical Anthropology (30,31)*. This is a widely used introductory lab manual that has gone through several editions, where many students of physical anthropology get their first introduction to a "scientific" approach to racial classification of unknown individuals in forensic contexts. In the first edition *(30)*, France and Horn (p. 30) provide a summary of seven cranial morphologic and metric characters that can be used to classify an unknown individual as "Negroid," "Caucasoid," or "Mongoloid." In the fourth edition *(31)* of the lab manual, (p. 123, fig. 4.21) the same seven cranial morphological and metric characters are used to classify the unknown as being of "African," "European," or "(East) Asian" ancestry. The underlying assumptions are the same, but the terminology has changed.

3. FORENSIC IDENTIFICATION OF POPULATION AFFINITIES

Generally, the investigation of human variation has followed two major methodological approaches, morphological and metric.* There has been some discussion about which is easier to apply with less training and which approach results in higher allocation accuracies *(33,34)*. The choice of method is almost entirely dependent on what variation is being observed. Some skeletal variation can be easily measured, and some variation can only be adequately assessed with a morphological approach (presence/absence or pronouncement of characters). Under the next two subheadings, metric and morphological methods for race determination are discussed, respectively.

3.1. Discriminant Function Approaches

In the early 1960s, Giles and Elliot *(35)* revolutionized "race" determination with the publication of their discriminant functions using samples of

---

* Three-dimensional digital approaches that combine both metric and morphological information are being developed for investigating patterns of human variation (*see* ref. *32* for a forensically relevant example). However, methods that are widely applicable in forensic cases are not currently available.

"Blacks" and "Whites" from the Hamann-Todd and Terry collections, and an aboriginal sample from Indian Knoll (*see* ref. *34* for details on applying these methods). Most metric methods developed since the mid-1960s, including recent computer based methods, are based on Giles and Elliot's approach involving discriminant functions (for example, *see* refs. *36–40*). Generally, cranial methods are considered the most reliable, pelvis and long bone combinations are less reliable, and other skeletal elements are considered the least reliable *(17,41)*.

Subsequently, Birkby *(42)* described several problems with Giles and Elliot's functions and with the entire approach for allocating individuals to a limited number of racial groups. He tested the Giles and Elliot method with aboriginal archaeological samples from across North America and found that they performed poorly. Only 52% of the crania where classified correctly because of two theoretical problems with metric race methods *(42)*. First, an unknown individual is forced into one of three categories regardless of whether that individual fits into any of those categories. Second, a category such as "American Indian" is not a single homogenous category. The allocation accuracies for most of the test samples were between 20 and 78%. The notable exception was the relatively high allocation accuracy (92%) for the test sample from Indian Knoll, the same population used by Giles and Elliot to develop their equations. Birkby's results suggest that it may be possible to determine ancestry and allocate an unknown individual to a specific biocultural group defined by geographic and temporal parameters, in this case, the Indian Knoll population. However, the method performed very poorly when it was applied to samples outside the reference sample used to develop the original method because racial categories consist of many heterogeneous populations that are not fixed through time.

In addition to Birkby's study, Giles and Elliot's method was tested using various identified and archaeological samples *(34,44)*. In all the studies, the methods performed poorly on the respective American Indian samples (accuracies ranged from 14 to 30%), and confirmed Birkby's conclusion that the Indian Knoll sample cannot be considered a proxy for the pattern of variation in numerous populations that are included in the group American Indian *(34,43,44)*.

Two of the tests of Giles and Elliot's method included forensic cases, and they resulted in allocation accuracies of 71.4 and 76.4%, lower than Giles and Elliot's original published accuracy *(34,44)*. Based on a review of the test results, allocation accuracy approaching the level described by Giles and Elliot could be achieved if Amerindian samples were left out of the test and if the Black–White sectioning point for males was modified *(34,44)*. For analytical purposes, knowing the allocation accuracy for each race and sex subsample in the test is important. However, on a practical level, when applying the method to *one* unknown individual, what matters is whether the method can be applied with confidence in that one case. When dealing with a true unknown, for example, a forensic anthropologist in North America has no way of knowing if a given analysis is a case where the Black–White situation applies, whether the individual may be Amerindian or whether Giles and Elliot's sectioning point or the modified sectioning point should be used. The independent tests suggest that Giles and Elliot's method can be expected to give erroneous information in at least one out every four cases with no indication of when the method is providing incorrect information.

Other methods for determining race are available *(45)*. In many cases, the methods are based on relatively small sample sizes with uneven subsamples (few females and/or one group overrepresented), have not been tested with independent samples or have ignored Birkby's conclusions regarding the lack of homogeneity within a racial group and the problems associated with a forced allocation into only one of three categories. In cases when methods have been comprehensively tested, the resulting allocation accuracies have been low *(40,46–49)*. For example, in a comprehensive test of femur and tibia methods *(50)* using a large forensic sample from the Forensic Anthropology Databank (FDB), the allocation accuracy for "Whites" was worse than randomly guessing, and the high accuracy for "Blacks" was misleading because the functions simply classified almost everyone as "Black" *(46)*. As with methods that use only leg bones, methods that used the pelvis and leg bones *(37)*, had a tendency to classify most individuals as "Black," and a number of "Whites" were classified incorrectly *(46)*.

The general poor performance of both metric sex- and "race"-determination methods when tested with large independent samples has been attributed to problems with the representativeness of reference collections, specifically, the widely used Terry and Hamann-Todd collections *(46)*. The major problems with these collections have been noted for decades *(51,52)*. More recently, secular change has been described as an additional problem with the collections and a reason for the poor performance of forensic identification methods developed from these collections *(46)*. The FDB was established to address the poor performance of various "race"- and sex-determination methods and to address the problems with the older reference collections by providing an alternative source of data for the development of forensic methods *(46)*.

The FDB consists of data collected in forensic cases and submitted by various anthropologists, as well as a sample of individuals from the Terry Collection and a small number of individuals from the Hamann-Todd Collection who where born in the 20th century *(40,46)*. Although an electronic database is not a substitute for a skeletal collection, the FDB has enormous research potential *(46)*. An example of this potential is the computer application known as FORDISC, which can be used to determine "race" and/or sex. FORDISC has several features that make it more useful than all other previous discriminant function approaches. First, unique discriminant functions are calculated based on what measurements can be collected from an unknown individual. Second, posterior and typicality probabilities are calculated in addition to the discriminant function score. The posterior probability is a measure of group membership, assuming that the unknown individual is in fact one of the options selected. The typicality probability is a measure of whether the unknown individual could belong to any of the groups selected in the analysis. This statistic addresses one of the major problems with all discriminant function approaches. Although the discriminant function score may force a placement into one of the selected groups, a typicality score of 0.05 or lower indicates that the unknown is not typical of any of the selected groups *(40)*. Aside from the interface, there are several substantive differences in the second version of the program. With FORDISC 2.0, infracranial measurements can be used, and there is the option of using Howells' *(53,54)* data instead of the FDB as the reference sample for the calculation of discriminant functions *(40,46,55)*.*

In contrast to the good results in an early test of FORDISC 2.0 *(55)*, when the method has been comprehensively tested with large independent samples, allocation accuracies when determining race are low (less than 60%) or do not follow any pattern of classification regardless of whether Howells' data or the FDB is selected as a reference sample *(48,49,56–58)*. Well-documented archaeological samples (i.e., continental origin was known) were used in several of these tests and may account for the low accuracies when the FDB data were used as the reference sample. This is a liability that was anticipated and clearly articulated by the developers of FORDISC *(40)*. However, in practice, when a forensic anthropologist is presented with an unknown individual there is no *a priori* way of knowing if the method should not be applied. Despite the confidence placed in FORDISC, there is little evidence that FORDISC performs at the 90% accuracy that has been reported *(55,59)* or performs any better than the earlier nonelectronic methods that rely on discriminant functions.

---

* FORDISC 3.0 has been recently released, but it could not be reviewed in time to be included here.

Because of the widespread confidence in FORDISC *(55,59)*, research on "race" and ancestry determination has largely been relegated to areas of the skeleton that are not included in the FDB and thus not available for analysis with FORDISC (for examples, *see* refs. *17* and *60–65*). In most cases, these methods provide reasonable allocation accuracies (generally more than 80%) for the sample used to develop the method. However, in cases where independent samples are used to test the methods *(47–49,64,65)*, allocation accuracies decrease to levels that undermine the applicability of the methods in actual cases. In one example *(65)*, the allocation accuracy of 75% for the test sample is misleading. The results follow a pattern for the femur previously described *(46)*, where every bone is classified as "Black." In another case, there are considerable differences in allocation accuracy by sex *(64)*. An allocation accuracy of 100% for females in the original sample dropped to 57% on a test sample of forensic cases. In tests of multiple methods, allocation accuracies were low, and there was no consistency between different methods when they were applied to the same individual *(47–49)*. For example, one unknown was classified as "Black" with the Giles and Elliot *(35)* method, "White" with the Gill *(17)* method, "Japanese" with FORDISC using the FDB data, and "from the Philippines" with FORDISC using the Howells' data *(48)*.

Discriminant function approaches have not resulted in highly reliable methods for race determination for various reasons. These problems are not restricted to the discriminant function technique, but they are exacerbated by this metric approach. Some of the contradictory results and low allocation accuracies result from limitations of the reference sample used to calculate a given discriminant function *(55)*. The Terry and Hamann-Todd collections and *all* reference collections, including the FDB, present some problems that are derived from how the collections were amassed *(66)*, but these are not insurmountable problems for developing forensically relevant methods *(67)*.

The poor performance of "race"-determination methods tested with the FDB data have been attributed to secular changes *(46)*. But there is some evidence that secular change observed in these skeletal collections may be a result of sampling error when data from separate collections are combined *(24,66)*. When trying to reproduce the results of Meadows, Jantz, and Jantz *(68)*, it was found that the increases in femur length occurred when the source of the data (i.e., collection) changed *(24,66)*. The differences in femur length between collections that are coincidently separate in time have been attributed to secular changes. Regardless of how this variation in reference collections is interpreted, research conducted in the first half of the 20th century, using living individuals and a sample from the Hamann-Todd Collection, demonstrated the nonconcordance between race and morphology when secular change was not a confounding factor in reference collections *(69)*. The different patterns of cranial and infracranial morphology attributed to, for example, "White" males born in the 20th century vs "White" males born in the 19th century *(46)*, clearly demonstrates that skeletal variation is not fixed or genetically based for the group "White males." If the changes are secular changes, 100 yr (or roughly five generations) is too little time for such significant changes in morphology to be because of genetic variation. If the variation that has been attributed to secular changes is in fact because of sampling error derived from the methodology for sampling and limitation in the reference collections *(24)*, the different pattern of variation for "White" males born in the 20th century vs "White" males born in the 19th century clearly shows that the "White" group is not a valid category for apportioning human variation.

Although racial categories may not be a biological reality, it may be possible to use a statistical association in the reference sample to allocate unknowns *(15,40,70,71)*. The independent test results from various samples over the last 40 yr presented previously clearly indicate that regardless of how robust the statistical association is in the reference sample, this association does not result in a method that can be confidently applied to cases outside the reference sample used to develop the method. There are two reasons for this. First, the parameters used to define the groups do not correspond with the real patterns of human variation. Based on phenotypic variation, an unknown individual is forced into a group that is defined by *variable* social criteria and not phenotypic or genotypic parameters. Second, variation because of age, sex, cause of death, living conditions, and so forth, is incorrectly apportioned to a race (*see* the pelvis example under Subheading 4.2.).

3.2. Morphological Characters

There is also a long tradition in physical anthropology of using morphological characters of the skull to assign individuals to population groups. Historically, this attention derives from anatomists who had a broader interest in human physical variation as early as the 17th century *(72)*. In the 1920s, the anthropologist Ernest Hooton developed a recording form for such characters during his tenure at the Peabody Museum of Harvard University. Hooton's recording form is believed to have had a major influence on subsequent students and researchers in North America studying skeletal samples or forensic cases *(73)*.

There are two main kinds of morphological characters of the skeleton relevant to this discussion, anthroposcopic traits and nonmetric traits. *Anthroposcopic traits* are features of shape observable in all skeletons, such as a particular form of the palate or the position and height of the bridge of the nose, whereas *nonmetric traits* are minor skeletal and dental variants that may or may not be present. When discovered, nonmetric traits appear to be curious anomalies, and are assumed to cluster in large or small population groups. Several hundred nonmetric traits have been reported for the skull and infracranial skeleton *(72,74,75)*. Table 1 offers a sample listing and descriptions of some anthroposcopic and nonmetric traits. Unfortunately, the forensic anthropology literature uses either term interchangeably *(76)* or inclusively (e.g., ref. *77* refers to all traits as "anthroposcopic," whereas ref. *78* refers to all traits as "nonmetric"). Whereas the word *anthroposcopic*, literally defined, means "to see human," the distinction between these two terms is necessary because there is a long and separate tradition of research in biology and physical anthropology on nonmetric traits as population descriptors.

Many early workers would classify certain nonmetric traits as characteristic of specific groups and name them accordingly so that we have features, such as the "os inca" or "os japonicum." Ossenberg *(74)* considered the question of whether a battery of nonmetric traits might separate world population groupings when she used 24 cranial traits to compare samples of Native American Indians, Eskimos, African Americans, and African Blacks. The calculated distance statistics were found to be higher between the major groups than within them. However, this was tested further when Wijsman and Neves *(79)* examined whether the frequencies of nonmetric traits would mirror the genetic distances between Brazilian Blacks, Whites, and mulattos, and a model of genetic population admixture. They found significant deviations in the pattern of nonmetric trait distances from a linear model of genetic distance, and in support of this observation, many nonmetric traits have been found to have low estimates of heritable variation *(80,81)*. More recently though, Hanihara and colleagues *(82)* reported a comprehensive study of the frequencies of 20 nonmetric cranial traits in several thousand individuals from many populations from around the world. Using multivariate statistical analyses to calculate distances, they found the variation to be, at least in part, because of geographical factors rather than environmental factors, and similar to distances calculated from genetic or craniometric data. Hence, there is some evidence that traits cluster in regional world populations, but that variation forms a minimal portion of the total worldwide variation, most of which is within local populations *(29)*. One also cannot expect trait frequencies to reflect directly genetic allele frequencies because they are phenotypic features far from the genome with a different model of inheritance.

Early work with laboratory animals developed the quasicontinuous model of inheritance for the genetic control of these minor skeletal variants *(83)*. A good illustration of this model is Grüneberg's thorough study of the absence

Table 1
Sampling of Anthroposcopic vs Nonmetric Traits

Anthroposcopic traits[a]	Definition	Comments
1. Sutures	Scored as "simple," "medium," or "complex" on the basis of the sutures tracing a path deviating from a hypothetical straight line	It is not clear how to judge the difference between "simple," "medium," and "complex". Byers (77) shows diagrams for simple and complex patterns only.
2. Nasal opening	The opening is triangular, flared widely at the base, or flared centrally and at the base as well.	Rhine (76) and Byers (77) provide diagrams, but the boundaries between triangular and flared may still be difficult to judge.
3. Nasal form	Horizontal contour across the nasal root are either (a) low and rounded; (b) low to moderate in height, with relatively straight sides and angled in the midline; or (c) high, somewhat pinched in, with a break in contour at or near the naso-maxillary suture	Described by Brues (73), this trait is illustrated with photographs but still creates difficulties with judgment.
4. Nasal depression	The deepest point of curvature of the nasal bones just inferior to nasion is deeply depressed, slight depressed, or straight.	What constitutes a "slight depression"?
5. Nasal sill	Located where the vertical maxillae may create a sharp ridge separating the nasal cavity from the maxillae. If the ridge is high, the score is "deep;" if shallow, it is scored as "shallow;" and if a sharp ridge is lacking, it is "blurred." A smooth curve leading from the maxillae into the nasal aperture without interruption is "guttered."	The greatest difficulties appear to lie with judging "shallow" and "blurred" sills (see ref. 77, Fig. 7.5). Note that all nasal features are likely to be highly correlated with one another.

(continued)

Table 1 (Continued)

Anthroposcopic traits[a]

6. Alveolar prognathism	Scored as "large," "medium," or "none," depending on the amount of alveolar projection.	The degree of prognathism may be difficult to judge, but *see* Fig. 7.3 in Byers (77).
7. Canine fossa	A depression in the maxilla at the root of the canine.	What constitutes a "minimal" expression?
8. Shape of the chin	The chin is "bilobate" (with a central sulcus), "blunt" (smoothly rounded), or "pointed," as viewed from above.	How does one decide when a case appears equivocal?

Nonmetric traits[b]

| 1. Inca bone | Defined as a suture running from asterion to asterion dividing the squamous portion of the occipital approximately in half. Sutures cutting off smaller portions of the occipital are not scored as Inca bones. | The occipital squama inferior to the highest nuchal line is ossified in cartilage; the superior portion is ossified in membrane. Union of the two parts is said to occur in the third intrauterine month. If the parts fail to unite the upper portion is known as the os Inca. Wormian bones are common in the lamboid suture, and naïve workers have confused other variants — the os apices, the lambdic bone, or the lamboid wormians — for the os Inca, the rarest variant. |
| 2. Os Japonicum | Defined by a horizontal suture running from the zygomaticotemporal suture anteriorly to the zygomaxillary suture isolating and inferior section of the zygomatic bone. | This trait is probably easiest to identify of this list, although the observer has to be careful of postmortem alterations to the region. Difficulties may arise with identification of "barely discernable" traces of the suture. |

292

Trait	Definition	Reference
3. Shoveling of the incisors	In the upper central and lateral incisors, the lateral margins fold sharply backward, so that the tooth resembles a miniature scoop or shovel.[c]	Recording criteria vary. The most comprehensive are those of Dahlberg (86a), who provided model casts of many dental traits.
4. Carabelli's cusp	Accessory cusps located on the mesiolingual cusps of maxillary molars. Most prominent on the first molar.	Readers of the many studies of this trait will recognize that there are several gradations of expression, including a pit.
5. Mandibular torus	A torus on the inside of the body of the mandible. Seen as a small "lump," either unilateral or bilateral.	There is strong evidence that the appearance of this trait is affected by biomechanical factors (Ossenberg [86b]).
6. Supraorbital foramina	The supraorbital nerves, which supply the frontal region, may be encased in one of more foramina along the superior medial margin of the orbital border, or there may be a "notch" or the area may be smooth.	Ossenberg (86c)
7. Mylohyoid bridge	Accessory bridge of bone covering the mylohyoid groove on the medial surface of the body of the mandible.	Ossenberg (86c)
8. Paracondylar process		Ossenberg (86c)

[a]Definitions of anthroposcopic traits are taken from Gill and Rhine (45). Only a sampling of cranial–skeletal and dental traits was selected for this table even though there are many infracranial traits.

[b]Traits were selected based on frequent references to them in forensic anthropology sources. However, the last three traits—supraorbital foramina, mylohyoid bridge, and paracondylar process—have been identified as significant in separating groups.

[c]This definition is taken from St. Hoyme and Iscan (14).

293

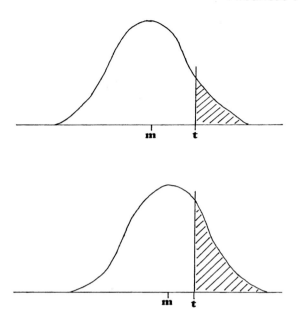

Fig. 1. Quasicontinuous model of inheritance taken from ref. *75*, pp. *97*. Printed with permission.

of third molars, a trait also found in humans. He observed that the absence of the tooth is a discontinuous character arising from an *underlying continuous distribution* (Fig. 1), the size of the tooth rudiment. Tooth germ size is determined by the individual's genome and influenced by the genetic constitution of the mother, the maternal environment, and prenatal and postnatal environmental factors. Usually, the genes involved are multiple genes with additive effects. Tooth absence occurs if germ size falls below a critical level, shortly after birth in the case of mice. Thus, the expressions of size variations are affected by generalized and localized factors; whatever influences size will indirectly affect the presence of third molars. (For reviews of the problems and potential of nonmetric traits in population studies, *see* refs. *75* and *84–86*.)

Whereas some writers have admonished researchers for scoring nonmetric traits as discrete (present or absent) because they will vary in expression, Grüneberg's early model had already established that underlying continuity of liability was the correct way of interpreting them. Presence or absence recording usually improves the precision of observations (consistency in recording), whereas consistency in observation is probably the greatest difficulty with anthroposcopic traits (*see* comments in Table 1 and Fig. 2). This

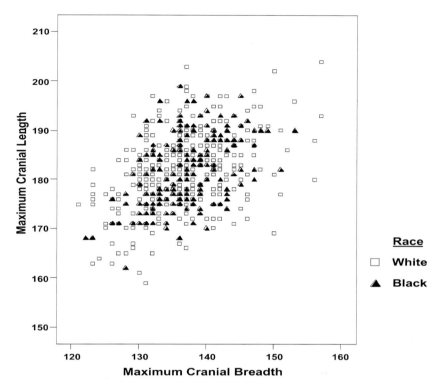

Fig. 2. Scatter plot of cranial length and width measurement by "race" of males and females from the Terry Collection and the Coimbra Collection (*n* = 526, *see* Table 2 for further details on sample composition). Note how the range of variation of the "Black" sample is entirely within the range of variation of the "White" sample.

can be said despite the main argument for using morphological traits to identify ancestry in forensic casework, which is ease of observation and recording *(76–78)*. Visual assessments require no expensive or delicate equipment and can be completed rapidly but could be useless if the collected data are faulty and imprecise. In addition, most texts will tell the student that considerable experience with recognizing traits and skill in forensic anthropology are necessary before employing traits to judge a forensic case. This contradicts the claim that they are easy to employ and warns us that the method may, in fact, be quite difficult.

What many seem to forget or neglect to mention is that the genetic backgrounds of trait causation can vary from individual to individual and from group to group. Common features may cluster in members of a large family. Major gene effects can modify skeletal or dental development and produce traits that are produced by other genetic factors in other individuals and populations. The discovery that different mutations can produce the same phenotypic effect was recognized long ago in the field of genetics but seems to be ignored in forensic anthropology.

Most of the forensic anthropology literature on the subject of ancestry informs the reader that the goal is to assign individuals to one of three major groups: White (or Caucasoid), Black, or Asian (including North American Indian) *(76,77)*. This is reflective of the American literature, which is where most of this information is published and where ancestry determination seems to be a significant goal of forensic casework. In fact, the American publications also refer to Hispanic as a "neorace" *(76)*, and these persons are defined as of mixed European and Native American heritage. Rhine reported on a test of a list of 45 mixed, anthroposcopic, and nonmetric features that were observed on a sample of 87 documented skulls with known backgrounds. Rather than report success rates of race assignment against documented race, he reported the frequencies of traits in the different groups (defined based on written documentation), including a listing of traits found in 30% or more and 50% or more of each sample, along with a notation of expectations. He recognized that the classification of the group samples could be problematic, stating, "We are not dealing with unmixed populations," and "not only is there a great deal of systematic populational variability (racial variability), there is a considerable amount of idiosyncratic variability as well." In fact, of the 45 traits in this study, 37 were found to be 30% or more frequent in more than one group. Six of the remaining eight traits were simply too rare and not found in this sample.* However, in conclusion, Rhine pointed out that even though there is a continuum of variation for morphological characters, making them hard to assess, they are of value in forensic cases where one cannot be confident of measurements because of fragmentation or postmortem alteration to the remains. On the other hand, some readers would interpret these results as disappointing, suggesting that the exercise of ancestry assessment from anthroposcopic and nonmetric traits should be rejected.

Even though recent forensic anthropology texts caution that there is no such thing as a pure ethnic group, race, or ancestral group, and that there is considerable overlap of traits that characterize different groups (as shown in previous paragraph) so that "the attribution of ancestral group is one of the

---

* A large portion of, but not all, ambiguity occurred within the Hispanic sample.

most difficult assessments made for skeletal remains" *(77)*, many in the field still claim that the anthropologist *must* communicate this information to law enforcement personnel, the general public, and students. It is worthwhile reconsidering this basic claim.

Byers' *(77)* recent text in forensic anthropology states that, when possible, forensic anthropologists should give an assessment of ancestry from skeletal remains with the categories of "White," "Black," "Asian," "Native American," and "Hispanic." This is an American text referring to categories used by many law enforcement agencies in the United States. In comparison, in Canada, the situation does not appear to be so straightforward. Canada is a country of immigrants, and the 1996 and 2001 censuses report people originating from Europe, the Middle East, Western Asia, Southern Asia, Eastern and Southeast Asia, Africa, the Pacific, and the Caribbean. In addition, the proportion of persons reporting multiple continental origins is 36%!

Whereas it seems that, particularly in the United States, the imperative to identify ancestry is tied to issues of racism, in Canada, missing persons lists use a two-variable category relating to ancestry, White or nonWhite *(87)*. Ascribing an unknown to either of these two categories will undoubtedly assist in narrowing the possible matches for identification, but it is not the only important variable. More research on establishing careful estimates of other biological parameters, such as age at death and stature, can do much to improve the success of individual identification. The authors illustrate with an example. In the spring of 2001, one of the authors (S. Saunders) was called to a rural road outside of Hamilton, Ontario, by police investigators. The partially skeletonized remains of an individual had been discovered under melting snow. Foul play was evident from the presence of perimortem trauma to the skull.

After assisting with the recovery, both authors evaluated the remains with anthropological methods. A suggestion was made that the individual might be of Southern Asian ancestry based on prominent presence of alveolar prognathism, convexity to the nasal profile, concavity beneath the border of the nasal spine, and moderate shoveling of the maxillary incisors. In the meantime, police investigators were researching the sources of some clothing and jewelry items found at the scene. In addition, they were attempting the rehydration of fingerprints from some preserved skin. Ultimately, the woman was identified by the recovered fingerprints matched to a criminal record. The suggestion of ancestry had been of some help in narrowing the investigation, but it was the combination of recovered information from a variety of investigated sources that led to the solution of the murder. In fact, the investigators considered the anthropologists' estimation of age at death of the victim to be of equal or greater significance in contributing to identification.

4. INTERPRETING THE SOURCES AND PATTERNS OF VARIATION IN REFERENCE COLLECTIONS

Despite the more recent prominence of the FDB, arguably, the most important collection for the development of "race" and ancestry-determination methods has been, and continues to be, the Terry Collection. The Terry Collection has been continuously available for research for more than 60 yr; it is an important component of the FDB and FORDISC *(40,46)*, and it has been a major source of data for the "race"-determination methods that have been widely used for the last five decades *(35–37,39–41,88–90)*.

Using data from the Terry Collection and the Coimbra Collection (a cemetery-derived identified collection from Portugal), one cranial example and one infracranial example are presented here to illustrate some of the potential problems with identifying and interpreting sources of variation in reference collections. The first example illustrates the lack of concordance between cranial variation and racial categories or continental origin. Using the pubic bone, the second example illustrates that statistical significance, without historical and biocultural context, may lead to the apportionment of variation to the wrong source. Both examples illustrate the theoretical and methodological limitations of determining social or bureaucratic race from skeletal remains, and how expected patterns of variation have been described in scholarly literature and popular discourse even when the data did not support the perceptions *(91)*. This second issue is analogous to Walker's *(92)* observations on sex determination, where results can be driven by the expectations of researchers rather than actual observable patterns of variation.

4.1. Example 1: Patterns of Variation in the Cranial Index

For more than 150 yr, the cranial index and the cephalic index were used as tools for investigating human variation and to classify individuals into racial categories *(6).** The *cranial index* is defined as cranial breadth divided by cranial length multiplied by 100. The cranial index is calculated with data collected from skeletal material, and the *cephalic index* is the equivalent col-

---

* By the early 20th century, Boas's *(93)* research showed that cranial shape as approximated by the cephalic index was influenced by environmental factors and was not fixed. Two separate reanalyses of Boas's original data have reignited the debate over the plasticity of cranial shape *(94–97)*.

Table 2
Mean Cranial Indices and Sample Sizes by Unit of Analysis
(Collection, "Race," Sex)

Unit of analysis	Mean	n	Standard deviation	Standard error	Minimum	Maximum
Co males	73.4	116	3.03	0.282	66.8	83.3
Co females	74.4	118	2.77	0.255	67.6	82.5
Te "Black" males	74.6	84	3.41	0.372	67.9	83.0
Te "Black" females	76.0	91	2.63	0.276	68.8	82.4
Te "White" females	77.5	68	2.84	0.344	71.8	84.2
Te "White" males	77.5	49	4.06	0.580	68.9	88.8

Co, Coimbra Collection; Te, Terry Collection.

Note how the Terry Collection "Blacks" are intermediary between the Coimbra Collection sample and the Terry Collection "Whites" and the range of Terry Collection "Blacks" falls within the range of the Coimbra Collection sample.

lected on living subjects (98). These measurements have been used to calculate cranial index scores, and these scores are often converted into categories of cranial shape that range from long crania to hyperround crania: dolicocranic, up to 75; mesocranic, 75–79.9; brachycranic, 80–84.9; and hyperbrachycranic, 85 or greater (98).

Data for this example were collected from the Terry Collection (8) and the Coimbra Collection (99,100). The sample was selected to include and account for a wide range of variation associated with age at death and year of birth (67). Details regarding sample size are available in Table 2. Figure 2 is scatter plot of maximum cranial length by maximum cranial breadth from both collections combined into racial categories. There is no pattern in the distribution of variation by "race" and the range of variation of the "Black" sample is entirely within the range of variation of the "White" sample.* In contrast, Fig. 3 is a scatter plot of the same data but coded by sex instead of race. As expected when considering sexual dimorphism in *Homo sapiens*, there is a clear clustering by sex and overlap in the ranges of both sexes. In other words, there is a clear pattern of variation in cranial morphology by sex but not by "race."

When looking at the cranial index instead of its component parts, racial categories still do not explain the variation in the samples. Figure 4 is a plot

---

* The data follow the same pattern, complete overlap between races, when it is graphed for each sex separately for the Terry Collection alone (not shown here). Sex differences are not obscuring "race" differences.

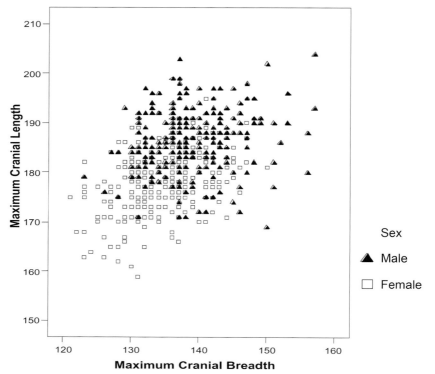

Fig. 3. Scatter plot of cranial length and width measurement of males and females from the Terry Collection and the Coimbra Collection (*n* = 526, *see* Table 2 for further details on sample composition). Identical data from Fig. 2 are displayed but coded by sex. Note how there is a clear cluster of data by sex.

of the 95% confidence intervals of the mean of the cranial index by unit of analysis (samples divided into collection–"race"–sex groups). The mean cranial index does not follow cited racial patterns. "Blacks" are usually described as dolicocranic *(17,31,36,41,90,98,101)*. "Whites" are alternatively described as dolicocranic *(101)*, mesocranic *(17,31)*, both dolicocranic and mesocranic *(90)*, brachycranic *(36)*, and as spanning the mesocranic and brachycranic categories *(41,98)*. The results from the current analysis show that the mean for "Black" males (74.6) is only marginally dolicocranic, and the mean for "Black" females (76.0) is mesocranic. The means for the European-born Coimbra Collection females (74.4) and males (73.4) are in the dolicocranic range, whereas the means for the Terry Collection "White" females (77.5) and males (77.5) are in the mesocranic range. Based on the mean cranial index,

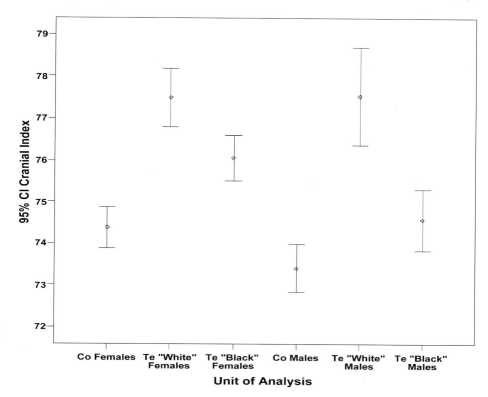

Fig. 4. Plot of 95% confidence interval of mean of cranial index by unit of analysis (collection–"race"–sex). Mean cranial shape as approximated by the cranial index does not follow often cited racial patterns (*n* = 526). Co, Coimbra Collection; Te, Terry Collection. Note: For each sex, the Terry Collection "Blacks" follow a pattern that falls between the Terry Collection "Whites" and the Coimbra Collection.

"Whites" from the Terry Collection are more similar to the "Blacks" from the Terry Collection than they are to the European-born Coimbra Collection sample. When the range of the cranial index is considered for each of the units of analysis, the entire range of variation in the Terry Collection "Black" sample falls within the range of variation in the Coimbra Collection sample. The similarities between the Coimbra Collection and the "Blacks" from the Terry Collection are not unexpected because these two samples are derived from the most disadvantaged segments of their respective communities *(66,102)*. Using a one-way analysis of variance with the Tukey honest

significant test *post hoc*,* the means of the Terry Collection "Whites" and the
Coimbra Collection are significantly different ($F = 24.981, p < 0.0001$) from
each other, whereas the Terry Collection "Blacks" are intermediary between
the two "White" samples. Because of the sampling methodology (which controlled for age at birth and age at death), the significant differences between
Terry Collection "Whites" and Coimbra Collection individuals are likely not
because of age factors or secular changes (67). This pattern of results,
nonconcordance between cranial morphology and skin pigmentation, is not
unique to the Terry Collection. Todd and Tracy (11) studied various facial
traits, cranial traits, and the cranial index from samples of American "Blacks,"
an archaeological sample from Africa, and an archaeological sample from
Europe. They found there was considerable overlap in variation between the
three samples, and African and American "Blacks" did not cluster into one
group just as American and European "Whites" did not cluster in the current
example.

   Although the components of the cranial index are rarely used alone for
race determination, these measurements are the foundation for several prominent approaches (35,40), and the cranial index categories are widely described
as racial characters (17,31,36,41,90,98,101). These differences between Terry
Collection "Whites" and the European-born Coimbra Collection sample illustrate that morphometric variation in the cranial index or its components is
not concordant with racial categories or continental origin. This example is
consistent with Relethford's (21,25,29) conclusions regarding the lack of association between skin color and human variation, which is theoretically incompatible with a more widely held view (15,70,71) that it is possible
determine "race," continental origin, or skin color with a reasonably high
accuracy outside of the reference sample used to develop the method.

4.2. Example 2: Variation in Pelvic Dimensions and the Misinterpretation of Mortality Bias as Racial Variation in the Terry Collection

   Data for this second example were collected only from the Terry Collection (8), and as in the example above, the sample was selected to control

---

* Tukey's honest significant test was selected because it is neither too conservative
(as with the Scheffe or Bonferroni tests) nor too liberal (as with the least significant test) in assessing significant differences, and Tukey's honest significant test is
both a multiple comparison test (pairwise comparisons are made between means to
identify significant differences) and a range test (similar means are grouped into
homogeneous subsets).

Table 3
Mean Age at Death for the Entire Terry Collection
and for the Subsamples Used in the Current Analysis

Unit	Entire Terry collection[a]			Current sample		
	n	Mean[b]	SD	n	Mean[c]	SD
Black females	366	51.75	19.05	80	36.35	9.15
White females	306	65.39	14.21	50	45.98	11.34
Black males	531	47.44	15.88	56	45.66	12.45
White males	453	59.30	13.37	37	50.46	12.96
Total	1656	229				

[a] Includes individuals 18 yr of age and older whose age is certain and who where classified as "White" or "Negro/Black" on original morgue documents.

[b] All means in this column are significantly different from other means in the same column at the $p < 0.0001$ level.

[c] The mean age for "White" females is significantly higher than "Black" females ($t = 5.317$, $p < 0.0001$). There are no significant differences in the mean age of "Black" males and "White" males ($t = 1.790$, $p = 0.077$).

for age-at-death and year-of-birth effects (67). In Table 3, the mean age at death for this sample is compared with the Terry Collection as a whole for each unit of analysis. The summary statistics for the entire Terry Collection are based on individuals 18 yr of age and older whose age is certain, and who where classified as "White" or "Negro/Black" on original morgue documents (8). There is a clear age bias in the Terry Collection that is confounded with racial designations, year of birth (YOB), and procedures for adding to the collection (8,103). For the entire collection, the mean age at death for each unit of analysis is significantly different from the mean for every other unit of analysis ($p < 0.0001$). The methodology used to select the sample for this study has reduced some of the effects of age at death and YOB: the mean age for "White" females is still significantly higher than "Black" females ($t = 5.317$, $p < 0.0001$), but the difference in mean age is lower; there are no significant differences in the mean age of "Black" males and "White" males ($t = 1.790$, $p = 0.077$).

After the skull, the pelvis has been considered a good source of information for determining ancestry or "race" (36,37,39,41,88,89). For this example, an alternative measurement of the pubic bone known as superior pubis ramus length was collected (67). A significant cubic relationship was found between age and the superior pubis ramus length ($r^2 = 0.18$, $F = 8.61$, $p < 0.0001$), but

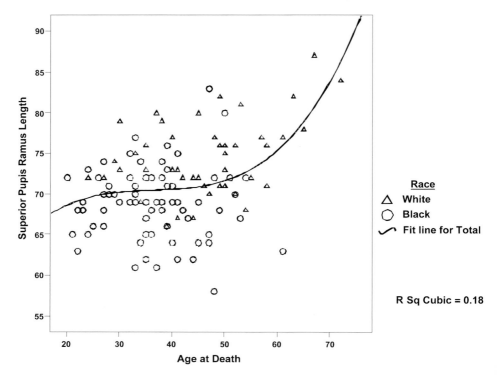

Fig. 5. Scatter plot of superior pubis ramus length by age at death for a subsample of females from the Terry Collection. *See* Table 3 for details regarding sample size. The line represents the cubic relationship between the variables for all the females. Note how the "White" females have consistently larger pelvic dimensions, but they are also consistently older.

only in females, and this relationship is graphically illustrated in Fig. 5.* This difference in pattern by sex is expected for biological and sampling reasons. The association between age at death and pelvic dimensions in females in archaeological and reference collection samples has been investigated, and various explanations have been suggested *(104,105)*. In this example, the significant association between age at death and pelvic dimensions is likely because of a mortality bias. Death resulting from complications from childbirth is not listed as the cause of the death for any females in the Terry Collec-

---

* An analysis of other pelvic measurements indicates the same pattern in the most sexually dimorphic elements of the hip bone including the iliac breadth.

tion. Rather, the correlation of pelvic dimensions with age is likely a nonspecific health indicator for females. Females with larger pelves likely had better living conditions during the period of their growth and development and also lived longer. The attribution of the variation in the pelvis to race is because a disproportionate number of younger females with smaller pelves were socially described as "Black" when they were included in the collection, and a disproportionate number of older females with larger pelvises were socially described as "White" when they were included in the collection.

Different selection pressures on the pelvises of males, who obviously will never bear children, result in a different pelvic morphology and different patterns of variation under various environmental conditions *(106–108)*. Additionally, the sample selection methodology described above was more successful in minimizing the age bias in the male sample *(see* Table 3). This current analysis actually understates the age–YOB–"race" bias in the Terry Collection. The sample selection methodology for this example reduced but did not eliminate the effects of age at death and YOB.

Pelvic "race"-determination methods that use samples drawn from the Terry Collection *(36,37,39,88,89)* allocate unknown individuals on the basis of age-related variation in the pelvis, which has incorrectly been attributed to "race." These race-determination methods work best to allocate females from the Terry Collection *(36,39,88,89)*, the samples where age-at-death and YOB differences are greatest in that collection because of historical accidents in how the collection was assembled. With one method, when age was recognized as an issue there was an attempt to statistically eliminate the effects of the "aging process" from the method *(89)*. Whereas the reductions in allocation accuracy were considerable for the adjusted functions, particularly for females who were most affected by age at death, the methodology for controlling for effects of age did not necessarily control for the true effect of age *(109)*, and the authors assume rather than demonstrate that the rest of the variation is because of "racial, and thus genetic, differences" *(89)*. Statistically significant association without any biocultural context for the variation has resulted in the apportionment of variation to the wrong source, and the resulting methods cannot be confidently applied to real forensic cases.

5. GENETIC IDENTIFICATION OF POPULATION AFFILIATION: RELEVANCE TO FORENSIC ANTHROPOLOGY

DNA fingerprinting (a technique for identifying individual organisms based on the uniqueness of their genetic pattern) is a method of identifying perpetrators and victims of crime and is now widely accepted as scientifically valid and acceptable as evidence in court. The emphasis has always been on individual identification or the matching of the sample of DNA to a specific person. More recently, however, as a result of the development of large public and private databases of genetic information and demand from the public, genetic ancestry testing (or, allocation of an individual to a specific population group) has become a growth field in the United States *(110)* and is having an influence on forensic investigations (*see* ref. *111*, and example in the following paragraphs).

There are large numbers of North American peoples wishing to trace their genealogical roots, and this has fostered the appearance of a number of private companies offering to trace personal genetic histories (PGH) by comparing individual samples to genetic data on human genetic polymorphisms from a variety of human populations. As of August 2004, there were 11 sources listed on the Internet offering fee-for-service tests of genetic ancestry *(110)*. Currently, there are two methods of tracing PGH: lineage-based tests, which amplify mitochondrial DNA (mtDNA) and the nonrecombining Y chromosome, and biogeographical ancestry (BGA) or autosomal marker-based tests, which purport to use genetic markers on the autosomal chromosomes informative of ancestry (ancestry-informative markers) to place people within biologically and geographically defined populations. Most existing tests are lineage-based, taking advantage of the fact that mtDNA and Y chromosome DNA do not recombine at fertilization (the genetic material comes either from the mother or the father), are more likely to accumulate marker mutations within lineages because of the smaller number of ancestors (a smaller effective population size, and have higher mutation rates, contributing to substantial variability. The results of the tests currently offered are designed to determine whether an individual has paternal or maternal lineages that originate from Native American, European, African, or Asian populations. The less common BGA tests aim to estimate a person's ancestry in terms of the proportional representation of ancestry-informative markers from a selection of reference databases treated as representing ancestral populations. Determination of ancestry is based on statistical tests of probability of ancestry by the maximum likelihood approach (a statistical concept used to quantify the probability that a certain hypothesis or model is correct given a set of data).

BGA tests have been applied to a recent forensic case. In the spring of 2003, the murders of five women in Louisiana had been linked through sample analyses of forensic DNA samples by short-tandem-repeat marker panels (also called microsatellite markers, these are short DNA sequences, typically from one to four nucleotides long, that are tandemly repeated several times) to implicate a single perpetrator of the crimes. However, there were no hits when the genetic sequence was compared with the national combined DNA index system (CODIS) database of convicted felons. The police had restricted their investigations to White men, screening more than 600 individuals. Then they sought the assistance of a company offering PGH screening. The results of the BGA tests indicated that the perpetrator of the murders was mainly of West African descent. This ultimately led to the arrest of a suspect whose short tandem repeat profiles matched those of the perpetrator.

Considering that geneticists attempting ancestry determinations are working from basic DNA code, it would seem that this approach would have great advantages over anthropological assessment of bones to identify a victim or unidentified decedent. The DNA of body cells is not altered during an individual's lifetime (except for cases of homeoplasy or somatic mutations within mtDNA) or subject to environmental influences. Once sequenced, DNA results should be uncontested; observations of sequences are not subjective or variable as with skeletal traits. In addition, the statistical calculations applied to estimating ancestry from genetic data are far more exacting and sophisticated than any methods currently used for nonmetric or morphological traits (metric methods are comparable, limitations lie with the reference samples as discussed under Heading 4). However, an examination of the scientific literature on genetic ancestry determination reveals a number of limitations to the approach and provides an object lesson to forensic anthropologists wishing to assign ancestry affiliation from skeletal remains. Many of the limitations described for genetic data are applicable to, or instructive for, forensic anthropology.

5.1. Limitations of Genetic Methods

Those in the field of PGH lament the fact that there needs to be an increase in the number of markers used for analysis because the more markers used, the higher the probability of estimating affiliations correctly. Theoretically, this applies to forensic anthropology too. A nonmetric or metric description of only the nasal area will provide considerably less information than a thorough examination of the entire skull. However, there are statistical problems with dealing with correlated data when many forensic traits are used.

More important than markers is the need in the genetics field for improvement, increase in size, and the sharing of genetic databases *(110)*. A few years ago, a European researcher identified the fact that there were many errors in a large public database of mtDNA sequences *(112–114)*. More recently, a similar claim has been made by others *(115)*. Not only do many genetic databases contain recording errors, but also, few have even considered the problems of quality of the background data on individuals whose DNA sequences are included in the databases. The gatekeepers of genetic databases often give no details about the number and geographical spread of samples included, so it is difficult to even assess the quality of databases. The problems are just as prevalent within genetics as have been described for forensic anthropology.

For lineage-based tests, the maternal and paternal lineages sought do not represent the entire genetic make-up. For example, an individual's mtDNA comes from his or her mother, who received it from her mother, and so on. At the great-grandparental generation, only one of eight individuals of the great grandparents (mother's mother's mother) is being sampled. In forensic anthropology, all of the phenotypic data represent recombined genetic data from all ancestors, and the nature of the morphology observed becomes the basic problem. Forensic anthropology texts state that remains that exhibit ambiguous (or mixed) ancestral groupings should be assigned to the group that is considered the minority (example in United States: a skeleton that exhibits both White and Black "features" should be assigned as "Black") because this is how they would have been classified in life. Now the forensic anthropologist (and the geneticist) becomes mired in social definitions of race. How many cases are there of mixed heritage individuals who functioned in their own "chosen" racial group or even changed designation several times in their lifetimes?

These limitations illustrate that PGH estimation is far from being an exact science, as some of the practitioners admit *(110)*. They also show that highlighting genetic differences among people might unfortunately reinforce the stereotypic features of these identities, a risk to forensic anthropology as well because judging the unknown to come from a specific group can limit the investigation as well. Nevertheless, the desire on the part of many to link genetic phenomena to ancestry or race cannot be ignored. Many want PGH estimation to justify their socially mediated constructions of population differences. In the medical field, a resurgence of interest in race relates to questions of risk for various disease conditions and the risks of blood transfusion reactions for those of different population origins *(111)*. Surely, a clearer understanding of the complexities of biological population diversity can only illuminate the debates that swirl around these issues.

6. CONCLUSIONS

The reality of human variation is not consistent with how forensic anthropologists have used, and many continue to use, human variation to identify unknown individuals, and the substitution of various terms without a critical reanalysis of the underlying assumptions has not remedied the situation. With no biological basis for racial categories, how can forensic anthropologists determine social race or bureaucratic race? Several authors have suggested that such a contradiction is not an impediment to determining "race" and that high allocation accuracies are possible with various "race"-determination methods *(15,70,71)*. The claim of 90% accuracy that has been reported for "race"-determination methods *(15,17,59)* is unsubstantiated. Despite the relatively high-allocation accuracies (often more than 80%, but rarely more than 90%) and the strength of the statistical significance that are noted when various methods are first described, the comprehensive independent tests of "race"-determination methods consistently result in low-allocation accuracies. Some forensic anthropologists have argued that race determination is a forensic necessity, and forensic anthropologists would be either derelict in their professional responsibilities or ill equipped to positively identify an unknown individual if the assessment of "race" is not investigated *(15,17,31,70,71)*. False or misleading information is far worse than a lack of information. The relatively high risk of false information outweighs the value that determining "race" may possibly have for the positive identification of an unknown individual.

Cranial and infracranial variation in different groups living under various biocultural conditions through time and space is a reality, but this variation does not neatly cluster into two to five racial categories or by continent. A racial approach for identifying unknown individuals in a forensic context will be typological because:

1. It ignores the heterogeneous patterns of phenotypic variation in the highly plastic species *H. sapiens*.
2. It runs contrary to the genetic evidence that there is a great deal of genetic homogeneity in *H. sapiens*.
3. It ignores the fact that both phenotypic and genotypic variations are continuous.
4. It tries to categorize continuous phenotypic and genotypic variation into a few *socially* constructed categories.

New methods or updates of older methods, new collections, and new terminology (use of ancestry without a reevaluation of the underlying concepts) will not solve the problems associated with "race"-determination methods if these four issues are not considered.

The greater problem is that racial designations are part of various folk taxonomies that are related to social and economic issues and inequality rather than any phenotypic or genotypic reality. As Brace *(70)* notes when referring to the various waves of migration to North America of African, Asian, and European peoples, "the social barriers between these three *artificially distinct* human constituents of the Western Hemisphere have ensured the perpetuation of discrete identity of those components despite an increase in the blurring around the edges, and this is what constitutes the 'reality' that is the 'something there' for the forensic anthropologist to discover" (p. 174, emphasis added). Socially, race is relevant and law enforcement authorities continue to ask about race because it plays a prominent role in personal identification and racial issues are prominent in the justice systems in various jurisdictions. In Canada, a country of great population diversity, law enforcement personnel are as aware of the problems of inferring geographic and population background as are the anthropologists. The simple argument that "investigators require it" is not sufficient to justify the claim for a noncritical application of anthropological methods. The authors think that the law enforcement field can be receptive to critical explorations of the complex interrelationships between sociopolitical processes and the scientific knowledge affecting our understanding of human physical diversity because the police are having to deal with such explorations within their own ranks.

REFERENCES

1. Brace, C. L. The roots of the race concept in American physical anthropology. In: Spencer, F., ed., A History of American Physical Anthropology, 1930–1980. Academic, New York, NY, pp. 11–29, 1982.
2. Blakey, M. L. Skull doctors: intrinsic social and political bias in the history of American physical anthropology with special reference to the work of Aleš Hrdlièka. Crit. Anthropol. 7:7–35, 1987.
3. Blakey, M. L. Beyond European enlightenment: towards a critical and humanistic human biology. In: Goodman, A. H., Leatherman, T. L., eds., Building a New Biocultural Synthesis: Political-Economic Perspectives on Human Biology. University of Michigan Press, Ann Arbor, MI, pp. 379–406, 1998.
4. Armelagos, G. J., Goodman, A. H. Race, racism, and anthropology. In: Goodman, A. H., Leatherman, T. L., eds., Building a New Biocultural Synthesis: Political-Economic Perspectives on Human Biology. University of Michigan Press, Ann Arbor, MI, pp. 359–378, 1998.
5. Armelagos, G. J., Van Gerven, D. P. A century of skeletal biology and paleopathology: contrasts, contradictions, and conflicts. Am. Anthropol. 105:53–64, 2003.
6. Gould, S. J. Mismeasure of Man. Norton, New York, NY, 1996.
7. Thompson, D. D. Forensic anthropology. In: Spencer, F., ed., A History of American Physical Anthropology, 1930–1980. Academic, New York, NY, 357–369, 1982.
8. Hunt, D. R., Albanese, J. History and demographic composition of the Robert J. Terry anatomical collection. Am. J. Phys. Anthropol. 127:406–417, 2004.
9. Todd, T. W. Age changes in the pubic bone: I. The male White pubis. Am. J. Phys. Anthropol. 3:285–334, 1920.
10. Todd, T. W. Age changes in the pubic bone: II, the pubis of the male Negro-White hybrid; III the pubis of the White female; IV the pubis of the female Negro-White hybrid. Am. J. Phys. Anthropol. 4:1–70, 1921.

11. Todd, T. W., Tracy, B. Racial features in the American Negro. Am. J. Phys. Anthropol. 15:53–110, 1930.
12. Terry, R. J. The clavicle of the American Negro. Am. J. Phys. Anthropol. 16:351–379, 1932.
13. Washburn, S. The new physical anthropology. Trans. NY Acad. Sci. 13:298–304, 1951.
14. St. Hoyme, L. E, Işcan, MY. Determination of sex and race: accuracy and assumptions. In: Işcan, M. Y., Kennedy, K. A., eds., Reconstruction of Life from the Skeleton. Wiley-Liss, New York, NY, pp. 53–93, 1989.
15. Sauer, N. J. Forensic anthropology and the concept of race: if races don't exist, why are forensic anthropologists so good at identifying them? Soc. Sci. Med. 34:107–111, 1992.
16. Goodman, A. H. Bred in the bone? Sciences 37:20–25, 1997.
17. Gill, G. W. Craniofacial criteria in the skeletal attribution of race. In: Reichs, K., ed., Forensic Osteology. Charles C. Thomas, Springfield, IL, pp. 293–317, 1998.
18. Keita, S. O. Y., Kittles, R. A. The persistence of racial thinking and the myth of racial divergence. Am. Anthropol. 99:534–542, 1997.
19. Cartmill, M. The status of the race concept in physical anthropology. Am. Anthropol. 100:651–660, 1998.
20. Templeton, A. R. Human races: a genetic and evolutionary perspective. Am. Anthropol. 100:632–650, 1998.
21. Relethford, J. H. Global analysis of regional differences in craniometric diversity and population substructure. Hum. Biol. 73:629–636, 2001.
22. Brown, R. A, Armelagos, G. J. Apportionment of racial diversity: a review. Evol. Anthropol. 10:34–40, 2001.
23. Lieberman, L. How "Caucasoids" got such big crania and why they shrank—from Morton to Rushton. Curr. Anthropol. 42:69–95, 2001.
24. Albanese, J. The use of skeletal data for the study of secular change: methodological implication of combining data from different sources. Am. J. Phys. Anthropol. 34:36, 2002.
25. Relethford, J. H. Apportionment of global human genetic diversity based on craniometrics and skin color. Am. J. Phys. Anthropol. 118:393–398, 2002.
26. Molnar, S. Human Variation: Races, Types, and Ethnic Groups, 5th Ed. Prentice Hall, Upper Saddle River, NJ, 2002.
27. Livingstone, F. On the non-existence of human races. Curr. Anthropol. 3:279–281, 1962.
28. Lewontin, R. The apportionment of human diversity. Evol. Biol. 6:381–398, 1972.
29. Relethford, J. H. Craniometric variation among modern human populations. Am. J. Phys. Anthropol. 95:53–62, 1994.
30. France, D. L., Horn, A. D. Lab Manual and Workbook for Physical Anthropology. West, St. Paul, MN, 1988.
31. Francem D, L. Lab Manual and Workbook for Physical Anthropology, 4th Ed. Wadsworth Thomson Learning, Belmont, CA, 2001.
32. Ross, A. H., Slice, D. E., Ubelaker, D. H., Falsetti, A. B. Population affinities of 19th century Cuban crania: implications for identification criteria in South Florida Cuban Americans. J. Forensic Sci. 49:11–16, 2004.

33. Hooton, E. The Indians of Pecos pueblo: a study of their skeletal remains. Yale University Press, Andover, MA, 1930.
34. Snow, C. C., Hartman, S., Giles, E., Young, F. A. Sex and race determination of crania by calipers and computer: a test of the Giles and Elliot discriminant functions in 52 forensic science cases. J. Forensic Sci. 24:448–460, 1979.
35. Giles, E., Elliot, O. Race identification from cranial measurements. J. Forensic Sci. 7:147–157, 1962.
36. Işcan, M. Y. Race determination from the pelvis. OSSA 8:95–100, 1981.
37. DiBennardo, R., Taylor, J. V. Multiple discriminant function analysis of sex and race in the postcranial skeleton. Am. J. Phys. Anthropol. 61:305–314, 1983.
38. Işcan, M. Y., Cotton, T. S. The effect of age on the determination of race from the pelvis. J. Hum. Evol. 14:275–282, 1985.
39. Schulter-Ellis, F. P., Hayek, L. A. Predicting race and sex with an acetabulum/pubis index. Coll. Antropol. 8:155–162, 1984.
40. Ousley, S., Jantz, R. L. FORDISC 2.0: Computerized Discriminant Functions. University of Tennessee, Knoxville, TN, 1996.
41. Krogman, W., Işcan, M. Y. The Human Skeleton in Forensic Medicine. Charles C. Thomas, Springfield, IL, 1986.
42. Birkby, W. H. An evaluation of race and sex identification from cranial measurements. Am. J. Phys. Anthropol. 24:21–27, 1966.
43. Fisher, T. D., Gill, G. W. Application of the Giles and Elliot discriminant function formulae to a cranial sample of Northwest Plains Indians. In: Gill, G. W., Rhine, S., eds., Skeletal Attribution of Race. Maxwell Museum of Anthropology, Albuquerque, NM, pp. 59–64, 1990.
44. Ayers, H. G., Jantz, R. L., Moore-Jansen, P. H. Giles and Elliot race discriminant functions revisited: a test using recent forensic cases. In: Gill, G. W., Rhine, S., eds., Skeletal Attribution of Race. Maxwell Museum of Anthropology, Albuquerque, NM, pp. 65–72, 1990.
45. Gill, G. W., Rhine, S. Skeletal Attribution of Race. Maxwell Museum of Anthropology, Albuquerque, NM, 1990.
46. Ousley, S., Jantz, R. L. The forensic data bank: documenting skeletal trends in the United States. In: Reichs, K., ed., Forensic Osteology. Charles C. Thomas, Springfield, IL, pp. 441–458, 1998.
47. Billinger, M. S. Geography, Genetics and Generalizations: the Abandonment of "Race" in the Anthropological Study of Human Biological Variation. Masters Thesis, Carleton University, Ottawa, Ontario, 2000.
48. Ginter, J. Dealing with Unknowns in a Non-Population: the Skeletal Analysis of the Odd Fellows Series. Masters Thesis. University of Western Ontario, London, Ontario, 2001.
49. Ginter, J. Issues of skeletal identification: ancestry determination of the Odd Fellows series. Abstract. Can. Assoc. Forensic Sci. J. 35:41, 2002.
50. Işcan, M. Y., Cotton, T. S. Osteometric assessment of racial affinity from multiple sites in the postcranial skeleton. In: Gill, G. W., Rhine, S., eds., Skeletal Attribution of Race. Maxwell Museum of Anthropology, Albuquerque, NM, pp. 83–91, 1990.

51. Terry, R. J. On measuring and photographing the cadaver. Am. J. Phys. Anthropol. 26:433–447, 1940.
52. Giles, E. Sex determination by discriminant function analysis of the mandible. Am. J. Phys. Anthropol. 22:129–135, 1964.
53. Howells, W. W. Cranial Variation in Man. Peabody Museum of Archaeology and Ethnology Papers. Harvard University Press, Cambridge, MA, 1973.
54. Howells, W. W. Skull Shapes and the Map. Harvard University Press, Cambridge, MA, 1989.
55. Ubelaker, D. H. Book review: Personal computer forensic discriminant functions. Int. J. Osteoarchaeol. 8:128–123, 1998.
56. Fukuzawa, S., Maish, A. Racial identification of Ontario Iroquoian crania using FORDISC 2.0. Can. Assoc. Forensic Sci. J. 30:167–168, 1997.
57. Belcher, R., Williams, F., Armelagos, G. J. Misidentification of Meroitic Nubians using FORDISC 2.0. Am. J. Phys. Anthropol. 34:S42, 2002.
58. Leathers, A., Edwards, J., Armelagos, G. J. Assessment of classification of crania using Fordisc 2.0: Nubian X-group test. Am. J. Phys. Anthropol. 34:S99–S100, 2002.
59. Snow, C. C. Murder most foul. Sciences 35:16–21, 1995.
60. Marino, E. A. A pilot study using the first cervical vertebra as an indicator of race. J. Forensic Sci. 42:1114–1118, 1997.
61. Smith, SL. Attribution of foot bones to sex and population groups. J. Forensic Sci. 42:186–195, 1997.
62. Byers, S. N., Churchill, S. E., Curran, B. Identification of Euro-Americans, Afro-Americans, and Amerindians from palatal dimensions. J. Forensic Sci. 42:3–9, 1997.
63. Duray, S. M., Morter, H. B., Smith, F. J. Morphological variation in cervical spinous processes: potential applications in the forensic identification of race from the skeleton. J. Forensic Sci. 44:937–944, 1999.
64. Holliday, T. W., Falsetti, A. B. A new method for discriminating African-American from European-American skeletons using postcranial osteometrics reflective of body shape. J. Forensic Sci. 44:926–930, 1999.
65. Trudell, M. B. Anterior femoral curvature revisited: race assessment from the femur. J. Forensic Sci. 44:700–707, 1999.
66. Albanese, J. Identified Skeletal Reference Collections and the Study of Human Variation. McMaster University, Hamilton, Ontario, 2003.
67. Albanese, J. A metric method for sex determination using the hipbone and the femur. J. Forensic Sci. 48:263–273, 2003.
68. Meadows Jantz, L., Jantz, R. L. Secular change in long bone length and proportion in the United States, 1800–1970. Am. J. Phys. Anthropol. 110:57–67, 1999.
69. Cobb, W. M. Race and runners. J. Health Phys. Ed. 7:1–9, 1936.
70. Brace, C. L. Region does not mean "race"—reality versus convention in forensic anthropology. J. Forensic Sci. 40:171–175, 1995.
71. Kennedy, K. A. But professor, why teach race identification if races don't exist? J. Forensic Sci. 40:797–800, 1995.

72. Hauser, G., De Stefano, G. F. Epigenetic Variants of the Human Skull. Schweizer-bartsche, Stuttgart, 1989.
73. Brues, A. M. The once and future diagnosis of race. In: Gill. G. W., Rhine, S., eds., Skeletal Attribution of Race. Maxwell Museum of Anthropology, Albuquerque, NM, pp. 1–8, 1990.
74. Ossenberg, N. S. Within and between race distances in population studies based on discrete traits of the human skull. Am. J. Phys. Anthropol. 45:701–716, 1976.
75. Saunders, S. R. Nonmetric skeletal variation. In: Işcan, M. Y., Kennedy, K. A., eds., Reconstruction of Life from the Skeleton. Liss, New York, NY, pp. 95–108, 1989.
76. Rhine, S. Nonmmetric skull racing. In: Gill, G. W., Rhine, S., eds., Skeletal Attribution of Race. Maxwell Museum of Anthropology, Albuquerque, NM, pp. 9–20, 1990.
77. Byers, S. N. Introduction to Forensic Anthropology. Allyn and Bacon, New York, NY, 2002.
78. Gill, G. W. Challenge on the frontier: discerning American Indians from Whites osteologically. J. Forensic Sci. 40:783–788, 1995.
79. Wijsman, E. M., Neves, W. A. The use of nonmetric variation in estimating human population admixture: A test case with Brazilian Blacks, Whites and mulattos. Am. J. Phys. Anthropol. 70:395–405, 1986.
80. Sjovold, T. Non-metrical divergence between skeletal populations. OSSA 1:S1–S133, 1977.
81. McGrath, J., Cheverud, J., Buikstra, J. Genetic correlations between sides and heritability of asymmetry for nonmetric traits in rhesus macaques on Cayo Santiago. Am. J. Phys. Anthropol. 64:401–411, 1984.
82. Hanihara, T., Ishida, H., Dodo, Y. Characterization of biological diversity through analysis of discrete cranial traits. Am. J. Phys. Anthropol. 121:241–251, 2003.
83. Grüneberg, H. Genetical studies on the skeleton of the mouse. IV. Quasi-continuous variations. J. Genet. 51:95–114, 1952.
84. Rösing, F. W. Discreta of the human skeleton: a critical review. J. Hum. Evol. 13:319–323, 1984.
85. Scott, G. R., Turner, C. G. The Anthropology of Modern Human Teeth: Dental Morphology and its Variation in Recent Human Populations. Cambridge University Press, Cambridge, 1997.
86. Tyrrell, A. Skeletal non-metric traits and the assessment of inter- and intra-population diversity: past problems and future potential. In: Cox, M., Mays, S., eds., Human Osteology. Greenwich Medical Media, London, pp. 289–306, 2000.
86a. Dahlberg, A. A. 1951. The dentition of the American Indian. In Laughlin, W. Ed. (ed.): Papers on the Physical Anthropology of the American Indians. Viking Fund, New York: pp. 138–176.
86b. Ossenberg, N. S. 1969. Discontinuous Morphological Variation of the Human Cranium. Ph.D. thesis, University of Toronto.
8bc. Ossenberg, N. S. 1981. An argument for the use of total side frequencies of bilateral nonmetric skeletal traits in population distance analysis—the regression of symmetry on incidence. Am. J. Physical Anthropol. 54:471–479.

87. Public Safety and Emergency Preparedness Canada. http://www.psepc-sppcc.gc.ca/index_e.asp. Last accessed Mar. 7, 2006.
88. Işcan, M. Y. Assessment of race from the pelvis. Am. J. Phys. Anthropol. 62:205–208, 1983.
89. Işcan, M. Y., Cotton, T. S. The effects of age on the determination of race. Coll. Antropol. 8:131–138, 1984.
90. Rogers, SL. Personal Identification from Human Remains. Charles C. Thomas, Springfield, IL, 1987.
91. Jackson, F. L. C. Anthropological measurement: the mismeasure of African Americans. Ann Am. Acad. Pol. Soc. Sci. 568:154–171, 2000.
92. Walker, P. L. Problems of preservation and sexism in sexing: some lessons from historical collections and palaeodemographers. In: Saunders, S. R., Herring, A., eds., Grave Reflections: Portraying the Past Through Cemetery Studies. Canadian Scholars Press, Toronto, pp. 31–47, 1995.
93. Boas, F. Changes in bodily form of descendants of immigrants. Am. Anthropol. 14:530–562, 1912.
94. Sparks, C. S., Jantz, R. L. A reassessment of human cranial plasticity: Boas revisited. Proc. Natl. Acad. Sci. USA. 99:14,636–14,639, 2002.
95. Gravlee, C. C., Bernard, H. R., Leonard, W. R. Boas's changes in bodily form: the immigrant study, cranial plasticity, and Boas's physical anthropology. Am. Anthropol. 105:326–332, 2003.
96. Gravlee, C. C., Bernard, H. R., Leonard, W. R. Heredity, environment, and cranial form: a reanalysis of Boas's immigrant data. Am. Anthropol. 105:125–138, 2003.
97. Sparks, C. S., Jantz, R. L. Changing times, changing faces: Franz Boas's immigrant study in modern perspective. Am. Anthropol. 105:333–337, 2003.
98. Olivier, G. Practical Anthropology. Charles C. Thomas, Springfield, IL, 1969.
99. Rocha, A. Les collections ostéologiques humaines identifiées du Musée Anthropologigue de l'Université de Coimbra [in Portuguese]. Antropol. Port. 13:7–38, 1995.
100. Cunha, E. Testing identification records: evidence from the Coimbra Identified Skeletal Collections (nineteenth and twentieth centuries). In: Saunders, S. R., Herring, A, eds., Grave Reflections: Portraying the Past Through Cemetery Studies. Canadian Scholars Press, Toronto, pp. 179–198, 1995.
101. Skinner, M., Lazenby, R. A. Found! Human Remains. Archaeology Press, Simon Fraser University, Burnaby, British Columbia, 1983.
102. Santos, A. L. A Skeletal Picture of Tuberculosis. Ph.D. Thesis. University of Coimbra, Coimbra, Portugal, 2000.
103. Trotter, M. Robert James Terry, 1871–1966. Am. J. Phys. Anthropol. 56:503–508, 1981.
104. Tague, R. G. Maternal mortality or prolonged growth: age at death and pelvic size in three prehistoric Amerindian populations. Am. J. Phys. Anthropol. 95:27–40, 1994.
105. Fuller, K. Adult females and pubic bone growth. Am. J. Phys. Anthropol. 106:323–328, 1998.

106. Stini, W. A. Adaptive strategies of human populations under nutritional stress. In: Watts, E. S., Johnston, F. E., Lasker, G. W., eds., Population Adaptation. Mouton, The Hague, pp. 19–41, 1975.
107. Stini, W. A. Sexual dimorphism and nutrient reserves. In: Hall, R. L, ed., Sexual Dimorphism in *Homo sapiens*. Praeger, New York, NY, pp. 391–419, 1982.
108. Stinson, S. Sex differences in environmental sensitivity during growth and development. Yearb. Phys. Anthropol. 28:123–147, 1985.
109. Norušis, M. J. SPSS 12.0 Statistical Procedures Companion. Prentice Hall, Upper Saddle River, NJ, 2003.
110. Shriver, M., Kittles, R. Genetic ancestry and the search for personalized genetic histories. Nat. Rev. Genet 5:611–618, 2004.
111. Duster, T. Buried alive: the concept of race in science. In: Goodman, A. H., Heath, D., Lindee, M. S., eds., Genetic Nature/Culture. University of California Press, Berkeley, CA, pp. 258–277, 2003.
112. Rohl, A., Brinkmann, B., Forster, L., Forster, P. An annotated mtDNA database. Int. J. Legal Med. 115:29–39, 2001.
113. Forster, P. To err is human. Ann. Hum. Genet. 67(Part 1):2–4, 2003.
114. Budowle, B., Allard, M. W., Wilson, M. R., Chakraborty, R. Forensics and mitochondrial DNA: applications, debates, and foundations. Annu. Rev. Genomics Hum. Genet. 4:119–141, 2003.
115. Yao, Y. G., Bravi, C. M., Bandelt, H. J. A call for mtDNA data quality control in forensic science. Forensic Sci. Int. 141:1–6, 2004.

Chapter 13

Estimation and Evidence in Forensic Anthropology

Determining Stature

Lyle W. Konigsberg, Ann H. Ross, and William L. Jungers

Summary

Identifications in forensic anthropology occur in two rather different contexts. One context is that of "estimation," when a biological profile from unidentified remains is built in the hope of eventually identifying said remains. Another context is in evidentiary proceedings, where biological information from the remains is used to contribute to a probability statement about the likelihood of a correct identification. Both of these contexts can occur when stature is the biological parameter of interest, and so the authors take data related to stature as the example in this chapter. The unifying method in both contexts is the application of Bayes' theorem. Therefore, this chapter opens with a review of some of the characteristics of a Bayesian analysis.

The authors show how a Bayesian analysis can be used to estimate stature from either an informative or uninformative prior distribution of stature and reference sample information on the scaling of long bone lengths against stature. This reference sample may be either large in size, in which case it can be assumed that the regression parameters are known, or small, in which case the uncertainty of the regression parameters must be incorporated. The authors also show how to calculate likelihood ratios that compare the probability of obtaining the long bone lengths if the identification is correct vs if the individual was randomly sampled from the "population at large."

Key Words: Allometry; Bayesian analysis; Gibbs sampler; likelihood ratio; long bone lengths; WinBUGS.

From *Forensic Anthropology and Medicine:*
Complementary Sciences From Recovery to Cause of Death
Edited by: A. Schmitt, E. Cunha, and J. Pinheiro © Humana Press Inc., Totowa, NJ

1. INTRODUCTION

Stature is one of the biological characteristics often used in forensic anthropology (FA), both to help build profiles for unidentified individuals and to support putative identifications. With acts of genocide resulting from the recent wars in the former Yugoslavia and Rwanda and other mass fatalities incidents like the tsunami in Southeast Asia in 2004, demographic indicators such as stature are increasingly important in the search for missing persons. Because current standards are based on aging US skeletal samples and may not be applicable with any accuracy to other ethnic groups, the development of local population criteria and a multidisciplinary approach are critical aspects of contemporary forensic science (1,2). Forensic pathologists, because of the number of cases of both known and unknown individuals processed at their facilities, are in a unique position to contribute to a standards database. Although the collection of metric data from skeletal remains is not always practical, especially if the remains have to be macerated, a potential source of data could be obtained from radiographs, given that radiographs are generally already part of the medical examiner's protocols.

Broadly, there are two possible applications where information on stature may be of use in FA. The first problem is one of estimation in which (typically) long bones are used to estimate stature. The second problem is an evidentiary one in which (typically) a stature estimated from long bones is shown to be consistent with the "known" stature for a particular individual (quotations around the word *known* are meant to indicate that the living or cadaver stature may itself be an estimate rather than a precisely known quantity). Another possible problem that will not be dealt with in this chapter is variation in limb proportions in relation to stature among different populations. Recent studies of secular change and allometry have observed differential limb proportionality between sexes and among populations, which could affect the accuracy of stature equations depending on the skeletal elements used to calculate such estimates (3–6). Meadows-Jantz and Jantz (4) concluded that it is not likely that changes in function are solely responsible for differences in proportional relationships. Differential limb proportionality among populations should not be surprising because different parts of the human body are known to mature and achieve adult proportions at different rates (7,8). At the age of peak growth velocity, the upper limbs are more developed than the lower limbs, and the distal segments, such as the tibia and fibula and forearm, precede the proximal segments (8). Thus, along with genetics, nutritional and/or disease stresses at a particular developmental and growth stage would affect the various biological systems differently, resulting in limb proportion variation among populations. These results suggest that considerable variation exists among populations that might normally be considered similar and further stress the need for local standards.

Regardless of the context, whether as a problem in estimation or presentation of evidence, the argument is made here that Bayesian methods *(9)* are appropriate. Whereas Bayesian methods are quite commonplace in most of the forensic sciences *(10–12)*, they have been virtually unheard of in FA until quite recently. Consequently, in this chapter, the authors first describe some very basic Bayesian analyses as preamble to discussing applications specific to stature. Virtually all of their presentation makes use of the program WinBUGS 1.4.1 *(13)*, which is available at http://www.mrc-bsu.cam.ac.uk/bugs/welcome.shtml.

2. ESTIMATION IN A SINGLE-PARAMETER PROBLEM

In this chapter, the authors make extensive use of humerus and femur maximum length measurements from 19 African pygmies *(14)*. The third author took all of the measurements as well as estimated statures for the skeletons, using the Fully technique *(15)*. Of these 19 individuals, 11 are males and 8 are females. In this section, the authors demonstrate how a Bayesian analysis can be used to estimate a single parameter or present "evidence" based on a single parameter. As is discussed under Heading 5, stature estimation is a multiparameter problem, so the authors pick a simpler problem that contains a solitary parameter. For this problem, they look at estimation of the proportion of males in the sample of 19 pygmies.

The essentials of a Bayesian analysis are the specification of prior distributions and likelihood functions. The prior distribution is just some probability function (in the case of a discrete parameter) or a probability density function (in the case of a continuous parameter). The proportion of males in the sample of 19 pygmies is a continuous parameter problem as the true population proportion of males from which the small sample of 19 was drawn could take any value between 0 and 1. A statement of ignorance about the true proportion would be to say that all values between 0 and 1 are equally likely, which is a uniform distribution on the interval from 0 to 1. Equivalently, the same uniform distribution can be specified as a $\beta(v = 1, \omega = 1)$ distribution *(16)*. The likelihood function is defined as proportional to the probability of getting the observed data (in this case, 11 males out of 19 individuals) given a fixed value of the parameter, in this case, a fixed value of the population proportion of males. The authors are careful to state that this proportion is unlikely to be the actual proportion of living males, as anatomists and anthropologists have typically collected male skeletons with greater frequency than they have female skeletons *(17)*. For maximum likelihood estimation, one would examine different possible values of the proportion and select the value with the greatest likelihood. In this case, one would find that the maximum likelihood estimate occurs, quite logically, at 11 ÷ 19.

By Bayes' theorem, the posterior probability density is proportional to the product of the prior density with the likelihood function. The posterior density represents knowledge about the underlying parameter based on the initial knowledge (the prior) and what can be gleaned from the collected data through the likelihood function. For the current example, this can be written as:

$$f(p|x) \propto U(0,1) \times Bin(x|p), \tag{1}$$

where $U(0,1)$ is a uniform distribution on the interval from 0 to 1 and represents prior information, $Bin(x|p)$ is the likelihood function that is the binomial probability of getting x (=11) successes out of n (=19) trials if the population probability is p, and $f(p|x)$ is the posterior density of p given the data. Thus, Eq. 1 tells us that the posterior density is proportional to the product of the prior density and the likelihood. For technical reasons, a different prior known as Haldane's prior *(18)* is used, which is $\beta(\nu = 0, \omega = 0)$. In the β distribution, both shape parameters must be greater than 0, so for the following analysis the authors instead use $\beta(\nu = 10^{-5}, \omega = 10^{-5})$. The β probability density function is proportional to $p^{(\nu-1)}(1-p)^{(\omega-1)}$, so it is a simple matter to graph the density function with a computer spreadsheet. With Haldane's prior, the posterior density is:

$$f(p|x) \propto B(10^{-1},10^{-5}) \times Bin(x|p), \tag{2}$$

where $B(10^{-5},10^{-5})$ is the β prior density.

The program WinBUGS is a Windows version of BUGS, which stands for *B*ayesian analysis *u*sing *G*ibbs *s*ampling. Gibbs sampling is a type of Markov chain Monte Carlo simulation that successively samples from full conditional distributions in order to obtain the posterior distributions for all parameters in a particular model *(19)*. As the model here has a single parameter, there is no conditioning on other parameters, so WinBUGS will sample directly from the posterior density, $f(p|x)$. To do this, we need to specify the prior distribution for p and the probability of getting the observed count *(11)* on 19 trials at a fixed value of p (i.e., the likelihood). Additionally, the "data" (which is just the count of 11) is given and an initial guess as to the value of p (for which 0.5 is used). This is all specified in the BUGS code below, where the "sharp sign" is a tag for comment lines:

```
Model {
# Haldane's prior
  p ~ dbeta(1.E-5,1.E-5)
# Likelihood
  x ~ dbin(p,19)
}
```

Data
```
list(x = 11)
```

Inits
```
list(p=.5)
```

The above code can be copied and pasted into a new file in WinBUGS. The syntax is then checked, the data loaded, the program compiled, and the initial guess of 0.5 also loaded (this is all covered in "WinBUGS–the movie!"; http://www.statslab.cam.ac.uk/~krice/winbugsthemovie.html). Running 30,000 iterations of WinBUGS will produce a mean p across the iterations of 0.5795, which agrees well with $11 \div 19$ (=0.5789). The variance of the 30,000 iterates is 1.22×10^{-2}, which agrees well with $11 \div 19 \times (1 - 11 \div 19) \div 19$ (=1.28×10^{-2}). A useful value that can be monitored in WinBUGS is the "deviance," which is -2 multiplied by the log-likelihood for the entire model. The minimum deviance value across the 30,000 iterations is 3.3980. This number has no particular use on its own, but is extremely important when comparing alternative models, as is shown below.

An alternative model for the data would be to assume that the actual population proportion of males was 0.5. This can also be modeled with a β prior for which $\beta(v = 10^{99}, \omega = 10^{99})$ is used. This β distribution has a point mass of 1.0 at the value of $p = 0.5$, so the prior will entirely dominate the likelihood. Therefore, the posterior distribution for p is also a point mass of 1.0 at $p = 0.5$, so WinBUGS will always simulate a value of 0.5 for p. Consequently, the authors only run two iterations in order to find the deviance for this model, which is equal to 3.8736. Now the likelihood ratio for the two models is equal to $\exp[(3.8736 - 3.3980) \div 2] = 1.2684$. This agrees well with the theoretical calculation, which is $\exp\{11 \times [\ln(11 \div 19) - \ln(0.5)] + 8 \times [\ln(8 \div 19) - \ln(0.5)]\} = 1.2685$. The likelihood ratio can be interpreted as meaning that the obtained data (11 males out of 19 individuals) are about 1.268 times more likely to be obtained if the real population proportion of males was equal to $11 \div 19$ rather than 0.5. This is rather weak evidence for arguing against the real proportion being equal to 0.5. In fact, the deviances for the two models can also be used in what is known as a likelihood ratio test. In this setting, the difference between the two deviances asymptotically follows a χ-square distribution with 1 degree of freedom. A χ-square value of 0.4756 (the difference between the two deviances) has an associated p value of about 0.49, so in a frequentist setting, one would fail to reject the null hypothesis that the population proportion of males was equal to 0.5. The strong preference in the remainder of this chapter is to use likelihood ratios rather than their associated tests. The likelihood ratios have very direct interpretations in evidentiary settings, whereas statistical tests typically do not.

3. MULTIVARIATE ESTIMATION OF STATURE WHEN THE REGRESSION OF LONG BONES ON STATURE IS KNOWN

In the next example, the authors estimate stature from two variables (maximum femur length and maximum humerus length). The statistical basis for this is given in Konigsberg et al. *(20)*. Specifically, they show that the typical regression of stature on long bone lengths that is used in FA *(21)* is identical to a Bayesian analysis. In this analysis, the likelihood is proportional to the product of a prior distribution for stature and the probability of getting the observed long bone lengths given a particular stature. The prior distribution in this case is a normal density, with mean and variance equal to the reference sample used to derive the regression of long bone lengths on stature. In the setting described here, the authors take the reference collection as being so large that all of its parameters are known, so that the mean stature and long bone lengths and the variance–covariance matrix among these measurements are known without error. When the mean and variance of stature in the reference sample are used as an informative before estimating stature on a new case, then one assumes that the new case was sampled from the same (statistical) population that provided the reference sample. For the following example, data on 2053 individuals from the Terry Anatomical Collection US World War II data, and the Forensic Databank at University of Tennessee (*see* ref. *20* for further information on this sample) is used. The example case is from the 19 African pygmies, so the 2053 individuals do not provide a reasonable prior. Consequently, an uninformative prior for stature (a normal distribution with a very large variance) can be taken, in which case the estimated stature is the maximum likelihood estimate. A final and more logical alternative makes use of the fact that the test case is from an African pygmy; we can make use of this fact and use a prior appropriate for the case. This was the strategy used by Ross and Konigsberg *(1)* to derive new stature estimators for the Balkans. For the

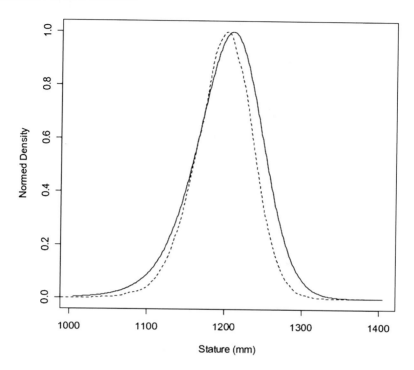

Fig. 1. Comparison of normalized profile likelihood (solid line) to WinBUGS output (dotted line) for an example with 19 pygmies for calibration, a diffuse prior for stature, and femur and humerus lengths of 329 and 241 mm, respectively.

current example, Dietz et al. *(22)* provide stature summary statistics for 53 adult Efe pygmies, from which a pooled mean stature of 1406 mm, with a variance of 1816 was obtained.

In Appendix 1, the WinBUGS code for the example is listed. A few of comments are in order. First, instead of variances WinBUGS uses "precisions," which are the inverse of variances (similarly for a multivariate normal the variance–covariance matrix is inverted to find the matrix of precisions). Second, Fig. 1 shows three different possible priors. Of these, only one should be "uncommented" in an actual run. When applied to an actual case with a femur length of 378 mm and humerus length of 278 mm (and Fully stature of 1436 mm), WinBUGS estimated the stature at 1494 mm, with a standard deviation of 40.84 when the (incorrect) informative prior from the 2053 individuals was used. This estimate and its standard deviation are based on 50,000 iterations. This estimate agrees with the estimate of 1494 mm from "inverse calibration" and standard deviation of 41.10 obtainable from that of Konigsberg et al. ([20] Table 4). Using an uninformative prior, the WinBUGS estimated stature is 1424 mm, with a standard deviation of 46.59, which again agrees with the estimate from Konigsberg et al. ([20] Table 4: 1424 mm and a standard deviation of 46.90). Finally, using the prior distribution for stature from the Efe pygmies, WinBUGS estimated the stature at 1414 mm, with a standard deviation of 31.38. The authors cannot evaluate this result within that of Konigsberg et al. ([20] Table 4) because they did not consider informative priors other than that from the 2053 individuals.

In terms of closeness to the Fully stature, using an informative prior for stature from the 2053 individuals in the reference sample produces an overestimate of 5.8 cm, which is clearly unacceptable. Using an uninformative prior leads to an underestimate of only 1.2 cm, whereas the informative prior from the Efe pygmies produces an underestimate of 2.2 cm. There are a number of others issues that could be addressed in detail here, but for the sake of brevity will not. In particular, the authors can also examine the predicted distribution for the long bone lengths in each of their three models. If done so, the model with an informative prior from the 2053 individuals does a particularly poor job of recovering the actual long bone lengths of 378 and 278 mm. Given this fact, it would be desirable to have the standard deviation (really the standard error) around the mean estimated stature be related to the disparity between long bone lengths and their predictions in a particular model. Brown and Sundberg (23) and Brown (24) discuss this problem at length, whereas Konigsberg et al. (20) discuss diagnostics documented in the previous two references. In the example, it is considered that the pygmy case has an R_x value of 9.55 that, with 1 degree of freedom on a χ-square test, gives a p value of about 0.002. The R_x statistic tests for extrapolation, an event that has certainly occurred in applying a non-pygmy prior for stature. The R statistic for this case is 0.16 that, with 1 degree of freedom, gives a p value of about 0.693. The R statistic tests for shape difference between the test case and the reference sample. However, an unfortunate side effect of using such a large reference sample is that confidence intervals are not influenced by the size of the R statistic. In other words, forensic cases that have major shape differences from the reference sample will have the same width confidence interval as cases that are shaped like the reference sample (where shape here refers to proportionality of the bones to one another). In fact, the authors can produce an estimator for stature that is sensitive to shape differences if the estimation of the regression parameters is included in their model.

4. MULTIVARIATE ESTIMATION OF STATURE WHEN THE REGRESSION OF LONG BONES ON STATURE IS ESTIMATED

All three models used in the previous section (informative prior from the 2053 individuals, uninformative prior, and informative prior from the Efe pygmies) assumed that the regression of long bones on stature was known, and that the regression could be generalized across any group. In this section, the authors instead examine the case where there is a small sample of individuals who serve as a reference sample for the regression of long bones on stature and there is a reasonable prior distribution for stature. Appendix 2 shows the code for this latter example. Here, the long bone and Fully stature data from the 19 African pygmies and the informative prior distribution for stature from the Efe pygmy data is used. As written, the model first shows a multivariate regression of femur and humerus length on stature. For those not familiar with multivariate regression, the model is one where there are two ordinary linear regressions (one with femur dependent on stature and one with humerus dependent on stature) and a two-by-two variance–covariance matrix of regression errors after removing the effect of stature on long bone length. The prior distribution for the inverse of this variance–covariance matrix is a Wishart distribution *(16)*. Another difference from the authors' previous WinBUGS code is the inclusion of a rather long list of "data" following the model. The first list gives the sample size for the regression ($n = 19$), the parameters for the Wishart prior distribution, the parameters for the prior distribution for the regression coefficients, and the bone measurements for the first test case (femur length equals 329 mm, humerus length equals 241 mm.) Following this is a tabular list of data that gives the Fully stature in the first column, the femur length in the second column, and the humerus length in the third column. Note that the 18th case does not have a humerus measurement, so "NA" (not available) has been entered. WinBUGS is able to deal appropriately with such missing data.

The authors' first test case was generated by taking the shortest observed Fully stature among the 19 pygmies (1211 mm) and predicting the long bone lengths given the regression of bone on stature. In this first example, WinBUGS was run first with a diffuse prior, so this is a "classical calibration" using a small reference sample of 19 individuals. The authors use this diffuse prior for comparison to the likelihood profile method given in Brown and Sundberg *(23)* as their method should then give very similar results to the WinBUGS results. Figure 1 shows a comparison of the densities (normalized so that the maximum occurs at 1.0) from the profile likelihood method and from WinBUGS. WinBUGS produces a median stature of 1199 mm, which agrees well with the profile likelihood estimate of 1209 mm. The WinBUGS 2.5th percentile is at 1118 vs the profile likelihood estimate of 1115 for the 2.5th percentile. For the 97.5th percentile, WinBUGS reports a value of 1267 mm, whereas the profile likelihood method produces a similar value of 1285 mm. And as can be seen in Fig. 1, the distribution of estimate stature is very similar for these two methods.

The second example is designed to show what happens when an individual with very different long bone proportions (relative to the reference sample) is entered into the analysis. For this second example, a femur length of 329 is again used, but with a humerus length of 298 in place of the previous value. A humerus length of 298 is what would be predicted for an individual 1535-mm tall (the tallest individual in the sample of 19 pygmy skeletons). It is very unlikely that such an oddly proportioned individual would exist, but if bones were accidentally commingled, then this could lead to attempts to estimate stature where the bones give very different results. Analysis in WinBUGS gives a median of 1436 mm with the 2.5th and 97.5th percentiles at 1264 and 1587 mm. This is an unacceptably large interval of 32.3 cm vs the interval of 14.9 cm from the previous example. Even the 14.9-cm interval is rather wide, a result of using the diffuse prior for stature.

5. INFORMATIVE PRIORS AND PRESENTATION OF EVIDENCE

Whereas the authors used a diffuse prior in all of the stature analyses so far, it is a very simple matter to return to the WinBUGS code listed in Appendix 2 and substitute an informative prior from the Efe pygmies. More to the point, if long bone lengths are used in evidentiary problems, it is generally necessary to have some informative prior distribution for stature. In this section, the use of long bone lengths as evidence in identification cases is discussed. Konigsberg et al. *(25)* argue that the proper use of osteological evidence in the courts is to provide likelihood ratios, and as was seen in the very first example, it is relatively easy to use WinBUGS to obtain these ratios. As an example, the authors consider the first of the 19 skeletons in the pygmy reference data listed in Appendix 2 (the individual with a Fully stature of 1436 mm and femur and humerus lengths of 378 and 278 mm, respectively). If stature is estimated with the routine in Fig. 2 for someone with these long bone lengths and with the Efe pygmy informative prior, an estimate of 1410 mm, with a 95% confidence interval of from 1359 to 1461 mm is yielded. This interval includes the actual stature of 1436 mm, so the long bone lengths are consistent with the "identification." However, there is the question of how likely the data (long bone lengths) are if the identification is correct vs how likely the data are if the individual was drawn from the "population at large."

To find this, the deviance within two different models in WinBUGS must be calculated. The following code shows how to do this:

```
Model {
# stature ~ dnorm(1406, 5.507E-4)
 stature<-1436
 pred[1] <- alpha[1] + beta[1] * stature
 pred[2] <- alpha[2] + beta[2] * stature
 bone[1:2] ~ dmnorm(pred[1:2],tau[,])

Data
list(tau=structure(.Data=c(0.0157,-.01057,
  -.01057,.04065),.Dim=c(2,2)),
alpha=c(36.46,28.37),beta=c(.242,.1765),
  bone=c(378,278))
```

In the above WinBUGS code, the regression parameters were estimated from the Appendix 2 code, so τ, α, and β are taken directly from WinBUGS output. The commented-out line takes the Efe pygmy stature distribution as an informative prior. If this line is substituted for the fixed stature (of 1436 mm), then the estimated stature from WinBUGS is 1411 mm, with a 95% confidence interval of from 1365 to 1457 mm. This is very similar to the estimates from Appendix 2, as the only difference is that the variance on the regression parameters is lost. More to the point, the deviance from this model is 11.2318. If the fixed stature of 1436 mm is then taken, then one finds the deviance in WinBUGS is 11.8966. Half the difference between these two deviances is 0.3324, which when written as an exponential is equal to 1.39. Thus, the analysis shows that if the "correct identification" is made, the data are only 1.39 times more likely than if the individual was drawn from the "population at large." Thus, for this particular example the long bone data are consistent with the actual stature, but they do little to "make" the identification.

6. CONCLUSION

Likelihood, and more specifically, Bayesian approaches, now have a firm foothold in the forensic sciences. In fact, Lindley (*[26]* p. 42) succinctly summarizes the use of likelihood ratios by noting that, "The responsibility of the forensic scientist in acting as expert witness is to provide this ratio." As a result, the authors expect that in the near future a "positive identification" made by a forensic anthropologist acting as an expert witness will be challenged in a court of law. It is therefore absolutely critical that forensic anthropologists learn how to work with likelihood ratios. When the task is instead that of "building a profile" in order to narrow the possibilities on identification, familiarity with likelihood and Bayesian procedures may be less critical. Still, as was argued in the introduction to this chapter, forensic anthropologists are increasingly coming into contact with cases for which they do not have appropriate reference samples. In such instances, a basic knowledge of Bayesian procedure again becomes absolutely essential.

This chapter has shown how a Bayesian approach can be applied both in estimation and evidentiary problems, using stature as the specific example. If the authors were allowed to number this chapter, they would have done so, as they expect to make future contributions to the literature in a similar vein, but focusing on different attributes. This series was begun with stature, as this is the simplest application. The intention is that the next contribution will focus on age at death. This is a more difficult application because the prior distribution for age at death is more complex than for stature. The third intended application will be in the analysis of categorical variables such as sex and "ancestry," and the fourth and final application will be in the analysis of time since death.

APPENDIX 1

Model
```
{
# Prior——
# Use Pygmy mean stature (and "precision") for prior
# This from pooled mean and variance on 53 Efe pygmies
# (mu = 1406, var = 1816, precision = 5.507*10^(-4))

  stature ~ dnorm(1406, 5.507E-4)

# Use mean and precision from the 2,053

# stature ~ dnorm(1725, 1.376E-4)

# Uninformative prior

# stature ~ dnorm(1725, 1.0E-40)

# Likelihood——-
# From regression of humerus and femur on stature
  in 2,053
# individuals

    femur   <- 0.2877579 * stature - 30.38238
    humerus <- 0.1891334 * stature + 5.745
```

```
        pred[1] <- femur
        pred[2] <- humerus

        tau[1,1] <- 7.5864E-3
        tau[1,2] <- -5.3323E-3
        tau[2,1] <- tau[1,2]
        tau[2,2] <- 11.4437E-3

        bone[1]<-378
        bone[2]<-278

        bone[1:2] ~ dmnorm(pred[1:2],tau[,])
    }
```

APPENDIX 2

Model

```
{
# Priors for Multivariate Regression
  alpha[1:2] ~ dmnorm(mean[1:2], prec[1:2,1:2])
  beta[1:2] ~ dmnorm(mean[1:2], prec[1:2,1:2])
  tau[1:2,1:2] ~ dwish(R[,], 2)

# Multivariate Regression
  for(i in 1:N){
    Y[i,1:2] ~ dmnorm(mu[i,], tau[,])
    mu[i,1] <- alpha[1] + beta[1] * x[i]
    mu[i,2] <- alpha[2] + beta[2] * x[i]
  }
# MLE (diffuse prior)
  stature ~ dnorm(1700,1.E-40)

# Bayesian estimate of stature for new case using
  Efe data
# stature ~ dnorm(1406, 5.507E-4)
  pred[1] <- alpha[1] + beta[1] * stature
  pred[2] <- alpha[2] + beta[2] * stature
  bone[1:2] ~ dmnorm(pred[1:2],tau[,])
}
```

Data

```
list(N=19,R=structure(.Data=c(0.01,.005,.005,.1),
  .Dim=c(2,2)),mean=c(0,0),
```

```
prec=structure(.Data=c(1.0E-6,0,0,1.0E6),
  .Dim=c(2,2)),
bone=c(329,241)
)
```

x[]	Y[,1]	Y[,2]
1436	378	278
1361	365	272
1362	360	270
1419	371	278
1372	367	273
1443	385	283
1338	378	262
1533	409	302
1498	397	298
1535	413	293
1430	396	289
1315	351	265
1374	361	273
1211	332	243
1353	359	261
1388	391	274
1437	366	266
1402	369	NA
1485	405	297

```
END
```

Inits
```
list(stature=1500)
```

REFERENCES

1. Ross, A. H., Konigsberg, L. W. New formulae for estimating stature in the Balkans. J. Forensic Sci. 47:165–67, 2002.
2. Steadman, D. W., Haglund, W. D. The scope of anthropological contributions to human rights investigations. J. Forensic Sci. 50:23–30, 2005.
3. Meadows, L., Jantz, R. L. Allometric secular change in the long bones from the 1800s to the present. J. Forensic Sci. 40:762–67, 1995.
4. Meadows Jantz, L., Jantz, R. L. Secular change in long bone length and proportion in the United States, 1800–1970. Am. J. Phys. Anthropol. 110:57–67, 1999.
5. Ross, A. H. Cranial and Post-Cranial Metric Variation: Regional Isolation in Eastern Europe. Ph.D. Thesis, University of Tennessee, Knoxville, TN, 2000.
6. Ross, A. H., Jantz, R. L., Owsley, D. W. Allometric relationships of Americans, Croatians, and Bosnians. Am. J. Phys. Anthropol. 28:S236, 1999.
7. Humphrey, L. Growth patterns in the modern human skeleton. Am. J. Phys. Anthropol. 105:57–72, 1998.

8. Norgan, N. Body-proportion differences. In: Ulijaszek, S., Johnston, F. E., Preece, M. A., eds., The Cambridge Encyclopedia of Human Growth and Development. University Press, New York, NY, pp. 378–379, 1998.

9. Gelman, A., Carlin, J. B., Stern, H. S., Rubin, D. B. Bayesian Data Analysis. Chapman & Hall/CRC Press, Boca Raton, FL, 2004.

10. Evett, I. W., Weir, B. S. Interpreting DNA Evidence: Statistical Genetics for Forensic Scientists. Sinauer, Sunderland, MA, 1998.

11. Aitken, C. G. G., Stoney, D. A. The Use of Statistics in Forensic Science. Harwood, New York, NY, 1991.

12. Aitken, C. G. G., Taroni, F. Statistics and the Evaluation of Evidence for Forensic Scientists. Wiley, New York, NY, 2004.

13. Spiegelhalter, D., Thomas, A., Best, N., Lunn, D. WinBUGS User Manual (vers. 1.4.1), 2004. Available via http://www.mrc-bsu.cam.ac.uk/bugs/winbugs/geobugs.shtml.

14. Jungers, W. L. Lucy's length: stature reconstruction in *Australopithecus afarensis* (A.L. 288-1) with implications for other small-bodied hominids. Am. J. Phys. Anthropol. 76:227–231, 1988.

15. Fully, G. Une nouvelle methode de determination de la taille [in French]. Ann. Med. Legal Criminol. 35:266–273, 1956.

16. Evans, M., Hastings, N. A. J., Peacock, J. B. Statistical Distributions. Wiley, New York, NY, 2000.

17. Weiss, K. M. On the systematic bias in skeletal sexing. Am. J. Phys. Anthropol. 37:239–250, 1972.

18. Lee, P. M. Bayesian Statistics: an Introduction. Arnold, New York, NY, 1992.

19. Konigsberg LW, Herrmann NP. Markov chain Monte Carlo estimation of hazard model parameters in paleodemography. In: Hoppa, R. D., Vaupel, J. W., eds., Paleodemography: Age Distributions from Skeletal Samples. Cambridge University Press, New York, NY, pp. 222–242. 2002.

20. Konigsberg, L. W., Hens, S. M., Jantz, L. M., Jungers, W. L. Stature estimation and calibration: Bayesian and maximum likelihood perspectives in physical anthropology. Yearb. Phys. Anthropol. 41:65–92, 1998.

21. Byers, S. N. Introduction to Forensic Anthropology: A Textbook. Allyn and Bacon, Boston, MA, 2005.

22. Dietz, W. H., Marino, B., Peacock, N. R., Bailey, R. C. Nutritional status of Efe pygmies and Lese horticulturalists. Am. J. Phys. Anthropol. 78:509–518, 1989.

23. Brown, P. J., Sundberg, R. Confidence and conflict in multivariate calibration. J Roy. Statist. Soc. Ser. B 49:46–57, 1987.

24. Brown, P. J. Measurement, Regression, and Calibration. Oxford University Press, New York, NY, 1993.

25. Konigsberg, L. W., Herrmann, N. P., Wescott, D. J. Commentary on: McBride DG, Dietz MJ, Vennemeyer MT, Meadors SA, Benfer RA, and Furbee NL. Bootstrap methods for sex determination from the os coxae using the ID3 algorithm. J. Forensic Sci. 47:424–426, 2002.

26. Lindley, D. V. Probability. In: Aitken, C. G. G., Stoney, D. A., eds., The Use of Statistics in Forensic Science. Harwood, New York, NY, pp. 27–50, 1991.

Chapter 14

Pathology as a Factor of Personal Identity in Forensic Anthropology

Eugénia Cunha

Summary

In many forensic anthropology cases, the biological profile is not sufficient to achieve positive identification. In those cases, bone pathology is a paramount criterion. Besides being crucial for identification, it can also give insights into cause and manner of death.

This chapter aims to prove the potential of pathology as an identification factor. It is illustrated with practical cases and some procedures to maximize the results are suggested. Furthermore, examples of some diseases that may leave marks on bone are given, with some of their key features provided, and emphasis on the importance of interdisciplinarity for their interpretation.

Key Words: Pathology; bone lesions; antemortem; identification; biological profile; diseases; differential diagnosis.

1. INTRODUCTION

In forensic anthropology (FA), parameters such as sex, age at death, and stature, which allow biological identity, are often attained. However, for positive identification, such an identity is not enough because the same biological profile can be shared by various individuals.

Thus, one has to rely on unique skeletal features, ones that distinguish one person from another. Bone lesions can work as such. In this chapter, the usefulness of bone pathology for the success of an FA case is advocated.

From *Forensic Anthropology and Medicine:*
Complementary Sciences From Recovery to Cause of Death
Edited by: A. Schmitt, E. Cunha, and J. Pinheiro © Humana Press Inc., Totowa, NJ

Furthermore, it is argued that observations on pathology and other abnormal conditions not only can assist identification, but also give insights into cause and manner of death. It is important to keep in mind that even though the customary role of forensic anthropologists is identification of decomposed human remains, they are frequently called on to provide evidence about circumstances that surrounded a particular death *(1)*.

The aims of the chapter are to prove the potential of pathology as an identification factor, to illustrate it with practical cases, and to present some procedures to maximize the results. Furthermore, examples of some diseases that may leave marks on bone are given. Although the purpose is not to give the features of those disorders apparent on bone, in order to illustrate their potential and their usefulness, some of the key features are given. Dental diseases will not be approached because the author argues that they should be discussed in preference by a forensic odontologist. Yet, in many instances, no dental records are available, and thus, pathology can be the only way to obtain identity.

In some situations, the remains of the individuals recovered from some graves (war crimes) share an identical biological profile. Komar *(2)* illustrates this situation by reporting a case where all the skeletons from a mass grave are adult males of a single ethnic affinity, sharing similar causes of death and postmortem intervals. Even in a routine case of FA, it is possible to achieve the four big parameters of identification—sex, age, ancestry, and stature—and yet, positive identification cannot necessarily be retrieved. This can happen when all the persons from the missing list share the same profile or when, in opposition, there is no individual in the missing list with the biological profile retrieved at the autopsy. In those cases, the anthropologist has to strive to go beyond those parameters.

Indeed, in addition to generating osteobiographies, anthropologists have to reach individualization by focusing on identifying unique features such as antemortem fractures or other skeletal pathologies, evidence of surgical interventions, and dental anomalies *(2)*. Even in the extreme case where two skeletons, A and B, are from the same sex, age, height, and ancestry, because there are no two skeletons alike, it is possible to find out the characteristics that will work as personal indicators of identity. These may include previous disease, earlier fractures, congenital abnormalities, handedness, gait, or sporting injuries *(3)*. Both cranial suture patterns and frontal sinuses, through their uniqueness, can also provide positive identification.

However, the search for some of these factors of individualization is not straightforward. Therefore, finding the characteristics that differentiate skeleton A from skeleton B requires some background/training.

1.1. Pseudopathologies

When a bone alteration is noted, a triple discrimination has to be performed. First, it is important to distinguish between ante- and postmortem alterations; it is well known that taphonomic factors cannot only mimic certain bone characteristics, but also produce alterations that are easily confounded with pathologies. Therefore, in a first procedure, these so-called pseudo-pathologies have to be discarded. Animal bites often confound forensic interpretation and/or mimic bone lesions or other important identification clues. Roots can also produce effects on the bone surface that are easily misinterpreted as bones lesions. Further, regular circular small holes in long bones diaphyses can be the result of microfauna action *(4)*. The author dealt with a case where the symmetric destruction of the proximal epiphysis of both tibias appeared to have been produced by perimortem trauma; however, it was likely because of knee position in the inhumation. The distinction between perimortem and postmortem can be even more complex. Subscribing to Sauer *(5)*, labeling injuries antemortem or postmortem can also be informative regarding the death event, like a homicide. This is discussed here under Heading 11.

In addition, postmortem alterations can also give clues on postmortem interval (time since death), one of the parameters needed by law enforcement agents in their investigations of death *(6)*. That is the case with root lengths *(7)*, which can indicate the minimum time of deposition of the remains, eventually suggesting whether it is a forensic case or remains from a past population. Another important aspect, still in the context of postmortem actions, is the detection of cuts on the bone in relation to dismemberment or mutilation *(8)*.

1.2. Antemortem Alterations

Once taphonomic modifications are discarded, one is faced solely with antemortem alterations within which one has to perform another distinction, namely the one between morphological and pathological modifications. There are four main different types of morphological skeletal variations: accessory ossicles (lambdoid ossicles, bregmatic bone), nonfusion anomalies (no vastus on the patella), accessory foramina (canalys condylarius intermedium), and miscellaneous anomalies (foramina mentalia bipartitae*)*. Some of these nonmetric skeletal variations, also called discrete traits, if not correctly identified can be confounded with pathologies. This is the case of septal aperture of the humerus, a hole through the olecranon fossa, or congenital sternal perforation (Fig. 1), among others. Nonfusion of bone elements, such as os acromial, can also be misdiagnosed as fractures. Discrete traits can be excellent factors of individualization, in particular when dealing with very rare ones.

Fig. 1. Sternal perforation in a male individual, a quite rare, discrete trait.

However, positive identification will be dependent on the existence of ante-mortem data with which to compare. Like this, the "uniqueness" of these features is problematic, because there are no published frequencies of these biological characters in modern populations, the matching of these elements can lead to positive identification. Furthermore, as some of these traits have a genetic inheritance, as is the case with the persistence of metopic suture, their presence on the victim, as well as on some close relatives, can be seen as an aid in identification (may provide more information on decedents). As they are atypical skeletal conditions, these morphological variations may be documented in medical records, thus enhancing their potential for identification.

Given that the frontiers between morphological and pathological variation are, in a way, wide and fluid, the author argues that the experience or training of the anthropologists is paramount. Forensic anthropologists must possess a broad breadth of knowledge of the variety of these deviations because the subevaluation of discrete traits can lead to false pathological diagnosis.

Having eliminated morphological variation, pathological alterations must be examined.

2. PATHOLOGY: LIMITS AND POTENTIALS

This science dealing with the study of diseases, which leave traces on bones, can be very important for achieving positive identification. In this respect, the forensic anthropologist, being familiar with the range of normal variation of human bones and their anomalies, as well as the pathological manifestation on the skeleton, can give crucial clues.

However, reading pathology from bare bones has its limitations that must be taken into account. Not only the limits, but also the potential of the pathological interpretation based on the skeletal remains has to be discussed. A skeleton is always less informative than a fresh cadaver. Furthermore, in most instances, the skeleton is the ultimate body system to respond to an "aggression." This means that there are many diseases that do not leave any sign on bones, and that those that do leave a signature tend to be the chronic ones. In other words, in general, and with exception of those pathologies that start in the bone, time is needed to let the agent, usually a bacteria, reach the bone. When dealing with bone pathology "the absence of evidence is not evidence of absence." This is particularly important when dealing with forensic cases. In the final case report, it is important to separate observation from inference, to keep description distinct from speculation *(9)*, and to state clearly whether bone lesions are detected. In the case of absence, the inference should never be that the victim did not suffer from any disease.

Another important consequence: if acute diseases do not leave any bony sign, cause of death will seldom be perceivable solely based on bones. A further and not less important limitation of the interpretation of diseases from skeletal remains concerns the uniformity/monotony of bone reaction. In effect, bone cells when "attacked" will react by means of bone formation (osteoblasts) or through bone destruction (osteoclasts, or both phenomena). The lack of specificity of bone reaction means that the same bone manifestation can be linked to a variety of etiologies. In other words, because of the almost lack of pathognomic osseous reactions, differential diagnosis is a mandatory step in any pathological analysis of skeletal remains. Moreover, it is important to keep in mind that in some cases the diagnosis may even be impossible.

The limited number of disorders that can be read from the skeleton is generally divided into a number of broad categories. These categories include infectious diseases, circulatory disturbances, hematopoietic disorders, metabolic disorders, endocrine disturbances, congenital abnormalities of the skeleton, skeletal dysplasias, degenerative diseases, and trauma *(10)*. The prevalence of some of the disorders included in the just mentioned categories is obviously very diverse, and this has obvious consequences for their potential in identification. For example, whereas osteoarthritis lesions are frequently seen in human remains, a huge metastatic tumor will be an abnormal finding. Inherently, the rarer the lesion, the higher the probability of achieving a positive identification. That is, whereas osteoarthritis lesions seldom provide identification, an osteosarcoma, theoretically, has a higher potential for attaining identity. Even when dealing with body parts or commingled remains, such as the cases of mass disasters, the detection of a skeletal lesion or bone prosthesis is an outstanding way of identification. It is important to keep in mind, particularly with badly decomposed bodies, that skeletal characteristics may provide the only evidence for identity or to help at triage for accurate inventory when dealing with commingling remains *(11,12)*. Among lesions, healed traumatic ones are possibly one of the most helpful of all antemortem bone changes as far as positive identification is concerned *(13)*.

The main disease categories are revised here, giving at least one example of a "forensically" important disorder within each group. Again, the aim is not to give the key elements for the diagnosis of those diseases, but to discuss some features of those disorders that might be helpful for forensic purposes.

3. DEGENERATIVE DISEASES

3.1. Osteoarthritis

As already referred to, osteoarthritis (OA) is the most widespread degenerative pathology found in skeletal remains; therefore, its presence its not enough for identification. It is the distribution pattern and the severity of the lesions that are more helpful. It is significant to differentiate between primary (idiopathic) OA and secondary OA. Whereas the former is mainly because of age and biomechanical efforts and can affect several articulations, the second can be caused by traumatic injuries and involves a sole articulation. A severe OA lesion in the elbow will more likely be included in the second category, whereas a symmetric OA on the knees would more likely be a primary OA. The severity of the lesions has to be accurately recorded because a case with severe porosity, subcondral bone sclerosis, and eburnation can be more useful for identification than one with only slight OA lesions. The lesions on the spine, namely the osteophytes, can work as identity factors because osteophytes are never identical. Their form, contour, and extension, when compared with antemortem X-rays, can provide identification *(14,15)*. Furthermore, OA deformities can give insight on asymmetry or overuse of some part of the skeleton, which can be another important element in identification. A severe OA on the hip, for example, will probably have important effects on gait.

3.2. Enthesopathies

Lesions on the enthesis can give information on the amount of physical effort, thus, on the type of activity, which, in turn, can eventually give an

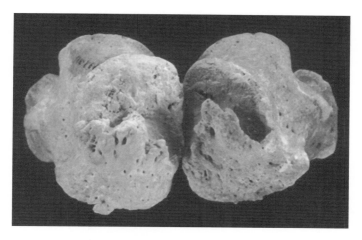

Fig. 2. Symmetric severe enthesopathies on the insertion of Achilles tendon, most probably caused by diffuse idiopathic skeletal hyperostosis.

insight on the occupation of an individual. The lesions on muscle and tendon insertion sites are recognized as markers of occupational stress *(16)*. This category can include bone facets, hypertrophies, and lytic lesions.

Again, the interpretation is not straightforward: an enthesopathy does not always indicate muscle overuse. There are some disorders such as diffuse idiopathic skeletal hyperostosis (DISH) and some spondyloarthropathies that lead to the development of symmetrical enthesopathies. In DISH, for instance, symmetric enthesopathies on calcanea (as those shown on Fig. 2), rotulas, and upper ulnas are characteristic features. Thus, one has to discard such disorders, like DISH and spondyloarthropathies, before making any inference about muscle overuse. Only after that, a lesion on the Achilles tendon insertion possibly indicates that the individual might have been an athlete. An asymmetry in muscle attachments on upper limb bones can indicate handedness.

4. CONGENITAL DISORDERS

Congenital abnormalities are a consequence of pathological alterations suffered during intrauterine life, some of which are inherited and have genetic disturbances as the main etiology. A considerable percentage of these anomalies affect the skeleton *(17)*. Congenital defects on the skull and on the spine, hyperplasias of the members, and congenital dislocation of the hip are some examples. Cleft palate and craniosynostosis (premature fusion of sutures of

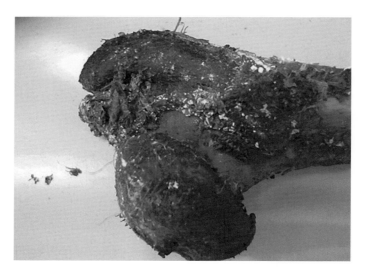

Fig. 3. Right femur of a young female displaying characteristics compatible with congenital dislocation of the hip.

the skull) are examples of cranial or craniofacial lesions that can be detected. Klippel-Feil syndrome with congenital fusion of two or more vertebral segments, namely cervical ones, into a block with a single spinous process, neural arch, and vertebral body *(17)* illustrates the usefulness of this type of malformation in the spine for the success of an FA case. Congenital dislocation of the hip is an example of a disorder that affects the postcranial skeleton, whose features and consequences on gait have a great potential for identity. The author dealt with a case where a skeleton of a young female displayed all the features compatible with that disorder (Fig. 3). However, any of the missing persons had reference to that defect or to gait problems and thus, the case remains open *(18)*. In another forensic case of a quite complete male skeleton with several malformations on the spine, namely two vertebral blocks (Fig. 4) plus unilateral costal fusion (the first two ribs), associated with a scoliosis and bone asymmetry, led to the identification of the victim *(19)*.

5. METABOLIC DISTURBANCES

In this group, scurvy and rickets are well known for their typical marks on the skeleton. However, for FA purposes, in industrialized countries, these disorders are rare because of adequate nutrition. This means that if these diseases, because of vitamins C and D deficiencies, respectively, are found on

Fig. 4. Thoracic vertebral ankylosis with scoliosis. This was one of the features that led to the victim's identification.

the skeletal remains, one has to suspect that one might be dealing with remains from a past population. However, in countries with problems of malnutrition, such as some African ones, these diseases do occur. In opposition, other metabolic diseases are much more frequent; therefore, they have little value for identification. That is the case with osteoporosis. Yet, its presence can inform us that we are dealing with an older individual or, if associated with other disorders such as spondyloarthropathy, could mean that the individual was immobile most of the time.

Intoxications, namely by fluoride, can also leave marks on the skeletal remains that can be valuable elements for both identification and evaluation of the general health status. In fluorosis, the skeletal axis can be severely affected with multiple loci of irregular new bone formation *(17)*.

Iron deficiency can provoke a well-known bone reaction on the skull bones known as cribra orbitalia, pitting of the roof of the orbit and porotic hyperostosis. Enlargement of the diploe because of bone marrow hyperplasia can be caused by anemia, which results in a pit appearance of the bone.

Fig. 5. Large osteoma in a middle-aged male skull.

6. NEOPLASIAS

Bone neoplasias can work as important individualization factors. Among neoplasms, we have to distinguish between benign and malignant tumors. The former, the osteomas, are better delimitated and can have a capsule. Bone osteomas, in the form of a button, are more frequent in males during the fourth and fifth decade (Fig. 5). Their detection when compared with antemortem records can help with identification.

Malignant lesions are much more invasive and have a very irregular form. Femur osteosarcoma, because of its low prevalence, can help in positive identification.

Many malignant osseous lesions are metastasis. The vertebrae, the pelvis, the ribs, and the skull are some of the more affected bones. Prostate carcinoma usually produces osteoblastic lesions or spiculae formation. Lung and breast cancers provoke both osteolytic and osteoblastic lesions, which can lead to the formation of mixed lesions. The bones of the axial skeleton that are closer to the affected organs have more lesions.

Again, the age and sex of the victim are important features for the diagnosis of the type of tumors.

In Fig. 6, an exuberant lesion on a left scapula corresponding to a benign tumor can be seen. It concerns a 1992 forensic anthropology case where four

Fig. 6. Left scapula of a male adult individual displaying an exuberant benign tumor.

human bones were found in a towel. Despite its potential for identification, identity was not found because no missing person reported such a lesion *(20)*.

7. Rheumatic Diseases

The seronegative spondyloarthropathies is a group of arthropathies characterized by inflammatory involvement of the spine and enthesis of peripheral joints that leave typical features on the skeleton. Of these, ankylosing spondylitis (AS) is the best known. The paramount features of AS are prominent sacroiliac abnormalities and spinal ligamentous calcification and ossification in a uniform pattern (bamboo spine; *see* Fig. 7 and refs. *21* and *22*). Sacroiliitis is the hallmark of AS, occurring early in the course of disease, therefore allowing the diagnosis of early cases at the autopsy table. Alava and collaborators *(23)* report a forensic case where this disease led to identification. It concerns a senile male with total fusion of the vertebral column, pelvis, and the entire thorax, including both clavicles. AS was suspected and the diagnosis coincided with the data provided by family members on the pathology of his vertebral column since the age of 30 and his significant loss of movement in the final years of his life.

Epidemiological data on this and other diseases can be helpful for the victim identification. The onset of AS generally occurs between the ages of 15 and 35 yr. The prevalence in the general population is approx 0.1%. AS affects males two to four times more often than females *(22)*.

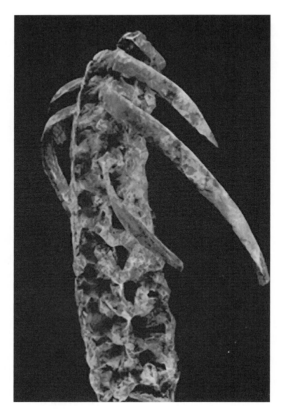

Fig. 7. Bamboo spine typical of ankylosis spondylitis with spinal ligamentous calcification and ossification in a uniform pattern.

Because this disease leads to bony ankylosis, namely of the sacroiliac joints and of the spine, AS is a good example of a disease for which the consequences on the daily life of the individual should be well described. An individual with fusion of the spine will not be able to move normally. Moreover, if the immobility occurred for a long period, the individual might have developed osteoporosis. This could easily be inferred from the bone analysis.

8. DIFFUSE IDIOPATHIC SKELETAL HYPEROSTOSIS

As DISH does not involve either the cartilage or the synovium, it is not a true arthropathy. However, because it can lead to ligament ossification, it can also produce ankylosis of the spine, although without intervertebral dis-

Fig. 8. Vertebral body displaying syndesmophytes typical of diffuse idiopathic skeletal hyperostosis in an old male skeleton.

ease *(17,21)*. Flowing ossifications along the anterolateral aspect of at least four contiguous vertebral bodies, namely thoracolumbar ones, involving mainly the anterior and right features and the absence of apophyseal fusion are the key characteristics of this disorder *(24)*. As already referred to, symmetrical and periphereal enthesopathies involving the posterior heel (*see* Fig. 2), superior patella, and oleocranon are extraspinal criteria that are very useful for a more accurate diagnosis *(21,24)*. DISH is rarely detected before 40 yr of age, and about two-thirds of the cases are males. Skeletal manifestations of this disorder had been found in some autopsies of old male skeletons (Fig. 8).

9. INFECTIOUS DISORDERS

Periosteal new bone formation, commonly termed "periostitis," is a proliferative lesion for which etiology is not specific. Periostitis is one of the symptoms of several diseases. Furthermore, both trauma and infection *(10)* can lead to the formation of new layers of bone. However, in some cases, the location and severity of the lesions can allow the diagnosis of the cause, as reported by Pinheiro and collaborators *(25)*, where extensive speculated thickening of the periosteum of both tibia and fibula of an old woman, consistent

Fig. 9. Close-up of the extensive speculated thickening of the periosteum of both tibia and fibula from an old woman who suffered from venous chronic insufficiency. (*See* Fig. 6, Chapter 7 to learn more about this case.)

with extensive reactive ossifying periostitis, led to the suspicion of venous chronic insufficiency (Fig. 9). The woman's family subsequently confirmed she suffered from this condition.

Periostitis is one of the nonspecific indicators of skeletal stress that have been used as signs to human rights abuses had taken place *(26)*.

When, in addition the periosteum, the cortex and marrow are also affected, there is a more severe lesion known as an osteomyelitis. Although it is primarily a bone disease, the infectious agent may reach the marrow by other causes *(10)*.

Some specific infections can be detected based on the skeletal analysis. That is the case of bacterial diseases, such as tuberculosis, brucellosis, lepra, and treponematosis, which when present, do contribute to positive identification.

The eventual diagnosis of those diseases can give more data on the victims or, in opposition, the previous knowledge of information about the eventual victims can help in the identification. Brucellosis as a disease transmitted from animal to human (zoonosis) may suggest occupational factors *(27)*. The most common alteration is in the spine—the lumbar spine in particular—and in the sacroiliac joint. Lytic cavitations of lumbar vertebra are one of the earliest signs of the disease.

9.1. Tuberculosis

Another important chronic infection, which can also be transmitted by animals, is tuberculosis. *Mycobacterium* mainly affects spongy bone; therefore, vertebral bodies and bone epiphysis are the favorite targets. Autopsy cases report that at least two adjacent vertebra are affected (vertebral bodies) *(10)*. Bone formation on visceral surfaces of ribs has also been suggested to be the result of chronic pulmonary disease *(28)*, which again, can provide elements for identification.

9.2. Treponematosis

Among the treponemal infections, acquired or venereal syphilis is one of the variants that can leave typical features on the bones. The most common location of syphilitic lesions is the skull with the characteristic "caries sicca," i.e., advanced sclerotic healing. An exceedingly prominent osteosclerotic response to the infection can also affect the long bones, provoking both thickening and deformity *(17,10)*.

9.3. Smallpox

Smallpox (variola) is one of the very few viral infections that can leave marks on the bones. Indeed, virus-induced bone infection is extremely rare *(17)*. Skeletal involvement is not seen in adults, being the lesions restricted to the limb bones. Articular infection in the elbow with coexistence of other osseous changes can happen. Whereas the detection of disease will be quite improbable in industrialized countries, in third-world countries it can occur.

10. Circulatory Diseases

Some conditions may produce osteochondrosis of the epiphysis. Legg-Calvé-Perthes disease has been chosen to illustrate the usefulness of some circulatory diseases in forensic contexts.

It is an uncommon disease, occurring unilaterally in 90% of the cases, that is, much more frequent in boys than in girls and more frequent in Asian and Central European groups *(10)*. The proximal epiphysis becomes extensively necrotic, after which the head of the femur flattens and the femoral neck becomes thicker. At the end, there is a mushroom-shaped femoral head. Although this is a typical characteristic, confusion can arise with other diseases, such as with slipped femoral capital epiphysis, among others. Again, it will be the epidemiological data (the second disorder occurs between the ages of 10 and 17 yr in boys), and some small details in bone manifestation that may be crucial for the differentiation.

11. TRAUMATIC LESIONS

Even if it is more likely that cases with skeletonized remains will provide clues to manner of death rather than cause of death, associating a skeletal injury with the time of death is one of the most crucial considerations in a forensic evaluation of trauma *(5)*. If it is true that many of violent deaths do not leave any trace on the skeleton, it is also true that a significant number of them do leave important key marks on the bones.

When there is no evidence for osteogenic reaction, the pattern of injury is crucial. The differences between a green-bone response and a dry-bone response have to be taken into account. More oblique fractures with cutting edges and smooth surfaces will be more compatible with green-bone fractures, whereas more transverse fractures with irregular surfaces will be more indicative of a dry-bone response *(29)*. During the detailed analysis, it is important to pay attention to clues, such as discoloration at the edges of fractured lines, bleeding signs at the fracture edges, and ecchymosis on the skull. Despite these clues, there are cases where it is virtually impossible to distinguish between perimortem or postmortem fractures.

Gunshots wounds, blunt trauma, and sharp forces are known to produce typical features on the bones that allow the differentiation among these three types of traumas that could be associated with the death. Furthermore, trauma caused by weapons and firearms is seen as skeletal evidence of physical abuse *(26)*. These issues will be approached in this book in Chapter 5.

On both cranial and postcranial skeleton, healed lesions, namely osseous callus formation, and marks of surgical interventions are among the most helpful factors of individualization. Various types of prostheses and other devices, such as implants, can be found with the human remains. The value of these devices is that they can be traced back to their manufacturer *(13,30)* and are often issued with a unique serial or production lot number. It is worthwhile to remind here the importance of following a series of procedures when leading with an FA case. Ubelaker *(31)* reports a case where a long bone diaphysis with both epiphyses destroyed by carnivores displayed an extensively remodeled fracture that had been bridged with a surgically implanted metal brace. Attempts to identify the surgeon and the hospital where the surgery had taken place failed because one of the initial questions to be addressed, whether it is a human bone or not, was not previously assessed: "The orthopaedic surgeon had not been located because the surgery had been conducted by a veterinarian" *([31]* p. 234). Yet, although medical treatment can provide key details for identification, the author was able to find old forensic cases, namely a case from 1965, where an implant

Fig.10. Despite the great potential of this device on the left tibia of a middle-aged male, this feature was useless for identification (1965 case).

applied on the left tibia of a middle-aged male (Fig. 10) was useless for identification purposes *(32)*.

In addition, evidence for remodeling associated with a skeletal lesion indicates that the injury occurred at least a week before death *(5)*. Even for fractures, a differential diagnosis has to be performed because they can either be pathological or be caused by trauma. Osteoporosis, cancer, and tuberculosis are some of disorders that can lead to vertebral fractures.

Still in the context of traumatic events, myositis ossificans traumatica can be valuable for identification purposes because of the irregular calcified bone masses produced, representing most of the time calcified crushed muscles. DiMaio and collaborators *(33)* report a case of heterotopic ossification in the musculature of the pelvis and femora in unidentified skeletal remains, which provided clues as to how the victim lived and events in his life and, ultimately, led to his identification.

Many of the previously mentioned disorders can offer insight into the general status of health of an individual. It is important to note that assessment of health from skeletal remains is significant in a number of forensic matters, and it may also give a clue on the socioeconomic status *(3)*. In addition, pathological lesions, as it is been argued previously, may help in elucidating the geographic origin, sex, age, and even occupation of the victim *(26)*. On the other hand, when severe lesions affect the skeletal areas that allow age-at-death estimation, we should avoid using those areas as age indicators.

A good example of this is ankylosis spondylitis: when the sacroiliac joint is severely damaged by lesions, auricular surface and pubic symphysis should not be used to infer age *(34)*.

12. PROCEDURES

In order to maximize the quality and quantity of the results, the author argues that a series of steps should be followed in any pathological analysis of the skeletal remains.

To answer the well-known series of questions to be addressed in any anthropological case *(35)*, such as whether the sample is human, the assessment of the biological profile should always be followed in the same sequence. Otherwise, as previously illustrated with the case of the animal bone, errors can be committed.

Paleopathological diagnosis should always start at the recovery scene. Because of this, the forensic anthropologist should be called into a case as early as possible. In the case of mass graves, only the most careful excavation will preserve the physical relationship of ligatures or blindfolds to the body *(9)*. Recovery is always the first step in any anthropological examination *(3)*. Because of the poor preservation of some skeletal remains, many observations done in the field are irreproducible. This means that some pathological diagnosis, if not done in the field, cannot be done anyplace else (Fig. 11). This also applies to routine cases of forensic anthropology whenever bone lesions are found. The affected area is particularly fragile and needs particular care when being handled. Therefore, all the details of the lesions should be registered before the affected bone piece is removed.

Despite that, in some countries, such as Portugal, in the majority of FA cases, the expert in FA is not usually called to the recovery scene. In a routine case, the remains normally arrive "inside a body bag" to the autopsy room like the one shown in Fig. 12. One of the first procedures in the examination, in the laboratory, should be to submit the whole body to an X-ray. After that an excavation of the human remains inside the body bag at the autopsy table should be performed. Bones should be separated as much as possible before maceration. The pieces of bone with lesions should be handled and treated with particular care while being cleaned. Brushes should not come into direct contact with the affected area, and water should be avoided. For instance, a thin layer of reactive bone will easily be lost if it comes in contact with water.

A detailed description of the completeness of the remains is crucial. Incompleteness of the skeletal remains precludes, in many instances, the positive diagnosis.

Fig.11. Detection of a skull with holes compatible with gunshot wounds during a mass grave excavation in East Timor (2003).

Fig. 12. Human remains at the autopsy table, immediately after the aperture of the body bag.

Whenever possible, that is, when the completeness of the skeletal remains allow it, the biological profile of an individual should be known before starting the paleopathological interpretation. Being an adult or nonadult, for instance, does matter for the interpretation of lesions because bone remodeling is different in a child than in an older person.

12.1. Lesions Description

It is emphasized that a good and objective description of the lesions is paramount. One has to provide a concrete description of the bone alterations in order to allow the diagnosis of pathology by someone else who may read the report later on. Descriptive rigor is essential in case studies of skeletal pathology *(36)*. It is important to keep in mind that a lesion is not a pathology. A *lesion* is an answer to a disease or an aggression, whereas *pathology* is the study of disease *(35)*.

When all the bone elements are disposed of at the autopsy table, lesions should be recorded following Ortner *(10)* recommendations. That is, the distribution of lesions within the skeleton has to be recorded followed by the location of abnormal bone in the skeleton. The exact location on the bone, such as whether it is "proximal" or "distal," needs to be provided. The inspection of each bone of the skeleton should be done slowly and closely while holding each bone in different positions and with good light *(37)*.

The type of bone abnormality has to be described as specifically as possible, making clear whether it is a lytic, proliferative, or deformative type. Regarding lytic lesions, one has to check whether there are perforations, where they are located, and how many there are. Registering whether there are Schmorl's nodes on the superior and inferior surfaces of the vertebral bodies is also important. With proliferative lesions, it is necessary to pay attention to spurs on bone, osteophytes, syndesmophytes, and others. Furthermore, one has to verify the existence of calluses on the bones, which indicate a healing or healed antemortem break. The previously mentioned button osteomas also have to be checked.

Abnormal bone shape is included in "deformative lesions."

Size and shape are two other important parameters to be noted. In many instances, it is important to measure the holes both externally and internally. In addition, the margins are adjacent to abnormal bone destruction and cannot be forgotten. Do they have sharp edges or are the margins smooth? It is also significant to record whether the lesions are healed because this could be informative regarding whether the disease was active or not at the time of death.

Pictures of relevant aspects should always be taken. Given that a radiographic image is one of the most important tools for analyzing paleopathological skeletons, whenever needed, X-rays analysis should be requested. Histological analysis can also be considered.

Also important in this phase is to note whether the lesions show signs of ever having been treated. Ubelaker *(38)* points out that the finding of a very severe case of osteomyelitis might belong to an ancient society without any knowledge of medical care, precluding it as a forensic case. In other words, pathology can also help in the chronological contextualization of remains.

Remember, one has to be as objective as possible in order to allow an independent diagnostic opinion based on one's descriptions.

12.2. Lesion Interpretation/Differential Diagnosis

This is a quite different phase, which inclusively can be performed later on, and not necessarily at the autopsy table. Further, it is essential that any description of the skeletal defects be clearly separated from any interpretation of their meaning or significance *(39)*.

Differential diagnosis is mandatory. It is important to bear in mind that the same pathology can have different expressions, depending on its developmental stage. Early stages can be different from more advanced ones. Pay attention to the possibility of the coexistence of different types of diseases, as is the case with some rheumatic ones. Some lesions, such as the ones provoked by osteoarthritis, can mimic the signs of other disorders. Furthermore, to exclude a certain pathology as the cause of the lesions under analysis, there has to be incompatibility among the lesions and the disorder, otherwise, that disease cannot be excluded. This means that if one is not sure about the diagnosis, a judgment should not be advanced as certain. This could lead to misidentification of the victim.

For the differential diagnosis of some pathologies, one has to rely on details such as the differentiation between spinal osteophytes accompanying spondylosis deformans and other bony outgrowths of the vertebral column. This is the case of the outgrowths of ankylosing spondilitis, which are typically thin and vertically oriented (whereas osteophytes are horizontal) and are termed syndesmophytes *(21,22)*. This requires training and experience.

When dealing with the interpretation of lesions besides the diagnosis of the disease underneath the observed lesions, there needs to be description of lesions' effect on the individual, in that individual's mobility, locomotion, and way of life. The forensic anthropologist has to try to describe the condition as it would probably be observed in a living person *(39)*. The conversion of the alterations detected on bare bone to disorders of the living is, sometimes, a complex task, which should ideally be performed simultaneously by the forensic anthropologist and forensic pathologist. Interdisciplinarity in this

task is necessary; both the forensic anthropologist and the forensic pathologist have to read the skeleton in its entirety, checking for lesions over the
entire skeleton.

The incorporation of medical interpretation in forensic reports is important, but the training of physical anthropologists, with hundreds of pathological cases from past populations, is not any less essential. The crossing over of
the knowledge of these two specialists is therefore very beneficial. As already
mentioned, differential diagnosis is particularly difficult because the exclusion of certain pathology as the most probable etiology of the observed lesions
can only be made when the lesions' pattern is clearly incompatible with that
disease. In practice, the incompleteness of the skeleton, taphonomic alterations, and bone fragmentation preclude many diagnoses. For example, rheumatoid arthritis: for an accurate diagnosis, bones of both hands* have to be
preserved, which is indeed a very infrequent occurrence. On the other hand,
skeletal remains from mass graves and mass disasters are very often severely
damaged, which means that the diagnosis will not be reached. However, for
these latter cases, the second important point of lesion interpretation can be
achieved, that is, the translation of the lesions effect on the individual's life.
Key elements are evidence of medical treatment, such as medical prostheses.
Healed traumatic lesions, even if observed in an isolated bone, can be quite
important. Gait of an individual with a large, healed traumatic injury on the
leg can be an important element for identity. In this respect, the experts should
be as exhaustive as possible. One has to keep in mind that the victim's relatives sometimes have difficulties in accepting that the skeletal remains under
question belong to their relative. In such instances, any particular individual
characteristic, such as pathology, can become crucial *(39)*.

The significance of medical interpretation in forensic reports is thus paramount. One has to avoid technical terms when dealing with the victim's family.
Saying, for instance, that the victim suffered from an enthesopathy on the
Achilles tendon may not mean anything to the relatives. However, arguing
that the victim might have overused his feet while performing some continu-
ous/repetitive physical effort might indeed shed some light on the victim's
identification. Yet, many of the persons who are found in decomposed condition in routine cases have a lifestyle that offers little evidence of past medical
treatment and diagnosis. It is also possible that many of them lack medical
files *(39)*.

---

* Rheumatoid arthritis typically affects multiple synovial joints (polyarticular) in a
  symmetric manner, the joints in the hands and feet being the more affected *(22)*.

Fig. 13. Male individual displaying a lesion in the process of healing on the left parietal. Despite this, the individual was not identified.

Above all, one has to bear in mind that identification is a comparative process. It is a matter of matching up features with known preexisting conditions, and depends on the availability of a potential match. If there are not any missing persons or any data about the missing persons, no matter how severe and rare the pathology is, there is no way to achieve positive identification (Fig. 13). Consequently, it is indeed very important to have standard inquiries *(2)* about the missing persons accurately filled by the victim's relatives. Particular attention should be given to medical information. As correctly pointed out by Komar *(2)*, "gathering medical information from relatives with little or no medical background results in understandably nonspecific descriptions of past ailments."

Pathological conditions are a challenge for the forensic anthropologist. Each FA case is unique, which means that we always have to adapt the procedures to the case under analysis *(26)*. Moreover, one has to keep in mind that an autopsy can never be repeated.

REFERENCES

1. Sauer, N. J., Simson, L. R. Clarifying the role of forensic anthropologists in death investigations. J. Forensic Sci. 29:1081–1086, 1984.
2. Komar, D. Lessons from Srebrenica: the contributions and limitations of physical anthropology in identifying victims of war crimes. J. Forensic Sci. 48:713–716, 2003.

3. Black, S. Forensic Anthropology. An introduction and summary of procedures. 2004. www.bahid.org/docs/NCF_Anthro.html. Last accessed Dec. 31, 2005.
4. Cunha, E., Umbelino, C., Tavares, T. Necrópole de São Pedro de Marialva. Dados antropológicos [in Portuguese]. Patrimon. Estud. 1:139–143, 2001.
5. Sauer, N. The timing of injuries and manner of death: distinguishing among antemortem, perimortem and post-mortem trauma. In: Reichs, K., ed., Forensic Osteology. Charles C. Thomas, Springfield, IL, pp. 321–332, 1998.
6. Ubelaker, D. Taphonomic applications in forensic anthropology. In: Haglund, W., Sorg. M, eds., Forensic Taphonomy. The Postmortem Fate of Human Remains. CRC Press, Boca Raton, FL, pp. 77–88, 1988.
7. Willey, P., Heilman, A. Estimating Time since death using plant roots and stems. J. Forensic Sci. 32:1264–1270, 1987.
8. Reichs, K. Postmortem dismemberment: recovery, analysis and interpretation. In: Reichs, K., ed., Forensic Osteology: Advances in the Identification of Human Remains, 2nd Ed. Charles C Thomas, Springfield, IL, 1998.
9. Skinner, M., Alempijevic, D., Djuric-Srejic, M. Guidelines for international forensic bio-archaeology monitors of mass grave exhumations. Forensic Sci. Int. 134: 81–92, 2003.
10. Ortner, D. Identification of Pathological Conditions in Human Skeletal Remains, 2nd Ed. Academic, New York, NY, 2003.
11. Budimlija, Z., Mechthild, K., Zelson-Mundorff, A., et al. World Trade Center Human Identification Project: experiences with individual body identification cases. Croat. Med. J. 44:259–263, 2003.
12. Kahana, T., Ravioli, J., Urroz, C., Hiss, J. Radiographic identification of fragmentary human remains from a mass disaster. Am. J. Forensic Med. Pathol. 18:40–44, 1997.
13. Steyn, M., Iscan, M. Y. Bone pathology and antemortem trauma in forensic cases. In: Siegel, J. A., Saukko, P. J., Knufer, G. C., eds., Encyclopedia of Forensic Sciences Academic, San Diego, CA, pp. 217–227, 2000.
14. Angyal, M., Derczy, K. Personal identification on the basis of antemortem and postmortem radiographs. J. Forensic Sci. 43:1089–1093, 1998.
15. Valenzuela, A. Radiographic comparison of the lumbar spine for positive identification of human remains. A case report. Am. J. Forensic Med. Pathol. 18:215–217, 1997.
16. Kennedy, K. Assessment of occupational stress. In: Siegel, J. A., Saukko, P. J., Knupfer, G. C., eds., Encyclopedia of Forensic Sciences. Academic, San Diego, CA, pp. 212–217, 2000.
17. Aufderheide, A., Rodríguez-Martín, C. The Cambridge Encyclopedia of Human Paleopathology. Cambridge University Press, Cambridge, 1998.
18. Cunha, E. A Paleopatologia como factor de individualização em antropologia forense. Lição de síntese. Provas de agregação [in Portuguese]. Universidade de Coimbra, 2001.
19. Cunha, E., Mendonça, M. C. Anthropologie médico-légale: contribution de la paléopathologie à un cas des Açores. In: Vieira, D. N., Rebelo, A., Corte-Real, F., eds., Temas de Medicina Legal II [in Portuguese]. Centro de Estudos de Pós-Graduação em Medicina Legal, Coimbra, pp. 121–126, 2000.

20. Manuel, R., Cunha, E., Pinheiro, J., Ribeiro, I., Santos. J. C. Revisiting old forensic cases from Lisbon: two interesting cases. Poster presented at the 1st meeting of Forensic Anthropology Society of Europe. Frankfurt, 2004.
21. Resnick, D., Niwayama, G. Diagnosis of Bone and Joint Disorders. Saunders, Philadelphia, PA, 1988.
22. Cunha, E. Aproximación paleopatológica a algunas enfermedades reumáticas. In: Isidro, A., Malgosa, A., eds., Paleopatología. La Enfermedad no Escrita [in Spanish]. Masson, Barcelona pp. 209–220, 2003.
23. Alava, R. A., Azcárate, C. G., Soler, M.-C. B., Etxeberria, F. G. El valor de la patología ósea en la identificación personal, a propósito de un caso de espondilitis anquilosante [in Spanish]. Cuad. Med. Forense 22:53–58, 2000.
24. Resnick, D. Bone and Joint Imaging, 2nd Ed. Saunders, Philadelphia, PA, 1998.
25. Pinheiro, J., Cunha, E., Cordeiro, C., Vieira, D. N. Bridging the gap between forensic anthropology and osteoarchaeology: a case of vascular pathology. Int. J. Osteoarchaeol. 14:137–144, 2004.
26. Hunter, J. R., Brickley, M. B., Bourgeois, J., et al. Forensic archaeology, forensic anthropology and human rights in Europe. Sci. Just. 41:173–178, 2001.
27. Roberts, C. A. Forensic anthropology 2: positive identification of the individual; cause and manner of death. In: Hunter, J., Roberts, C., Martin, A., eds., Studies in Crime: an Introduction to Forensic Archaeology. Berttler and Tanner, London, pp. 122–137, 1996.
28. Roberts, C. A., Boyslston, A., Buckely, L., Chamberlain, A., Murphy, E. Rib lesions and tuberculosis: the paleopathological evidence. Tuber. Lung Dis. 1998, 79:55–60, 1998.
29. Etxeberria, F. Patología traumatica. In: Isidro, A., Malgosa, A., eds., Paleopatología. La Enfermedad no Escrita [in Spanish]. Masson, Barcelona, pp. 195–204, 2003.
30. Bennett, J. L., Benedix, D. C. Positive identification of remains recovered from an automobile based on presence of an internal fixation device. J. Forensic Sci, 44:1296–1298, 1999.
31. Ubelaker, D. Skeletons testify: Anthropology in forensic science AAPA luncheon Ardes: April 12, 1996. Yearb. Phys. Anthropol. 39:229–244, 1996.
32. Macedo, M. C., Cunha, E. When an obvious factor of individualization becomes useless. Poster presented at the 1st Forensic Anthropology Society if Europe meeting. Frankfurt, 2004.
33. Dimaio, V. J., Francis, J. R. Heterotopic ossification in unidentified remains. Am. J. Forensic Pathol. 22:160–164, 2001.
34. Rissech, C., Schmitt, A., Malgosa, A., Cunha, E. Influencia de las patologias en los indicadores de edad adulta del coxal: estúdio preliminar [in Portuguese]. Antropol. Port. vol. 20–21, 2003–2004.
35. Pickering, R., Bachman, D. C. The Use of Forensic Anthropology. CRC Press, Boca Raton, FL, 1997.
36. Barnes, E. Developmental defects of the axial skeleton in paleopathology. University of Colorado Press, Denver, CO, 1994.
37. Mann, R., Murphy, S. Regional Atlas of Bone Disease. Charles C. Thomas, Springfield, IL, 1998.

38. Ubelaker, D. Interpretación de las anomalías esqueléticas y su contribución a la investigación forense [in Spanish]. Cuad Med. Forense 33:3542, 2003.
39. Maples, W. The Identifying pathology. In: Ratbun, T. A., Buikstra, J. E., eds., Human Identification: Cases Studies in Forensic Anthropology. Charles C. Thomas, Springfield, IL, pp. 363–370, 1984.

Chapter 15

Personal Identification of Cadavers and Human Remains

Cristina Cattaneo, Danilo De Angelis,
Davide Porta, and Marco Grandi

Summary

Personal identification is a field where pathology, anthropology, odontology, and even genetics must merge. Specific features and descriptors (such as scars, moles, gross anomalies) may be sufficient for identification. However, in more complex cases, four main disciplines are involved in the identification of human remains: DNA, fingerprint analysis, odontology, and anthropology (or better yet, osteology). Genetic and fingerprinting methods give a quantitative result, or at least statistics have been performed on the specific traits studied, which allow one to answer in a quantitative manner on the probability of two individuals having similar characteristics—in the first case, for the distribution of different alleles within a population, and in the second, for the frequency of minutiae on the finger. Forensic anthropology and odontology methods, which compare the status and shape of teeth and bones, are valid alternative methods. Methods include comparison of dental work, bone, and tooth morphology, in particular frontal sinus patterns, and craniofacial superimposition. They are advantageous methods because faster and less costly; however, they may suffer, in the view of some judges, from the qualitative and nonquantitative responses they give.

Personal identification must always be carried out with a set of data, after having carefully evaluated the limits and the possible sources of error of each method.

Key Words: Identification; DNA; fingerprinting; odontology; anthropology.

From *Forensic Anthropology and Medicine:*
Complementary Sciences From Recovery to Cause of Death
Edited by: A. Schmitt, E. Cunha, and J. Pinheiro © Humana Press Inc., Totowa, NJ

1. INTRODUCTION

An unidentified body comes in many different forms, ranging from a well-preserved corpse to skeletal or badly burned human remains. This is one of the reasons why the process of personal identification is another area where pathology, anthropology, odontology, and even genetics must merge. The previous chapters have focused on the most important steps in achieving a biological profile, i.e., aging, sexing, determining stature, and ancestry, recording every single detail of the remains that may provide a thorough "identikit" of the person, from scars or tattoos visible on bodies with soft tissue residues (one should never forget to always clean the skin of charred or putrefied remains thoroughly so as to not miss any similar details) to bone pathology and dental restorations. This procedure can be completed with facial reconstruction from the cranium in cases of badly decomposed remains. In this way, such a complete identikit can be provided to investigating authorities and the media (newspapers and television) in order to try to achieve a possibility of identification in the case that somebody recognizes the biological profile. In the better-organized countries, this kind of information can be inserted into a postmortem database, which will then be crossmatched with an antemortem database containing data from missing persons in order to reach a prospect of identity or at least possible matches for those specific human remains. At times, circumstantial evidence can help, in the sense that the remains have already arrived at the pathologist's attention with a supposed identity (for example, a burned body in a car whose owner is known).

The previous chapters have all dealt with the steps involved in creating such a profile and reaching a possible identity. The present chapter aims to give general guidelines for everything that happens after that, i.e., definitive personal identification. Whatever the case may be, the forensic anthropologist, pathologist, or odontologist is faced with the necessity of comparing antemortem with postmortem data in order to finalize the identification process.

Identification of a body, even if it is well preserved, is not an easy procedure, and it is necessary for the operator to have a good knowledge of all available methods that can be applied to that particular case. In most countries, before autopsy of a normal identified body, a formal identification of the victim is performed by relatives or friends who officially are considered "responsible" for this identification on a *bona fide* basis. However, in all cases of badly preserved remains or in cases of well-preserved cadavers for which no one can perform a reliable visual identification, biological identification must be performed. Visual identification of well-preserved cadavers carried out by acquaintances in some countries is the only adopted and accepted criterion. However, many times this procedure has proven unreliable. Even in well-preserved cases, it is advisable to carry out identification with a combination of criteria and not to depend only on visual identification. In particular circumstances, in fact, this could be invalidated by the emotional condition of the relatives or acquaintances, or by slight postmortem alterations. Thus, particularly in cases of human remains that cannot be visually identified because they have been altered by putrefactive processes, fire, or dismemberment, magistrates must be advised against performing visual identification or identification by means of personal belongings or documents (e.g., identity card, driver's license). The magistrate's awareness of this problem must be seriously stimulated.

How is positive biological identification achieved? Interpol identification guidelines state that an accurate identification can be obtained by comparing ante- and postmortem data, both circumstantial (clothes, personal belongings, and so on), along with the findings from the external examination of the corpse (physiognomic traits, fingerprints, and so forth) and by means of postmortem examination (clinical, dental, DNA data). It is the authors' opinion that even circumstantial information may be dangerous on its own. It may happen that, both by error or intentionally, the personal belongings of a person are found on the remains of another person. Thus, they must be considered as circumstantial indications of identity, but not definite proof. It is clear that the risk posed by each case must always be carefully evaluated.

Within this perspective, one should consider physical biological evidence as the foundation of identification. For this reason, any form on which such data (the so-called descriptors) is collected must be extremely detailed. This implies drawing up, at the external examination, an accurate description both of clothing/personal belongings and body data: sex, height, constitution, skin color, and the like. Some of these features, which are general and observer-dependent, are potentially misleading. However, there are more specific features and descriptors (such as scars, moles, gross anomalies) that often may be sufficient for identification. Finally, within the context of the autopsy, it is possible to carry out a dental examination, to verify organ anomalies, and to take blood samples and samples of other tissues for genetic examination, together with samples and radiographs of bone tissue.

Apart from the issue of identifying a well-preserved cadaver with personal descriptors such as physionomy, tattoos, and so on, there are four main disciplines involved in the identification of human remains: DNA, fingerprint analysis, odontology, and anthropology (or better yet, osteology).

Genetic and dactyloscopic (fingerprinting) investigations are better known to criminal investigation departments and to the magistrates. In the first case, one compares the genetic asset of the remains with those of the presumed relatives (children, parents, siblings) or with that obtained from residual cells on the personal belongings used by the person in life (for example, razors, combs, toothbrushes, and so forth). The genetic investigation techniques are certainly very effective and have great potential. However, at times they may not be applicable as there could be problems in the extraction of DNA from skeletal remains, or relatives suitable for a genetic comparison may not be available—this is often the case of non-European immigrants. On the other hand, concerning the use of dactyloscopic methods, the problem consists sometimes in the fact that the fingerprint is poorly detectable (even if this problem can be partly overcome with techniques to be discussed further on), and that the person's fingerprints need to have been taken in life. This frequently means that he or she has to have a criminal record, is part of the military, or the country of origin registers fingerprints on identity cards. Many European countries have a database (automated fingerprint identification system, or AFIS) that permits one to compare the fingerprints inserted in a databank with those of subjects already fingerprinted in life. Once the fingerprint of the cadaver is entered, this computerized system will return a series of possible matches, which the fingerprint expert will then evaluate.

Forensic anthropology and odontology methods, which compare the status and shape of teeth and bones, are valid alternative methods. They are advantageous methods because they are faster and less costly; however, they may suffer, in the view of some judges, of the qualitative and nonquantitative responses they give. Genetic and fingerprinting methods give a quantitative result, or at least statistics have been performed on the specific traits studied that allow one to answer in a quantitative manner on the probability of two individuals having similar characteristics—in the first case, for the distribution of different alleles within a population; in the second, for the frequency of minutiae on the finger. In the case of morphological methods (such as the odontological and anthropological ones), a unanimous and clear agreement on the quality and quantity of the characters necessary in order to achieve personal identification does not exist. The recurrence of discordant characters settles the case by excluding the identity; some or many concordant characters, particularly if not uncommon within the population, can only permit expression of a judgment of compatibility or possibility; few characters or a combination of characters, rare among the population, will allow one to express a judgment of high probability or certainty.

The authors' experience in Milan from 1995 to 2003 shows that of 312 cases of remains requiring identification, only 218 have been identified. Of these, 81 were badly preserved and required biological methods of identification. The disciplines that resulted in being more useful in identification were, in decreasing order, odontology, dactyloscopy, anthropology, and DNA. Thus, although one must not underestimate the potential of biomolecular techniques, in the past years, because of the high number of immigrants from northern Africa and the East, anthropological and odontological methods have resulted in being increasingly useful.

It is not the purpose of this chapter to deal with the genetic aspects of identification, which are of a more specialized and technical nature. Suffice it to say that adequate sampling from the human remains must be performed (usually blood [if fresh], muscle, bone) and stored at −20°C, at a minimum.

Positive identification possibilities by means of dactyloscopic, odontological, and anthropological methods will be discussed.

2. DACTYLOSCOPY

Identification by fingerprint analysis is not a task for the forensic pathologist or anthropologist; qualified police personnel exist for this purpose. However, the biomedical expert dealing with the remains should be aware of the potential for a fingerprint even in badly decomposed human remains. In some countries, it is, in fact, the pathologist or anthropologist who tries to enhance fingerprints on the cadaver, or at least guides investigating authorities in doing so. Thus, the following paragraphs provide guidelines for the treatment of decomposed fingers.

Dactyloscopy carried out on a well-preserved corpse is easy and fast to apply, and for these reasons is the primary approach to identification. Once fingerprints are taken, if the person has a criminal record, the automated fingerprint identification system will find the appropriate identity in a few hours.

The problem arises when the fingertips are compromised by putrefactive and/or decomposition processes (mummification, corification, saponification) or by postmortem factors (such as fire), in such a way that immediate fingerprinting is impossible. Depending on the case, the papillary crests can present deformations consisting of folds of the epidermal or dermal layer (as in mummification), or can be flattened/thinned because of erosive effects of environmental phenomena, or dehydrated, and therefore retracted and fragile, as in the case of exposure to high temperatures and flames. In these cases, specific methods should be used in order to enhance the papillary design.

Very different techniques have been developed to recover the papillary design *(1)*. Chemical–physical techniques (methanol solutions, sodium hydroxide, ethylenediaminetetraacetic acid) are applied to soften and rehydrate the skin, and as a result, extend the fingertip and allow the inking of the papillary crests. Once the finger is softened, subcutaneous injections of glycerin or saline solution can be performed to reinflate the finger. Good results have been obtained also by putting the finger in a saturated saline solution with the addition of sulfuric acid. In spite of the validity of these chemical and physical techniques, they are potentially destructive, complex, and require constant monitoring, solution preparation, pH control, or amputation of the fingers.

In the postmortem transformation context, it is possible to recognize two distinct situations, one characterized by conditions of humidity (as for putrefaction and saponification), the other by shortage of water or dehydration (as for carbonization and mummification). This distinction is necessary because in the former case, the treatment has to be carried out quickly in order to stop the putrefactive processes, whereas for the latter case, this aspect will be less important.

2.1. Mummification

Mummification implies the loss of liquid from tissues. The fingertips thus show more or less pronounced folding that prevents the application of the normal techniques of fingerprinting. A technique frequently used in these cases consists in softening and reinflating the finger. This is obtained by carrying out alternated incubation in 90% methyl alcohol and 5% sodium hydroxide solutions. The immersion times vary from minutes to hours, depending on the cases. However, the sodium hydroxide treatment is destructive for the skin, and it is not advisable to repeat it. Once the fingertip is softened, it is possible to reinflate it by means of saline injections. When the folds have flattened and the papillary design becomes sufficiently readable, it is important to try to ink it or, if it is impossible, to take a photograph with tangential lighting.

Alternatively, a simple method that gives more satisfying results in a very short time has been devised. The method consists in spreading a thin layer of latex on the fingertip (Fig. 1). This latex film, once hardened, can be gently removed from the finger, set on a frame, and inked.

2.2. Carbonization

This implies dehydration, soiling by soot, loss of superficial skin layers, and thinning of the papillary crests. Even with bodies heavily damaged by the

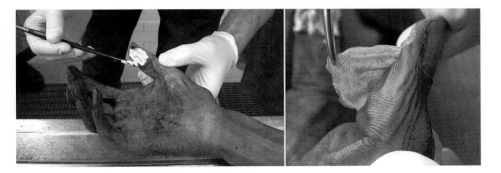

Fig. 1. Spreading a film of latex on mummified fingers, with subsequent removal of the latex film.

combustion process, it is possible to recover fingerprints because, on account of the heat, the fists tend to be clenched, thus preserving the fingertips. In these cases, it is necessary to remove the fingers in order to clean them and work on them. Cleaning is carried out by degreasing the finger with ether and by removing the layer of soot on the fingertip with a soft brush. It is possible to use the technique of rehydration and of reinflation described for the mummified fingers, but the latex method is by far the most effective.

2.3. Putrefaction

Putrefaction leads to peeling off of the skin with a consequent progressive loss of the papillary design. The first step in this case is to block the putrefactive process by hardening the skin via immersion in ethanol for a time ranging from a few minutes to 1–2 h. Dehydration because of the immersion in alcohol, although necessary, introduces serious problems, such as the thinning of the papillary crests, which are already compromised. At this point, it should be sufficient, once the epidermal glove (i.e., the peeled-off skin) has been worn by the examiner, to ink the fingertip and transfer the fingerprint on paper.

2.4. Saponification

Saponified fingers (left in water) present skin flaking, flattening of the papillary crests, and, at times, hardening of the whole finger. The technique recommended in this case is still that of reinflating and inking.

It is clear that sometimes it is necessary to combine these methods, depending on the different and mixed preservation conditions. Finally, it is convenient for the operator (pathologist or anthropologist) to be in close contact with the fingerprint expert who will carry out the identification, to explain what he or she is looking at. For example, the fingerprint obtained from the latex film has to be inverted in "place and colored" before fingerprint comparative analysis.

3. ODONTOLOGICAL IDENTIFICATION

Teeth are extremely resistant to decomposition, environmental factors and, to a certain extent, fire. They are therefore of crucial importance for identification, particularly in cases where soft tissues have been altered for various reasons. In addition, teeth, because of all their possible variations in shape, size, and position, constitute a three-dimensional apparatus that is characteristic of each individual. Genes, nutrition, environment, pathology, and dental treatment act synergistically in decreasing the possibility that two sets of teeth may be identical, and thus allow one to express a statement of identity of an unknown corpse.

Odontological identification is based on the comparison between postmortem evaluation and antemortem data concerning the dental status.

Characters such as malformations, anomalies, pathological and traumatic alterations, and therapeutic peculiarities (avulsions, fillings, root canals, caps, dentures) are by many authors considered among the most important factors for personal identification (2–4). However, morphology is also important. One has to consider the fact that improving oral health conditions decreases the need for dental work, particularly in young individuals, and thus leads to the need for identification methods based on simple morphological traits.

3.1. Postmortem Odontological Assessment and Data Collection

In the greatest number of cases, odontological identification is carried out on corpses that have been deeply traumatized, burned, decomposed, or skeletonized. These conditions make the dental arch particularly fragile and impose on whoever is handling the corpse the need for the utmost attention. Before moving the body from the scene of crime, it is advisable to proceed to an initial dental analysis and photographic survey. It is also appropriate to inspect the environment where the remains were found, because dental elements or prosthetic devices may have been moved by larvae or small animals after decomposition. Above all, in the case of highly decomposed cadavers (when the periodontal ligament cannot anchor the tooth to the socket) or burned remains, it is necessary to preserve the teeth so that precious information is not lost during transportation to the morgue. For this purpose, a fixative spray can be used on the teeth and dental arches, which may be further protected with soft material (gauze) kept in place by a surgical mask.

Before proceeding to the dental examination, a series of photographs of the dental arches, both in occlusion (frontally and laterally) and of the occlusal surfaces (superior and inferior), should be taken, using labial retractors and mirrors for intraoral photography. In the case of a mass disaster, the preparation of a photographic file, possibly in a digital format, greatly facilitates the identification phases and often avoids a second dental inspection.

Although the odontological examination is normally carried out after the autopsy and is therefore facilitated by the removal of the tongue and of the larynx, access to the oral cavity of the corpse is not always easy. When faced with fairly well-preserved bodies, rigor mortis often prevents sufficient opening of the mouth; in these cases, it is possible to practice an intraoral incision of the chewing muscles or overcome the rigor by using levers or a special mouth-opening device, taking care not to damage the dental elements (obviously an alternative could be waiting for the resolution of rigor mortis).

In cases of severely traumatized bodies, decomposed, or charred remains, disarticulation or the resection of the lower jaw may be necessary: after having exposed the osseous surface of the lower jaw, a cut is practiced with a Stryker saw on the ascending branch of the mandible (paying attention not to damage the third molars). If necessary, even the superior maxilla can be removed with a Stryker saw and by working a parallel section to the occlusion level, sufficiently cranial not to damage the dental apex. In case it is necessary to remove the mandible and maxilla from a well-preserved body, one may proceed to an accurate dissection (flap) of the soft tissues from the facial skeleton. The parts removed can be substituted by adequately modeled artificial volumes in such a way so as to provide support to the soft tissues; alternatively, the maxilla and mandible can be repositioned after odontological analysis.

After having accurately cleaned the dental elements, using a probe and a dental mirror, one should proceed to the examination of the dental arches, taking note of any anatomical, pathological, and therapeutic characteristics, and in particular:

1. Presence/absence of each dental element, specifying if it is missing, if the loss occurred antemortem (recent or remote) or postmortem.
2. Periodontal status, presence of calculus, pigmentations, abrasions.
3. Anomalies of shape, number, position.
4. Occlusion.
5. Position, morphology, technique, material and conservation state of each filling.
6. Accurate description of fixed and removable prostheses and osteointegrated implants.
7. Orthodontic treatments.

When possible, the prosthetic devices have to be removed in order to be able to observe the characteristics both of the prosthesis and of the dental elements to which it is anchored. The use of a UV light points out aesthetic restorations otherwise difficult to see.

When the dental arches are not removed *in toto*, it is advisable to make a cast, using materials commonly adopted in dentistry (alginates and silicones). The hardening time for these materials will be greater because of the lower temperature of the oral cavity in a dead body.

Radiographic surveys must be carried out with equipment and material commonly used in odontology and, when possible, they should be restricted to the search for the peculiarities observed in the antemortem comparison materials, such as the presence of endodontic therapy, osteointegrated implants, morphological, and radicular peculiarities of the osseous trabecula and of the pulp chambers. All data collected are then summarized on an appropriate form (Interpol, FBI, Computer-Assisted Postmortem Identification System) that will serve afterwards to facilitate the comparison with the antemortem information.

In Europe, the most frequently used charts are the ones pertaining to the Interpol forms (yellow for collecting data of missing persons, pink to collect corpses' data), which are subdivided in various sections (http://www.interpol.int/Public/DisasterVictim/Forms/Default.asp). Those related to the odontological identification are sections F1 and F2. In section F1 of the pink section, a number and an identification mark is inserted, related to the body, sex (when it is possible to determine it), and various information related to the state of the human remains, to the place and to the circumstances of their finding. In section F2, the dental survey related to the corpse is reported. In the designated squares, all treatments and other particularities can be found. It is important to fill in such forms in a clear manner, using odontological terminology to avoid misinterpretations. In the odontogram, the morphology of each dental restoration is drawn using black for fillings with amalgam, red for gold, and green for aesthetic material. Existing prostheses are always drawn. With regard to missing teeth, it must be specified if the loss is postmortem or antemortem. All the radiographic exams carried out must be indicated with reference to the tooth that is being observed. Finally, an estimation of age, specifying the methods used, is carried out.

3.2. Antemortem Data Collection

The antemortem information, at best, will come from the odontologist who treated the presumed victim in life, who may provide a case history, orthopantomographs, intraoral photographs, and casts. However, even a simple estimate concerning the treatment carried out or an interview with the dentist of the presumed victim could be of fundamental importance in the identification phases. With regard to dental casts, in addition to precious information concerning dental morphology and therapeutic particularities, they also provide information on palatal rugae, which, in view of their interpersonal variability and morphological stability with time, could be utilized for identification purposes.

In the cases in which clinical odontological material is not available, useful information could be obtained from skull radiographs and from photographs of the person smiling (in other words, exposing the teeth). Obviously, because this is not material from a dental clinic, various difficulties in singling out the dental peculiarities useful for identification will be encountered; in a radiograph of the skull in a laterolateral projection, for example, the dental elements are all visible, but the right hemiarches are superimposed to the left ones. In spite of this, precious information on avulsions, root canals, prostheses, and fillings are, however, readable and can be located.

All antemortem data are then summarized in the antemortem identification form that differs very little from the postmortem one for a subsequent comparison. The antemortem form may arrive already filled in by another odontologist, particularly in the case of mass disasters involving subjects of several nationalities; the sources used for filling in the form should always be available for verifying correctness of data. In filling out the antemortem form, each observation (e.g., filling, avulsion) should refer the source and the date on which the source was created. The dental apparatus, mainly for pathological reasons and for medical interventions, is in fact in constant evolution; therefore, the increase of the time interval between antemortem and postmortem data often increases the probability that such characteristics have changed. The in-depth knowledge of the possible evolution of various dental pathologies and of odontological therapy is thus indispensable for a correct interpretation of antemortem and postmortem data. In addition, it has to be taken into consideration that dental nomenclature varies not only among different odontologists, but also among different countries.

3.3. Personal Identification: Comparison of Antemortem and Postmortem Odontological Data: Dental Charts

The antemortem and postmortem forms are then placed side by side and, tooth after tooth, consistencies and inconsistencies are analyzed.

In case there is only one anatomical, pathological, or therapeutic inconsistency among the forms (for example, the presence of a dental element in the postmortem card not reported in the antemortem one, or a therapeutic particularity incompatible with the natural history of the dental element), a judgment of exclusion is expressed. In cases where the antemortem or post-mortem information is lacking or insufficient in number, the comparison among forms leads to a judgment of possibility or compatibility. Further investigations are then necessary in order to arrive at a positive identification. Finally, the simple comparison of forms in cases where the pathological and therapeutic peculiarities are numerous leads to positive identification.

3.4. Personal Identification: Comparison of Antemortem and Postmortem Odontological Data: X-Rays

When the comparison among forms is not sufficient to establish a definite identification, the antemortem and postmortem radiographs can be compared. In the case that the postmortem radiographs are taken with the same spatial orientation of the antemortem ones, a superimposition of the images can help in a positive identification. In comparing two radiographic images, the smallest anatomical, pathological, and therapeutic characteristics must be looked for; even one periapical image rich in peculiarities can lead to a definite identification (Fig. 2).

3.5. Dental Superimposition

Unfortunately, it is not always possible to recover suitable antemortem odontological documentation, both for the lack of regulations obliging the odontologist to register and keep dental charts of patients and in the cases when the suspected victim may have never been to a dentist (a increasingly frequent circumstance, considering the increment of legal and illegal immigrants). On these occasions, photographs of the face of the suspected victims, particularly when the dental elements are clearly visible, are of great importance. Such photographs, supplied by relatives and acquaintances of the missing person, can be used for an identification study based on computer-assisted superimposition between the person's face and the skull of the corpse to be identified or, better yet, when possible, between the dental elements visible in the photograph and a dental cast of the corpse. Craniofacial superimposition is based on the controversial correspondence between soft tissues and a skeletal structure; however, a comparison among dental elements can overcome this problem, because these are the only "skeletal" elements visible during the life of a person. The identification procedure of the dental superimposition can be summarized as follows.

After having selected among the pictures of the missing person those presenting a better visualization of the oral zone, one proceeds to analyze the spatial orientation of the dental arch of the subject in such a way so as to be able to

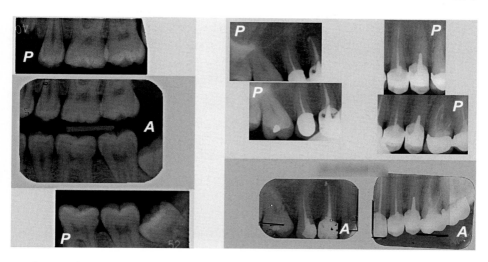

Fig. 2. Identification by means of intraoral radiographs (A refers to antemortem images; P to postmortem ones). To the left, in the absence of therapy, the morphological characteristics of the single dental elements (crowns, roots, pulpar chambers) and their reciprocal positions (third left inferior partially included and mesioinclined); notice also the lesion from caries on the distal surface of the first inferior molar. To the right one can notice the similarities of root canal and dental restorations between A and P.

photograph the cast of the teeth of the remains in the same position. The picture of the cast is then superimposed to the antemortem photograph (photo retouching software allows one to enhance more clearly the areas of major interest during the overlap). It is at this moment that it is possible to study the trend of the superimposition of the profile of each tooth and to express a judgment on the correspondence of the dental profiles examined (Fig. 3).

Discrepancies, if not caused by morphological modifications because of pathological, traumatic phenomena, or dental work, will lead to an exclusion.

4. ANTHROPOLOGICAL AND OSTEOLOGICAL IDENTIFICATION

In order to identify a person, it is also possible to compare the shape of bones *(5–19)*, just as though each bone were a fingerprint, even if, as has been mentioned, these methods are not standardized. It is clear that the comparison, as always, must be carried out between antemortem and postmortem radiographs of different skeletal districts. Thus, if radiographs of the various osseous

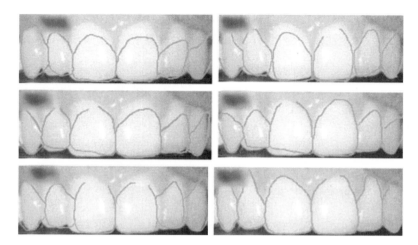

Fig. 3. Some examples of dental superimposition. In the background, one can note the antemortem dentition to which the black profile of the postmortem cast is superimposed. The only matching superimposition is on the bottom right.

districts (for example, head, thorax, limbs, abdomen, and the like) are available, it will be possible to compare the morphology of the skeletal elements visible in the radiograph, with the same osseous elements belonging to the human remains (both working on the actual osseous elements, and on their radiographs).

Apart from exceptional morphological peculiarities (osteophytes, bone calluses, and so on), the difficulty consists in determining which and how many are the morphological elements sufficient for a definite identification. The literature states that personal identification in this way is carried out by means of a meticulous comparison of details. However, a minimum number of points do not exist—as they exist instead for fingerprints—in order to carry out an identification. Usually, it is intended that one to four characters, without evident discrepancies, are considered sufficient for identification. The problem is that an agreement does not exist yet on what exactly is meant by a "significant" character. It is clear that the areas compared must be scarcely modifiable in time. However, the peculiarity of the character and the consistency between the antemortem and postmortem shape is left, in part, to a subjective evaluation and to the experience of the operator.

The most hailed districts in the literature are the frontal sinus and the vertebrae. For the comparison of frontal sinuses, there are even algorithms that allow one to achieve a judgment of identity; the shape of frontal sinuses is so peculiar that it is even different in homozygous twins (like fingerprints). For the other districts, such precise indications do not exist.

4.1. Superimposition of the Frontal Sinuses

As previously mentioned, for this particular skeletal district there are several algorithms *(5,6)*. Particularly famous is that of Yoshino et al. *(6)*. An antemortem radiograph is used where the frontal sinuses are clearly visible. A postmortem radiograph is then carried out on the skull or head, which is oriented in a similar position to the antemortem picture by means of progressive approximations, aimed at obtaining identical ratios between lines drawn on a transverse and coronal plane, between craniometric points. Briefly, on the radiograph, it is possible to draw two lines parallel to the median sagittal plane running between alveolare and nasion. Subsequently, on the transversal plane, a line is traced tangent to the occlusal border of the central superior incisors and another line going through the most cranial point of the edge of the orbits. The ratios between these distances are then calculated. The skull is radiographed in different positions, similar to those of the antemortem plate, until a positioning is found that gives ratios that can be superimposed to those of the antemortem radiological picture.

It is then possible to proceed with different classification systems in addition to evaluating the natural morphological concordance or discordance of sinus morphology. The Yoshino method is based on the attribution of specific scores for each of the following parameters: asymmetry index (ratio between the area of the smaller frontal sinus A1 and the larger one A2, calculated with a special software); left sinus larger than the right sinus or vice versa; trend of the profile of the superior edge of the left and of the right sinus; presence of the number of arches per septum; presence and location of partial septa; presence and location of supraorbital cells; and so on. To all these traits a score is given. This is a classical example of a method trying to quantify the morphological closeness of osteological traits. However, once the cranium has been properly oriented and radiographed, a qualitative comparison of sinus morphology may be sufficient (Fig. 4).

4.2. Comparison and Superimposition of Other Skeletal Districts

As previously stated, it is possible to compare the forms of other osseous districts *(7–19)*. Among the most utilized are the vertebrae. Of these, the transverse processes and the spinal process, which present very different shapes from one another, are particularly useful. However, there are no algorithms

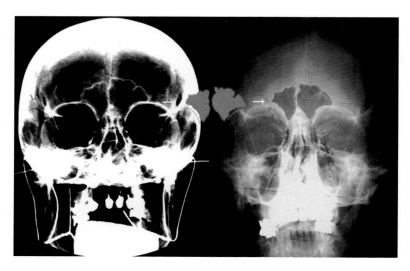

Fig. 4. To the left, the postmortem radiograph of skeletal remains, to the right the antemortem radiograph of the subject to whom it was assumed the skeleton belonged. The margins and shape of the frontal sinuses, identical in both pictures, can be recognized.

yet that allow a quantitative or semiquantitative estimate of the comparison. The answer is left to the morphological evaluation of the observer. It is evident that it is necessary to carry out the comparison of two structures oriented in the same manner; therefore, an orientation of the postmortem material must be found so that it best approaches the antemortem radiograph.

4.3. Craniofacial Superimposition

A "last-chance" possibility should be craniofacial superimposition. It consists of the superimposition of a photograph of the skull with a photograph, similarly oriented, of the face of the living person. The correspondence between two subjects is evaluated based on the correspondence of several anatomical landmarks that can be found on the skull and on the face. As can be easily understood, this superimposition has far less credibility than dental superimposition. In dental superimposition the same elements—teeth antemortem and teeth postmortem—are superimposed; in craniofacial superimposition, the soft tissues are compared with the skeleton. For the sake of completeness, Fig. 5 illustrates a general example that summarizes most proposed methods and whose aim is to demonstrate the difficulty in matching specific landmarks.

The supporters of this method report a reliability of 96% whenever the possibility exists of both frontal and lateral superimposition, but the discrepancy among numerous anthropologists concerning the degree of certitude supplied by this type of investigation is large. In the authors' opinion, this method should never be used alone for identification because there are several problems to overcome in the comparison between a structure with soft tissues (face) and a structure made of hard tissue (skull). It should be used only for excluding identity if gross incompatibilities are present.

5. CONCLUSIONS AND GUIDELINES

This chapter concludes with an outline summarizing possible solutions (at present) for performing positive identification of human remains by comparing antemortem and postmortem data, with the relative advantages and disadvantages.

5.1. Well-Preserved Body

Even if the purpose of this chapter is not to deal with the identification of the well-preserved cadaver by means of the comparison of facial physiognomy, it should be stressed that it may be more difficult to compare a dead face with the picture of a living face in the attempt to declare that it is the same person. This is confirmed by the difficulties encountered by anthropologists dealing with the identification of living individuals on photographic material (for example, on video surveillance recordings of bank robberies, and the like). In these cases, it is necessary to compare the physiognomic traits of the person represented on tape or on a photograph with the face of the suspected thief or assailant. Whereas this appears to be a banal and intuitively simple activity, it is anything but simple. Comparing the morphological and metric traits of two images for arriving at a definite identification of the subject is still complex; this is because of differences in orientation of the two images and of the lack of standardization of such procedures. In the same manner, in the case of a well-preserved cadaver to be compared with a photograph of a living person, serious problems in determining the traits that may be crucial for identification can turn up. It is for this reason that it is important to support a mere resemblance with specific descriptors such as scars, tattoos, moles, and so forth.

5.2. Putrefied, Burned, Partly or Completely Skeletonized Human Remains

For this type of material, depending on which districts are better preserved, the following methods should be applied.

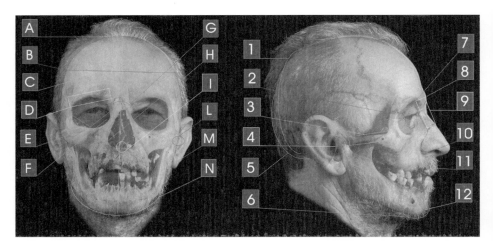

Fig. 5. Craniofacial superimposition. After having selected images of the missing person, proper spatial orientation of the skull and enlargement of the picture (trial and error) are achieved. Then superimpositions are usually performed in the frontal and lateral views. The figure shows an example of craniofacial superimposition in the frontal and lateral position. The letters (frontal) and the numbers (lateral) indicate the landmark for which the correspondence between face and skull is evaluated. At the points where the graphic indication is absent, the corresponding landmarks are not detectable. The observed criteria for the comparison in norma frontalis, marked with letters A to N are the following: A, the length of the skull from bregma to mention must be included in the face—the bregma is generally covered with hair; B, the width of the skull must match the forehead area: C, the temporal line, if visible on the face, should correspond to the temporal cranial line; D, the eyebrows generally follow the superior edge of the orbit to the medial and central third—they continue superiorly to the lateral third, whereas the edge of the orbit deviates inferiorly; E, the orbits contain the eye entirely; F, the lachrymal groove, if distinguishable on the photograph, lines up with the osseous groove; G, the width of the nasal bridge must correspond in the two images; H, the width of the nasal aperture falls within the external margins of the nose; I, the nasal spine is situated above the inferior edge of the medial nasal crus; L, the external auditory meatus is medial to the tragus—this can be adequately evaluated by a marker inserted in the ear; M, the oblique line of the mandible, if visible on the face, corresponds to the same line on the skull; and N, the mandibular curve is similar to the curve visible on the face. In norma lateralis: 1. The skullcap must coincide with the height of the head. 2. Sometimes it is possible to notice the margin of the frontal process of the zygomatic bone that should match the one on the cranium. 3. The margin of the zygomatic arch of the skull is also superimposable to that of the face. 4. The porion is slightly behind the tragus and below the

5.2.1. Significant Descriptors

This is the case of putrefied bodies presenting countermarks (or features) so singular that they may be used for identification purposes. Examples of these identification instruments are residues of tattoos, scars, bone prostheses or anomalies, unusual mutilations, or surgical operations.

5.2.2. Dactyloscopy

It is always worthwhile trying to restore the papillary crests in order to be able to obtain sufficient dactyloscopic data for the comparison of fingerprints. This, however, presumes that the subject's prints were taken during lifetime and that antemortem fingerprints of the subject are available.

5.2.3. Odontology

If a detailed antemortem dental chart, dental radiographs, or other clinical dental data exist, they can be used for comparison with the dentition of the human remains. Such data, however, must be available and the dentition of the remains fairly well preserved. The advantages of this method are its rapidity and low costs. One disadvantage, compared to DNA analysis, could be the inability to quantify the result. For example, it is almost impossible to provide a judge with the numerical probability that two different individuals may share the same dentition. Many odontologists, however, feel that quantification of the result would be useless and that morphological methods are based on the operator's experience and common sense *(4)*.

5.2.4. DNA

This is the most popular method, and the most expensive. It is necessary, nevertheless, to be able to extract the DNA from the remains, and in the case of dry bone, this can be difficult for the presence of PCR inhibitors and

---

helix crus. 5. The occipital curve is placed inside the margin of the nape. 6. The anterior protuberance of the mandible is behind the chin. The chin form corresponds to the mandible form. 7. The lateral margin of the eye is situated within the orbit. 8. The profile of the glabella both of the skull and of the face must be similar. 9. The glabella, the nasal bridge, and the region of the nasal bones are the most significant. The prominence of the glabella and the depth of the nasal bridge follow closely the contour of the thin layer of overlying skin. The nasal bones fall within the margins of the nose. 10. The front nasal spine is situated posteriorly with respect to the base of the nose, close to the more posterior portion of the lateral septum cartilage. 11. The prosthion is posterior to the anterior margin of the superior lip. 12. The pogonion is posterior to the indenting noticeable in the chin where the orbicularis oris crosses the chin muscle.

degradation. Furthermore, there may be no adequate relatives for DNA comparison or objects such as toothbrushes or combs from which to extract the individual's antemortem DNA may not be retrievable (as in the case of vagrants and illegal immigrants). The advantages of this method are being able to supply a quantitative result because of studies on the distribution of the alleles of specific loci within a certain population, which makes it possible to provide the probability that another person shares the same genetic asset. Other possible setbacks may be that it is more expensive and requires more time.

5.2.5. *ANTHROPOLOGY–OSTEOLOGY: IMAGE SUPERIMPOSITION*

These methods are applied when the above-described methods are not applicable. Superimposition can be dental or craniofacial. As already mentioned, the dental superimposition requires the existence of a decent-quality photograph of the living subject (smiling) in order to be able to compare the subject's profile with that of the human remains. Craniofacial superimposition, where craniometric points of the soft tissues are compared with craniometric points of the remains, is less reliable. These investigations require good-quality photographs. In the case of dental superimposition, the methodology, although incapable of quantifying the error, at least compares the same structures.

Radiological comparison of frontal sinus shape or the morphological correspondence between the shapes of any bones (e.g., vertebrae) can be a valid method of identification, although one must be very cautious in matching the orientation of the antemortem and postmortem radiographs and in looking for sufficient corresponding traits.

In conclusion, results always need to be carefully examined by an experienced observer. Personal identification has to be carried out with a set of data, after having carefully evaluated the limits and the possible sources of error of each method.

REFERENCES

1. Kahana, Y., Grande, A., Tancredi, D. M., Penalver, J., Hiss, J. Fingerprinting the deceased: traditional and new techniques. J. Forensic Sci. 46:908–912, 2001.
2. Bernstein, M. L., Cottone, J. A. Forensic Odontology. CRC Press, Boca Raton, FL, 2005.
3. Clarke, D. H. Practical Forensic Odontology. Butterworth-Heinemann, London, 1992.
4. Acharya, A. B, Taylor, J. A. Are a minimum number of concordant matches needed to establish identity in forensic odontology? J. Forensic Odontostomatol. 21:6–13, 2003.

5. Kirk, N. J., Wood, R. E., Goldstein M. Skeletal identification using the frontal sinus region: a retrospective study of 39 cases. J. Forensic Sci. 47:318–323, 2002.
6. Yoshino, M., Miyasaka, S., Sato, H., Seta, S. Classification system of frontal sinus patterns. Can. Soc. Forensic Sci. J. 22:135–146, 1998.
7. Adams, B. J., Maves, R. C. Radiographic identification using the clavicle of an individual missing from the Vietnam conflict. J. Forensic Sci. 47:369–373, 2002.
8. Angyal, M., Derczy, K. Personal identification on the basis of antemortem and postmortem radiographs. J. Forensic Sci. 43:1089–1093, 1998.
9. Brogdon, B. G. Radiological identification of individual remains. In: Brogdon, B. G., ed., Forensic Radiology. CRC Press, Boca Raton, FL, 1998.
10. Goodman, N. R., Himmelberger, L. K. Identifying skeletal remains found in a sewer. J. Am. Dent. Assoc. 133:1508–1513, 2002.
11. Kahana, T., Goldin, L., Hiss, J. Personal identification based on radiographic vertebral features. Am. J. Forensic Med. Pathol. 23:36–41, 2002.
12. Kahana, T., Ravioli, J. A., Urroz, C. L., Hiss, J. Radiographic identification of fragmentary human remains from a mass disaster. Am. J. Forensic Med. Pathol. 18:40–44, 1997.
13. Mann, R. W. Use of bone trabeculae to establish positive identification. Forensic Sci. Int. 98:91–99, 1998.
14. Owsley, D. W., Mann, R. W. Positive personal identity of skeletonized remains using abdominal and pelvic radiographs. J. Forensic Sci. 37:332–336, 1992.
15. Smith, D. R., Limbird, K. G., Hoffman, J. M. Identification of human skeletal remains by comparison of bony details of the cranium using computerized tomographic (CT) scans. J. Forensic Sci. 47:937–939, 2002.
16. Sudimack, J. R., Lewis, B. J., Rich, J., Dean, D. E., Fardal, P. M. Identification of decomposed human remains from radiographic comparisons of an unusual foot deformity. J. Forensic Sci. 47:218–220, 2002.
17. Valenzuela, A. Radiographic comparison of the lumbar spine for positive identification of human remains. A case report. Am. J. Forensic Med. Pathol. 18:215–217, 1997.
18. Dean, D. E., Tatarek, N. E., Rich, J., Brogdon, B. G., Powers, R. H. Human identification from the ankle with pre- and postsurgical radiographs. J. Clin. Forensic Med. 12:5–9, 2005.
19. Rogers, T. L., Allard, T. T. Expert testimony and positive identification of human remains through cranial suture patterns. J. Forensic Sci. 49:203–207, 2004.

PART V

Particular Contexts: Crimes Against Humanity and Mass Disasters

Chapter 16

Forensic Investigations Into the Missing

Recommendations and Operational Best Practices

Morris Tidball-Binz

Summary

Over the last 20 yr, a new and growing field for the application of forensic sciences has emerged in support of investigations of violations of human rights and international humanitarian law.

These investigations are often carried out under international jurisdiction and present challenges and opportunities for forensic practitioners worldwide.

The purpose of this chapter is to summarize international principles of best practice guiding forensic investigations into the missing, in particular the guidlines adopted by the International Committee of the Red Cross in 2003.

Key Words: Missing; identification; guidelines investigation; mass graves.

1. INTRODUCTION

The role of forensic sciences in helping clarify the fate of the missing, including the identification of the living and of the dead, has evolved remarkably over the past 20 yr. In addition, since the early 1990s, a series of

From *Forensic Anthropology and Medicine:*
Complementary Sciences From Recovery to Cause of Death
Edited by: A. Schmitt, E. Cunha, and J. Pinheiro © Humana Press Inc., Totowa, NJ

forensic standards have been developed by the concerned scientific community and adopted by the United Nations to assist and guide investigations into deaths in custody, mass graves, and torture *(1–3)*. In 2003, the International Committee of the Red Cross (ICRC) organized an international conference that adopted recommendations based on existing best practices worldwide, including on forensics, to help resolve the tragedy of the missing *(4)*.

This chapter summarizes some of the relevant recommendations for forensic practitioners investigating the missing believed to be dead.

1.1. The Tragedy of the Missing

According to the ICRC, the missing are "people unaccounted for as a result of armed conflict or internal violence." *(5)*

Worldwide, hundreds of thousands of families live in anguish as a consequence of a missing relative, struggling for their right to know about the whereabouts and fate of their loved ones.

Regardless of their cultural, religious, and social background, the relatives of the missing usually coincide in expressing that the death of a family member—however painful—can be accepted; but not knowing the fate of a loved one is far worse than almost any other possible experience.

The following testimonies help illustrate the above:

"When visiting my son's grave and crying near his tombstone, I feel my grief become lighter. But I can't find any comfort for the pain that constantly burns my heart, the pain of my missing son."

> —Testimony to the ICRC from a mother of two soldiers, one of whom was killed and the other went missing in 2001 during the armed conflict between Armenia and Azerbaijan over the territory of Nagorno Karabakh.

"During all these years I knew he could not be alive, but one can never completely give up the dream that he might come home one day. I don't know if there is any worse torture than that. Burying my son, with his name on a gravestone above his tomb, has curiously, paradoxically, rescued him for us. He came out of the fog of persons unknown."

> —Testimony of Juan Gelman, Argentine poet, after the funeral of his son Marcelo Gelman, who went missing after his detention by the military in 1976 and whose remains, bearing skeletal injuries consistent with torture and execution-style trauma, were recovered and identified in 1989 *(6)*.

1.2. Legal Framework

The emotional trauma caused by the disappearance of a person to his or her loved ones, particularly in the context of armed conflict, is growingly recognized and acknowledged, including by courts, as a cause of grave suffering, for which the authorities responsible for the disappearance also bear responsibility. It is also acknowledged that this suffering may be remedied, at least in part, by the truth about the whereabouts of the missing person *(7)*. This has been established in jurisprudence of international human rights law.

For example, in 1999, the Inter-American Court of Human Rights ruled that: "The forced disappearance of Mr. Nicholas Blake caused his parents and brothers suffering, intense anguish, and frustration in the face of the Guatemalan authorities' failure to investigate and cover up of what occurred. The suffering of the family members, in violation of Article 5 of the American Convention on Human Rights [prohibition of torture and ill-treatment], cannot be disassociated from the situation created by the forced disappearance of Mr. Nicholas Blake that lasted until 1992 when his mortal remains were located. The Court, in conclusion, holds that the grave moral damage suffered by the four family members of Mr. Nicholas Blake is completely proved." *(8)*

International humanitarian law (IHL), the branch of law applicable at times of armed conflict, recognizes and protects the right of families to know the fate of their missing loved ones. The very detailed body of IHL is contained in the four Geneva Conventions (GCs) of 1949 and their two Additional Protocols (AP) of 1977. One hundred ninety-one countries are signatories of the GCs up to date.

The ICRC, a Swiss-based international organization established in 1863, is the originator and custodian of IHL worldwide. It directs and coordinates international relief activities in situations of conflict, and it endeavors to prevent suffering by promoting and strengthening humanitarian law and universal humanitarian principles around the world.

Acting on the basis of the mandate conferred on it by the four GCs and their two APs, the ICRC also aims to prevent all disappearances, to restore family ties when they have been broken, and help ascertain the whereabouts of people about whom their families have no news, including the need to identify the remains of those who die in direct or indirect relation to an armed conflict or internal violence.

In addition to specifically protecting the right of families to know the fate of their missing relatives (API: Art. 32), the treatment of the dead and graves is addressed in detail in the following provisions of IHL:

1. Whenever circumstances permit, and particularly after an engagement, all possible measures must be taken, without delay, to search for and collect the dead,

without adverse distinction (GCI: Art.15; GCII: Art. 18; GCIV: Art. 16; API: Art. 33).

2. Each party to the conflict must treat the dead with respect and dignity and prevent their being despoiled (GCI: Art. 15; GCII: Art.18; GCIV: Art. 16; API: Art. 34).

3. Each party to the conflict must take measures to identify the dead before disposing of their remains (GCI: Arts. 16, 17; GCII: Arts. 19, 20; GCIII: Arts. 120, 121; GCIV: Arts. 129, 131).

4. The dead must be disposed of in a respectful manner and their graves respected (GCI: Art. 17; GCII: Art. 20; GCIII: Art. 120; GCIV: Art. 130; API: Art. 34[1]).

5. Burial should be in individual graves, unless unavoidable circumstances require the use of collective graves. All graves must be marked (GCI: Art. 17; GCII: Art. 20; GCIII: Art. 120; GCIV: Art. 130; API: Art. 34).

6. At the commencement of hostilities, the parties to the conflict must establish an official Graves Registration Service to see to the dead, including burials, and to record the particulars for identification of graves and those there interred (GCI: Art. 17[3]; GCII: Art. 20[2]; GCIII: Art. 120[6]; GCIV: Art. 130[3]).

7. Each party to the conflict must take all possible measures to provide information to the appropriate authorities or to the family of the deceased regarding the deceased's identity, location, and cause of death (GCI: Arts. 16,17; GCII: Art. 19; GCIII: Art. 120; GCIV: Art.130; API: Art. 33).

8. Upon the outbreak of a conflict and in all cases of occupation, each party to the conflict must establish an official Information Bureau:

    a. To centralize, without adverse distinction, all information on the wounded, sick, shipwrecked, dead, protected persons deprived of their liberty, children whose identity is in doubt and persons who have been reported missing and to provide this information to the appropriate authorities, through the intermediary of the Protecting Powers and likewise of the ICRC Central Tracing Agency (GCI: Arts. 16, 17[4]; GCII: Arts. 19[2], 20; GCIII: Arts. 120, 122, 123; GCIV: Arts. 130, 136–138, 140; API: Art. 33[3]; HRIV: Arts. 14, 16).

    b. To be responsible for replying to all enquiries concerning protected persons and for making any enquiries necessary to obtain information that is asked for if this is not in its possession (GCIII: Art. 122[7]; GCIV: Art. 137[1]; API: Art. 33[3]; HRIV: Art. 14).

    c. To act as an intermediary for the free transport of matter, including correspondence, sent to and by protected persons (and whenever requested through the ICRC Central Tracing Agency) (GCIII: Art. 74; GCIV: Art. 110; HRIV: Art. 14).

9. Information recorded on protected persons deprived of their liberty or on deceased persons must be of such a character as to make it possible to identify the person exactly and to advise the next of kin quickly (GCI: Art. 16; GCII: Art. 19; GCIII: Arts. 120, 122; GCIV: Arts. 129, 138[1], 139; API: Art. 34).

10. Within the shortest possible period, each of the parties to the conflict must transmit to the Information Bureau the following information, when available, on each wounded, sick, shipwrecked, or dead person (GCI: Art. 16; GCII: Art. 19):

    a. Full name.
    b. Army, regimental, personal, or serial number.
    c. Date of birth.
    d. Any other particulars figuring on the identity card or disc.
    e. Date and place of capture or death.
    f. Particulars concerning wounds/illnesses or cause of death.

11. In case of death, the following must be collected and transmitted to the Information Bureau with (GCI: Arts.16, 17, 40[2]; GCII: Arts. 19, 20, 42[2]; GCIII: Art. 120; GCIV: Arts. 129, 130, 139; HRIV: Arts. 14, 19; API: Art. 34):

    a. Date and place of (capture and) death.
    b. Particulars concerning wounds/illnesses or cause of death.
    c. All other personal effects.
    d. Date and place of burial with particulars to identify the grave.
    e. When applicable, half of the identity disc must remain with the body and the other half transmitted.

12. Each party to the conflict must endeavor to facilitate the return of the deceased's remains and personal effects to the home country at its request or at the request of the next of kin (API: Art. 34[2][c]).

Many of the above provisions of IHL also represent customary international law applicable to the management of human remains in wider contexts.

1.3. The ICRC and the Missing

In 2002, the ICRC launched a process aimed at better addressing the plight of people who are unaccounted for as a result of armed conflict or internal violence and of their relatives.

This was done in cooperation with government representatives, other components of the International Red Cross and Red Crescent Movement, international, regional, and national governmental and nongovernmental organizations, representatives of families of missing persons and a variety of experts.

The ICRC's objectives in launching this process were to:

1. Review all methods of preventing persons from becoming unaccounted for in armed conflict or internal violence, and of responding to the needs of families who have lost contact with their relatives.
2. Agree on common and complementary recommendations and operational practices with all those working to prevent persons from becoming unaccounted for, and to respond appropriately when people are missing because of armed conflict or internal violence.

3. Heighten concern about the issue among state authorities, the United Nations, and nongovernmental organizations.

The initial phase of the process, which comprised eight workshops and three studies, was carried out with the involvement of academic institutions, numerous experts, and representatives of governmental and nongovernmental organizations *(9–18)*. It resulted in a series of practical recommendations on legal and operational matters designed to help prevent people going missing in the context of armed conflict, to ascertain the fate of missing persons, and assist their families.

In a second stage, the ICRC organized an international conference of governmental and nongovernmental experts that was held in Geneva from February 19–21, 2003, and that provided an opportunity to share the outcome of this work with a wide array of participants. The *Observations and Recommendations (4)* made at the conference were then included in the *Agenda for Humanitarian Action (19)* adopted by the 28th ICRC and Red Crescent in December 2003.*

Existing recommendations and best practices relate to topics such as international and domestic law, means of identification for civilians and noncivilians, the treatment of persons deprived of their liberty, the exchange of family news, and the proper handling of human remains and information on the dead.

The recommendations about forensic investigations into the missing are central to the ICRC's proposals to help resolve this humanitarian tragedy worldwide. These recommendations and best practices resulted from three specialized international workshops organized by the ICRC during the process *(21)*. They recognize that humanitarian considerations are indispensable in forensic investigations into the missing, and they note the particularities of situations of armed conflict or internal violence, their effect on the role and responsibilities of humanitarian organizations, on forensic work, and how to adapt accordingly.

The ICRC is usually not directly involved in forensic investigations, but it endeavors to promote and support the implementation of standards of best practice, such as those reflected in this chapter, wherever in the world they might be needed. The ultimate responsibility for their implementation lies with the concerned authorities and, more specifically, with the forensic community, which is thus offered an additional challenge and opportunity to help remedy human suffering and failings.

---

* The ICRC and Red Crescent bring together not only the National Red Cross and Red Crescent Societies, but also the governments of the 191 states party to the GCs.

2. ROLE AND RESPONSIBILITIES OF FORENSIC SPECIALISTS INVESTIGATING THE MISSING

2.1. Introduction

The collective term "forensic sciences" used in this chapter includes a range of disciplines applicable to investigations into the missing, such as forensic pathology, forensic archaeology, forensic anthropology, forensic odontology, forensic entomology, forensic radiology, paleopathology, criminology, forensic fingerprint science, taphonomy, forensic photography, molecular biology, and mortuary science. They are truly complementary and evolving sciences in this field, from recovery to cause of death and, as importantly, for identification and proper management of the remains.

The role that forensic specialists play in their domestic context cannot be automatically extrapolated to an international context involving investigations into missing persons; there are some important differences. In the domestic context, forensic specialists work within the legal system of their country. Identification of remains is an integral part of medicolegal investigation and goes hand in hand with ascertaining the cause of death.

However, in the case of investigations into missing persons related to armed conflict or internal violence, especially when these involve exhumations of mass graves, the cause of death of victims buried in them may be far easier to ascertain, given the particular context, than their identity. In effect, in many such cases, identification of the victims is often the most difficult and resource-intensive forensic task. As a result, exhumations may readily satisfy the need for evidence of the cause and manner of death of the deceased, even if these are not identified. This can sometimes lead to the unfortunate situation whereby remains are exhumed and their cause of death established but because the process of identification is much more time- and resource-consuming, the bodies remain unidentified. This situation is unacceptable from a humanitarian point of view, as it prevents the concerned families from knowing the fate of missing relatives and from recovering their remains. Identification of human remains is therefore as important as the collection of evidence for criminal investigations. It is a duty of investigators, in recognition of the right to know of concerned families, as enshrined in IHL.

In summary, whereas forensic specialists may feel comfortable from an ethical perspective investigating violations of IHL and international human rights law, by helping secure evidence on the cause and manner of death of victims, they should also always endeavor to identify the victims.

2.2. General Challenges

Forensic specialists working in humanitarian contexts involving missing persons must demonstrate a level of professionalism that goes beyond simply assuring standards of practice. A highly professional approach to the sensitive issue of human remains can provide the necessary basis for a much-needed dialogue between two parties locked in conflict. In addition, professionalism among forensic specialists involved in such investigations can be a major factor in promoting IHL, international human rights law, accountability, and a process of reconciliation.

In particular, when applied to investigations into the missing, professionalism implies a degree of respect and impartiality that transcends conflict. For this purpose, correct guidelines can serve to empower forensic specialists working in new, difficult, or highly political circumstances.

Forensic specialists working in contexts involving missing persons have a duty to share and transmit their knowledge and experience to colleagues and professionals from other fields working with human remains, and should endeavor to promote local capacity building.

The authorities have well-defined and often clear legal and administrative obligations concerning the issue of missing persons in the context of armed conflict. Forensic practitioners interested in working in such cases should familiarize themselves with those obligations, among other things, to prevent any misuse or manipulation of the results of their work, which might affect or undermine their own professional standing.

Forensic practitioners investigating the missing should thus seek clarity from the authorities and other relevant stakeholders about some basic questions affecting their work before embarking on investigations in any particular context, namely:

1. How criminal justice works in the domestic and international contexts applicable to violations of IHL and international human rights law under investigation.
2. Applicable jurisdictions, laws, rules, regulations, and responsibilities concerning forensic investigations into the missing.
3. How to inform and return remains to families.
4. How to inform and return remains to the concerned authorities.
5. How their work will affect the legal and political process.

Forensic specialists must recommend that a mechanism be put in place whereby the remains that have been positively identified are swiftly returned to the family either by the authorities or by some other relevant stakeholder who is competent to do so. Thought must be given to the whole process before the forensic practitioner becomes involved; it cannot be assumed that the entire chain of responsibility that usually exists in a domestic context is in place and will be effectively operational.

Forensic practitioners wishing to become involved in cases involving violations of IHL and international human rights law must be aware that they may be called on to work in difficult conditions. Their role and responsibilities may entail examining those who have been killed or injured in circumstances of torture or illegal imprisonment, or other circumstances that amount to such violations. This can place forensic specialists in extremely compromising situations, which in certain circumstances may be tantamount to helping to obstruct justice. Forensic practitioners could find themselves doing this:

1. Willingly, by consciously failing to record and effectively document findings, including signs of abuse, or by failing to ensure that abuse is reported to the appropriate authorities able to stop, investigate, and punish it.
2. Reluctantly, where their own or professional values are outweighed by pressure or threats from the state authorities or from others.
3. Unconsciously, where insufficient training or skills results in failure to recognize and properly record relevant findings.

Any form of involvement and/or complicity in the obstruction of justice amounts to a breach of the forensic practitioner's professional ethical obligations, as well as a violation of applicable law.

In short, it must be recognized that it is a mark of civilization to identify the dead. Forensic practitioners must be qualified and competent to work in contexts involving missing persons, and they should only work within their respective sphere of expertise; they have an ethical duty to advocate actively for an identification process (which includes the collection of ante-mortem data and in certain contexts of blood samples from the family). When examining remains, forensic specialists have an ethical duty to observe and record all information potentially relevant to identification, and the procedures followed must not destroy material that may be used later. Forensic practitioners must consider the families' rights and needs before, during, and after exhumation. Human remains comprise both complete bodies and body parts, and consideration must be given to the disposal of unidentified remains in a way appropriate to the context. Forensic practitioners must be familiar with the pertinent provisions of IHL and international human rights law, and should advocate their incorporation into the basic training of forensic specialists; they have a duty to abide by the ethics of their profession and be aware of the challenges and threats they might face in contexts involving missing persons *(21)*.

2.3. Forensic Teams, Contracts, Employers

The authorities have ultimate responsibility for the management, exhumation, and identification of human remains. However, in contexts involving persons missing as a consequence of armed conflict, others may have to undertake this role and bring forensic specialists to the area.

When forensic practitioners move from their everyday domestic context to work in an international context and foreign jurisdiction, often for the first time, a specific person with relevant experience needs to be placed in charge of the examination of the remains. This person needs to have the qualifications, skills, and experience required to determine the identity of the human remains, the pathologies (including trauma) present, and the probable cause and manner of death.

The findings, conclusions, and reports signed by the forensic specialist in charge should be both formally valid and accepted as credible by local officials, the families, and (national and international) tribunals.

Before starting, the forensic specialists should make sure that the following questions are addressed when they are briefed or advised by the employer (whether a government service, international organization or other agency) and the relevant authorities. What is the legal framework within which they will be working? (The answers to other questions may determine this):

1. Which domestic and international law applies?
2. What part of the proposed work may be legal and what part may be illegal if performed by a foreign forensic specialist? For example, it may be lawful to watch a postmortem examination being performed by a local pathologist but unlawful under national law to conduct an exhumation.
3. Do the authorities recognize the forensic specialists' qualifications?
4. Is the contract with the employer recognized by the authorities?
5. What legal support is available if the forensic specialists are arrested (whether justifiably or unjustifiably) for doing their work?
6. Is the work, in fact, being done in a context that is unlawful or might be deemed unlawful in domestic law?
7. What is the mandate and legal standing of the employer (if not the authorities) in the context?
8. Can it be assumed that such work performed under the mandate of an international organization (i.e., the United Nations) automatically preempts domestic law?
9. Has the forensic work been incorporated into any kind of peace process to which the parties to the conflict are committed?

Forensic specialists must understand the different contexts and priorities the employer may attribute to their work. They must fully understand the employer's mission, including the broad legal and political framework of its operations and whether the employer is recognized as competent and credible and is willing to work with others. Forensic specialists should also be aware of the wider agenda the employer organization may have:

1. The promotion of human rights and the investigation of violations (organizations involved in human rights advocacy, such as Amnesty International, Physicians for Human Rights, and Human Rights Watch).
2. The promotion of IHL while preserving neutrality and impartiality (for example, the ICRC).
3. The question of criminal accountability (such as in the case of the International Criminal Court).

Much of the above relating to the role and responsibilities of forensic practitioners should be recognized by the employer and reflected in the contract. A contract by which a forensic practitioner is engaged to work in a context specifically involving missing persons should include the following:

1. An affirmation of professional qualifications.
2. A commitment to work by standard guidelines relating to exhumation, autopsies, and identification.
3. A commitment to, if necessary, exhume the remains, identify the body, and establish the cause of death on an impartial and objective basis.
4. A commitment to give equal consideration to the family in all matters pertaining to human remains and to ensure that the authorities or the employer have done everything possible to make sure that the families are informed and supported.
5. A commitment to treat any remains with due respect.
6. A commitment to brief any forensic specialist replacing him/her and to affirm the obligation that that person must continue to work by the same guidelines.
7. An indication of how this work will fit in with the mandate and legal status of the employer.
8. A clear understanding of who bears ultimate responsibility for exhuming remains, making the identification, and issuing a death certificate if the authorities are unable or unwilling to do this.
9. An assurance that the employer has obtained or will obtain security guarantees from the authorities.
10. A reference to the handling and preservation of all evidence by standard means.
11. An understanding that exhumation will include both identification and establishing the cause of death.
12. A clear indication of whether or not the forensic specialist is expected to present findings in court.
13. A commitment that health and safety procedures will be followed.
14. A commitment that adequate insurance coverage—such as malpractice insurance—has been provided for all eventualities, as the coverage pertaining to the specialist's domestic work may not apply.

15. In keeping with standard forensic practice, an agreement that the practitioner has the right to copy documents and photos for which he/she was responsible, subject to an undertaking of confidentiality, and acknowledgement that copyright lies with the employer.
16. Work-load forecasts for any action or investigation must be both realistic and professional.

Consideration of these points will help forensic practitioners work within a sound and ethical framework while promoting the application of IHL and international human rights law and at the same time minimizing the families' distress.

Failure to take account of these points could undermine the forensic practitioner's own credibility.

In short, the terms of reference or contract must ensure that the employer's mandate is compatible with the ethical and professional practice of forensic specialists.

All forensic work must be carried out within the framework of a clear mandate. This includes consideration of the legitimacy and lawfulness of the work and other short- and long-term considerations.

The mandate must be underpinned by the principles of neutrality and impartiality.

The employer must recognize the role and responsibilities outlined previously and the need to adhere to best-practice guidelines.

The employer must provide adequate background information about the context, including political, cultural, and security information.

The security of the investigating team and contributors has priority over the provision of evidence and identification.

2.4. Specialized Guidelines

Specific best-practice guidelines help forensic practitioners to act within the ethical and professional boundaries applicable to investigations into the missing and ensure they are observed in all circumstances. They must therefore be disseminated and promoted within the forensic community.

Best-practice guidelines should, wherever possible, accommodate local skills and expertise, and they should also contemplate the need for local capacity building, including the training of nonspecialists and partially qualified personnel; such training should be planned in the early stages of any mission or project.

Well known international guidelines include the *UN Manual on the Effective Prevention and Investigation of Extra-Legal, Arbitrary and Summary Executions* (Minnesota Protocol) *(22)* and the Interpol Disaster Victim Identification (DVI) protocol *(23)*.

The ICRC's own recommendations and operational best practices complement and expand existing references and guidelines for investigations into the missing.

One of the shared objectives of existing guidelines is, whenever possible, to subject human remains to one examination only. Examinations should not have to be repeated because previous examinations were incomplete. The same examination should serve to establish the cause and probable manner of death and to record the information needed to make a positive identification.

With regard to the use of the Minnesota Protocol *(22)*, some of its advantages are that it is widely recognized and comprehensive, and it represents standards of best practice. Some of its disadvantages are that it describes a standard autopsy and, therefore, contains much information that is redundant for a qualified forensic pathologist; is difficult to apply to all situations; it does not provide the means to document findings; it is difficult to read as a checklist for an inexperienced examiner; it does not discuss in detail the examination of skeletal or partial remains; and it has no information technology support tool.

With regard to use of the Interpol DVI autopsy protocol in contexts involving missing persons, some of the advantages are as follows: it is widely recognized and adapted for international use, and it has been translated into a number of official languages; it is easily translatable into an electronic format; it serves as a checklist; it provides an easy means to document autopsy findings; and it has an effective information technology support tool.

Its disadvantages are twofold: the section relating to missing body parts is not useful in relation to the examination of partial remains in all contexts, and it does not permit the systematic documentation of findings pertaining to relevant case history, injuries, and cause of death in most contexts of the missing.

Concerning antemortem data and postmortem data forms for identification purposes, these can be developed and adapted for particular contexts (*ad hoc* forms), with due consideration of the relative advantages and disadvantages of existing models, including the Minnesota Protocol and the Interpol DVI autopsy forms. Such *ad hoc* forms should:

1. Be designed to serve as both checklist and data collection form.
2. Be designed to be compatible with the development of appropriate software.
3. Be mutually compatible.
4. Be written in an international language and be able to accommodate a local language.
5. Use recognized terms in a consistent manner permitting translation.
6. Permit the inclusion of an autopsy report and a conclusion.

7. Include a reference to the chain of custody for the samples taken.
8. Be able to accommodate future revisions.
9. Be accompanied by specific training in its use.

Disadvantages of developing *ad hoc* forms include the further work required to prepare them and the fact that development and implementation will slow down the overall process of investigations, a point to be borne in mind when planning and funding the corresponding mission.

2.5. Exhumation of Human Remains

The main general phases are listed here and should be followed in strict order whenever possible, or otherwise the reasons should be documented accordingly:

1. Locating the gravesite.
2. Establishing a security perimeter.
3. If permitted, photographing and documenting surface features/evidence.
4. Establishing the boundaries of the grave.
5. Removing the overburden and topsoil covering the remains.
6. Exposing the remains with forensic archaeology methods and techniques suitable for the case and context.
7. Mapping and photograph the remains.
8. Noting the position of the remains, labeling distinctly, and keeping separate any personal effects or other objects not attached to the remains (e.g., keys, bullets).
9. Labeling all remains distinctly and individually, whether parts or whole bodies.
10. Removing the remains (while keeping them as an entire body if possible).
11. Transporting and storing the remains in a safe container and place.
12. If appropriate and whenever possible, allowing the family immediate visual access for the purposes of identification (*see* discussion regarding steps for identification in the following subheadings).

2.6. Conducting Forensic Work When Only External Examination Is Possible

In contexts involving missing persons, forensic pathologists may sometimes find themselves unable to perform a full autopsy because of extreme constraints, including security. It may be necessary under such difficult conditions, with little time and without access to mortuary facilities, to examine a number of bodies with an aim to both identify them and establish the cause of death. This would pose a problem for any forensic specialist, but performing only an external examination would be compatible with professional conduct given the constraints, as long as the supporting reasons are duly noted and recorded.

The objective of such an abbreviated examination is to collect and preserve as much information as possible within the constraints of the case, with an aim to maximize the chances of later identification.

A forensic pathologist is best qualified to perform such an abbreviated examination of recently dead bodies, whereas forensic anthropologists might be best equipped to examine skeletal remains.

2.7. Responsibility and Accountability for the Identification of Human Remains

Identification is a central aspect of the investigation into a suspicious death, which complements the answers to other key questions, such as the cause, time, and manner of death.

Human remains are usually examined and identified by means of a team effort, under the overall responsibility of a professional with the necessary qualifications, skills, and experience required for identification procedures. It is therefore highly preferable that this person be a fully competent and qualified forensic practitioner, and normally (if available), a forensic pathologist, as this reflects legal arrangements in most parts of the world.

Ultimately, the authorities bear the responsibility of ensuring that human remains are identified by qualified and competent people.

It is the responsibility of the head of the forensic team to decide which methods of identification are most appropriate in a given context. It is also his or her responsibility to ensure that relatives, the community, and the authorities are well and fully informed about the limitations of the methods chosen to identify human remains, to minimize unrealistic or false expectations.

Constraints on resources—whether human, financial or logistical, or particular circumstances of a mission—may justify a lapse in the standards. This does not absolve the person in charge and/or the overall employer of responsibility for the approach and means used to identify human remains and the corresponding results.

When there is no competent authority, regional or international organizations can be instrumental in supporting families or close acquaintances through the process of identifying human remains and in preserving as much information as possible about missing persons, human remains that have not been identified officially, and unidentified human remains.

2.8. Means of Identifying Human Remains

Human remains are identified in three main ways: visually, by circumstantial evidence, and/or by scientific/objective methods.

1. Visual or customary (i.e., relatives or acquaintances viewing the remains, identity documents, or tags).
   a. Visual identification may be the only pragmatic option (i.e., in difficult security situations, with recently killed, complete bodies, where the families are present and no other possibility for formal identification exists). However, it is known to carry a significant risk of misidentification, and should only be resorted to when the bodies are well preserved and there is a good idea as to who the victims are. Otherwise, more objective methods should be used.
   b. Where visual identification is used, consideration should be given to collecting a sample for later DNA analysis should the need arise; however, even this apparently simple measure may be difficult to perform in the field.
2. The weight of circumstantial evidence (e.g., matching of antemortem data with information collected during the examination). When the identification is made by matching antemortem data with postmortem data and associated evidence (i.e., clothing), some "hard" features, such as previous medical conditions and frontal sinus radiology, equate with "scientific" means. Without such hard identifiers, there is a risk of misidentification (which, in fact, represents declaring a presumptive identification to be an identification, but also wrongly excluding a positive identification).
3. Scientific/objective methods (dental records, X-rays, fingerprints, unique medical conditions, or DNA).

    These three steps do not necessarily follow one after another, but normal practice is that, as identification becomes more difficult, the emphasis moves from point 1 to point 2 to point 3.

    The condition of the remains should be taken into account in order to adopt the most efficient means of identification in situations: whether the bodies are whole, few, or numerous, commingled or partial; degrees of decomposition; and whether there are few or numerous skeletal remains.

    Means of identifying human remains may of course be combined for more-reliable results:

4. Identification by visual/normal/customary means plus matching of antemortem data with postmortem data. This is appropriate in situations similar to those described in 1, above, but where there is more time available, doubt about identity, or the family is not present immediately and scientific/objective means cannot be used. Any positive identification should be agreed on, if possible, by two qualified people.
5. Identification by visual/normal/customary means plus a scientific/objective means. This is appropriate in situations similar to point 1, above, but in which scientific/objective means can be used, there is more time or doubt about identity, or there is a dispute with legal implications. This may be appropriate in cases of re-exhumation.
6. Identification by matching antemortem data with postmortem data only. This means should only lead to positive identification if there are matching hard identification features. The identification should be concluded by agreement between

two qualified people. Without hard identification features, matching antemortem data with postmortem data may be used to supplement both 1 above and 2 below.

7. Identification by matching antemortem data with antemortem data plus scientific/objective means. Identification by these means is the most certain route to true identification.

8. Identification by scientific/objective means only. This refers to matching of fingerprints, matching of antemortem dental records with postmortem dental examination, or DNA analysis. Each has its advantages and disadvantages in contexts involving missing persons:

  a. All require additional expertise and possibly laboratory resources:
  b. Fingerprints can lead to the rapid identification of fresh bodies if antemortem prints are available; the principal disadvantages of using fingerprints are that it requires soft tissue on the hands of the remains and the existence of antemortem records, which are rarely available in the many contexts considered in this chapter.
  c. Matching of antemortem dental records with postmortem dental examination is most appropriate when the remains are burned, skeletal, or in an advanced state of decomposition; as with fingerprints, antemortem dental records are a prerequisite, and they are rarely available in the contexts considered here.
  d. DNA is the only means, apart from those alluded to in 2, above, of making an objective/scientific identification if there are skeletal remains but no antemortem records; DNA analysis sometimes provides the only reliable means of identifying and assembling partial remains.

Whenever possible, a visual (normal or customary) identification should be supplemented with identification by one of the other two methods.

Human remains should be identified with DNA analysis when other investigative techniques of identification are inadequate and the legal and ethical conditions defined for the use of DNA have been fulfilled (*see* Subheading 2.9.).

Governments, regional, and international intergovernmental and nongovernmental organizations and the ICRC must exercise greatest care not to introduce double standards in the methods used to identify human remains, ensuring that whatever the approach to identification, it must be adapted to the context, a process that may have security, political, financial, cultural, legal technical and/or scientific ramifications, and it must be agreed to by all those involved before the identification process starts. In addition, it must:

1. Include decisions and protocols regarding the collection of antemortem data and, possibly, of samples for DNA analysis.
2. Include autopsy and identification protocols.
3. Be implemented under the responsibility of the head of the forensic team.

2.9. The Use of DNA Analysis to Identify Human Remains in the Contexts Considered in This Chapter

DNA analysis must not preclude the use of other objective means of identification and should therefore not be considered as the first and sole method available for making a positive identification because it is not always feasible from a financial and/or operational perspective; it raises unfounded expectations and demands from families of the missing, who might thus dismiss other sound methods of identification; and handling and laboratory errors (e.g., contamination, inadequate standards, incorrect labeling of samples, etc.) cannot be ruled out, thus making crosschecking of results, including the use of traditional methods of identification, mandatory.

The decision to use DNA analysis should therefore be based on sound scientific and practical considerations within the identification process strategy defined for a given context. It should not be based only on demands for DNA analysis generated by individuals, families, communities, organizations or governments; laws must not be enacted requiring mandatory DNA analysis for the purpose of identification; requests by governments, organizations or individuals for the re-exhumation of remains previously identified with traditional means for the purpose of DNA analysis should be decided on a case-by-case basis; and even if the laboratory is of the highest standard, it may not have the technical or personnel capacity to undertake an increased workload at short notice.

In the preliminary phases of investigations into the missing, the social, religious, and cultural characteristics of the community concerned must always be taken into consideration. The families and the community will accept the outcome more readily if they have confidence in the investigation, without undue demands for DNA analysis when this is not necessary.

When DNA analysis is deemed necessary for identification, it must be performed in laboratories that:

1. Are accredited with international standards of quality, such as the International Standard Organization (ISO) 17025.
2. Handle remains, samples, and data in accordance with the rules governing the protection of personal data and human remains, which include the protection of antemortem data and DNA samples and results.
3. The laboratory performing the analysis must not operate based on maximum profit.
4. Commercial considerations should be minimized, and the accounts must be externally audited.
5. Any contract with a laboratory must include a reference to the rules governing the protection of personal data and human remains.

6. The use of anonymous data collected during DNA analysis for the purposes of research, for example, to establish allele frequencies, should be duly consulted and be in full accordance with applicable national and international standards.

2.10. Preconditions for Including DNA Analysis in a Program to Identify Human Remains

The conditions under which DNA samples are collected should be clearly defined beforehand and in accordance with international standards, and investigators have a duty to ensure that donors of reference samples are duly informed about the rules governing the protection of personal and genetic information (informed consent). It is the responsibility of the head of the forensic team to seek compliance of these rules by all those involved in the investigations, including the laboratory.

An expert evaluation or appraisal of the need for DNA analysis must be carried out when the identification strategy for a given context is drawn up. This will determine, to some extent, the resources required. The DNA techniques proposed should be feasible and practicable in the given context, and they should be reliable and scientifically valid. The forensic laboratories and the DNA database used should be accredited or in compliance with standards such as the ISO Guide ISO/IEC 17025. The information technology used to analyze and match DNA samples must be appropriate for the context. The financial costs must also be considered; these will vary substantially depending on the number and type of analyses required (i.e., nuclear DNA, mitochondrial DNA, an so forth). The additional costs and complexity involved in using DNA must be outweighed by the anticipated results as well as by the additional social benefit of the investment.

Prior consideration should also be given to the positive and negative unintended impact on preexisting legal and forensic services. Strategies must be established for dealing with errors of identification and with partial, commingled, or unidentified human remains.

In relation to resources and logistics:

1. The logistical implications include collection, storage, transport, and a chain of custody agreed to by all those concerned.
2. The number of those involved, including the number of laboratories, should be kept to a minimum.
3. There is an important distinction between samples taken for DNA analysis to be performed within the country and those taken for analysis abroad.
4. If there is no overall coordinating body in charge of collecting and labeling samples, it should be clearly established how those samples are to be transported and analyzed, and this should be stipulated in advance according to competencies and in a written contract.

All those involved in the process must agree on communication, information, and counseling strategies for the communities and individuals concerned. The information must be realistic but should not discourage participation.

With regard to DNA, it should be mentioned that it is not always required for identification, it is not always possible to extract DNA from remains, and positive results will not always be achieved.

Appropriate mechanisms providing, for example, for confidentiality, follow-up, and services must be established for informing the families about the process.

Finally, there should be an "exit strategy" for any program using DNA analysis to identify human remains, including planned transferal of facilities and expertise once the investigation is completed.

2.11. Community and Family Involvement in an Exhumation and/or Identification Process: General Principles, Including for the Collection of Antemortem Data

All forensic investigations into the missing resulting from armed conflict or internal violence, including exhumations, must be carried out in constant interaction with the concerned communities and with the families or their representatives, who should be consulted accordingly and kept fully informed of the process and results. The notion of "family," including its size and the roles of those included in it, may vary considerably in different cultural contexts. This needs to be borne in mind in order to help ensure the best possible interaction with the families of the missing persons, including for the optimal collection of antemortem data.

Communities and families are usually deeply traumatized when their members go missing in the context of armed conflict or internal violence, and the process of identifying remains may simply add to the trauma. The social and psychological affect of investigations on communities and families should therefore be assessed as part of their planning. Preventive measures should be adopted accordingly.

Investigators must be also aware that any undignified or unskillful handling of remains and information (real or perceived) may further traumatize the families of the missing.

The relationship between the forensic specialists and the communities and families is always complex. A forensic specialist may feel either constrained or empowered within this relationship, which is influenced by the following:

1. How information about investigations is transmitted to the communities and families.
2. The purpose of the investigation, i.e., whether it focuses on the identification of remains or on a criminal investigation.
3. The extent and timescale of the investigation.
4. Who is conducting the investigation—the police, the military, a government body, an nongovernmental organization, an international forensic team, a United Nations body, and so forth (forensic practitioners holding official positions in government alleged to be involved in atrocities may generate considerable suspicion or outright animosity).
5. Whether the perpetrators are still at large (this will affect the security of witnesses and may affect the relatives' own readiness to help locate graves, testify, or provide antemortem data).
6. Whether the families believe any information resulting from the investigation will be used for their benefit or in the genuine interests of justice.
7. Whether and how the forensic specialists and other team members interact with the community, including attending the funerals of the people whose remains they have identified.

The extent to which the communities or families are involved in the exhumation should be decided on a case-by-case basis taking into account:

1. The results of any consultation with the communities and families.
2. Whether the family wishes to be present or represented by a qualified person.
3. The overall possible benefit to the families.
4. The possibility that the investigation will be compromised, including by political interference.
5. The possibility that the families may suffer further trauma, especially if they perceive the investigation as being unnecessarily prolonged, the information collected in an insensitive way, or the remains perceived to be handled unprofessionally, in an undignified manner, or disrespectfully.
6. Security considerations.

In addition, the community or family may know where remains or graves are or are likely to be situated (including in territory controlled by the former enemy), facilitate identification of remains after recovery, provide security at the site of the investigation, and/or wish to veto the exhumation (this requires careful consideration).

Informing the communities and families about the exhumation requires a communication strategy. Realistic appraisals must be given of the outcome, and information should be updated regularly. Investigators should be aware that family observation of the exhumation process may lead to easier acceptance of the results; religious or community leaders (who are not connected to the authorities) should be contacted and consulted in some contexts; it may be appropriate to discuss some form of memorial for the victims at an early stage; and any psychiatrists, psychologists, social workers, or traditional healers who might be working with the families addressing their particular needs should be contacted and consulted accordingly.

Establishing a good relationship with the families of those missing is essential for meaningful antemortem data collection.

The collection of antemortem data may not involve forensic specialists, but the data and samples collected will be of no value unless they can be compared with the findings of and by forensic specialists.

In principle, therefore, before any antemortem data are collected, a framework for the exhumation and identification process must be defined and agreed to by all those involved, particularly concerning the legal rules governing the protection of personal data and human remains, which include the protection of antemortem data, and ownership and management of the antemortem data.

In principle, therefore, antemortem data should not be collected outside the framework of a planned process to collect, exhume, and identify remains. The fact that antemortem data are collected from a family suggests that the missing relative is dead and induces great hope that the remains will be found; if no such data are being collected but there is a strong suspicion of death, the family's tracing request must be exhaustively completed as the recollection of important details fades with time.

Once the prerequisites have been met, the collection process must be well prepared and coordinated with all those concerned. Staff in charge of the collection process must be identified, selected, trained, and supported to avoid secondary trauma.

Psychological support for the families or individuals must be systematically planned and provided as an integral part of the collection process in order to help avoid retraumatization.

In principle, the aim should be to carry out only one interview with the family (even if conducted in several phases). Multiple interviews and subsequent requests for further information might further traumatize the family.

Whenever possible, the process of collecting antemortem data should be organized for groups of people who became unaccounted for in the same circumstances or during a specific event and/or whose remains might be expected to be found in the same location. This should facilitate the planning of exhumations and speed up the process of identification.

A communication strategy that is agreed to by all those concerned must be implemented. The communities and families must be realistically informed about the processes by which antemortem data and DNA samples are collected and remains exhumed and identified.

3. CONCLUSION

In observing the humanitarian implications of their profession and following existing guidelines, recommendations, and operational best practices for investigations into the missing, such as those adopted by the ICRC, forensic practitioners help fulfill the right of the families to know the fate of their loved ones and to relieve their suffering. They also help develop and expand the value and scope of action of applicable and complementary forensic knowledge, including forensic archaeology, pathology, and anthropology.

REFERENCES

1. UN Manual on the effective prevention and investigation of extra-legal, arbitrary and summary executions, 1991—unpublished. Sales No. E.91.IV.1 (doc.ST/CSDHA/12).
2. Guidelines for the conduct of United Nations inquiries into allegations of massacres, 1997—unpublished. Sales No. E.97.1.21.
3. Istanbul Protocol: Manual on the Effective Investigation and Documentation of Torture and Other Cruel, Inhuman or Degrading Treatment or Punishment, 2001—unpublished. Sales No. E.01.XIV.1.
4. International Conference of Governmental and Non-Governmental Experts (Geneva, 19-21.02.2003), Outcome in: The Missing: Action to resolve the problem of people unaccounted for as a result of armed conflict or internal violence and to assist their families—Documents of Reference, http://www.icrc.org/Web/eng/siteeng0.nsf/htmlall/881CB6F1912554CDC1256CD40041F954/$File/TheMissing_Conf_022003_EN_1AND82.pdf. Last accessed Mar. 7, 2006.
5. ICRC Report: The Missing and Their Families—Summary of the Conclusions arising from Events Held prior to the International Conference of Governmental and Non-Governmental Experts (19–21 February 2003) (ICRC/TheMissing/01.2003/EN/10;http://www.icrc.org/Web/eng/siteeng0.nsf/htmlall/5JAHR8/$File/ICRC_TheMissing_012003_EN_10.pdf). Last accessed Mar. 7, 2006.
6. A Glimpse of Hell: Reports on Torture Worldwide. Duncan Forrest, London, 1996.
7. Report submitted by Mr. Manfred Nowak, independent expert charged with examining the existing international criminal and human rights framework for the protection of persons from enforced or involuntary disappearances, pursuant to paragraph 11 of Commission resolution 2001/46, UN Commission on Human Rights, Fifty-eighth session, E/CN.4/2002/71. 8. Inter-American Court of Human Rights, Blake Case. Reparations (Art. 63[1] of the American Convention on Human Rights), Judgment of January 22, 1999. Series C No. 48.

9. The legal protection of personal data & human remains, Electronic Workshop, 02.04.2002–06.05.2002: Final report and outcome (ICRC/TheMissing/07.2002/EN/1).
10. Member of armed forces and armed groups: identification, family news, killed in action, prevention, Workshop, 06.05.2002–07.05.2002, Ecogia ICRC Training Center, Geneva, Switzerland: Final report and outcome (ICRC/TheMissing/08.2002/EN/2).
11. Human remains and forensic sciences, Electronic Workshop, 02.2002–03.2002; Human remains: Law, politics and ethics, 23.05.2002–24.05.2002 and Human remains: management of remains and of information on the dead, 10.07.2002–12.07.2002, Workshops, Ecogia ICRC Training Center, Geneva, Switzerland: Final report and outcome (ICRC/TheMissing/10.2002/EN/3).
12. Support to families of people unaccounted for, Workshop, 10.06.2002–11.06.2002, Ecogia ICRC Training Center, Geneva, Switzerland: Final report and outcome (ICRC/TheMissing/08.2002/EN/4).
13. Means to prevent disappearances and to process missing cases, Workshop, 24.07.2002–26.07.2002, Ecogia ICRC Training Center, Geneva, Switzerland: Final report and outcome (ICRC/TheMissing/10.2002/EN/5).
14. Mechanisms to solve issues on people unaccounted for, Workshop, 19.09.2002–20.09.2002, Ecogia ICRC Training Center, Geneva, Switzerland: Final report and outcome (ICRC/TheMissing/12.2002/EN/6).
15. Mourning process and commemorations. Study—Report and recommendations, Drawn up under the direction of Yvan Droz, Doctor of Ethnology, associate professor at the Geneva Graduate Institute of Development Studies (IUED), in cooperation with Sylvain Froidevaux, Doctor in Social Sciences, commissioned by the IUED (ICRC/TheMissing/10.2002/EN/7).
16. Overcoming the tensions between family needs and judicial procedures. Study—Report and recommendations by Ms Vasuki Nesiah, Senior Associate, International Center for Transitional Justice (ICRC/TheMissing/09.2002/EN/8).
17. Study on existing mechanisms to clarify the fate of people unaccounted for. Report and recommendations by Jean-François Rioux, Professor of conflict studies at Saint-Paul University, Ottawa, Canada and Marco Sassòli, Professor of public international law at the Université du Québec à Montréal, Canada, with the assistance of Mr. Mountaga Diagne and Ms. Marianne Reux, research assistants at the Université du Québec à Montréal (ICRC/TheMissing/01.2003/EN/9).
18. The missing—events. http://www.icrc.org/Web/eng/siteeng0.nsf/htmlall/section_ihl_missing_persons?OpenDocument. Last accessed Mar. 23, 2006.
19. The Missing: Action to resolve the problem of people unaccounted for as a result of armed conflict or internal violence and to assist their families—Documents of Reference or at http://www.icrc.org. Last accessed Mar. 7, 2006.
20. Human remains and forensic sciences—Electronic workshop 02–03.2002; Human remains: Law, politics and ethics 23–24.05.2002; and Human remains: management of remains and of information on the dead 10–12.07.2002 (ICRC/TheMissing/10.2002/EN/3); http://www.icrc.org/Web/eng/siteeng0.nsf/htmlall/5CALR3/$File/ICRC_TheMissing_102002_EN_3.pdf. Last accessed Mar. 7, 2006.

21. World Medical Association statement on forensic investigations of the missing, adopted by the WMA General Assembly, Helsinki 2003 (http://www.wma.net/e/policy/m34.htm).
22. United Nations Manual on the Effective Prevention and Investigation of Extra Legal, Arbitrary or Summary Executions ("Minnesota Protocol"), United Nations Publication, ISBN 92-1-330132-4, 1991.
23. Interpol Disaster Victim Identification Guide. http://www.interpol.int/Public/DisasterVictim/Guide. Last accessed Mar. 7, 2006.

Chapter 17

Crimes Against Humanity

Dario M. Olmo

Summary

This chapter discusses how forensic anthropology enables the examination and documentation of crimes against humanity long after they have been committed. It shows how to obtain the evidence to sustain the criminal prosecution of people who are responsible. The development of forensic anthropology, particularly in the context of the post-1970s Argentine experience, is discussed. Furthermore, two recent cases that illustrate in detail the field's methods are given.

Key Words: Crimes against humanity; biological anthropology; archaeological anthropology; Argentina.

1. INTRODUCTION

Crimes against humanity are not new, nor are they exclusive to any historical period. Rather, they are a type of social behavior that can be found across the historical and geographical board. It is only in recent times, however, that increased global interdependence has resulted in the creation of supranational juridical figures, among them that of "crimes against humanity." The phrase refers to offences against individuals and communities, which, given their nature, offend humankind as a whole. There is no statute of limitations to them; their criminal prosecution must be carried out irrespective of where and when the crimes were committed, and they do not contemplate "due obedience" to higher orders as an exculpatory argument *(1)*.

This chapter analyzes the possibility of examining and documenting these crimes long after they have been committed and obtaining the evidence to

From *Forensic Anthropology and Medicine:*
Complementary Sciences From Recovery to Cause of Death
Edited by: A. Schmitt, E. Cunha, and J. Pinheiro © Humana Press Inc., Totowa, NJ

sustain the criminal prosecution of those responsible for them. The delay is usually explained in political terms. In most cases, it takes a considerable amount of time before the political circumstances in a country or region change to facilitate the investigation. However, nature will take its course. When years elapse between the actual murders and their investigation, there is usually a definitive and irreparable loss of soft tissues in the human remains. A forensic pathologist can hardly work without them.

In these cases, it is necessary to resort to the tools afforded by sciences such as archaeology and its auxiliary disciplines. In North and South America, a traditional approach to labor division among the forensic disciplines placed the examination of hard tissues in the field of biological anthropology. Forensic anthropology results from a synthesis of biological anthropology and archaeology, and can be defined as the application of knowledge on human variability to the medicolegal field with the purpose of contributing to the investigation and documentation of human rights violations *(2)*. This chapter will trace the development of forensic anthropology, particularly in the context of the post-1970s Argentine experience, and then present two more recent cases that will illustrate the field's methods in some detail.

2. CRIMES AGAINST HUMANITY: A BRIEF HISTORY

Romanian jurist Eugene Aronèanu posits *(3)* that crimes against humanity arise from the criminal exercise of sovereign authority. Genocide as well as other "crimes of lese-humanity" (e.g., war crimes, summary or extrajudicial executions, torture and forced disappearances, and so forth) are now considered crimes not only against international law (*crimina juris gentium*), but also against customary international law.

The phrase "crimes of lese-humanity" was first used on May 2, 1915, by the Allied Forces (the governments of the United Kingdom, France, and Russia) to refer to the Armenian genocide carried out by the Ottoman Empire (Turkey). Through a joint declaration, these three governments described the Armenian genocide as a crime against humanity and civilization, and announced that they would hold personally responsible not only those among their agents who were implicated in the massacre, but also all the members of the Ottoman government. By contrast, the United States and Japan strongly opposed advances in international legislation in this regard *(1)*.

The Treaty of Sèvres (August 10, 1920) marked the first appearance of crimes against humanity as a juridical figure in an international covenant; Article 230 states that the Turkish government should hand over to the Allied Powers the persons responsible for the massacres (committed not only against the Armenian people but against Turkish nationals as well) to be tried by *ad hoc* tribunals *(4)*. This treaty was never ratified by the Turkish government.

The first characterization of crimes against humanity as an effective instrument of international criminal law has to be found in the Statute of the International Military Tribunal at Nuremberg in the aftermath of World War II. Since the Holocaust, a large number of incidents have been deemed serious enough to qualify as crimes against humanity. Some of them have resulted in the creation of international tribunals to try those responsible for the crimes, as was the case in Rwanda and in the former Yugoslavia. One of the most accurate documents in this regard is the "Draft Code of Crimes against Peace and Security of Mankind" produced by the UN International Law Commission *(5)*. Article 18 of the Draft Code defines crimes against humanity as "any of the following acts: murder, torture, enslavement, enforced disappearance of persons, among others...committed in a systematic manner or on a large scale and instigated or directed by a Government or by any organisation or group." A comprehensive description of crimes against humanity is also made in Articles 5 and 7 of the Rome Statute of the International Criminal Court (Fig. 1) *(6)*.

Despite international sanction, however, at the national level, the process of incorporating this legislation has proved slow and painful. The most recent—and notorious—setback in this regard has been the current Bush administration's refusal to accept the jurisdiction of the International Criminal Court over United States citizens. Recent reports around the world cast a pessimistic shadow, but at the same time lead to a search for new ways of preventing and punishing such criminal acts.

3. The Interface of Forensic Anthropology and Human Rights: The Argentine Case

Argentina offers a case that required one such new approach in the search for justice as well as an experience that is characteristic of recent human rights violations in the context of political turmoil.

As Argentina emerged from years of dictatorship in the mid-1980s, the international scientific community (and particularly the US forensic community) decided to allocate the financial and human resources to help trace the whereabouts of thousands of victims of crimes against humanity. In fact, the Argentine case was one of the first in which internationally sponsored forensic methods were applied systematically, to the extent that the experience laid the foundation for a practice that would become common in the years to come. It also served as a model for other Latin American countries to imitate, with a

---

Article 5. Crimes within the jurisdiction of the Court

1. The jurisdiction of the Court shall be limited to the most serious crimes of concern to the international community as a whole. The Court has jurisdiction in accordance with this Statute with respect to the following crimes:
    a) The crime of genocide
    b) Crimes against humanity
    c) War crimes
    d) The crime of aggression

(...)

Article 7. Crimes against humanity

1. For the purpose of this Statute, "crime against humanity" means any of the following acts when committed as part of a widespread or systematic attack directed against any civilian population, with knowledge of the attack:
    a) Murder
    b) Extermination
    c) Enslavement
    d) Deportation or forcible transfer of population
    e) Imprisonment or other severe deprivation of physical liberty in violation of fundamental rules of international law
    f) Torture
    g) Rape, sexual slavery, enforced prostitution, forced pregnancy, enforced sterilisation, or any other form of sexual violence of comparable gravity
    h) Persecution against any identifiable group or collectivity on political, racial, national, ethnic, cultural, religious, gender as defined in paragraph 3, or other grounds that are universally recognized as impermissible under international law, in connection with any act referred to in this paragraph or any crime within the jurisdiction of the Court
    i) Enforced disappearance of persons
    j) The crime of apartheid
    k) Other inhumane acts of a similar character intentionally causing great suffering, or serious injury to body or to mental or physical health.

Fig. 1. Rome Statute of the International Criminal Court, section on crimes against humanity.

subsequent expansion of the field to other regions of the world facing similar situations. It might be helpful at this point to provide further background to help understand how the different actors converged in time and place, and how this convergence evolved in the context of a timely political atmosphere that made this scientific contribution feasible.

In the mid-20th century, Argentina was embroiled in an alternation of civilian and military governments. The armed forces, and the army in particular, considered it their natural right to exert "guardianship" over representative democracies that it viewed as no longer reliable. This view was tradition-ally shared by the dominant sectors of Argentine society, which usually encouraged military "interventions," proof of which is the fact that only one case of constitutional succession (in fact a reelection) took place between 1930 and 1983. The latest coup by the armed forces led to the regime that ruled over the country between 1976 and 1983—a regime that, among other features, engaged in the terrorist practice of political persecution of targeted sectors of the population. The military ignored every legal constraint on their actions; they committed flagrant, massive violations of human rights, i.e., what has been defined as crimes against humanity.

The systematic violation of human rights was the response of the domi-nant sectors of Argentine society to mobilization of, and questioning from, vast sectors of the population, among them organizations that challenged the state's monopoly on the use of force. The Argentine Army openly adhered to the contemporaneous counterinsurgency doctrines applied by European and American colonial powers in North Africa and Southeast Asia; however, whereas these operated against foreign and remote populations, the Argen-tine (and Guatemalan) Armed Forces operated at home and against conationals. In *a posteriori* accounts of what happened during their rule, the military con-firmed this conceptual genealogy. These doctrines promoted the practice of the enforced disappearance of persons, which was considered an efficient tool to discourage and terrorize the subversive movement.

This practice was an outrageous mockery of the international legislation on armed conflicts, whether regular or irregular, and a dramatic retreat from the principles that emerged from the Nuremberg trials. It is worth noting that, for the last quarter of the 20th century, Amnesty International reported the practice of enforced disappearance in more than 70 countries. Argentina was among those at the top of the list for the abuse of human rights at the hands of a state whose heads were violating every law they claimed to defend.

With minor differences depending on the locale, the pattern of illegal abduction, clandestine imprisonment, torture, and execution of thousands of citizens spread through the country in the mid-1970s. These crimes were per-petrated by various intelligence sectors of the armed and security forces with the support of the military institutions and the government they represented. In 1982, the regime further engaged in a military adventure against a NATO member—the United Kingdom—for the possession of the Malvinas, an archipelago in the South Atlantic, which ended in disaster with the military government debilitated beyond recovery. This provided a window of oppor-tunity for a return to democracy and for a revision, although timid, of the recent past.

What is most disturbing about the repression strategy is probably the clandestine nature of military activities. This aspect was of great concern in a society that was not used to massive manifestations of state terrorism. On the grounds of vague, often inconsistent imputability criteria, targeted citizens were abducted and confined to clandestine detention centers where they were denied every constitutional right. Torture was regularly used to undermine the prisoners' convictions and obtain information that was in turn used toward new abductions. Finally, the fate of the detained was decided by one of the men in charge of the repression groups; this was usually summary execution, with no review by the legal system. Nevertheless, the state consistently denied engaging in illegal detentions; in the same spirit, the courts of justice rejected the *habeas corpus* petitions presented by the relatives of the "disappeared."

Each murder entailed the problem of disposal of the body, a kind of aftereffect to be taken care of. The army's organizational division of national territory is a crucial starting point when trying to determine the fate of the bodies of the people who were abducted and murdered. In regions where air transportation was available, the bodies were dumped from planes into the nearest sea or river (mainly the Mar Argentino or the Río de la Plata). However, task groups were sometimes instructed not to dispose of the bodies in this manner, but to abandon them in suburban wastelands instead. The district's officer in command would then issue a press release informing about an "armed struggle" between "irregulars" and government forces invariably resulting in the death of the former. The bureaucratic procedure indicated that the bodies should be labeled "of unknown identity found in a public space," and the routine generated a series of documents reproduced by this typically impassive, indifferent bureaucracy. Most of these bodies ended up in "No Name" (NN) or "John Doe" graves at the closest public cemetery. A body was occasionally retrieved from the sea and buried as NN at the district cemetery. The stripping of the victims' identity was the hallmark of the system.

One of society's unanticipated responses was the emergence of a number of collectives organized by people affected by state terrorism, generally relatives of the "disappeared." When they assembled to inquire about the whereabouts of their loved ones in open confrontation with the state, they acted on the moral force of their blood ties and emotional bonds, as reflected in the names of the organizations they formed: Madres de Plaza de Mayo (Mothers of Plaza de Mayo), Abuelas de Plaza de Mayo (Grandmothers of Plaza de Mayo), Familiares de Detenidos y Desaparecidos por Razones Políticas (Association of Families of the Detained and "Disappeared" for Political Reasons), and so on. The self-styled nature of these collectives and their members' political inexperience turned out to be a tactical advantage: their movements were neither predictable nor easy to control.

Abuelas de Plaza de Mayo is an organization formed by grandmothers of persons disappeared along with their children or, in many cases, of couples who were expecting a child at the time of their abduction. A peculiar feature of the Argentine case is the frequency with which children were appropriated, a crime known as *sustracción de identidad* (literally, "identity robbery"): after the abduction and clandestine murder of their parents, these children were handed over to families of, or related to, the military or the police, who claimed them and raised them as their own. In the late 1970s, Abuelas toured a number of capital cities of the world to report on the Argentine situation. One of their claims resonated in the scientific community: the need for a tool to establish consanguinity. The imperative spurred a number of projects in this line, such as the determination of histocompatibility antigens (or HLA system) to establish consanguinity between grandparents and grandchildren, a method that is typically used to assess the viability of organ transplantation but which, at the request of the Abuelas, is still being used to verify their biological relationship with abducted children.

In 1984, when the new democratically elected government was already in power, there was frequent news of judicially mandated exhumations at many public cemeteries. These resulted from the growing volume of allegations that bodies buried as NN belonged to the citizens whose enforced disappearance had been reported mainly between 1976 and 1977. After 8 yr, the remains thus exhumed were fully skeletonized; they bore no traces of soft tissue. Moreover, the absence of adequate exhumation techniques or correct treatment and study of the remains led to careless excavations, the commingling of remains and, ultimately, to irreparable damage.

At the joint request of Abuelas de Plaza de Mayo and an Investigative Commission (Comisión Nacional sobre la Desaparición de Personas, i.e., National Commission on the Disappearance of Persons) appointed by the constitutional government, the American Association for the Advancement of Science* summoned a number of US forensic specialists who went on to visit Argentina and contribute their expertise to the ongoing projects. Headed by Eric Stover, the group included, among others, forensic anthropologist Clyde Collins Snow, a prominent figure in the American forensic community.

Snow had long claimed that the work of forensic anthropologists should begin not at the laboratory, but at the exhumation site to ensure the proper

---

* An interdisciplinary research association founded in the 19th century by Lewis Morgan, the father of modern anthropology.

recovery of skeletal remains for careful examination. His line of reasoning led him to request the assistance of archaeologists, used to recovering valuable material by means of meticulous techniques to prevent the loss of information. Faced with such primitive exhumations, Snow further asked the Argentine Anthropology Association (Colegio de Graduados en Antropología) to select a group of local professionals to help exhume the remains and prevent future damage. The Association ignored his request; he never received a reply.

In view of the situation, Snow welcomed the aid of a group of anthropology and medicine students, some of whom had experience in prehistoric archaeology and were acquainted with the routine care of recovered remains. Their joint work proved to be useful, and the results were substantially different from those of prior investigations, permitting a significant number of positive identifications and the return of the remains to their families to end the indefinite, devastating uncertainty inflicted by the enforced disappearances.

Beyond scientific methods *per se*, there is an aspect of forensic work that is essential to a positive identification from the study of bone remains: the retrieval of accurate, reliable documentation on the persons involved (such as X-rays of old fractures and/or dental records) that may provide features that are easy to identify on hard tissues. These antemortem data are correlated with postmortem data, i.e., the information collected at the laboratory after careful analysis of the remains.

After initial success by the group that Snow had trained, however, it became increasingly difficult to obtain antemortem data. This forced the group to retrieve bureaucratically generated information stored in the archives of a terrorist state. Thus began a new stage of their work involving a whole new meticulous learning process that eventually permitted the identification of several additional hundreds of disappeared citizens and the return of their remains to their families.

The original group of students continued to work in close collaboration with Snow to gain further experience in the field; in time, they became full-time researchers and formed the Argentine Forensic Anthropology Team (Equipo Argentino de Antropología Forense [EAAF], www.eaaf.org). As they continued to work in Argentina, the EAAF traveled to various countries where political conflict had led to a similar perpetration of crimes against humanity by the state. The successful investigation into the fate of the disappeared in Argentina became known, and the restitution of identified remains provided the solid evidence that was necessary to bring those responsible for committing crimes to trial in Argentina and elsewhere.

As reports of their work spread first to neighboring countries and then to more distant regions, the EAAF was summoned to help solve similar problems around the world. Their institutional policy was to accept any request based on solid and convincing grounds, as well as to foster the Argentine model where needed. Given their independence from the state—an essential characteristic of the EAAF—the Team has been able to do their work without committing to official institutions frequently suspected of complicity with the people under investigation. Additionally, the Team has systematically stressed their interdisciplinary and collective character.

As long as changes in the political situation have permitted it and brought with them the need to come to terms with the past, other Latin American countries that were emerging from similar dictatorships have evaluated the possibility of creating expert groups, as was the case in Argentina. The Team has encouraged and contributed to the formation of similar research teams in countries like Chile and Guatemala, where they attended the introductory courses for local investigators conducted by Dr. Snow. Similar groups were also formed in Perú and Colombia.*

But what does a forensic anthropologist actually do on the field? By way of illustration, the next section consists of two summary case reports of complex investigations in Central America, a region besieged by decades of political violence involving the systematic violation of human rights. The purpose of this inclusion is to illustrate briefly the method, the typical complexity of such cases, and the number and variety of actors usually involved in this kind of investigation.

4. CASE REPORT NO. 1: EL MOZOTE, EL SALVADOR (1992)

4.1. Background of the Case

The massacre at El Mozote[†] is possibly one of the most devastating in the history of El Salvador, a country that endured a 12-yr civil war between 1980 and 1991. In December 1981, the whole population of El Mozote—a

---

* In the course of their 20-yr experience, the EAAF has conducted investigations not only in Latin America (Bolivia, Brazil, Chile, Colombia, El Salvador, Guatemala, Haiti, Honduras, México, Panama, Paraguay, Perú, Uruguay, and Venezuela) but also in Eastern Europe (Bosnia, Croatia, Kosovo, and Romania), Asia (Georgia, Indonesia, Iraqi Kurdistan, and East Timor), Africa (Angola, the Ivory Coast, the Democratic Republic of Congo, Ethiopia, Kenya, Sierra Leone, South Africa, Sudan, and Zimbabwe), and Oceania (French Polynesia and the Philippines).

[†] The massacre was named after El Mozote because it was the first village to be attacked and the one with the most victims.

little town in the province of Morazán—was devastated by the Salvadorean Army.

According to eyewitness accounts, as well as reports by human rights organizations, between December 6th and 16th, the Salvadorean Army launched an offensive against the civilians in the north of the province of Morazán. Known as Operation Rescue (Operación Rescate), the offensive was carried out by an elite group (the Atlacatl battalion) trained by US military advisors as a counterinsurgency force. The main purpose of the operation was to eliminate the guerrillas, who had a training base in a place close to El Mozote called La Guacamaya. When the guerrillas abandoned the area, the operation moved to El Mozote, with the suspicion that the villagers were harboring them. On December 11th, the forces killed all the villagers with machine guns and machetes; they only held young women temporarily as cooks, then raped them and finally killed them as well. By December 13th, the army had massacred the entire civil population of five other neighboring villages: La Joya, Cerro Pando, Jocote Amarillo, Ranchería, and Los Toriles. Before leaving each town, the soldiers also killed the domestic animals and burned down houses and crops. In the aftermath of the incidents, some of the victims were buried in common graves, whereas some were left where they died. The majority of the survivors fled to Honduras, and for years lived in a refugee camp in Colomoncagua; others moved to other areas or joined the Frente Farabundo Martí para la Liberación Nacional (Farabundo Martí National Liberation Front). At the time of exhumation, all the towns involved in the massacre were still deserted.

Concerning the role of the local press, Americas Watch reported that little information was generally available to the Salvadorean public at the time of the massacre as to the nature of military operations in the countryside; nothing like an independent press existed, and all information was controlled by the armed forces. Only one local daily, *La Prensa Gráfica,* reported on December 9, 1981, that the International Red Cross, journalists, and the population in general were barred access to the area, which was under strict control of the army to avoid regrettable or unpleasant acts.

4.2. The Investigation

In 1989, Tutela Legal, the Human Rights Office of the Archdiocese of San Salvador, started a thorough investigation of the massacre. They placed the estimated number of victims at a minimum of 792, which the EAAF itemized by gender, age, and distinctive physical characteristics. Eighty percent (690 individuals) of the total were children or women and men over the age of 56; as many as 40% were children under 10. In October 1990, they provided legal assistance to Pedro Chicas, Rufina Amaya, and another three survivors who filed a lawsuit before the Second Court of First Instance in San Francisco Gotera, Morazán, against the Atlacatl Battalion. In the absence of local forensic experts, Tutela Legal requested the technical assistance of the EAAF to take care of the forensic aspects of the case.

On January 16, 1992, the government of El Salvador and the Frente Farabundo Martí para la Liberación Nacional signed an historic peace accord in Mexico, which ended the 12 yr of civil war. From February 1 of that year through the next 3 mo., three members of the EAAF (P. Bernardi, L. Fondebrider, and M. Doretti) coordinated the exhumations at El Mozote. Once they had examined the information available, the EAAF presented a preliminary work plan and schedule to Mateu Llort, Director of the Medico-Legal Institute, and Mr. Portillo, the judge on the case.

On July 13th, the UN Truth Commission started working in El Salvador on the peace agreement's mandate that the violent events occurred from 1980 to 1992* should be investigated. The massacre at El Mozote was among the more important cases. The three commissioners in charge of the work nominated the EAAF members along with other experts as forensic consultants in this case.

On October 13th, after overcoming a number of obstacles and thanks to the efforts of the UN Commission, as well as other organizations, the exhumation work finally began (Fig. 2). This time, the EAAF stayed from the first days of October until December 20th, during which time they organized the participation of a group of forensic experts: forensic anthropologist Clyde Snow, forensic pathologist Robert Kischner, radiologist John Fitzpatrick, archaeologist and ballistics expert Douglas Scott, and archaeologist Melissa Connor, all of whom came from the United States to participate in the laboratory analysis of the remains and of ballistic evidence for 2 wk.

It was decided to start the exhumations at the site known as "The Convent," a one-room rectangular building adjacent to the village church where the priest used to sleep when he was in town. It was made of adobe and stone, and had a tiled roof and floor. The excavation took more than 1 mo, from October 13th to November 17th. The working area was under surveillance by the police and UN Observer Mission in El Salvador's military division around

---

* The only cases that were actually investigated (a very small minority if one considers the magnitude of the atrocities) were those not within the scope of the amnesty that was declared under the auspices of the UN Observer Mission in El Salvador and as part of the peace agreements between the Frente Farabundo Martí para la Liberación Nacional and the Salvadorean government.

Fig. 2. Work at El Mozote, El Salvador. (Photograph courtesy of Mercedes Doretti and Stephen Ferry.)

the clock. The procedures were regularly monitored by officials of the UN's Human Rights Division and the Truth Commission.

The exhumations were conducted by the EAAF along with 30 members of the local medicolegal system and the Salvadorean Special Investigation Unit (Comisión de Hechos Delictivos). The local team rotated every week, so that by the end of the fourth week, the entire staff of the medicolegal system had learned the basics of forensic archaeology.

Laboratory work was conducted by the above-mentioned experts (Snow, Kirschner, and Fitzpatrick), the three members of the EAAF and a few local physicians, dentists and other technicians; the lab and the archaeological reports were written by the US scientists and by the EAAF members, respectively. Both reports were submitted to the judge in charge and to the UN Truth Commission and were included in the latter's final public report *(7)*. The exhumations were widely covered by the local and international press and became a cover story in many Latin American, North American, and European newspapers.

4.3. Methods

The work at the site had the following characteristics:

1. The excavation was performed according to a grid system specially designed for The Convent, which consisted of 20 grid squares of 1.5 × 1.5-m each; this enabled the assignment of a precise spatial position to each finding.

2. The stratigraphy of the site revealed three compact, clearly differentiated levels that covered the whole of the excavated area; they were essentially composed of, from top to bottom:

   a. Level 1: remains of the adobe walls that collapsed inside the room.
   b. Level 2: roof remains, mostly blackened reddish tiles, nails, and part of the beams, also burned.
   c. Level 3: human skeletons and a large number of bullet fragments and spent cartridges.

3. The floor surface had blackened areas, probably a result of the fire; a total of 38 holes from gunshots were counted (in some cases, the fragments of the bullets were still inside).

All the skeletons recovered from the site and accompanying evidence had deposited in the course of the same event inside a primary synchronous common interment. These findings excluded the possibility that site 1 had been used as a "graveyard" in which the bodies had been placed in different events over time, as stated by the local authorities.

4.4. Results and Discussion

At least 143 skeletons were found inside The Convent, 131 belonging to children under the age of 12 (average age, 6 yr). One of the adult skeletons belonged to a woman who was in her last trimester of pregnancy; fetal bones were found in her pelvic area.

It could not be established conclusively whether all the victims were alive when they arrived at The Convent. However, in at least nine of the cases, it was established that the victims had been shot inside the building while lying in a horizontal position. The bullets had gone through the clothing and bodies and been embedded in the ground. Some of the children may have been shot outside the building, although sufficient rounds of ammunition were found inside to account for all the deaths. The damage to the victims' bones, clothing, and personal effects was substantial. Most of the victims were dressed; some of them were carrying personal effects such as toys, marbles, medals, crosses, and coins.

Ballistics expert Douglas Scott contributed his invaluable expertise to the task of analyzing the evidence. The majority of bullet fragments (263) were found at the center and in the northeast corner of the room, embedded in or in direct relation to the bodies (Fig. 3). By contrast, most of the spent cartridges found (245) were in the southwest area of the room. All of this indicates that some shooters may have stood at the doorway on the west wall or in the southwest corner; they may have shot from the inside or the near outside to the center and northeast squares of the grid.

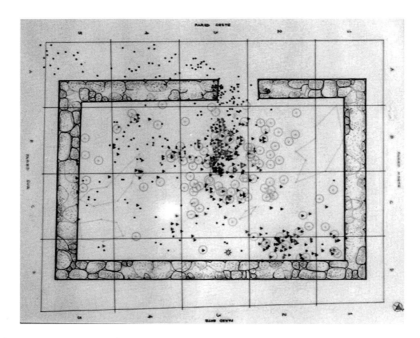

Fig. 3. A site map shows the concentration of bullet fragments (black triangle) in close relation to the recovered skeletons (gray circles). Spent cartridges are shown in black. (Picture courtesy of Claudia Bernardi.)

All of the cartridges but one belonged to 5.5-mm caliber NATO firearms. According to evidence, the bullet casings had been fired by M-16 military rifles manufactured in the United States; they bore an "L.C." stamp, which indicated that they were manufactured for the US Government at the Lake City Plant near Independence, Missouri. Analysis of the casings indicated that at least 24 individual firearms were used during the shootings.

The skeletons evidenced severe trauma, reflecting high-velocity gunshot wound injuries, postmortem crushing, and fire/heat damage. After cleaning, the manufacturing dates were still legible on 28 of the 33 coins and 185 of the 245 spent cartridges recovered: none had been manufactured later than 1981, which led to the presumption that the events took place soon after. It was also determined that one or more explosive(s) and/or incendiary device(s) had been thrown into the building after the shooting.

All the evidence collected at site 1 confirmed the massacre of civilians at El Mozote and was consistent with the testimony offered by the witnesses. The examination of findings at site 1, testimony by dozens of witnesses, as well as some military personnel and consultation of a number of archives in El Salvador and the United States, led the UN Truth Commission to declare the massacre fully proven. In terms of responsibility, the Commission stated that:

1. Despite public denunciation of the massacre and abundant evidence for it, Salvadorean officials did not order any investigation and constantly denied its existence.
2. [Salvadorean Minister of Defense and Chief of Staff] President Cristiani denied having information concerning the military units that participated in Operation Rescue, saying there are no files from those days.
3. The President of the Supreme Court had a biased political interference in the judiciary process, which started in 1990 in relation to the case *(8)*.

The Commission also considered sufficiently proven the slaughter of more than 300 additional civilians in the neighboring villages of La Joya, Los Toriles, Rancheria, Cerro Pando, and Jocotye Amarillo, at the hands of the military units that participated in "Operation Rescue" in the days that followed the massacre at El Mozote *(9,10)*.

5. *Case Report No. 2: Las Dos Erres, Guatemala (1994–1995)*

5.1. *Background of the Case*

In the past four decades, Guatemala has suffered the largest number of enforced disappearances in Latin America ever—45,000 in a country with a population of only 10 million. Most of missing were abducted from rural villages between 1978 and 1986 during a counterinsurgency campaign against the guerrillas by the military regimes of Generals Lucas García, Ríos Montt, and Mejía Vitores. The main objective of these campaigns was to eliminate support of the guerrillas by the villagers and to end opposition to the regime, whether organized or not. Besides the thousands disappeared and/or dead, many thousands more fled to Mexico or relocated elsewhere in the country.

Those responsible for the massacres were reportedly the Guatemalan Army along with paramilitary groups and civil patrols for "self-defense," locally known as Patrullas de Autodefensa Civil ([PACs] Patrols of Civil Self-Defense). These were organizations of peasants who, as part of their compulsory military service, were forced to keep order in rural areas. The PACs patrolled their own villages and, at times, took part in abductions and murders. Anyone who refused to join the PACs was identified as "subversive" and could disappear or be murdered.

Since the mid-1980s, the human rights situation has improved but remains critical. Although international organizations have recommended that paramilitary groups be dismantled, the agents accused of abuses remain in service and keep their status as army employees.

With UN mediation, in 1990, the Guatemalan administration started a series of peace negotiations with a coalition of guerrilla groups known as the Unidad Revolucionaria Nacional Guatemalteca (Guatemalan National Revolutionary Unit). In June 1994, the parties agreed to form a special commission for the investigation of human rights violations committed during the 30 yr of civil war, and a peace accord was finally signed in December 1996. By mutual agreement, the Guatemalan National Assembly went on to pass an amnesty law that, in the opinion of many human rights groups, would absolve both soldiers and the guerrillas of all responsibility for murders, abductions, and torture committed during the civil war.

The massacre at Las Dos Erres is characteristic of this period. This northern village in El Petén was founded by a group of indigent peasants who migrated from other areas of the country. In December 1982, under the Ríos Montt administration, the *Kaibiles* (an army elite counterinsurgency group) occupied the village and accused the people of sympathizing with the local guerrillas. Nearly 500 men, women, and children were murdered in a single day; in many cases, the bodies were dumped into the village well and others were left on the ground in the surrounding woodlands. All domestic animals were killed, and the village was subsequently burned down.

5.2. The Investigation

At the request of Grupo de Apoyo Mutuo (Group of Mutual Support) and the Coordinadora Nacional de Viudas de Guatemala (National Coordination of Guatemalan Widows), two local human rights organizations, the EAAF began work in Guatemala in 1991, exhuming the remains of people disappeared at two sites in Quiché, Chontala (1991) and San José Pachoa Lemoa (1992). These missions were partially sponsored by the American Association for the Advancement of Science as well as Physicians for Human Rights. EAAF members were appointed as forensic experts and worked for the judge overseeing the investigations.

In July 1994, the author and other EAAF colleagues (Patricia Bernardi and Silvana Turner) conducted a 20-d preliminary mission in El Petén. The mission was requested by Familiares de Detenidos y Desaparecidos de Guatemala ([FAMDEGUA] Association of Families of the Detained and "Disappeared" in Guatemala), a local human rights organization supported by the Legal Office of the Guatemalan Archbishopric.

The second mission to Las Dos Erres was carried out between May and July 1995 by the same three EAAF anthropologists and coordinated by FAMDEGUA, whose members were always present at the site. Human rights observers from the UN Military Observer Mission in Guatemala visited the excavation and provided crucial logistic support. The work was financed by the Dutch Catholic Organization for Development Cooperation (now Cordaid) and the Harry Frank Guggenheim Foundation in New York *(11)*.

5.3. Methods

Based on the evidence collected from witness testimony, the EAAF searched three areas of what was left of Las Dos Erres and conducted preliminary excavation in one of them, Pozo Arévalo, an abandoned well designated as site 1. The objective of this preliminary mission was simply to inspect the well. Because of time and logistical constraints, a primitive pulley system above the well was constructed, which was used to get people and tools in and out of it and to retrieve the remains.

The second mission started in May 1995. This time, and at the same time as the excavation and laboratory work proceeded, the EAAF members interviewed witnesses, relatives, and survivors for the purpose of gathering as much information as possible concerning the case. The local office of the Catholic Church helped them to make the interviews and to collect information on other massacres that took place in El Petén in the 1980s.

5.4. Results and Discussion

The first articulated remains were found at a depth of 20 ft, and 10 more skeletons 6.5 ft deeper; this allowed supposition that there were many more at greater depths. The retrieved skeletons belonged to male individuals of all ages, two of which presented lesions compatible with gunshot wounds. All were fully dressed, and some personal belongings were recovered from their pockets. From three of these items (some Guatemalan coins from 1977 and 1978, a 1982 calendar, and two IDs), it could be inferred that the killings and burials could not have taken place before 1982. One of the skeletons was positively identified as Albino Israel Gonzalez Romero, a 22-yr-old peasant who was subsequently buried at his family's request in 1995 during a collective burial of the victims of the massacre.

A large number of unarticulated bone remains and pieces of clothing were found scattered on the ground in two areas designated as sites 2 and 3. At site 2, a bullet fragment and two cartridge cases belonging to an Israeli-made Galil rifle, commonly used by the Guatemalan army at the time, were

Fig. 4. Argentine Forensic Anthropology Team (Equipo Argentino de Antropología Forense) workers and volunteers reinforce the work platform inside the well at El Pozo. (Photograph courtesy of Ana Aslan.)

found. The EAAF's first mission to Las Dos Erres yielded findings that were consistent with the information provided by witnesses.

The second mission involved a more thorough investigation: the deeper end of the well was reached, laboratory work was intense, and countless witness accounts were collected. As a result, the EAAF compiled a list with the victims' names (222 in all)* and physical traits to be correlated with lab analysis results.

5.5. A Detail of the Archaeological Work at Site 1 (El Pozo)

Site 1 consisted of a circular well[†] 7 ft in diameter at the surface level. For the second phase of the mission in 1995, the excavation plan was designed with the aid of an engineer and included the removal of earth around the perimeter of the well, which permitted the construction of a platform 20 ft down, which was lowered as the excavation proceeded, thus giving easier access to the remains and preventing possible damage (Fig. 4).

---

* Nearly half the victims were children under the age of 12 (105, or 47%); as their parents did not survive, their names could not be registered, so many were listed only by their surnames. Only 5.95% of the victims were over the age of 50.
[†] This was actually a well that was abandoned as it was being constructed.

Early in the project, the EAAF hired workers from the surrounding area to help with the excavation. At times, they used a backhoe provided by the mayor of La Libertad, a neighboring town. One of the constant problems was the frequent collapse of the walls of the well so that the platform needed to be propped up just as frequently. Once at the level of the remains, the excavation continued along the natural layers of the ground, which permitted the retrieval of articulated remains. However, because they were in a vertical position and highly intermingled, it was decided to excavate further in 20-in. artificial layers, starting at a depth of 33 ft. When the work at site 1 ended, the excavation had reached the depth of the well at the time of the massacre, 40 ft, with a bottom 3 ft in diameter. The well was then locked and the area of excavation leveled on the surface.

By mid-July 1995 when the work stopped, at least 156 skeletons had been retrieved* along with pieces of clothing and personal belongings, as well as firearm projectiles, which were significant evidence of the cause of death. Judging from the distribution of the remains and the depth at which they were found, it could be deduced that women and children were the first to be thrown in; their remains were at the bottom of the well, whereas the male skeletons were lying on top.

According to witness testimony, the residents of Las Dos Erres had been forced to leave the village in groups and executed in the woods. During the EAAF's preliminary investigation in July 1994, skeletonized remains, clothing, and ballistic evidence were found on the ground in two areas known as La Aguada and Los Salazares, both of them in the woodlands near Las Dos Erres. In May and June 1995, the EAAF returned to these areas for prospecting and collected the evidence scattered around over an area of 15,000 ft². The remains were disarticulated, incomplete, and in a poor state of preservation, mostly because of the damage caused by fire and other external factors, such as erosion or the existence of big scavengers such as dogs, cats, and vultures, or small ones like rodents and insects. Additionally, the dense foliage of the woodlands made it difficult to apply a system of coordinates to the entire area. The remains and associated evidence were marked with pennants of different colors, and the items that were close together were identified as a "concentration." A total of 18 concentrations were discovered and marked with this system. As a final step, the evidence in each concentration was collected for examination.

In spite of the dreadful condition of the remains, it was possible to recover evidence to establish cause of death. Some bones bore fractures compatible with lesions caused by firearm projectiles. The ballistic evidence associated with the remains included three cases of spent cartridges from a Galil rifle. It

---

* Subsequent lab analysis yielded a minimal number of individuals exhumed of 162.

was impossible to determine whether the victims were alive as they were taken to this area; however, the presence of cases near the remains and the nature of the lesions added to witness testimony to suggest strongly extrajudicial executions.

Comparing preliminary historical data with the results of forensic investigation, the EAAF found a discrepancy between the number of individuals listed on the former (222) and the minimal number of individuals recovered as established by the latter (162). This difference was particularly large in the category of children under the age of 12: there were 38 more children listed as victims than were recovered by archaeological work. This could be partly explained by the severely deteriorated condition of the children's skeletonized remains, as well as by other difficulties that arose during the investigation; it is for this reason that the EAAF only speaks of a "minimal number" of skeletons. It is also possible that the remains belonged to a larger number of individuals or that some of the children were not thrown into the well but buried or abandoned in the village.

Another important difference between the number of victims listed and the remains exhumed may be found among women in the 13- to 37-yr-old range, that is, adolescents and young women. For this age group, the victim list has 10 more names on it than corresponding remains found during the forensic investigation. The characteristics of the massacre can explain some of these findings: it was reported that a number of women were separated from the rest to cook the meals for the soldiers; the youngest may eventually have been taken to the woods, raped, and killed and their bodies abandoned there.

As stated previously, the remains recovered at sites 2 and 3 were in a dreadful state of preservation because of a variety of factors. A similar situation was observed at site 1, where the damage to the bones resulted from dumping the bodies into the well, as well as from the subsequent pressure exerted by other bodies and the ground itself; these factors explain the large number of peri- and postmortem fractures present.

In addition to these types of damage, the remains evidenced severe trauma caused by firearm wounds. At least 29 victims were shot, as determined by the recovery of projectiles associated to the remains and/or by the observation of lesions compatible with gunshots in the cranium or the thorax. Additionally, four individuals were found with their hands tied behind their backs and ropes around their necks.

5.6. Identification

Two fundamental sources of antemortem physical data were missing in this investigation. First, no antemortem data were available on Las Dos Erres victims because whole families were killed, and most of the victims had recently migrated from other regions of the country, which made it impossible to find relatives to contribute to the identification process. Second, clinical and dental records were also absent, because people had no access to medical assistance in the region. However, three positive identifications were eventually made based on external factors: the discovery of an ID, a picture, and a raffle ticket found in the clothes associated to the skeletons. These pieces of evidence enabled the investigators to establish a connection with the relatives of the victims, who provided relevant physical information that confirmed the identification.*

The investigation of the massacre at Las Dos Erres has thrown light on the repression that occurred at El Petén in the 1980s and is a fundamental step towards the consolidation of the peace process in Guatemala. Since then, FAMDEGUA has worked to bring General Ríos Montt to justice for the massacre of Dos Erres. The case has also been presented before the UN Truth Commission.

6. CONCLUSIONS

This chapter is aimed at offering a reflection on the legal and scientific efforts that have been made in response to the political violence involved in crimes against humanity. It is an unfortunate feature of anthropological and archaeological work, as is the case with forensics, that it is performed *a posteriori* of the conflicts and is thus confined to a concern with their dire consequences.

It is not within the scope of our endeavors as forensic professionals to modify the expression of contemporary societies, but the authors are positive that the contributions made by forensic professionals to the search for truth and justice helps to relieve the pain of the victims, as well as to discourage the all-too-common revisionist attitude of exculpating those responsible for the crimes that forensic professionals investigate.

ACKNOWLEDGMENTS

I am deeply grateful to João Pinheiro for inviting the EAAF to contribute to this volume, to Inés Macchi for the original translation, and to Ana Traversa and Mark Stein at Stonebridge Editing for their adaptation and corrections.

---

* On the morning of July 30, 1995, the Archbishop of El Petén, Monsignor Rodolfo Bobadilla, held a religious inhumation ceremony at the ruins of Las Dos Erres. The remains of the victims identified by the forensic analysis or recognized by their relatives were placed in individual urns and buried in a special section of a collective grave to facilitate future re-exhumations.

As ever, thanks to all Team members—Cecilia Ayerdi, Patricia Bernardi, Daniel Bustamante, Andrea del Río, Mimí Doretti, Sofía Egaña, Luis Fondebrider, Anahí Ginarte, Rafael Mazzella, Miguel Nieva, Maco Somigliana, and Silvana Turner—for the enormous privilege of sharing team-work through the years.

REFERENCES

1. Mattarolo, R. La jurisprudencia argentina reciente y los crímenes de lesa humanidad. In: Doswald-Beck, L., ed., Impunidad, Crimen de Lesa Humanidad y Desaparición Forzada (La Revista Comisión Internacional de Juristas) [in Spanish], 2001.
2. Krogman, W. M., Iscan, M. Y. The Human Skeleton in Forensic Medicine. Charles C. Thomas Springfield, IL, 1986.
3. Aronèanu, E. Le Crime Contre l'humanité [in French]. Librairie Dalloz, Paris 1961.
4. Armenian National Institute, "Treaty of Sèvres." Available at http://www.armenian-genocide.org/Affirmation.236/current_category.49/affirmation_detail.html. Last accessed Mar. 7, 2006.
5. UN International Law Commission, Draft Code of Crimes against Peace and Security of Mankind (UN Doc. AP/51/332 of July 30, 1996). Available at http://untreaty.un.org/ilc/texts/instruments/english/draft%20articles/7_4_1996.pdf. Last accessed Mar. 7, 2006.
6. "Rome Statute of the International Criminal Court" (17 July 1998) reproduced in 37 ILM (1998) 999. Available at http://www.un.org/law/icc/statute/romefra.htm. Last accessed Mar. 7, 2006.
7. United States Institute of Peace (1993). From Madness to Hope. Available at http://www.usip.org/library/tc/doc/reports/el_salvador/tc_es_03151993_toc.html. Last accessed Mar. 7, 2006.
8. Americas Watch Committee and the American Civil Liberties Union, Compilers. Report on Human Rights in El Salvador. Vintage Books, New York, NY, 1982.
9. Danner, M. The Massacre at El Mozote: A Parable of the Cold War. Vintage Books, New York, NY, 1994.
10. Equipo Argentino de Antropología Forense. Biannual Report 1992–1993. EAAF, New York, NY, 1994.
11. Equipo Argentino de Antropología Forense. Biannual Report 1994–1995. EAAF, New York, NY, 1996.

Chapter 18

Mass Disasters

Cristina Cattneo, Danilo De Angelis, and Marco Grandi

Summary

A mass disaster is commonly construed as an event (air, naval, railway, or motorway accident, flooding, earthquake, and so on), resulting in a large number of victims that need to be identified and subject to medicolegal investigation. Furthermore, depending on which continent one comes from, innumerous protocols and procedures are available, the Interpol Disaster Victim Identification form being the most frequently used one in Europe. Whatever the case may be, the procedure is the same, and it consists of a meticulous collection of both antemortem and postmortem data. Consequently, the identification modalities to be applied will vary according to the quality of the antemortem data available and preservation conditions of the victims. This chapter gives general guidelines, common to most protocols, for the management—strictly from a medicolegal point of view—of victims of a mass disaster. As mentioned, intervention protocols may differ greatly depending on the country in which the disaster occurs; furthermore, medicolegal intervention in a mass disaster is dependant on local authorities, such as the magistrate's court, the police, local health authorities, and so forth. These authorities decide, in many countries, what should be done and when. For this reason, it is always wise for medicolegal services and departments to create (ahead of time) contacts and connections with local authorities in order to avoid a confused conduction of the emergency. At the scene of the accident or disaster, when conditions allow it, medicolegal staff should contribute to the recording of victims' position and condition just as at any "normal" scene of crime situation, although time constraints must be respected. Once the remains have been removed from the disaster site, the bodies should be brought to a morgue for medicolegal activity. While the above-mentioned preliminary procedures are carried out, a place at which to interview relatives of the victims must be established. On every cadaver or human remains, a full autopsy

From *Forensic Anthropology and Medicine:*
Complementary Sciences From Recovery to Cause of Death
Edited by: A. Schmitt, E. Cunha, and J. Pinheiro © Humana Press Inc., Totowa, NJ

according to European standards should be performed, along with appropriate analysis and sampling from an odontological, genetic, anthropological, and a fingerprinting point of view according to the methods described in previous chapters. Adequate toxicological and histological sampling (if necessary) should also be performed for establishing (when necessary) manner and cause of death. Antemortem and postmortem data are then crossmatched in order to obtain best matches among the victims with every person that has been reported missing or who was on the passenger list. The modality of identification will depend on, in the end, the state of conservation and condition of the corpses and on the available antemortem documentation. It should always be kept in mind that visual identification on well-preserved cadavers in such cases should always be double-checked with another biological method.

Key Words: Mass disasters; identification; manner and cause of death; autopsy; Europe.

1. INTRODUCTION

Extensive literature exists concerning the medicolegal investigation of air traffic accidents and other mass disasters. Thus, various events, ranging from the scene of crime to the actual autopsy and identification of the victims, have been reported *(1–7)*. Furthermore, depending on which continent one comes from, innumerous protocols and procedures are available, the most frequently used one in Europe being the Interpol Disaster Victim Identification (DVI) form. Nonetheless, in the authors' point of view, what pathologists, odontologists, and other experts involved in mass disasters should realize is that the main factor in these cases is a profound knowledge of reliable and proper identification procedures in order to, according to the variables that one may encounter, be able to appropriately deal with the situation. From a medicolegal perspective, there are three main objectives with regard to the study of human remains: a good scene of crime investigation, with proper retrieval and registration of human remains, application of proper identification procedures; adequate autopsy techniques along with tissue sampling (e.g., toxicology) for eventually reconstructing cause; and manner of death. It may be very difficult, depending on the country and authorities involved, to place these activities in a set protocol. For example, in countries in which DVI teams are well organized and Interpol protocols known to all specialists involved, application of preset logistics and methodologies is fairly easy and automatic. In many other countries these *modi operandi* may not exist. For this reason, the authors, in this chapter, have focused on explaining what should be done, and how, rather than entering the detail of preordained protocols, which may not be applicable to all countries.

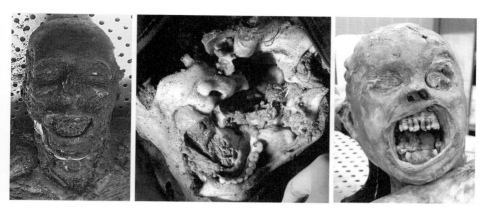

Fig. 1. Examples of types of remains (referring to the head and face) that can be encountered in mass disasters: on the left, burned remains; in the center, severely traumatized remains; on the right, badly putrefied.

A mass disaster is commonly construed as an event (air, naval, railway, or motorway accident, flooding, earthquake) resulting in a large number of fatalities (some authors consider an event to be a mass disaster when the number of victims is greater than 12), the remains of which, being often badly traumatized, burned or dismembered, have to be identified and subjected to medicolegal investigation (Fig. 1).

Mass disasters can be considered as a "closed" or "open" system. The first is a system in which a specific number of known individuals are involved, for example, an air disaster with a passenger's list. In this case, the work consists of mainly matching antemortem (AM) data of individuals on the passenger list with postmortem (PM) data from the victims. An open system, on the other hand, is much more difficult to manage. It is the case, for instance, of a sunken ship with illegal immigrants on board (and therefore without a formal passenger list) or the case of an explosion in a railway station or in the underground. In these cases, it is necessary to wait for information concerning missing persons that should have been in that place on that specific day. Many times, bodies remain unidentified for a large length of time.

Whichever the case may be, the procedure is the same, and it consists of a meticulous collection of both AM and PM data. Thus, the identification modalities to be applied will vary according to the quality of the AM data available and preservation conditions of the victims (for details on identification procedures, *see* Chapter 8). For example, in the case where the victims come from Western industrialized countries (for example, the Linate aircraft accident of October 8, 2001, which involved mainly northern European and Italian victims), it is often possible to apply odontological and genetic methods, considering that the recovery of suitable medical clinical data from dentists is feasible as is the acquisition of DNA swabs from suitable relatives. In the cases of victims from poorer countries from which it is very difficult to attain useful medical data or relatives, it is sometimes necessary (as in the case of the Albanian refugees traveling on the Kater Rades, which sunk on the coast of Brindisi, Italy in 1997) to identify individuals by other methods (age, morphological dental features, and so on). Sometimes in these cases, as in cases of victims of war crimes, a definite identity cannot be achieved.

First, it should be said that scene-of-the-crime investigations, from a medicolegal point of view, may be crucial for many reasons in cases of mass disasters. The first consists of the complete recovery of all remains. In the case, for example, of remains of an aircraft that has exploded in the air, remains may be scattered over a very large area. Only thorough searches performed with field-walking techniques, cadaver dogs, and expert personnel will lead to a complete recovery. Furthermore, a precise topographic positioning of all remains should be sought. This may be crucial in reconstructing the dynamics of the accident. Again, take as an example an aircraft explosion. If it is known where specific passengers were sitting, the manner of dispersal of their remains, once identified, may be important for reconstructing the point of origin of the explosion. This may be done with the help of a total station, which uses a laser beam to register topographic coordinates. Finally, pathologists, anthropologists, and odontologists should be present on-site during recovery. Only expert personnel will be able to accurately search for burned bones or teeth, for example. Furthermore, for the pathologist, it may be crucial to record the immediate environment around and position of the victims, if the pathologist later has to help reconstruct the modalities of death.

It is also crucial for expert personnel to be on-site before removal of the victims in order to protect fragile parts that are fundamental for identification, for example, in cases of badly charred victims.

2. GUIDELINES

What follows are general guidelines common to most protocols for the management, strictly from a medicolegal point of view, of victims of a mass disaster. As has already been mentioned, intervention protocols may differ greatly depending on the country in which the disaster occurs. Furthermore, medicolegal intervention in a mass disaster is dependant on local authorities, such as the magistrate's court, the police, local health authorities, and so on. These authorities decide, in many countries, what should be done and when. For this reason, it is always wise for medicolegal services and departments to create (ahead of time) contacts and connections with local authorities in order to avoid a confused conduction of the emergency.

2.1. Medicolegal Steps for the Mass Disaster

1. At the scene of the accident, when conditions allow it, medicolegal staff should contribute to the recording of victims' position, condition, and so forth, just like at any normal scene-of-the-crime examination, although time constraints must be respected. This should obviously take place after the intervention of emergency personnel (fire department, first aid, and rescue units). Once all has been registered, every victim should be assigned a number, photographed, and delicate areas should be protected. An example may be teeth in the case of burned remains. The dentition should be protected with fixative sprays or, preferably, a mask, in order to guarantee that further damage will not be inflicted during body removal and transportation to the morgue. All such activities should be carried out together with the police and other intervening bodies. Accurate search for all other remains should be performed.

2. Once the remains have been removed from the disaster site, the bodies should be brought to a morgue for medicolegal activity. If the accident is near a morgue, then already available structures can be used; otherwise, prefabricated, temporary, "mobile" morgues can be rented. One should always keep in mind that for very badly maimed or degraded bodies, it is also useful to have radiological equipment for identification purposes.

3. While the above-mentioned preliminary procedures are carried out, a place where to interview relatives of the victims must be established. Such information must be given to the media and to crisis centers in order to be able to inform relatives and to keep them constantly posted on how operations are proceeding. A list must also be prepared and published so that relatives can bring all necessary AM data. In the preordained area destined to the reception of relatives, the collection of all AM data useful for identification will be performed. A AM team (or several AM teams, depending on the number of victims), preferably constituted by a forensic pathologist, an odontologist, a geneticist, and a psychologist, for possible assistance to mourning relatives must be set up. This team is appointed to collect clinical and nonclinical data related to the victims, and to register the information on appropriate forms. Such AM data includes information on personal effects; clothing; jewelry worn; descriptors such as age, sex, height, race, hair and eye color, tattoos, scars, moles, malformations, prosthetic devices, osseous and dental pathologies; and any clinical, in particular radiological, and dental data (along with a contact name or number of physicians and dentists of the victim), pictures of the victim alive, possibly when smiling and displaying

the front teeth (in order to be able to carry out an identification via the dental profile). A list of useful items to be sent to the identification team later on and to a prearranged place must be given to the relatives. These are clinical medical and odontological records, radiographs, personal effects, such as combs, razors and toothbrushes used by the victims (useful for DNA analysis), and photographs. Medical data consisting of case histories and radiographs of any body district must be collected. For the odontological data, the victim's dentist is generally contacted in order to obtain dental charts, casts, endoral radiographs, ortho-pantomographs, dental-arch X-rays, or clinical photographs.

4. Collaterally, the programming of body examinations and autopsy (or anthropologi-cal examination, depending on the manner of conservation of the remains) is car-ried out. Thus, PM teams are organized for the autopsy and the collection of all data useful for identification of the human remains. This team is formed, prefer-ably, by a pathologist, an odontologist, an anthropologist, a geneticist, a toxicolo-gist, a morgue technician, and a secretary. The pathologist will perform the autopsy according to standard procedures for badly preserved human remains *(8)*. From the point of view of identification, the pathologist, on external examination, should clean the skin looking for scars, tattoos, and the like, and, once the autopsy has begun, should look for signs of surgery and important pathologies useful for iden-tification. Appropriate sampling for toxicological and other laboratory analyses should also be performed. Registration of identification features and sampling will be carried out according to the identification protocols already described and estab-lished by Interpol forms. The odontologist will perform a dental examination as described in Chapter 15 (Heading 4), with photographs, UV light testing, and so forth, the odontologist will make dental casts, perform X-rays, and excise the man-dible and maxillae if necessary. Minimal anthropological sampling should also be performed: this includes samples for aging (dental and osteological)—pubic sym-physes and fourth rib and one monoradicular tooth should always be taken. Aging may greatly aid in an initial matching of antemortem and PM data. X-ray analysis, if soft tissue is still present, will be useful in distinguishing the adult and subadult individuals. For this latter group, X-rays of the dental arches and of the hand and wrist will allow for quick age determination. Of course, if cadavers are skeleton-ized, the role of the anthropologists becomes more relevant as sexing, determina-tion of ancestry, and stature may be crucial, as well as full skeletal analyses. Finally, the geneticist will assist in collecting adequate samples of tissue for DNA extrac-tion. Of course, not all experts may be available, so various identification groups should always ask for sampling protocols if specific experts are not present. For each corpse, a form will be completed, complementary to the antemortem form, and the data are then transferred to a suitable computer program.

In this manner, appropriate analysis and sampling of the remains will guaran-tee optimal conditions for identification and study of the cause of death. One final comment that should be made is that often fingerprinting of the victim may be useful. Thus, fingerprints are taken, according to the state of preservation as described in Chapter 15, Heading 2.

In conclusion, on every cadaver or human remains, a full autopsy according to European standards *(8)* should be performed, along with appropriate analysis and sampling from an odontological, genetic, anthropological, and a fingerprinting point of view according to the methods described in Chapter 15. Adequate toxicological and histological sampling (if necessary) should also be performed for establishing (when necessary) manner and cause of death.

5. All collected data are then recorded on Interpol forms (as previously mentioned, many forms exists; however, because in Europe the Interpol form is the one most commonly used, it should always be used in cases where victims of different nations are involved). All data can then be put into a database. Interpol does have appropriate software for crossmatching data and selecting best matches; however, it is very expensive for nonpolice organizations, such as universities. For this reason, a simpler database for initial comparison can be used, such as Microsoft Excel or Access, on which one can then search for common descriptors. It should be kept in mind that frequent updates concerning which procedures are being used and what is being done should be released to the press in order to avoid extra pressure from relatives who may think they are being kept in the dark.

6. The AM and PM data are then crossmatched in order to obtain best matches among the victims with every person that has been reported missing or who was on the passenger list. The modality of identification will depend ultimately on the state of conservation and condition of the corpses and on the available AM documentation. It should always be kept in mind that visual identification on well-preserved cadavers in such cases should always be double-checked with another biological method.

7. Finally, according to each country's requirements, documents necessary for the burial and transportation of the body must be prepared. A direct channel with consulates and embassies in cases of foreign victims should always be kept. Most countries in Europe require a declaration of identity, cause of death, and magistrates' and civil statuses' permission to bury the body. Problems involving different legislations in different countries have been exemplified by Lunetta et al. *(9)*.

3. AN EXAMPLE: THE LINATE AIRCRAFT DISASTER OF OCTOBER 8, 2001

The logistics of the Linate mass disaster is possibly a good example of the organization of a non-DVI identification group, which, however, follows the above-mentioned guidelines.

On October 8, 2001, at 8:06 AM, a Scandinavian Airlines (SAS) MD 87 on its scheduled flight SK 686 from Milan-Linate Airport in Italy, to

Copenhagen, Denmark, collided on the ground with a Cessna Citation II business jet on takeoff. The small jet fragmented into two main portions and caught fire. The MD 87, after sliding for several hundreds of meters, crashed into an airport baggage hangar. Here, a posterior portion of the fuselage separated from the main body of the aircraft and caught fire within the hangar, whereas the more anterior portion, although severely warped, remained untouched by the flames.

The Milan Prefecture was responsible for the general emergency. The prefecture is an organization attached to the Ministry of Internal Affairs (Ministero dell'Interno), which deals with the logistics of all catastrophes and coordinates many police activities. The judicial authority in charge of the entire investigation of the mass disaster was a magistrate (Procuratore della Repubblica) from the Milan Magistrate's Court, whose territorial jurisdiction covers the airport area. The immediate emergency was dealt with by the fire department (Vigili del Fuoco) that arrived at the site of the MD 87 impact, assisted by police personnel from the airport (Polaria) and from the Milan Police Department (Squadra Mobile, Polizia Scientifica). Then, other law enforcement officers and rescue service personnel belonging to agencies generally involved in the management of mass disasters within the city and region (Carabinieri, Guardia di Finanza, Polizia Municipale, ASL, Croce Rossa, and so on) arrived at the scene.

The victim recovery procedures were handled mainly by the fire department, assisted by 10 specialists from the scene of crime personnel of the Milan Police Department (Polizia Scientifica della Questura) for photographic and video recording. Unfortunately, in this case, medicolegal personnel were not involved. Bodies were placed in numbered body bags supplied by the airport administration.

The entire recovery of victims from the wreckages took about 28 h. Although medicolegal personnel could not participate directly in the recovery operation, personnel of the identification team and forensic pathologists, all from the Institute of Legal Medicine, University of Milan, screened and performed preliminary examination of the bodies at a working station located within the airport in order to direct the badly burned or maimed bodies to the Institute of Legal Medicine (directly connected with the main morgue in Milan, which can hold more than 100 bodies) for further investigation, and the better preserved bodies to another smaller Milan cemetery morgue (Lambrate). This was possible because Linate Airport is only a few kilometers from the city of Milano.

The passenger list was provided to the Italian authorities by SAS on October 8th at 9:00 AM and included 104 passengers, plus six pilots and flight attendants. The Cessna jet had two pilots and two passengers on board; four other victims were airport employees working on the ground in the hangar at the time of the SAS MD 87 impact. Foreign embassies in Rome and the Consulates in Milan were informed by the Italian authorities that foreign citizens might be among the victims.

Scandinavian disaster teams arrived, almost unannounced, at the Institute expecting to find their equivalents of the Italian DVI team. This was not so because such a team in practice does not exist and because the Magistrate in charge of all operations had already appointed the Institute of Legal Medicine performing autopsies and identification of the victims. Italy, as many other European countries, has no official protocol for mass disasters. In Rome, forensic pathologists are affiliated with the Polizia Scientifica as Interpol DVI representatives, but there is actually no operative DVI team, and magistrates generally turn to experts at the nearest university department or institute of legal medicine.

Foreign experts, however, helped in the collection of AM data of the victims from their respective countries.

This leads to considerations on a present problem in identification, which recently emerged with the 2004 tsunami events in South East Asia. As previously mentioned, in cases of mass disasters, usually "political" forces are activated. These have, in most European countries, on a national logistic level, absolutely no contact with universities. It is well known that within the *Scientifiche* (i.e., forensic science services) of the police or *Carabinieri*, there are valid fingerprint and DNA experts, but no pathologists, odontologists, or anthropologists. Nor can such professional figures, present in several Italian universities, be recruited by police or *Carabinieri*—for beaurocratical and administrative reasons—within the logistics of the ministries of Internal Affairs or of Defense. In other words, expert and qualified personnel necessary for a thorough approach to identification procedures in mass disasters, paradoxically, will not be involved. This problem, which is present in most southern European countries, must be dealt with in the future, in order to avoid subsequent mishaps and inadequate *modi operandi* in mass disasters.

In the case of the Linate mass disaster, the prosecutor's main interest was identification of the victims; however, examination of the bodies and sampling was necessary in order to acquire data on manner of death, which may have been subsequently useful—particularly in the case of the Cessna victims—with regard to the issue of time of survival and delays of the rescue teams. After the accident, the magistrate ordered full medicolegal autopsies and laboratory investigations for the Cessna pilots and passengers and for all members of the SAS crew and attendants of the MD 87. Moreover, she ordered

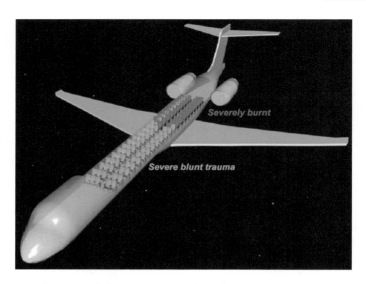

Fig. 2. Distribution of the victims within the MD 87 aircraft and mode of conservation of the body (Linate mass disaster). In black, bodies with severe blunt trauma; in gray, badly burned bodies.

external (and internal) examination of all other victims to collect data and samples necessary for identification and determination of cause of death.

The Milan-Linate aircraft disaster counted, in total, 118 victims: 104 SAS passengers (of which 58 were Italian, 17 Swedish, 16 Danish, 6 Finnish, 3 Norwegian, 1 Romanian, 1 British, and 1 South African), 6 members of the SAS crew (3 Swedish, 2 Danish, and 1 Finnish), 2 pilots (Italian) and 2 passengers (German) of the Cessna aircraft, and 4 Italian employees working on the ground in the hangar. Of the victims, 54 (46%)—those situated mainly in the rear section of the aircraft)—were badly burned, whereas others were maimed but still possessed recognizable facial features (Fig. 2).

Autopsies and external examinations were performed from October 10–19, 2001, according to the guidelines listed above. The proper collection, handling, storage, and processing of data allowed positive identification of the victims within 14 d. The identification team was composed of an AM and PM groups, working on-site and at the Institute of Legal Medicine, University of Milano. The AM group was composed of five specialists in legal medicine, five trainees in legal medicine, and two odontologists collecting data on Interpol AM forms and medical and dental history of the victims; one technician entering AM data into an Excel database file; and two geneticists collecting buccal swabs from relatives and personal effects of the victims that

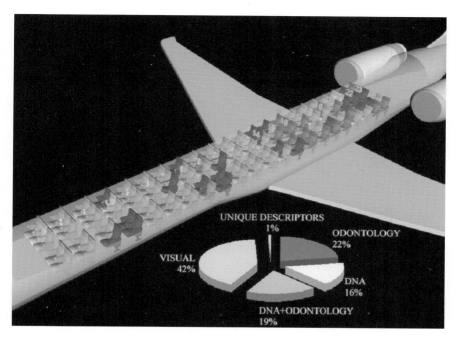

Fig. 3. Manner of identification of the bodies and distribution within the large aircraft (Linate disaster). As can be seen, in the rear portion of the aircraft where bodies were burned, DNA and odontology were the prevailing identification methods. Visual identification for bodies with a preserved physionomy was always assessed by biological means (e.g., descriptors). Unique descriptors were unusual tattoos and bone prosthetic devices.

could be useful for genetic identification. The PM team was composed of 12 specialists in legal medicine working on rosters for autopsies/external examinations, two dentists collecting information on the Interpol DVI form, one anthropologist collecting samples useful for age determination (e.g., pubic symphysis, 4th ribs, and diaphyseal shafts for microscopy), two geneticists collecting muscle and soft tissue samples, and one laboratory and three morgue technicians. Dental examinations were performed with UV light and X-ray facilities, and entire jaws were excised from badly burned victims. Pathologists and technicians were also engaged in entering PM data into the Excel database for subsequent comparison with AM data.

The collection of AM data from foreign victims was completed in 7 d and transmitted by fax or internet to Milano for comparison with PM data.

All victims were identified in the following manner: facial recognition (confirmed by anthropological and odontological analyses) (42%), odontology only (22%), DNA only (16%), combination of odontology and DNA methods (when one or the other was not sufficient for technical reasons [18%]), and tattoos and scars (2%) (Fig. 3).

The magistrate gave permission for the release and transfer of corpses on a daily case-by-case basis after identification. The transfer of foreign victims was then done according to the Berlin Convention that Italy signed and ratified in 1937.

4. CONCLUSION

In conclusion, mass disasters, regardless of the affiliation of the medicolegal experts involved, should be dealt with by qualified professionals from the scene of the accident to the subsequent autopsy and identification. Logistics and protocols for countries who do not have organized DVI teams may be more complex; however, if a general consensus and agreement on who does and needs what is reached among intervening authorities, proper identification and examination of the victims should not be impeded. Finally, pathologists must always keep in touch with the media (and therefore, relatives), explain what is being done, and justify the time needed for proper identification and autopsy to be performed in everyone's best interest.

REFERENCES

1. Interpol. Manual on disaster victim identification. International Criminal Police Organisation, Paris, 1992.
2. Brannon, R. B., Kessler, H. P. Problems in mass disaster dental identification: a retrospective review. J. Forensic Sci. 44:123–127, 1999.
3. Ludes, B., Tracqui, A., Pfitzinger, H., et al. Medico-legal investigations of the Airbus, A320 crash upon Mount Ste-Odile, France. J. Forensic Sci. 39:1147–1152, 1994.
4. Clark, M. A., Hawley, D. A., McClain, J. L., Pless, J. E., Marlin, D. C., Standish, S. M. Investigation of the 1987 Indianapolis Airport Ramada Inn incident. J. Forensic Sci. 39:644–649, 1994.
5. Timperman, J. How some medicolegal aspects of the Zeebrugge Ferry disaster apply to the investigation of mass disasters. Am. J. Forensic Med. Pathol. 12:286–290, 1991.
6. Valenzuela, A., Martin-de las Heras, S., Marques, T., Exposito, N., Bohoyo, J. M. The application of dental methods of identification to human burn victims in a mass disaster. Int. J. Legal Med. 113:236–239, 2000.
7. Moody, G. H., Busuttil, A. Identification in the Lockerbie air disaster. Am. J. Forensic Med. Pathol. 15:63–69, 1994.

8. Brinkmann, B. Harmonisation of medico-legal autopsy rules. Int. J. Legal Med. 113:1–14, 1994.
9. Lunetta, P., Ranta, A., Cattaneo, C., et al. International collaboration in mass disasters involving foreign nationals within the EU medico-legal investigation of Finnish victims of the Milan Linate airport SAS SK 686 aircraft accident on 8 October 2001. Int. J. Legal Med. 117:204–210, 2003.

Index

A

Abdominal wall, decomposition in, 90
Abuelas de Plaza de Mayo, 415
Accuracy defined, 226
Acetabular segment in sex determination, 228
Achilles tendon, 339
Achondroplasia, 61
Additional Protocols of 1977, 385
Ad hoc forms, 395–396
Adipocere
   in decomposition, 86, 87, 88f
   evaluation of, 88f, 100f, 107
   formation of, 99, 101–105
   identification and, 161, 170, 172
   in mummification, 106
   predator promotion of, 99
   in putrefaction, 96f
   in skeletonization, 97
Admissibility of evidence, 45
Adolescents
   age determination in, 50, 51, 60–62, 73, 248, 249
   in El Pozo, 427
   Tanner staging system, 60t, 61t
   teeth development in, 63
Adults, age determination in, 261, 262
Age-at-death assessment
   about, 259–262, 275
   articulations in, 264
   Bayesian analysis in, 273
   clavicles in, 268–270
   error analysis in, 263, 266, 267, 272, 275

fragmented body methodology, 271–274
iliac crest epiphysis in, 268, 269
Lamendin method of, 262, 264, 266–268, 272, 275
long bones in, 273, 274
methodology, 262–271
pathology in, 349
in populations, 252, 261, 269, 271–274
root translucency in, 264, 266–268
sacropelvic surface in, 272, 273, 275
from skeletons, 261, 268
Suchey-Brooks System (SBS) for, 262–264
Terry collection, 303t
two-step procedure for, 262, 263, 268, 275
ventral rim in, 264
Age determination
   about, 50, 51, 57
   in adolescents, 50, 51, 60–62, 73, 248, 249
   in adults, 261, 262
   in asylum seekers, 58
   biological vs chronological, 70–72, 244
   body mass index (BMI) in, 59, 61
   bone diaphyseal lengths in, 248
   in bones, 66–71, 75, 76
   in children, 58–63, 66, 67, 243, 244, 249–253
   error margins, 57, 68–69, 71, 72, 76, 77, 244, 247–248
   ethnicity in, 67, 72, 75, 245t, 249
   in Europe, 58

fourth rib method, 269, 271–273, 275
Guatemalan conflict and, 249–253
hand/wrist region in, 66–70, 75, 248, 249, 436
humerus in, 249
in immigrants, 58
in infants, 73, 246–248
infectious diseases in, 61
in living individuals, 74–76
malnutrition in, 61, 72, 252
manner of death and, 250–252
methods of, 72–77
nutritional deficiency diseases in, 61, 72
ortopantomographs in, 63, 64f
in perinates, 248
physical inspection in, 59–62
and pregnancy, 248
preservation of remains in, 262
puberty in, 59–62
quality control in, 75
radiography in, 68, 69, 73–76, 247, 436
skeletal, 66–70
from the skull, 271, 272
standardization in, 74
teeth in, 62–65, 72, 75, 244–247, 261
UNHCR guidelines, 58
variability in, 71, 72
Agenda for Humanitarian Action (ICRC), 388
A Guide to the Identification of Human Skeletal Material (Krogman), 8
Air
disarticulation in, 111
in putrefaction processes, 97, 98
in skeletonization processes, 110
Allometry, 318
Alveolar prognathism in ethnicity determination, 292t, 297
American Academy of Forensic Sciences (AAFS), physical anthropology section, 8, 40
American Association of Physical Anthropology, 7

American Board of Forensic Anthropology (ABFA), 9
American Board of Forensic Odontology (ABFO), 63, 64
Amputation
evaluation of, 197, 208, 209f
in fingerprint recovery, 364
lesions produced by, 212–214
Anatomical connections in primary deposits, 126–128
Ancestry
in age determination, 67, 72, 75, 245t, 249
determination of
about, 43, 47, 281–284, 308–310
alveolar prognathism in, 292t, 297
from bones, 235
in Canada, 297
canine fossa in, 292t
Carabelli's cusp in, 293t
chin shape in, 292t
decomposed/skeletonized remains, 261, 268
in diverse race children, 67, 249
FA's role in, 436
from femur, 286, 288
Inca bone in, 292t
incisor shoveling in, 293t, 297
from long bones, 285, 286
mandibular torus in, 293t
from mass graves, 334
morphological characters in, 289–298, 360
mylohyoid bridge in, 293t
nasal depression in, 291t
nasal form in, 291t, 297
nasal opening in, 291t
nasal sill in, 291t
Os Japonicum in, 292t
paracondylar process in, 293t
from pelvis, 285, 302–305
in SBS analysis, 263
from skull, 285, 289–298

supraorbital foramina in, 293t
sutures in, 291t
teeth in, 290, 294
from tibia, 286
in United States, 297, 308
WinBUGS, 328
error analysis, 288, 289, 299t, 307
literature regarding, 296, 297
and puberty, 60
reference collections, pattern/source
variation in, 298–305
in sex determination, 234–236
Anemia, 341
Animal bites in bone identification, 335
Ankylosing spondylitis, 343, 344
Antemortem data, 368, 369, 398, 404,
416, 433, 435
Anthropological examination described, 187
Anthroposcopic traits, 289–293
Appendicular skeleton
evaluation of, 185
fractures, 206, 207
Argentina, case study, 411–417
Arthropod activity, analysis of, 189
Articulations
in age-at-death assessment, 264
decomposition of, 133, 148
hips, evaluation of, 127, 128
labile vs persistent, 127
Aspartic acid racemization in dentine,
260, 272
Asphyxia, traumatic, 33
Asylum seekers, age determination in, 58
Atlantooccipital joint, 185
Autolysis in decomposition, 86
Autopsies
anthropological examination, 187
benefits of, 32–35
bones
individualization of, 182, 183
preparation for, 172–174, 350, 351f
cost(s) of, 30, 31
in diagnosis, 31

disarticulation procedures, 175–178
final report procedure, 188
homicides and, 29
in identification, 174, 175, 361,
431, 432, 437
inventory procedures, 186, 187
job accidents/disease, 24, 33
legal state of, 29–32
objectives of, 17–19
personnel conducting, 162–165
post–procedures, 188–192
prevalence, 27, 29, 30, 31
procedures, 167–193
quality control in, 27–29, 192
reconstruction, procedures, 180–182, 184f
soft tissues, washing/removal
procedure, 178–181
types of, 16, 17

B

Basilar occipital synchondrosis, 249
Bayesian analysis
about, 319, 327, 328
in age-at-death assessment, 273
single-parameter problem, 317–322
stature, multivariate estimated
parameter estimation,
325, 326
stature, multivariate known
parameter estimation,
322–324
Beatings, lesions produced by, 200t
Belgium
medical examiner qualifications in, 29
Biogeographical ancestry (BGA) tests,
306, 307
Biological profiles
creation of, 47, 48, 260, 317, 327, 328, 350
identical, 334
Biological race defined, 283
Biological vs chronological age, 70–72
Biopsy, 76

Blackman's head described, 93
Black tattoo described, 217f
Bodies. *See* Human bodies
Body diagrams, 188
Body mass index (BMI) in age
    determination, 59, 61
Body parts, identification of, 174, 175, 189
Bone diaphyseal lengths in age
    determination, 248
Bone necrosis, 209
Bones
    abnormalities, descriptions of, 352
    age determination in, 66–71, 75, 76
    ancestry inference from, 235
    antemortem alterations in, 335, 336
    autopsy, preparation for, 172–174,
        350, 351f
    cleaning procedures, 260, 350
    depth recording of, 125
    displacement
        coffins in, 137–139, 143–147
        gravity and, 129–131, 138, 139
        gutters in, 146
        in primary deposits, 129–132,
            140–144
        restraining effects in, 144–146
        in secondary deposits, 149–152
    environment, restitution of, 137–141
    forensic evaluation of, 43, 44, 49,
        118, 119
    fractures of, 202–207
    individualization of, 182, 183
    inventory procedures, 186, 187
    long (*See* Long bones)
    pathology of, 333–338
    in personal identification, 335, 371–375
    postmortem alterations in, 335
    recovery, pathologist's role in, 45, 46
    in sex determination, 225, 227–233, 238
    skeletonization of, 112
    washing/removal procedure, 178–181
Brain, mummification of, 106
Brazil
    buried remains, evaluation of, 100, 101
    forensic anthropologists in, 42

Breast cancer, 342
Broca, Paul, 5, 282
Brucellosis, 346
Brucellosis, 61
Bullets
    analysis, El Mozote massacre, 421, 422
    recovery of, 168f, 173f, 218
    wounds, evaluation of, 185, 214–216
Bureaucratic race defined, 283
Buried remains
    anatomical connections in, 126–128
    decomposition in, 87, 100, 101, 110, 251f
    evaluation of, 118, 120–125, 137
    filling in, 142
    recovery, pathologist's role in, 46
Burned remains
    evaluation of, 49, 433f
    identification of, 366, 367
    recovery, pathologist's role in, 46

C

Cadavers
    decomposition of (*See* Decomposition)
    environment, restitution of, 137–141
    fractures in, 202–207
    fresh, anatomical connections in,
        126–128
    identification of, 337, 361
    interior volume filling in, 142–144
    multidisciplinary evaluation of, 160–162
    nonfresh, forensic evaluation of, 20, 21, 25
    original position evaluation, 131–133
    state of, processes leading to, 119, 120
    teaching anatomy on, 34
Calcified cartilages, 205
Callus formation in identification, 348, 352
Canada, ancestry determination in, 297
Cancer, 342, 343, 349
Canine fossa in ethnicity determination, 292t
Carabelli's cusp in ethnicity
        determination, 293t
Carbonization
    in fingerprint analysis, 364, 365

Carving traces in secondary deposits, 148
Cause of death
    defined, 19, 49
    determination of, 17, 19–21, 160, 162,
        178f, 198, 202, 334, 348
    error margins, 33
    Las Dos Erres massacre, 427, 428
    in mass graves, 389
    mummification in, 107
    saponification in, 104
Cementum annulation, 272
Cemetery remains, recognition of, 47
Cephalic index defined, 298, 299
Certification requirements, AFBA, 9
Chain of custody, maintenance of, 170, 188
Charred remains. *See* Burned remains
Charts/forms in personal identification,
    368, 369, 395, 396
Chemical action in decomposition, 129
Child pornography, FA evaluation of, 51
Children
    age determination in, 58–63, 66, 67,
        243, 244, 249–253
    of diverse ethnicity, 67, 249
    identity theft, 415
    original position, evaluation of, 131
    putrefaction rate in, 97
    saponification in, 102f, 103
    sex determination in, 238
    skeletal development in, 247–249
Chin shape in ethnicity determination, 292t
Chop wounds, 212
Chronology in deposit evaluation, 150–152
Circulatory diseases, 347
Clavicles
    in age-at-death assessment, 268–270
    evaluation of, 143–145
    fractures in, 202, 206
Cleft palate, 339, 340
Clinical forensic medicine
    history of, 15, 16
    specialties in, 26

Clothing
    evaluation of, 169–171, 189–191
    in putrefaction, 97
    in sex determination, 250
CODIS system, 307
Coffins
    in bone displacement, 137–139, 143–147
    in decomposition, 101
Coimbra Collection, 295f, 298–302
Color differences in fracture evaluation, 203
Communication in investigations, 402–405
Communities in exhumation/
        identification, 402–405
Computer assisted skeletal age scores
        (CASAS), 69
Congenital abnormalities, 339, 340
Congenital disorders
    in age determination, 61
Conification
    in fingerprint analysis, 363
Consanguinity, establishment of, 415
Coroner system described, 22, 23
Costovertebral joints, 185
Cranial index, variation in, 298–302
Cranial suture closures, 260, 272
Craniofacial reconstruction, 48
Craniofacial superimposition, 370–372,
        374, 375
Craniosynostosis, 339, 340
Cranium. *See* Head
Credibility, maintenance of, 394
Cribra orbitalia, 341
Crimes against humanity
    about, 409, 410
    Argentina, case study, 411–417
    history of, 410, 411
Crime scenes
    investigation of, 165–167, 434
    pathologist's role in, 45, 46
Crushing trauma, lesions produced by, 200t

D

Dactyloscopy. *See* Fingerprints
Data collection for odontological
        evaluation, 367–369

Death cause/manner/mechanism. *See*
    Cause of death; Manner of death;
    Mechanism of death
Decapitation procedure, 177
Decomposition. *See also individual*
    process by name
  about, 85–89, 113, 114
  adipocere in, 86, 87, 88f
  and age determination, 247, 268
  of articulations, 133, 148
  autolysis in, 86
  body part identification, 174, 175
  bone displacement during, 129–132
  in buried remains, 87, 100, 101, 110, 251f
  chemical action in, 129
  coffins in, 101
  DNA fingerprinting and, 87
  earthworms in, 128, 129, 142
  epidermis, 91, 92, 111
  evaluation of, 20, 21, 25, 161, 433f
  of the face, 90, 93, 99, 104, 105f
  in filled spaces, 140, 141
  humidity and, 110
  in ligaments, 97, 111, 132, 136, 147f
  of organs, 94–96, 111
  predators in, 86, 128–129
  and reconstruction, 133–137, 367
  saponification and, 104
  in secondary deposits, 149
  in soft tissues, 86, 97, 105–108, 111, 152
  soil in, 101, 142, 144, 145
  traumatic wounds and, 98, 112f
  water in, 87, 99, 100
Decomposition processes
    and the PMI, 87–89, 104
Defense fracture, 206
Dehydration
  in fingerprint analysis, 364, 365
  of fresh cadavers, 127
  and mummification, 107
  in surface remains, 127
Delayed deaths, forensic evaluation of,
    18, 19

Demirjian's system, 63–65
Dental age, determination of. *See* Teeth
Dental arches, 366–368, 436
Dental casts, 369
Dental charts, 369, 370
Dentine sampling by tooth extraction, 76
Depth measurement in field
    evaluations, 124, 125, 145
DFA. *See* Discriminant function
    analysis (DFA)
Differential bone preservation, 148
Diffuse idiopathic skeletal hyperostosis
    (DISH), 339, 344, 345
Disarticulation
  described, 111
  in hands, 111, 134
  of mandible, 177, 178
  procedures, 175–178
  skeletonization procedures, 177
  in water, 111, 136
Discrete traits in individualization, 335, 336
Discriminant function analysis (DFA),
    228, 229, 233–237, 284–289
Diseases. *See also* Pathology
  autopsies of, 24, 33, 354
  circulatory, 347
  degenerative joint, 208, 209
  infectious (*See* Infectious diseases)
  Legg-Calvé-Perthes, 347
  nutritional deficiency, 61, 72
  protection from, 164
  rheumatic, 343, 344
DISH (diffuse idiopathic skeletal
    hyperostosis), 339, 344, 345
Dislocations
  evaluation of, 210, 211
  in primary deposits, 128
Displacement in multiple deposits, 150
DNA fingerprinting
  and decomposition, 87
  described, 48, 49, 305–308
  error analysis, 400, 401
  in identification of remains

about, 359, 361–363, 378, 398–402
ancestry, 283
mass disasters, 434, 436
procedures, 188, 189, 192
teeth, 176f
odontology and, 377
in sex determination, 234
Documentation in identification, 416
Dorsal rim in age-at-death
determination, 264
Dorsey, George A., 6, 7
Draft Code of Crimes against Peace and
Security of Mankind, 411
Drawing in field recording, 121–124, 153
Dry skeletal pathology, 197, 198, 218,
219, 247
Dwight, Thomas, 6

E

Earthworms in decomposition, 128,
129, 142
Education of forensic anthropologists,
40–45
Elderly adults, identification of, 261,
262, 268, 275
Electric shock, lesions produced by,
200t, 210, 211
Electronic Encyclopedia on Maxillo-
Facial, Dental and Skeletal
Development, 73, 74
El Mozote massacre, 417–423
El Pozo, 426–428
Employer contracts, 392–394
Empty spaces
corpse decay in, 137–139
original vs secondary, 139–140
Enforced disappearance, 411, 413, 415.
See also Guatemalan conflict
England. *See* United Kingdom
Enthesopathies, 338, =339, 345
Entrance wounds, 214, 215f

Environment
in decomposition, 101, 142, 144, 145
and dental development, 244, 246
evaluation, effects on, 218, 250
predators, 86, 128, 129, 189
restitution of, 137–141
Epidermis, decomposition of, 91, 92, 111
Epiphyseal fusion
in age determination, 261
assessment of, 75, 250
process of, 68, 69, 249
Equipment for forensic teams, 164, 165
Equipo Argentino de Antropología Forense
(EAAF), 416, 417, 419, 426f
Error analysis. *See also* Reliability
in age-at-death estimation, 263, 266,
267, 272, 275
age determination, 57, 68, 69, 71, 72,
76, 77, 244, 247, 248
ancestry determination, 288, 289,
299t, 307
avoidance, 4, 29
biological profile creation, 350
cause of death, 33
DNA analysis, 400, 401
historical sanctions against, 14
in identification, 187, 226, 361, 378
manner of death, 32, 33, 35
sex determination, 43, 46, 230, 236
stature determination, 322, 324, 325
Essentials of Forensic Anthropology
(Stewart), 118
Estimation
defined, 317, 318
multivariate, known parameters,
322–324
multivariate estimated parameter
estimation, 325, 326
single-parameter, 319–322
Ethanol, 365
Ethnicity. *See* Ancestry
Europe
age determination in, 58
autopsies, quality control in, 28
autopsy prevalence in, 27

charts/forms in, 368, 431, 437
forensic anthropologists in, 40–43
forensic anthropology in, 5, 6, 9, 15
medicolegal organizations in, 23
Evidence in estimation, 318, 326, 327
Examination guidelines, 395–397, 434–436
Exhumations
    in criminal investigations, 415, 416
    El Mozote massacre, 419–421
    El Pozo, 426–428
    procedures, 165–167, 192, 250, 350,
        389, 396
Exit wounds, 214, 215f
Explosives lesions, 216, 218
Exsiccation defined, 105
Extremities in age-at-death
    determination, 264

F

Face
    decomposition of, 90, 93, 99, 104, 105f
    filling of, 139f
    fractures in, 204, 205, 213
    identification by, 50, 370, 374–377
    mass disaster remains of, 433f
    reconstruction of, 48, 187
    trauma wounds, 20f
Families
    assistance of in criminal
                investigations, 343, 346,
                402–405, 414, 415
    in crimes against humanity, 252
    dealing with, 18, 19, 30, 260, 354,
                393–400
    genetics, 296
    identification by, 182, 188–190, 361,
                402–405
    of missing persons, 384, 385, 389
Fatty acid composition in
    mummification, 106, 107
Feet
    age determination by, 248, 249
    fractures in, 206

Fels method described, 69, 70
Females
    body characteristics described, 234
    cranial index in, 300f
    maturation of, 249
    pelvis of, 227, 228, 304, 305
    puberty in, 59–61
    saponification in, 102f, 103
    SBS phases in, 265f
    Tanner staging system for, 61t
    tooth development in, 244
Femur
    congenital disorders of, 339, 340f
    ethnicity determination from, 286, 288
    evaluation of, 138, 184
    fractures in, 202
    osteosarcoma of, 342
    stature estimation from, 322–324
Fibula
    development of, 318
    evaluation of, 185, 345, 346f
    fractures of, 207
Field recordings
    corpse position, evaluation of, 131–133
    in forensic evaluation, 118–120, 153, 154
    missing persons, 391
    multiple collective deposits, 150–153
    primary deposits, 125–131
    reconstruction in, 133–137
    secondary deposits, 146–150
    technical progress in, 120–125
Filling of volumes in corpses, 142–147
Final report procedure, 188
Fingerprints
    in identification, 297, 359, 362–366, 399
    limitations of, 362
    recovery of, 91, 92f, 174–176, 363–365
Fingers
    fingerprinting, 91, 92f, 174–176,
                363–365
    trauma in, 201, 206
Firearms
    evaluation of, 18, 104, 105f, 172, 348
    lesions produced by, 200t, 206, 214–
                218, 351f

Flail chest, 206
Flesh removal, 148
Fluids
    expulsion of in putrefaction, 92, 93f
    in primary deposits, 128, 129
    in putrefaction rate, 97
    in secondary deposits, 149
Fluorosis, 341
FORDISC 2.0 software, 233, 287, 288
Forelimbs
    development of, 318
    fractures in, 206, 207, 213
    position, evaluation of, 131
Forensic anthropologist
    described, 40–45
    roles of, 45–51, 161t, 189
    training of, 192, 193
Forensic anthropology
    defined, 3, 4, 39–45
    history of, 4–10
    in identification, 359, 362
    on nonfresh bodies, 25
    objectives of, 117–120
Forensic Anthropology Databank
        (FDB), 286–288
Forensic Anthropology Society of
        Europe (FASE), 9, 41, 193
Forensic medicine described, 14–16, 160
Forensic pathology
    described, 14, 35
    future of, 32–35
    legal issues in, 29–32
    role of, 160–162
    specialties in, 26, 33, 43, 44
Forms in personal identification, 368,
        369, 395, 396
Fourth rib, age determination from,
        269, 271–273, 275
Fractures
    appendicular skeleton, 206, 207
    in clavicles, 202, 206
    complications, 205, 208, 209
    defense, 206

evaluation of, 202–207, 218, 335,
        348–350
    in the face, 204, 205, 213
    in the feet, 206
    in femurs, 202
    in forelimbs, 206, 207, 213
    in the head, 204, 205, 354
    in humerus, 206, 209, 213
    in infants, 204
    in mandibles, 205
    neck, 205
    pelvis, 207
    repair of, 207, 208
    in rib cages, 205, 206
    sternum, 206, 336f
    vertebral column, 206, 349
    from violence, 206, 207
France
    age of imputability in, 58
    forensic anthropologists in, 42, 118
    identification issues in, 260
    medicolegal organizations in, 23, 24
Frontal sinuses, comparison of, 372–374

G

Gait in identification, 354
Geneva Conventions of 1949, 385
Genocides
    autopsy procedures, 159, 160, 170
    as crime, 410
    graves from, 152, 252
    victim identification, 17, 113, 318
Germany
    age of imputability in, 58
    forensic anthropologists in, 42
Gibbs sampling, 320
Giles and Elliot method, 284–289
G&P atlas (Radiographic Atlas of
        Skeletal Development of the Hand
        and Wrist), 66–68, 70, 75
Graves
    collective, 150–153
    evaluation of, 154
    IHL guidelines, 385–387

intersecting, 149
mass (*See* Mass graves)
secondary defined, 146, 148
sites, field evaluation of, 120–125
Gravity
and bone displacement, 129–131,
138–139
filling and, 142
Great Britain. *See* United Kingdom
Green abdominal stain, 90, 91f
Growth, assessment of, 59, 61, 71, 72, 74
Growth charts, 71, 75
Guatemalan conflict
and age determination, 249–253
investigation of, 423–429
Gutters in bone displacement, 146

H

Hamann-Todd collection, 285, 286, 288
Hands
age determinations, 66–70, 75, 248,
249, 436
autopsy procedures, 178, 179
in depositions, 150
disarticulation in, 111, 134
disease evaluation in, 354
field recovery of, 127, 129, 131, 250
fingerprinting, 175, 399
fractures in, 206
mummification in, 108f
skin slippage on, 92
Head. *See also* Skull
bullet wounds in, 214–216
fractures in, 203–205, 354
mass disaster remains of, 433f
position, evaluation of, 131, 132
Heart, putrefaction in, 96f, 97
Hips
articulation, evaluation of, 127, 128
bones in sex determination, 225,
227–233, 238
congenital disorders of, 339, 340f

Homicides
and autopsies, 29
evaluation of, 105f, 107, 111–113,
177, 335
methodology, 197, 212
murder by strangulation, 31
without lethal injuries, 20
Hooton, Ernest, 289
Hourglass effect, 142
Hrdlička, Aleş, 7, 8
Human bodies, disposal of, 414
Human rights investigation. *See also*
Crimes against humanity
clothing evaluation in, 190f
dislocations, 210, 211
FA's role in, 49, 50, 198
grave sites, 152
investigation of, 199, 206
pathology in, 346
sharp instrument wounds, 212–214
skeletonization processes in, 113
traumatic avulsion in, 209, 210
Human variation, investigation of, 282–305
Humerus
in age determination, 249
evaluation of, 134, 136, 139f, 144, 335
fractures in, 206, 209, 213
pathology in, 335
stature estimation from, 319, 322–329
Humidity
and decomposition, 110
in fingerprint analysis, 364
Hungary, medical examiner
qualifications in, 29
10-hydroxystearic acid, 102, 107
Hyoid bone, 205

I

Ice/snow and mummification, 106, 107
Identification
accountability/responsibility in, 397
and adipocere, 161, 170, 172
autopsies in, 174, 175, 361, 431, 432, 437
biological, 187, 260
of body parts, 174, 175, 177

of bones, 335, 371–375
of burned remains, 366, 367
of cadavers, 337, 361
callus formation in, 348, 352
of children, 243, 244
contexts of, 317
discrete traits in, 335–336
DNA analysis (*See* DNA fingerprinting)
documentation in, 416
of elderly adults, 261, 262, 268, 275
errors in, 187, 226, 361, 378
by face, 50, 370, 374–377
by families, 182, 188–190, 361, 402–405
fingerprints in, 297, 359, 362–366, 399
gait in, 354
IHL guidelines, 385–387
implants in, 348, 349
Las Dos Erres massacre, 428, 429
living individuals (*See* Living
        individuals)
mass disaster victims, 431–434
of missing persons (See Missing
        persons, identification of)
odontology in, 359, 362, 366–371
pathology in, 333–336, 346
personal (*See* Personal identification)
personal objects in, 170, 172f, 175,
        189–191, 362
physical inspection in, 59–62, 74, 75
of population affinities (*See* Populations)
of remains (*See* Remains,
        identification of)
secondary sex characteristics in, 59, 60
septal apertures in, 48
sex determination (*See* Sex
        determination)
of skeletons, 48, 49
surgery in, 348, 436
UV light for, 368
visual, 360, 361, 398
Identity theft, 415
Iliac crest epiphysis in age-at-death
        assessment, 268–269
Immigrants, age determination in, 58

Implants in identification, 348, 349
Imputability, determination of, 50, 58
Inca bone in ethnicity determination, 292t
Incised wounds, 18, 212
Incisor shoveling in ethnicity
        determination, 293t, 297
Indian Knoll population, 285
Infants
    age determination in, 73, 246–248
    fractures in, 204
    mummification in, 108, 109f
    putrefaction rate in, 97
Infectious diseases
    in age determination, 61
    evaluation of, 345–347
    protection from, 164
    and putrefaction, 97, 98
Infectious periostitis, 212
Infestation, 94, 95f, 98
Informative priors, 326, 327
Inheritance, quasicontinuous model of,
        290, 294–296
Insect activity, analysis of, 189
Intentionality, evaluation of, 125, 149, 150
International Committee of the Red
        Cross (ICRC), 384–388, 395
International humanitarian law (IHL),
        385, 386, 389, 390
Interpol Disaster Victim Identification
        (DVI)
    autopsy protocol, 395
    form, 431, 432, 437
Interpol identification guidelines, 361, 368
Inventory procedures, 186, 187
Investigation procedures, 165–192
Iron-deficiency anemia, 61
Ischiopubic segment in sex
        determination, 228
The Istanbul Protocol, 188, 197, 198
Italy
    age of imputability in, 58
    FA case time criteria, 47
    forensic anthropologists in, 41

J

Jaw. *See* Mandible
Job accidents/disease, autopsies of, 24, 33
Joints, confirmation of, 184, 185

K

Kater Rades case, 434
Kidney, putrefaction in, 95, 96
Klippel-Feil syndrome, 340
Krogman, Wilton, 8
Kvaal's intact method, 272

L

La Aguada, 427
Label verification, 170, 171f
Lamendin method of age-at-death
  assessment, 262, 264, 266–268,
  272, 275
Las Dos Erres massacre, 423–429
Latex in fingerprint analysis, 364, 365f
Latin America, forensic anthropologists
  in, 42
Legal medicine
  in autopsies, 29–32
  described, 14, 161
  forensic anthropology in, 45–51, 198
  history of, 15
  in identification of remains, 48, 49
  missing persons, 385–387, 390–392
  reliability, 226
Legg-Calvé-Perthes disease, 347
Lepra, 346
Lesions. *See also* Traumatic wounds
  amputation, 212–214
  defined, 352
  dry skeletal tissue procedures, 198–200
  evaluation of, 180–182, 219, 335,
    350–355
  explosives, 216, 218
  firearms, 200t, 206, 214–218, 351f
  pellet, 216, 217f

production of, 197, 200t, 201, 210, 211
  proliferative, 352
  sharp instruments, 200t, 212–214, 348
  shrapnel, 217f
  torture, 200t, 210–211, 213
Ligaments, decomposition in, 97, 111,
  132, 136, 147f
Likelihood ratio, 321
Linate aircraft disaster, 434, 437–442
Liver, putrefaction in, 95, 96
Living individuals
  age determination in, 74–76
  identification of
    about, 50, 57–59, 73
    physical inspection in, 59–62, 74, 75
    teeth in, 62–65
Localized subperiosteal thickenings,
  211, 212
Localized traumatic periostitis, 211, 212
Long bones
  adolescent age determination in, 249
  in age-at-death assessment, 273, 274
  DFA values for, 236
  ethnicity determination from, 285, 286
  evaluation of, 121, 144, 335
  sex determination from, 233, 234
  in stature estimation, 318, 322–326
Los Salazares, 427
Lung cancer, 342
Lungs, putrefaction in, 96f

M

Maggot infestation, 94, 95f, 98
Males
  body characteristics described, 234
  cranial index in, 300f
  maturation of, 249
  pelvis of, 227, 305
  puberty in, 59–61
  SBS phases in, 265f
  Tanner staging system for, 60t
  tooth development in, 244

Malnutrition in age determination, 61, 72, 252
Malpractice claims, 31
Mandible
  disarticulation of, 177, 178
  evaluation of, 132, 179f
  fractures in, 205
  reconstruction of, 185, 367
Mandibular ramus flexure, 226
Mandibular torus in ethnicity determination, 293t
Manner of death
  and age determination, 250–252
  defined, 19
  determination of, 17–20, 22, 23, 30, 49, 198, 219, 334, 348, 395, 397
  errors in analysis, 32, 33, 35
  exhumations and, 389
  in mass disasters, 432, 439
Manouvrier, Leonce, 5
The Manual on Effective Investigation and Documentation of Torture and Other Cruel, Inhuman or Degrading Treatment and Punishment–the Istanbul Protocol, 188, 197, 198
Marbling described, 91
Mass disasters
  bone individualization in, 182, 354
  data collection in, 367, 369
  defined, 431, 433
  FA's role in, 49
  guidelines, 434–436
  reporting, 191, 192
  victim identification, 431–434
Mass graves
  ethnicity determination in, 334
  IHL guidelines, 385–387
  investigation of, 49, 50, 252
  pathological, 350, 351f, 354
Maturity
  age and, 70–73
  determination of, 59–62, 73, 74, 264
  skeletal, 66–70

Mechanical asphyxia, lesions produced by, 200t
Mechanism of death, 13, 19
Medical examiners
  qualifications of, 28, 32
  system described, 22
Medical treatment in identification, 348, 354, 355, 436
Medicolegal organizations, 21–27
Metabolic disturbances, 340, 341
Metopic suture, 336
Microsatellite markers, 306, 307
Microscopic dental aging, 247
Military personnel in criminal activities, 411–423
Mindset in forensic evaluation, 43
Minnesota Protocol, 395
Missing persons, identification of
  about, 383–388
  accountability/responsibility in, 397
  best-practice guidelines, 394–396
  communities/families in, 402–405
  exhumation procedures, 396
  external examination only, 396, 397
  forensics in, 389–391
  team members in, 392–394
Morphological characters in ethnicity determination, 289–298, 360
Mortality bias, 304
Morton, Samuel, 282
MtDNA sequences, 306–308
Multidisciplinary team described, 162–165
Multiple collective deposits, 150–153
Multivariate regression in stature estimation, 322–326
Mummification
  adipocere in, 106
  in autopsy procedures, 170
  brain, 106
  in cause of death, 107
  dehydration and, 107
  described, 88f, 105–108, 126
  fatty acid composition in, 106, 107

in fingerprint analysis, 363–365
in hands, 108f
ice/snow and, 106, 107
in infants, 108, 109f
temperature in, 106, 110
Murder by strangulation, 31
Mylohyoid bridge in ethnicity
determination, 293t
Myocardial infarction, 30, 31
Myositis ossificans progressiva, 211
Myositis ossificans traumatica, 211, 349

N

Nasal depression in ethnicity
determination, 291t
Nasal form in ethnicity determination,
291t, 297
Nasal opening in ethnicity
determination, 291t
Nasal sill in ethnicity determination, 291t
National Institute of Legal Medicine
(NILM), 24–27
Neck fractures, 205
Necropsies. *See* Autopsies
Neoplasias, 342, 343, 349
Nonmetric traits, 290–293, 335
Nutritional deficiency diseases, 61, 72

O

Obesity, putrefaction rate in, 97
Obstruction of justice, 391
Odontograms, 187, 368
Odontology, 359, 362, 366–371
Oral cavity, accessing, 367
Orfila, Matthieu-Joseph-Bonaventure, 5
Organs
in case resolution, 185
collection of, 35
decomposition of, 94–96, 111
Origin of remains, determination of, 47
Ortopantomographs in age
determination, 63, 64f

Os coxae, evaluation of, 138, 139f, 145
Os Japonicum, 292t
Ossuaries, 110f, 149
Osteoarthritis, 209, 337, 338, 353
Osteochondritis, 210
Osteochondrodysplasias, 61
Osteochondroma, 211
Osteochondrosis, 347
Osteomas, 342
Osteometry, 234–236
Osteomyelitis, 61, 208, 353
Osteopathology, 219
Osteophytes, 338, 353
Osteoporosis, 341, 349
Osteosarcoma, 211, 338, 342
Overlapping values in DFAs, 236

P

Paracondylar process in ethnicity
determination, 293t
Paradoxical chronology, phenomena of, 146
Paré, Ambrosio, 15
Parkman, George, case of, 6
Patellae, evaluation of, 138
Pathology. *See also* Diseases;
individual disease by name
defined, 352
in identification, 333–336, 346
limitations/potentials of, 336–338
procedures, 350–355
Pearson, Karl, 5
Pellet lesions, 216, 217f
Pelvis
in autopsy procedures, 173, 177, 178
collapse, 130, 138, 145
ethnicity determination from, 285,
302–305
fractures, 207
neoplasms in, 342
sexual dimorphism of, 227, 228
People, identification of, 50
Perforating injuries, production of, 18

Perinates, age determination in, 248
Periodontal ligament, 63
Periodontosis, 266, 267f
Periostitis, 345, 346
Personal genetic histories (PGH),
    tracing, 306–308
Personal identification
    about, 359–363
    bones in, 335, 371–375
    charts/forms in, 368, 369, 395, 396
    factors affecting, 363–366
    teeth in, 366–371, 399, 434
Personal objects
    in identification, 170, 172f, 175,
        189–191, 362
    in sex determination, 250
PGH (personal genetic histories),
    tracing, 306–308
Phenice's method, 228
Phlyctenae, evaluation of, 91
Photography
    in field recording, 121–124, 153
    on forensic team, 164
    in odontological evaluation, 367, 369
    in reconstruction, 187
Photometric recording technique, 123
Physical inspection in identification,
    59–62, 74, 75
PMI. *See* Postmortem interval (PMI)
Populations
    affinities, identification of
        children, 244, 245t
        in examination, 187
        genetic methods, 305–308
        methodologies, 282–298
        sex determination, 227, 229, 233–236
    age-at-death estimations in, 252,
        261, 269, 271–274
    aging in, 73
    limb variation in, 318
Pornographic images, FA evaluation of, 51
Portugal
    autopsies, quality control in, 28,
        113–114, 192

FA case time criteria, 47
    forensic anthropologists in, 41, 42
    medicolegal organizations in, 24–27
    saponified bodies in, 104
Posterior probability defined, 287
Posthumous circulation described, 91
Postmortem data, 368, 369, 398, 416,
    433, 436
Postmortem interval (PMI)
    and decomposition processes, 87–89, 104
    determination of, 46, 47, 189
Posttraumatic osteodystrophy, 209
Posttraumatic osteoporosis, 209
Practical Anthropometry (Lombroso), 8
Predators
    activity, analysis of, 189
    in decomposition, 86, 128, 129
Pregnancy, 76, 248
Preservation of remains in age
    determination, 262
Primary deposition
    anatomical connections in, 126–128
    bone displacement in, 129–132, 140–144
    demonstration of, 126–131
    described, 125, 126
    dislocations in, 128
    field recordings, 125–137
    fluids in, 128, 129
    of human remains, 126–146
    putrefaction in, 128
    Testacella in, 128, 129
Professionalism in missing persons
    cases, 390, 391
Prostate, putrefaction in, 97
Prostate cancer, 342
Prostheses in identification, 348, 354, 368
Pseudoarthrosis, 208, 209f, 213
Pseudopathologies, 335
Puberty in age determination, 59–62
Pubic symphysis, 262–265, 272, 275
Pulp cavity index, 272
Putrefaction
    adipocere in, 96f
    air in, 97, 98

children, rate in, 97
clothing in, 97
described, 86, 87, 89–101
in fingerprint analysis, 363, 365
fluids in, 92, 93f, 97
heart, 96f, 97
in identification, 93, 94f, 99, 100
infants, rate in, 97
infectious diseases and, 97, 98
in kidney, 95, 96
in liver, 95, 96
in lungs, 96f
and obesity, 97
in primary deposits, 128
rate of, 97, 125
septicemia and, 97, 98
in spleen, 95, 96
temperature in, 97, 98f, 101
in uterus, 97

R

Race. *See* Ancestry
Radiographic Atlas of Skeletal
        Development of the Hand and
        Wrist (G&P), 66–68, 70, 75
Radiography
    in age determination, 68, 69, 73–76,
        247, 436
    in forensic evaluation, 164, 167, 187, 318
    in fracture evaluation, 204, 218
    in odontological evaluation, 368–374
    in pathology evaluation, 352, 353
    room, improvised, 168f
Reconstruction
    autopsy procedures, 180–182, 184f
    craniofacial, 48
    decomposition and, 133–137, 367
    of mandible, 185, 367
    photography in, 187
    of the rib cage, 185
    of skeletons, 134–136
    of vertebral column, 185
Red Crescent, 388
Reference collections, pattern/source
    variation in, 298–305

Refugees, age determination in, 58
Reliability. *See also* Error analysis
    cranial index, 300, 301
    defined, 226
    of discriminant values, 233, 285–288
    of DNA fingerprinting, 307, 308
    of Lamendin method, 267, 275
    in race determination, 309
    in sex determination, 228, 229, 232t, 235t
Remains, human
    forensic dissections of, 15, 43, 44
    identification of (*See* Remains,
                identification of)
    origin, determination of, 47
    primary deposition of, 126–146
    recovery of, 45, 46, 166
    secondary deposit of, 146–150
Remains, identification of
    autopsies in, 17, 187, 219
    clothing in, 169–171
    described, 48, 49, 74, 113, 114, 355,
                397–399
    field recording in, 124
    mummification in, 107
    putrefaction in, 93, 94f, 99, 100
    saponification in, 104, 105
Restraining effects in bone
                displacement, 144–146
Rheumatic diseases, 343, 344
Rheumatoid arthritis, 354
Rib cage
    flattening, 129, 130, 144
    fractures in, 205, 206
    neoplasms in, 342
    reconstruction of, 185
Rickets, 61, 340, 341
Rings, recovery of, 175
Rollet, Étienne, 5
Rome Statute of the International
        Criminal Court, 411, 412f
Root length/height defined, 266, 267f
Roots in bone identification, 335
Root translucency in age-at-death
        assessment, 264, 266–268

S

Sacroiliac joints, 185, 227, 260, 344
Sacroiliitis, 343
Sacropelvic surface in age-at-death
    assessment, 272, 273, 275
Saponification
    in autopsy procedures, 170, 173f
    in children, 102f, 103
    and decomposition, 104
    described, 99, 102f, 103, 108
    in females, 102f, 103
    in fingerprint analysis, 363, 365, 366
    in suicides, 102f
    temperature in, 103, 104
    water in, 103–105
Sauer's protocol, 213
Scapulae
    evaluation of, 138, 139f, 146
    neoplasms in, 342, 343
    shifting of, 139f
Scene of the crime officer (SOCO),
    163, 164, 190
Schmorl's nodes, 352
Sciatic notch in sex determination, 227
Scoliosis, 341f
Scurvy, 340, 341
Secondary degenerative joint disease, 209
Secondary deposit of human remains,
    146–150
Secondary sex characteristics, 59, 60
Secular changes in DFA analysis, 288, 289
Sediment, 138, 142
Senescence, 261
Septal apertures in identification, 48
Septicemia and putrefaction, 97, 98
Severe degenerative joint disease, 208
Sex determination
    about, 225, 226, 238
    clothing in, 250
    DFAs in, 233–237, 288
    error analysis, 43, 46, 230, 236
    hip bones in, 225, 227–233, 238
    probabilistic, principles of, 229–233
    from skeleton, 226, 227
    skull, 233, 238

Sexual assault, 27
Sexual dimorphism, 227, 228, 299
Sharp instruments, lesions produced by,
    200t, 212–214, 348
Shooting distance, estimation of, 216, 217f
Shoulders, compression in, 144
Shrapnel lesions, 217f
Skeletal biological methods,
    applications of, 282–284
Skeletonization
    dental aging and, 246
    described, 88f, 97, 108–113
    disarticulation procedures, 177
    and sex determination, 225
Skeletons
    age-at-death assessment from, 261, 268
    age determination in, 66–71, 75, 76, 244
    assembly of, 183–186
    children, development of, 247–249
    dry tissue procedures, 198–200
    excavation of, 120, 121
    forensic evaluation of, 43, 44, 49, 337
    health/development, assessment of,
        72, 349
    identification of, 48, 49
    incomplete, 148
    morphological variations in, 335
    pathology interpretation from, 337, 338
    reconstruction of, 134–136
    recovery, pathologist's role in, 45, 46
    sex determination from (*See* Sex
        determination)
    trauma, pathology of, 201–218
Skin blisters, evaluation of, 91
Skull. *See also* Head
    age determination from, 271, 272
    autopsy procedures for, 177, 179,
        181, 183f, 184f
    bullet wounds in, 214–216
    ethnicity determination from, 285,
        289–298
    fractures in, 203–205, 354
    neoplasms in, 342
    odontological evaluation of, 369
    sex determination from, 233, 238

Smallpox, 61, 347

Snow, Clyde Collins, 415, 416

Social race defined, 283

Sodium hydroxide treatment, 364

Soft tissues

decomposition in, 86, 97, 105–108, 111, 152

DNA testing of, 189

evaluation of, 43, 49, 170, 218, 367

filling of, 142–144

myositis ossificans traumatica, 211

washing/removal procedure, 178–180

Soil in decomposition, 101, 142, 144, 145

Solheim's intact method, 272

Spain

FA case time criteria, 47

forensic anthropologists in, 41, 42

medicolegal organizations in, 24

Spine. *See also* Vertebral column

brucellosis in, 346

fractures of, 206, 349

Spleen, putrefaction in, 95, 96

Spondyloarthropathy, 339, 341, 343, 344

Spondylosis deformans, 353

Stab wounds, 212

Stature

calculation, history of, 5

error analysis, 322, 324, 325

estimation of, 187, 191, 319–329

in profile building, 318

Statute of the International Military Tribunal at Nuremberg, 411

Sternal end of the fourth rib, age determination from, 269, 271–273, 275

Sternum

fractures, 206, 336f

perforations in identification, 48

Stigmata, evaluation of, 199

Stretching/suspension/positional torture, lesions produced by, 200t

Striae of Retzius, 247

Study Group on Forensic Age Estimation, 74, 75

Suchey-Brooks System (SBS) for age-at-death assessment, 262–264

Sudeck's atrophy, 209

Sue, Jean-Joseph, 5

Suffering, induction of, 197

Suicides

in France, 23

manner of death, determination of, 20, 21, 166f

methodology, 212

saponification in, 102f

Superimposition, craniofacial, 370–372, 374, 375

Superior depth marks, 125

Superior pubis ramus, 303, 304f

Supraorbital foramina in ethnicity determination, 293t

Surface remains, dehydration in, 127

Surgery in identification, 348, 436

Sutures in ethnicity determination, 291t

Syndesmophytes, 353

Syphilis, 347

T

Tanner and Whitehouse system (TW2), 68

Taphonomy described, 86

Tattoos, evaluation of, 175

Teeth

in age determination, 62–65, 72, 75, 244–247, 261

autopsy procedures for, 174–176, 187

dental arches, 366–368, 436

dental casts, 369

dental charts, 369, 370

in ethnicity determination, 290, 294

Lamendin method of age-at-death assessment, 262, 264, 266–268, 272, 275

in personal identification, 366–371, 399, 434

Temperature

in mummification, 106, 110

in putrefaction, 97, 98f, 101

in saponification, 103, 104

Temporomandibular joint, 132, 177, 179f, 185
Tendons, decomposition in, 97, 111, 132, 136, 147f
Terry, Robert J., 283
Terry collection, 285, 286, 288, 295f, 298–305
Testacella in primary deposits, 128, 129
Third mandibular molar, 64, 65, 74
Third molar root apices, 63–65, 74
Tibia
    development of, 318
    ethnicity determination from, 286
    evaluation of, 335, 345, 346f
Todd, T. Wingate, 283
Topinard, Paul, 5
Torture
    as crime, 410
    investigation of, 391
    lesions produced by, 200t, 210, 211, 213
    methodology, 197, 213
Traffic accidents in forensic history, 15, 16
Transversal compression, 144, 145
Traumatic avulsion, 209, 210
Traumatic wounds. *See also* Lesions
    classification of, 18, 49
    and decomposition rate, 98, 112f
    dry skeletal tissue procedures, 198–200
    evaluation of, 181, 182f, 433f
    pathology, 201, 348–350 (*See also individual wound type by name*)
    production of, 197, 200t, 201
Treaty of Sèvres, 410, 411
Treponematosis, 346, 347
Trunk fractures, 205, 206, 213
Tuberculosis, 346, 347, 349
Tukey's honest significant test, 301, 302
Turkey, medicolegal organizations in, 23
Turner's syndrome, 61
Two-step procedure for age-at-death assessment, 262, 263, 268, 275
TW2-RUS method, 68, 69, 70, 74
TW2 system (Tanner and Whitehouse), 68
Typicality probability defined, 287
Tyrolean Iceman, 106, 107

U

United Kingdom, 23, 33
United Nations High Commissioner for Refugees (UNHCR) age determination guidelines, 58
United States
    autopsies, quality control in, 28
    autopsy prevalence in, 27
    ethnicity determination in, 297, 308
    forensic anthropologists in, 40–42
    forensic anthropology in, 6, 7
    medicolegal organizations in, 21, 22
UN Manual on the Effective Prevention and Investigation Of Extra-Legal, Arbitrary and Summary Executions, 197, 199
Uterus, putrefaction in, 97
UV light for identification, 368

V

Variability in age determination, 71, 72
Variation, investigation of, 282–305
Ventral rim in age-at-death assessment, 264
Vertebral column. *See also* Spine
    ankylosis spondylitis in, 343, 344
    brucellosis in, 346
    DISH in, 344, 345
    dislocation of, 130–132, 136
    fractures in, 206, 349
    neoplasms in, 342
    reconstruction of, 185
    superimposition in, 373, 374
Violence
    as common ground, 16
    evaluation of, 27, 30, 92, 93f, 197, 199
    fractures from, 206, 207

W

Wall effect defined, 140, 141f, 145
War crimes investigation, 49, 50, 113
Water
    in decomposition, 87, 99, 100
    disarticulation in, 111, 136
    in saponification, 103–105

WinBUGS software, 320, 321, 323–330
World Trade Center attack, 189
Wrist/hand region in age determinations,
        66–70, 75, 248, 249, 436
Wyman, Jeffries, 6

X

X-rays. *See* Radiography

Y

Y chromosome DNA, 306
Yoshino method, 373
Yugoslavia, medical examiner
        qualifications in, 28

Z

Zacchia, 15